Science, Action, and Fundamental Theology

Science, Action, and Fundamental Theology

Toward a Theology of Communicative Action

Helmut Peukert
translated by James Bohman

The MIT Press, Cambridge, Massachusetts, and London, England

English translation © 1984 by the Massachusetts Institute of Technology. This work originally appeared in German as *Wissenschaftstheorie–Handlungstheorie–Fundamentale Theologie: Ana-
lysen zu Ansatz und Status theologischer Theoriebildung*, © 1976 by Patmos-Verlag, Düsseldorf,
Federal Republic of Germany.

© 1984 by The Massachusetts Institute of Technology

This book was set in Baskerville
by The MIT Press Computergraphics Department
and printed and bound by Halliday Lithograph
in the United States of America.

Library of Congress Cataloging in Publication Data

Peukert, Helmut.
  Science, action, and fundamental theology.

  Translation of Wissenschaftstheorie, Handlungstheorie, fundamentale Theologie.
  Includes bibliography and index.
  1. Theology—Methodology. 2. Communication.
3. Social sciences—Methodology. 4. Act (Philosophy)
5. Analysis (Philosophy) I. Title.
BR118.P4613 1984   230   83-24404
ISBN 0-262-16095-1

Contents

I
Theory of Science and Theory of Action

II
Theory of Action and Fundamental Theology

Translator's Introduction

The work of Jürgen Habermas has begun to exercise a perceptible influence on the conceptions of the tasks and methods of a number of disciplines. From the analysis of cognitive interests to the theory of communicative action,[1] he has both appropriated and transformed diverse fields of empirical and theoretical research. This book is marked by the same dual relationship to existing paradigms; however, for Helmut Peukert the work of Habermas is itself material to be appropriated and transformed. Thus, not only does Peukert reconstruct the foundations of theology in the light of Habermas's theory of communicative action; at the same time, he develops a critique of this theory from the viewpoint of theology.

With both thinkers the turn to the theory of communicative action as the path to normative foundations has a historical background in intellectual developments in postwar Germany. Just as Habermas's work must be viewed in relation to the earlier generation of the Frankfurt School, Peukert's must be viewed in relation to the earlier generation of political theology—specifically that of Johannes Baptist Metz. Further, their common concern with method is due in part to one of the most significant phenomena in recent German philosophy: the reception of Anglo-American "analytic" philosophy through the reimporting of originally German authors (Wittgenstein, Carnap, and Popper). Thus, to understand Peukert's theological appropriation of Habermas we must understand the systematic and historical interrelationships of critical theory, political theology, and the German reception of analytic philosophy of language and of science. The first part of this introduction will provide a sketch of these relationships; in the second part I shall trace the underlying argument of the book that binds together its vast complex of themes. With this background, the reader can decide how best to approach this study according to his interest in and acquaintance with the specialized literatures.

In light of the historical antagonism between "continental" and "Anglo-Saxon" philosophical traditions, perhaps the most striking phenomenon in current German philosophy is the increasing role played by the reception of "analytic" philosophy in all domains of inquiry. A perusal of professional journals in the Federal Republic indicates that German philosophy took, however belatedly and tentatively, a "linguistic turn" of its own sort in the early 1970s. This book takes the limit problems of these developments as the starting point for reflection on method in theology.

At a time when the project of using the philosophy of language to establish foundations for the empirical sciences is losing favor in Anglo-American circles, a new concern with the philosophical grounding of the sciences is developing in Germany. This foundationalism is, in fact, the perspective from which analytic philosophy has come to be reappropriated in German philosophy. Peukert shares this concern, which in theology takes the form of an attempt to provide foundations for the methods and results of the reflective discipline of "fundamental theology." He defines his task in light of the recurrent challenge to Christian thought in its relation to the changing modes and problems of Western philosophy: to rethink and criticize, and yet to preserve, the tradition in light of the demands of contemporary rationality. Thus, as Aquinas incorporated the emerging Aristotelianism of his time, theology today must be defined in relation to a scientific rationality that perceives itself as foreign, if not hostile, to it. Twentieth-century philosophical thought calls for a new approach to fundamental theology, an effort to rethink theology in an age of scientific rationality.

The recent turn to method in critical theory stems from an effort to consolidate and validate the insights of the earlier generation of thinkers who originated this style of thought. This may seem somewhat ironic in light of the fact that both Horkheimer and Adorno explicitly repudiated the idea of a foundation and a methodology for critical theory. Indeed, Habermas's theory of communicative action marks a new conception of method in critical theory and, ultimately, a wholly different basis for social criticism.

Horkheimer and Adorno had opposed the search for foundations as the modern, epistemological form of *Ursprungsphilosophie* (first philosophy, or the philosophy of origins). The concept of a "critical theory" could only be delineated negatively over and against "traditional theory." This critical theory was developed in two ways: in the Hegelian terminology of identity and nonidentity, dialectic and totality, and through the critique of instrumental reason. By contrast, Habermas's elaboration of the concept of critical theory has always been concerned with questions of method, particularly method in the social sciences. And it is the positivist assertion of the unity of method in all rational (that is, scientific) inquiry that has provided the foil for the development of Habermas's ideas. Accompanying this growing concern with method we also find an increased concern with language. In German as in Anglo-American philosophy this turn has suggested a new reading of the history of philosophy. Karl Otto Apel's account of paradigm shifts in philosophy—from ontology to consciousness to language—is one example. On his view the turn to language is the real achievement of the twentieth century.[2] Such revisionist historiography supplies the essential background for Peukert's attempt to rethink the conditions of possibility of reflection on the methodological foundations of theology. He is convinced that fundamental theology can today be carried out only by pursuing the logic of Apel's and Habermas's transformation of philosophy into the theory of the subject, of society, and above all of history. For Peukert, however, these theories are open to and in need of a theological foundation; they are not simply secular theories to which theological statements may be appended.

The most direct lineage of Peukert's book is to be found in Catholic theology in this century, specifically the political theology of Metz. Political theology has a chronology similar to that of postwar critical theory, to which it owes a clear intellectual debt. Metz first outlined the conception of political theology in *Theology of the World* (1966), in which he formulated a diagnosis of the contemporary social, cultural, and ecclesiastical crisis. In his view, the situation called for a critique of the false universalism of modern privatized religion and of the banality of the modern post-Enlightenment conception of emancipation.

Like the first generation of critical theorists, Metz has not supplied any systematic treatment of method or theory formation in theology. His key notions are in fact resistant to any such conceptualization. With his insistence on memory and narrative as central theological categories, there can be no conceptual, argumentative "mediation and reconciliation between actual and effective redemption on the one hand and the history of human suffering on the other."[3] In this way, Metz appropriates Adorno's negative dialectics of "nonidentity"[4] while criticizing any theology that would advance a universal history of salvation. Here political theology has reached the point of a strictly negative theology of history.

At the same time, Metz, following Ernst Bloch, insists on the utopian content of religious language in general and of the Judeo-Christian tradition in particular. His treatment of the apocalyptic content of early Christianity in *Faith, History, and Society* was inspired in part by Bloch's identification of novelty as the *sine qua non* of an authentic future and by his historical, eschatological, and political interpretation of the utopian potential of Judaism and Christianity. Much the same may be said of Metz's relation to Adorno and Horkheimer. Jewish mysticism and its negative theology and prohibition of images influenced their conception of an emancipatory philosophy of history. To be truly humane, such a theory had to incorporate the desire for redemption—to "think its impossibility for the sake of its possibility," as Adorno writes at the close of *Minima Moralia*.

While Metz utilizes theological language of the first generation of critical theory, his remarks on Habermas's attempt to reformulate the critical theory of society in terms of a theory of communicative action are overwhelmingly negative. For Metz, Habermas's assertion of finitude in *Legitimation Crisis*—that we must live "disconsolately" with the contingencies of fate and death—marks the banality of the Enlightenment conception of emancipation. It ignores entirely the historical dimensions of guilt, debt, and disappointed claims to happiness. The return to the Christian apocalyptic tradition in *Faith, History, and Society* is conceived as an implicit critique of the Enlightenment philosophy of history behind Habermas's conception of social evolution; on Metz's view, the conception dissolves the possibility of liberation in the constant, homogeneous process of evolutionary progression.[5] In effect, this criticism turns the negative dialectics and religious language of redemption of earlier critical theory against the universalist claims of Habermas's theory of rationality and method. Through opposing the modern conception of emancipation to the theological conception of redemption, Metz's political theology hopes to be able to criticize the false ideologies of both freedom and salvation.

In 1969, while a student of both Metz and Rahner, Peukert edited a volume of articles entitled *Diskussion zur politischen Theologie*, which marked the end of the first phase of the development of political theology.[6] In it he called for reflection on the methodological foundations of theology to secure Metz's programmatic and suggestive insights.[7] The present volume is his most sustained response to that need, and for this purpose he enlists the aid of a principal target of Metz's political theology: Jürgen Habermas.

Although theological reservations regarding the emancipatory philosophy of history also motivate Peukert to criticize Habermas, he nonetheless views the predominant Enlightenment conception of rationality as raising at least two decisive positive demands for theological method: that, if theology is to speak to modern experience, its discourse must be universally communicable and must be related to practice. Any theology that is to speak the language of contemporary rationality has to meet these requirements.

This attempt to give Catholic theology a modern articulation began in Rahner's rewriting of certain of its central categories in the modern philosophical vocabulary of transcendental philosophy, which awakened Catholic theology from its "dogmatic slumbers" of objectivist, antiquarian metaphysics. The critical reception of Kantian epistemology gave a new language to theology; in this respect, Peukert credits Rahner with a "transcendental-hermeneutic transformation of theology." Peukert's own undertaking can also be viewed as a hermeneutic transformation of theology, and one whose groundwork was laid by Rahner's discussion of the modern conception of intersubjectivity. However, Peukert's concepts are taken not from transcendental philosophy but from a new foundational discipline, the theory of communicative action, which opens up the possibility of reconstructing the "rational core" of theology in terms of a theory of the pragmatics of religious speech that emphasizes its temporal and innovative character.[8] In Peukert's review of the movement of the philosophy of science away from empiricism and positivism, Habermas's theory of communicative action emerges as the best candidate for this transformation of theology.

The history of the philosophy of science in this century culminates for Peukert in the theory of action [*Handlungstheorie*] in general and the theory of communicative action in particular. The problems of human action have always been the domain of "political theology." Peukert wants to argue that the contemporary discussion of rationality may no longer simply dismiss the possibility of theology out of hand. Thus, he attempts to identify the theological dimension of problems internal to scientific rationality after its turn to the theory of action. He hopes in this way to make good on his promise to formulate a modern conception of theology that is both public and related to practice.

At the very least, such a reconstruction of the "rational core" of theological statements would provide a contemporary access to the Christian tradition. Like Rahner in Catholic theology, Bultmann, with his program of demythologization and his use of Heideggerian categories from *Being and Time*, is the most radical predecessor of this theological undertaking in Protestant theology. However, Bultmann's tendency toward an almost literal application of Heideggerian categories to theology is something Peukert wants to avoid. Accordingly, he does not simply apply the concepts of the theory of communicative action already developed by Habermas; rather, he asks whether the conception of rationality developed in this theory must not ultimately have a theological dimension if it is to be consistent and coherent. This strong claim is developed primarily in part II, where Peukert attempts to unearth the contradictions that arise if the universalism that is so central to communicative ethics is extended to the dimensions of historical action. In this regard, the debate between Benjamin and Horkheimer concerning the philosophy of history becomes "one of the most theologically significant controversies of this century." Once the conception of rational community is given a historical dimension, the relation to the past, with all its setbacks and catastrophes, becomes fundamentally problematic for an otherwise thoroughgoing universalism. Thus, Peukert argues against the universalism of contemporary rationality on its own terms and finds in the search for normative foundations a new argumentative basis for the validity of theological categories. Here Peukert is following a strategy, suggested by Rahner's theological appropriation of modern philosophical categories, that is common to Neo-Thomist interpretations of Kant and to modern apologetics as a whole. Rather than argue against Habermas's explicit

statements about the overcoming of religion and theology, he seeks
to uncover necessary and implicit reference to a theological dimension
in the aporias of secular versions of universalism. Rahner has both
appropriated and criticized Kant, in such a way that the transcending
movement of intersubjectivity toward an unlimited horizon becomes
the framework for a new conception of theology. In his reading of
Habermas, Peukert too both appropriates and criticizes the theory of
communicative action, pushing its universalism one step further—
precisely the step that entails the admission of theological concepts
and delineates their sphere of validity. Indeed, he argues, central
concepts of the theological tradition—resurrection and redemption—
reemerge if the reflective foundations of modern science and the
Enlightenment practice of emancipation are interpreted radically.

On a formal level, then, Peukert's effort to rework theology in terms
of a theory of communicative action is influenced at least as much by
Rahner's transcendental theology as by Metz's political theology. It is
a synthesis of the two, and it finds in Habermas and Apel the conceptual
basis for a return within political theology to a "transcendental" conception of fundamental theology that asks the conditions of possibility
of existence in solidarity with others in the situation of historical and
social alienation. This theology starts from those aspects of the theory
of communicative action that Apel calls "transcendental-pragmatic"
and Habermas calls "quasi-transcendental." In his analysis of these
transcendental aspects of communication, Peukert discusses the contrast
between Apel's more Peircean concept of the "unlimited communication community" implicit in all communicative understanding and
Habermas's "ideal speech situation," the implicit suspension of force
and equality of chances supposed in every act of communication aimed
at understanding. It is certainly significant that he clearly sides here
with Apel's more strongly transcendental interpretation, according to
which the supposition of an unlimited communication community is
an almost existential commitment forced on every speaker who engages
in genuine communication. Fundamental to rational identity, this commitment becomes the basis for the theological dimension of communicative action. Although their strategies differ, there is nonetheless
a formal similarity in the mode of argumentation between Peukert
and Rahner. It is likely that those who find Rahner's critique of Kant
convincing will have the same opinion of Peukert's criticism of Haber-

mas; those who reject Rahner's arguments (both theologically and philosophically) may for similar reasons reject Peukert's.

Even if one does not accept Peukert's strong claim that the theory of communicative action is ultimately incoherent if not opened to a theological dimension, it is clear that he places theology in a new position with regard to intellectual culture and political life. It no longer appears insular, since its themes can be shown to be present in other disciplines. This, coupled with the use of theological language in the context of such a traditionally anti-theological conception of history as Marxism, raises a provocative question concerning the place of contemporary theology. An image from Benjamin's "Theses on the Philosophy of History" points to the tension at the heart of Benjamin's conception of "redemptive" or "rescuing" criticism. He compares theology to a dwarf who is "ugly and wizened, and kept out of sight." Yet the dwarf, hidden in an apparatus and posing as a chess-playing puppet, ensures victory against all comers. The puppet here represents the victims of the past. The turn to some agency (whether memory or God) to rescue the past seems still to be a ruse—the false hope and ideology of a religion that, as Marx said, refuses to "let the dead bury the dead." Peukert's politically situated religious language raises just this extreme hope, the hope for the past of all "redemptive" criticism. If Peukert is right about contemporary rationality, such a use of religious language can be judged only in pragmatic terms, not by some prior decision about the nature of "reality"; it must be judged in terms of theology's task of disclosing new dimensions of the communicative situation and new possibilities of action. The possibility of "rescuing criticism" hinges, then, on the theological dimension of the theory of communicative action.

As a glance at the table of contents reveals, this book has the encyclopedic scope its title suggests. Because it aims to bring together the converging problems of so many different areas of contemporary research, it involves extensive reviews of diverse literatures. The reader might best be served here by a précis of the overall structure of the argument that can be kept in mind throughout the book's detailed individual investigations.

In this translation, the order of the chapters has been altered in order to clarify the presentation. The more theologically informed reader may want to follow the original order by reading the appendixes after the author's preface. Some knowledge of the material in the appendixes is needed to understand the theological content of the chapters in part II. For the purpose of illustrating the "dialectical-reconstructive" method Peukert utilizes, my précis of his overall argument will follow the order of the original German edition.

The three parts of the German title—theories of science, theories of action, and fundamental theology—represent a dialectical progression of concepts, with the dynamic of internal contradictions generating ever fuller and more adequate content. Such "dialectical limit reflection" is the formal organizing principle of Peukert's theological phenomenology (in the Hegelian sense), an ordering of the historic search for foundations in recent theory of science. With the importance of the progression of concepts for such a dialectical argument, a great deal of weight is placed on reconstructing the development of the philosophy of science. Here Peukert relies heavily on Apel's treatment of the history of analytic philosophy and on all those philosophers who have critiqued the "received," positivist view.

The capstone of Peukert's reconstruction of recent theories of science, action, and theology is the claim that all these disciplines have converged in the theory of action. Theology reenters this dialectical-reconstructive scene rather late, in the final step to a fundamental theology. Just prior to theology, and the step that generates it, are problems of the normative basis of the theory of action, with its fundamental demand for universal solidarity. It is in response to these problems that theology claims its modern sphere of validity, as the dialectic comes to its end.

The introductory chapter and the appendixes discuss three major paradigms of fundamental theology, understood in the broad sense of "theological hermeneutics": Bultmann's conception of theology as "existential interpretation," Rahner's "transcendental-hermeneutic" transformation of theology, and Metz's "political theology." Taking Peukert's criticism and systematic interpretation of the large corpus of these theologians as a guide, we can see what he wishes to preserve from each. It will also become evident that in his view all these conceptions of fundamental theology suffer from a common, unresolved problem: "intersubjective communication," or communicative action.

Both existential and political theology supply a "corrective moment" to theological discourse. In the case of existential theology, this corrective is the insuperability of the finitude of human existence: Religious discourse, with its concepts of God and transcendence, should not be set apart from the structures of human existence. Bultmann, applying Heidegger's interpretation of the historicity of existence, saw the message of Jesus as a historic call to a decision to believe, a call revealed only in the believer's confrontation with his own death. For Peukert, Bultmann correctly located a hermeneutics of religious language in the analysis of the most extreme horizon of human existence. Nonetheless, owing to Heidegger's isolation of the death of the individual, Bultmann failed to see one of its important theological dimensions: its essential intersubjectivity. Only in the death of the other does Peukert see the furthest possibility of existence that demands interpretation in theological language. While preserving Bultmann's attempt to locate the theological dimension of human experience at its most extreme horizon, he endeavors to give it a new content derived from the furthest limits of an ethics of communicative action in history. Thus, the categories that for Bultmann are merely related to individual existence are now reinterpreted to refer primarily to historical action in its political and intersubjective dimensions.

The corrective function of political theology is found primarily in its category of *society*, which (like *existence*) has marked an unavoidable characteristic of discourse since the nineteenth century. In the present age, theology too must pass the tests of the hermeneutics of suspicion and the "critique of ideology." Though the introductory chapter serves mostly to frame the proper content of theology, it argues cogently for locating theological inquiry in the political field and in relation to problems raised by the philosophy of history and the social sciences. Three recurrent perspectives emerged from Peukert's reflections: the theories of history, society, and the subject. In each perspective the theory of communicative action furnishes the basic concept, which becomes the starting point for a theological hermeneutics: Habermas's idea of undistorted communication. In a theological context, this conception becomes the normative core of a theory of "anamnestic-liberating" and rectifying speech, or of a "pragmatics" of religious discourse.

Peukert tries to locate Rahner's transcendental theological hermeneutics within the limits of these corrections. In appendix 2 Peukert provides a long gloss on Rahner's "On the Unity of the Love of God and the Love of Neighbor,"[9] drawing on the theory of communicative action and on the correctives of existence and society. The theological analysis of intersubjectivity had already become the proper theme of theology for Rahner. On his view, the object of theological inquiry into the experience of "absolute mystery" is revealed in the inner-worldly experience of others in communication. Rahner speaks of God as the reality that "enables" and "empowers" action for others; this "enablement" is the key to the transcendental character of theology. As manifested in the Resurrection, this is a God who empowers those striving for the highest possibilities of human existence, a life in solidarity with others in the face of death. Peukert's theology can be understood as a systematic integration of Bultmann, Rahner, and Metz within the framework of this conception of intersubjectivity and the reality of God. It is the theology of a God who enables human beings to exist in solidarity in history.

On Peukert's understanding of theological hermeneutics, one of the tasks of fundamental theology is to provide the foundations for basic theological statements. As suggested above, these foundations cannot be developed today without consideration of the controversies surrounding the attempts to ground the various sciences. The progressive movement in the history of philosophy away from positivism and toward a "pragmatic turn" makes it possible for theology again to ask its questions in the language of contemporary rationality. Part I traces this development, from the negation of theology in Wittgenstein's *Tractatus* and the Vienna Circle (chapter 1) through the development of the foundations of logic and mathematics to the end of formalism in Gödel's theorem (chapter 2) and the consequent transformations in the conception of the theory of the empirical sciences (chapter 3) to the final "pragmatic turn," discussed in chapter 4 with special attention to the later Wittgenstein and to problems in linguistics. Similar problems can be traced through the development of the philosophy of the social sciences (chapter 5) and the constructivist theory of science of the Erlangen School (chapter 6). Readers familiar with the general inter-pertation of this development can skip over portions of part I without losing the thread of the main line of argument.

Peukert's strategy in part I becomes immediately clear in his treatment of the positivist negation of theology. Rather than argue directly against the critique of theology formulated by Wittgenstein and the Vienna Circle, he presents them as the starting point for a process of development of internal contradictions in the idea of science, beginning with the most radical questioning of the possibility of theology. The subsequent transformation of the theory of science itself supplies the grounds for overcoming this critique and its narrow conception of foundational reflection. A fundamental rupture in the seamless web of confident positivist science occurred in its bastion of certainty, mathematics, with the blow delivered by one of the Vienna Circle's own, Gödel. Even in mathematics, considerations of reflexivity, novelty, and temporality are necessary, since formal systems are never complete. Incompleteness always leaves room for reflective distance and choice; in this way, the critique of formalism initiates the turn to the thinking and acting subject behind science and mathematics.

A similar development may be traced in the history of the philosophy of the empirical sciences from Carnap to Kuhn and Feyerabend. The most important factor in this development is the failure of the reductionist program of early positivism, which was due to the recurring difficulties encountered by attempts to isolate a pure form of observation, or protocol sentences. Popper's *Logic of Scientific Discovery* is a key juncture in this historical process, with its admission of the conventional character of basic statements and methodological rules in science. Although on Peukert's view Popper himself retains a "positivist core," his new emphasis on convention led to a pragmatic conception of scientific rationality. Even for an empiricist like the later Carnap, the growth of scientific knowledge can only be judged by the weaker, pragmatic criteria of usefulness, coherence, and fruitfulness. The chief concern of the philosophy of science after the introduction of the fully historicized conceptions of paradigms and research programs by Kuhn, Lakatos, and others is not questions of observation and correspondence but the history of science and the "rational interaction" of the scientific community.

The pragmatic turn initiated by Wittgenstein in *Philosophical Investigations* made linguistic interaction the theme of the philosophy of language and entailed the next dialectical-historical step in the development of the theory of science. This turn reaches its conclusion in the contemporary theories of communicative action. Already in Wittgenstein's conception of language games and in Austin and Searle's speech-act theory there is a fundamental unresolved problem of innovative speech acts that change the very structure and background of agreements in linguistic interaction. The poetic-figurative use of language is to be counted among such innovative speech acts and also figures prominently in the pragmatic analysis of religious speech. Such speech acts both thematize and change the rules that are at the basis of social interaction. The analysis of such rules in interaction becomes the central problem of the philosophy of the social sciences (chapter 5), which becomes central to the philosophy of science after its pragmatic turn. Peukert analyzes the theoretical deficiencies of the various approaches to social inquiry, including problems raised by historical materialism, systems theory, and symbolic interactionism, and then lists the fundamental desiderata of a foundational theory of the social sciences developed simultaneously as a theory of society and a theory of history. Because human interaction is the domain of both theology and the social sciences (although the content differs), the foundational theories have similar structures.

In part II, Peukert tries to make good this claim by analyzing the theoretical contradictions that beset even the most adequate candidate for a foundational theory of the social sciences and of a fundamental theology: the theory of communicative action. He develops a critique of Habermas's views and, at the same time, a new conception of fundamental theology, for the contradictions revealed in his critique make clear the proper sphere and subject matter of theology.

Broadly speaking, Peukert's criticism of social-scientific theories of religion is an attempt to undermine their claim to self-sufficiency in analyzing the domain of social interaction and its normative foundations. Thus, the burden of the argument in part II falls on the modern theologian to develop those contradictions that require building a theological dimension into the theory of communicative action. For Peukert, these contradictions are to be found in the most extreme possibilities of a life lived in accord with the normative demand for universal solidarity, the highest ideal of modern secular visions of history. The utmost possibility of this solidarity is the death of the innocent who has struggled for the freedom of others.

Chapters 10 and 11 develop the promised dialectical transition from the theory of action to theology. This is done in two steps. First, Peukert identifies certain paradoxes at the core of the normative ideas of community and rational identity in the communicative ethics of Mead, Habermas, and Apel. These paradoxes reveal the limit experiences of communicative action in history. Second, he interprets the entire Judeo-Christian tradition from Exodus through exile to the prophets and the Gospels as expressing these very experiences in ever more radical ways. This progression within the Judeo-Christian tradition culminates in a theology of the communicative action of Jesus and the determination of God as the saving reality in the experience of the death of others. I shall expand briefly on these two steps, since they represent Peukert's most original contribution in this volume.

Beginning with Mead's conception of the constitution of self-identity in interaction, Peukert hopes to show that three normative claims are implied in the very structure of communication aimed at mutual understanding: equality, reciprocity, and solidarity. If they are to be constitutive for self-identity in social interaction, these claims require more content than the purely procedural, counterfactual suppositions Habermas's universal pragmatics give them. The arguments for the necessary supposition of the "ideal speech situation" and of the ideal of the "universal communication community" support the norm of universal solidarity in communicative action; accordingly, this norm represents "the highest ideal attainable in modern times." The paradox emerges when this ideal is incorporated in the emancipatory philosophy of history that is so central to the critical theory of society. Once the ideal is historicized in the context of the struggle for the realization of human freedom, the community to which this solidarity extends must include past generations—those to whom we owe the creation of the human possibilities we enjoy in the present. However, this sort of solidarity is unthinkable in modernity: How can we extend solidarity to the past, or even recognize our debt to it, if the past is past and the dead are finally and irrevocably dead? This is the "paradox of anamnestic solidarity," a phrase Peukert borrows from Christian Lenhardt's generational typology of relations to the past in the struggle for emancipation. According to Lenhardt, the denial of the past is tantamount to the denial of memory, of debt, and even of the past itself: "The conventional understanding of what solidarity is all about in the context of a secular theory of man and history has implied a wholesale erasure of memory."[10] As Horkheimer wrote to Benjamin, the solidarity with the past implied in Benjamin's conception of "empathetic memory" is ultimately theological. As Benjamin himself put it in his Theses, "The past carries with it a temporal index by which it is referred to redemption."[11]

What Peukert is arguing here is that it is impossible to maintain the dimensions of solidarity, inheritance, and justice that are so central to communication in periods of emancipatory action without also referring to their ultimate theological context. Viewed historically, these

concepts have their origins in the theology of *communio sanctorium* as
reinterpreted in nineteenth-century idealist philosophies of history.
Political literature as well is full of expressions of the "spiritual" character of solidarity with the past. One of the best examples of this is
Brecht's "An den Nachgeborenen," the appeal to future generations
to remember those struggling in the "terrible time" of social transformation.[12] In the context of specifically religious language, Peukert
sees the parables of the New Testament as just such innovative speech
actions aimed at disclosing such dimensions of the experience of
solidarity.

If anamnestic solidarity is the paradox of communicative action, its
explicit limit experience is the destruction of those who act in solidarity
with others. In the face of this experience, Peukert introduces his most
explicitly theological and Christian category: the Resurrection. One of
the strongest motives for historical amnesia is the impotence to do
anything about the past, a point of what Horkheimer called the "most
extreme despair and inconsolable grief" for those acting on behalf of
justice. In response to this grief, the primitive Christian community
had an unequivocal answer to their experience of the death of Jesus:
the saving reality of God in the Resurrection. The question of the
reality of God could then be systematically reconstructed in terms of
the redemptive reality nameable and identifiable in the furthest possibilities of communicative action, empowering human action to achieve
universal solidarity in history. This normative and religious dimension
of human action in solidarity with others is the "rational core" of
theological language, the end point of the broad search through the
history of foundational reflection constitutive of fundamental theology
itself.

The success of this entire line of argument depends on considerations
similar to those which Kant's *Critique of Practical Reason* raises in arguing
that the practical postulate of the reality of God is required for the
possibility of moral action. One of Peukert's achievements is to revive
this sort of practical argument for the reality of God in the new, "quasi-
transcendental" language of the theory of communicative action. In
this way, it is not surprising to see the reemergence of the theological
legacy of Kant's postulates in the context of the theory of communicative
action, which itself owes much to Kant's idea of the rational will.

Peukert also revives another important Kantian theme: the theology
of history with practical intent, linked to the increasing realization of

human freedom. This theology is precisely the antipode of the theological pessimism of Horkheimer, for whom perfect justice was the nightmare of history. Peukert's theology does not simply oppose the utopian content of the Judeo-Christian tradition to the brute facts of the world. Quite to the contrary, this content is found anew in the universalism of contemporary rationality with its practical counterparts: emancipation and solidarity.

Author's Preface

In our century theories of science have radically challenged the very possibility of theology. This challenge is radical in that these theories raise doubts about whether we have at our disposal even the linguistic means to pose questions with a theological dimension.

In this work I shall take up the debate within the theory of science in order to develop a proposal for a "fundamental theology," that is, a kind of foundational theory of theology. It is my view that a certain convergence can be established between contemporary reflection on the fundamental principles of theology on the one side and the results of research into the theory of science on the other. It seems to me that the point of convergence lies in a theory of communicative action. Accordingly, the basic idea behind this work is to develop a fundamental theology from the theory of communicative action. This should not be perceived as completely alien or new to theology; one might understand the thesis of Karl Rahner's "On the Unity of the Love of God and the Love of Neighbor"[1] as the starting point for a "formal and fundamental theology"[2] with a hermeneutic relevance for the whole of theology. This follows from an understanding of fundamental theology according to which fundamental theology is formal dogmatics and dogmatics as a whole is material fundamental theology.[3]

I shall proceed by attempting to develop the foundational problems of theories of science and theories of action to a point where both the theological dimensions of communicative action and the possibilities of theoretically grasping them become perceptible through a dialectical limit reflection.

The introduction and the two appendixes investigate fundamental conceptions of theology that can claim to develop a foundational theory for theology. The proposals of R. Bultmann, K. Rahner, and J. B. Metz are discussed as paradigms for such a theory.

Part I investigates the development of theories of science in the last decades, beginning with the radical questioning of the possibility of theology by the young Wittgenstein and—further intensified in the direction of empiricism—by the Vienna Circle. The resulting development is presented as a more and more radical recourse to communicative action as the basis of scientific rationality. This development is pursued in connection with general discussions of the theory of science and foundational problems of linguistics and sociology.

Against a background of considerations concerning both theology and the theory of science, part II attempts to open up the problem dimension in which responsible theological discourse has its original place. This involves the following steps:

• I argue that the normative postulates that are necessary and binding for all partners in every elementary interaction have the character of anticipatory, foundational actions that both make freedom possible and disclose reality.

• This normative theory of action reaches its own limits in the experience of the annihilation of the innocent other; the "paradox of anamnestic solidarity" marks the breakdown of the theory of action.

• The basic experiences of the Judeo-Christian tradition have to do with the determination of God precisely in the face of this experience.

• Accordingly, fundamental theology is to be understood as a theory of universal, anamnestic-solidaristic, communicative action and as a theory of the reality that is experienced and becomes nameable in this action.

Hence, fundamental theology is, on the one hand, the theory of science with respect to theology, insofar as it discloses the domain of its objects and clarifies the possibility of theoretically comprehending that domain. On the other hand, it is fundamental theology in the sense that it makes available basic theological propositions that have to be developed in theology as a whole and that have a hermeneutic function for this whole.

In this work I have not discussed the studies that would be necessary for elaborating the methodological implications of such a conception; briefly, they are the following.

• Out of a fundamental theology developed in discussion with sociological and linguistic theories of action, one could derive suggestions for an explicit theological hermeneutics and text theory. A theory of translation, on which I have published a few observations,[4] seems to me to be the test case for hermeneutic theory as a whole. Here we encounter the problem of the intercultural transposition of innovative, liberating, and situation-changing speech acts, to which a theological theory of language and hermeneutics must do justice. Certain consequences can be derived from chapter 4, which is concerned with a theory of dialogue that includes innovative and metaphorical, situation-related speech. It must be admitted that these questions involve problems of presentation, since questions of this complexity cannot be expounded briefly without the help of relatively elaborate formal means. The basic dialectical structure of dialogical action that is outlined briefly in chapter 4 needs to be developed further.

• If a proposal for a fundamental theology is to be developed by way of a theory of communicative action, how is such a proposal to be related to practical theology? I contend that a practical theology is most likely to be founded on the basis of an explicit theological theory of communicative action. In my university lectures I have discussed the issues of this relationship in light of the problem of a didactics of theology. I hope to publish attempts to work out these implications in the near future.[5]

• There are also consequences that can be drawn from this proposal for interdisciplinary studies in theology, that is, for the question of whether, along with a "logic of scientific discovery," there could be something like a "logic of interdisciplinary discovery"[6] that determines the relationship of theology to other disciplines in concrete scientific study. But perhaps such a section will not be too badly missed, since this investigation itself may be read as a practical proposal in this area.

Acknowledgments

A work dealing with foundational problems in various disciplines cannot be written without constant discussions with colleagues in other fields. It is impossible for me to name them all here. However, I must mention J. S. Petöfi and S. J. Schmidt of Bielefeld, in whom I found ready partners for conversations concerning questions in linguistics and the theory of science. L. Schäfer of Tübingen read parts of the manuscript and offered suggestions on many difficult questions. I was able to discuss with J. Habermas the limit questions of a theory of communicative action; he also alerted me to essential problems in the interpretation of texts of the Frankfurt School, especially in the work of Walter Benjamin.

This work would not have been possible without my theological mentors. Eighteen years ago I began studying systematic theology with Karl Rahner. In the last few years I have been able to study and work with J. B. Metz. To them I owe the impetus to take up this work, which I could never have finished without their encouragement and kindness over the years.

Many friends and unnamed helpers have contributed over the years to the completion of this work. That it was finally brought to a close is due in more than a literal sense to the excellent abilities of Mrs. L. Pischel.

I have also discussed many of the issues treated here with the students of the Department of Catholic Theology of the University of Münster. I wish to thank them for their stimulation and criticism.

Helmut Peukert

Introduction: On Political Theology

Theology and the Theory of Society

Not only a theology that sees itself as existential interpretation, and not only one that takes as its starting point a transcendental anthropology, but theology as a whole is confronted by questions resulting from the development of the sciences since the nineteenth century.

The great challenges to theology in modern times came first from the natural sciences—above all from physics and its application in astronomy. The names of Galileo and Copernicus have become symbols of this crisis. The nineteenth century completed the Copernican turn; through Darwin man received a biological history that linked him to evolution. The steadily mounting data produced by the expanding historical sciences disrupted the matter-of-factness of our own historical and cultural orientation. This cultural orientation was delivered over to a relativism that seemed impenetrable to reflection. Historical consciousness became historicist. From this followed first the suspicion and finally the insight that one's own consciousness is the product and sediment of historical development. This historical development shows itself to be pervasive and determinate in all basic human relationships, in the mechanisms of the biological and economic reproduction of life, in the common agreement as to what constitutes "normal reality," and in the forms of constitution of individual consciousness.

This presents problems that go to the very root of theology. In the face of such radical forms of suspicion, directed against consciousness and shrinking at nothing, how can one still take theology seriously enough to do it at all? Peter Berger, especially, has insisted that the new form of science, embodied above all in the sociology of knowledge, represents "the specifically contemporary challenge to theology"[1] — a challenge that cannot be ignored without serious concrete and cognitive consequences. "The challenges of the human sciences," Berger writes, "have been more critical, more dangerous to the essence of the theological enterprise."[2]

The threat to theology is twofold. First, theories arise that claim to be able to make transparent the function of religion in the historical evolutionary constitution of humanity and to give plausible explanations of religion in particular societies. Theology as "theory," as the reflective form of religious consciousness, is then itself deciphered in terms of its functionality at a definite stage of human evolution. Theology as "theory" is thus made obsolete by a metatheory whose explanatory power goes beyond the scope of theology. Second, a new concept of practice comes to the fore in the Enlightenment, in the practical-philosophical writings of Idealism, and in Marx: practice is no longer merely concerned with the change of individual relationships in a fixed whole; rather, it is concerned with the change in the status of the evolution of the species, and thus with change in the constitutive mechanisms of the existing society in all its dimensions. These dimensions include the dimension of consciousness, which had formerly given us the final guiding categories of our understanding of reality. The new notion of practice signifies nothing less than the transformation of religious consciousness, and of theology with it.

If, in a general way, one defines political inquiry with reference to the reality of the political field, political theory can be defined by the political field in three respects: Certain questions become decisive problems, for which definite alternative solutions are offered; within these alternatives, these problems allow for certain decisions, which must be concretely resolved; finally, these decisions must be carried out.[3] If this is the case, one can speak—against the background of developments since the Enlightenment—of an enormous expansion of what can be called "political." At the very least, it must be admitted that what is signified by the term "political" in a specific society (that is, what is assigned to various forms of communal responsibility and decision making) itself falls under the same process of decision making at all levels. For example, whether certain questions are perceived or accepted as a matter of choice, or whether certain eligible alternatives

are the only ones that are to be considered available, is, as a problem of the constitution of the political field, again a "political" question.

J. B. Metz's attempt to develop a "political theology"[4] can be understood only in light of this post-Enlightenment intellectual-historical and social-political development. The problems involved in the use of the term "political theology"[5] do not consist so much in the fact that since antiquity it has been used for forms of religion and their "theology" that served to legitimate specific forms of social domination. The conceptual change in the modern, post-Enlightenment use of the concept would then merely mirror the political change that has taken place. What is more questionable than this terminological difficulty is whether such a comprehensive concept of the political has so made its way into general consciousness that its use does not necessarily lead to misunderstandings. However, it may well be the case that the fundamental problems of our contemporary world society force the expansion of reflection and action into dimensions that make naive any simple separation of theology and existing political problems.[6]

How should the task of a theology adequate to this situation be determined? Since mankind has reached the stage of *animal historicum* within the process of evolution (that is, the species that possesses the capacity to store and communicate experiences, not just to live in an environment, but to construct out of these experiences a world that is self-made and humanized, comprising historical experiences by means of which the human species in the interchange with its natural life conditions determines itself as what it wants to be and is capable of being), is not the horizon within which theology is constrained to do its thinking precisely this human species, in its history and its open possibilities? The concept of society within this context signifies then not so much the static relationships within the social network, but more fully the very process of the development of society, and hence precisely this process of the self-constitution of the human species. Theological statements that would elucidate the historical experiences of humanity and its historical, epochally significant events could be interpreted only in relation to this process. Theology is thus necessarily related to society. What was heretofore defined in anthropology-oriented theology as transcendental experience must now be determined within the horizon of this process. Even where theology was previously aware of its social dimension it was confined in its categories to an almost exclusively "religious" realm and emphasized an individualized, transcending existence. Processes of socialization then had meaning as merely social, merely economic, merely political. Theology thus surrendered the possibility of seeing those processes in their full meaning and their multidimensionality. The consequence has been that the further development of categories of thought has been left to other disciplines. It is characteristic that Marx could understand *Capital* as a "critique of political economy" and, as such, a universal theory of the self-constitution of the human species. This universal theory has special significance. Despite the fact that Marx's exclusion of certain realms (above all his neglect of social interaction within symbolic systems of signs) is clear today in hindsight; despite the fact that after the experiences of this century the Critical Theory of society derived from Marx is no longer possible without psychoanalysis, social psychology, and general research into social interaction; despite the fact that Marx himself interpreted the entire process of the constitution of society on the model of social labor—despite all that, Marx's analyses and the analyses of this new type is science reach dimensions that were previously in the realm of theology in the classical sense. Thus, theology finds itself in a new situation in regard to the development of its system of categories.

Neither a hermeneutics that carries out its interpretations in the horizon of a theory of subjective experience nor a theory of intersubjectivity as an I-Thou relationship appears to be adequate to the sheer ponderousness of factual history and its events. Thinking in these categories is in danger of glossing over and losing sight of the density of historical growth, the resistance of sedimented relations, the penetration of traditional norms into the very consciousness of the individual. In contrast, the concept of *society* fulfills an inescapable hermeneutic function. Such a concept balances the tendency of idealism to conceive of intersubjectivity from the viewpoint of subjectivity, as a "realm of spirits" the very conception of which one cannot help but believe transcends its fundamental conditions. Independent of any discussion of the theoretical status of the concept of society, one can simply indicate elements given within it that a hermeneutic theory cannot ignore. (For the moment, I will leave aside the connections between a theory of history and a theory of society.)

• No theory of society can overlook the interdependence of human beings, both in the succession of generations and in primary and secondary socialization, which is internalized both biologically and in certain forms of behavior. Sociology has to deal with theories of social evolution and comparative behavioral research as well as with theories of the biological reproduction of the human species.

• Already in early forms of social life, the necessity of the exchange with nature as the condition of survival in cooperative "work" assigns roles according to the division of labor. The analysis of the conditions of production and reproduction as the analysis of labor in society cannot be neglected in a theory of the history of the human species and of the constitution of the field of meaning of human existence.

• Language, as the capability of communication that discloses the world and of the accumulation of experience and reflection on the immediate, historically realized situation, is the paradigm for the commonly acquired and internalized system of rules. This system of rules always leads us beyond an isolated existence; it is characterized by the capability of reflective self-definition as an activity performed in history and interaction. The linguistically mediated construction of reality is never the accomplishment of an individual alone; it is the accomplishment of a social process.[7]

• The development of more complex societies means at the same time the development of classes or strata in society and the unfolding of antagonisms that bring individual conflicts into existence. Their transformation is predicated on a change in other mechanisms determining the structure of the total society, such as the transformation of the conditions of production and of economic exchange.

• The formation of institutions is attributable on the one hand to the necessity of freeing a no longer instinctually guided species from the constant pressure of decision and on the other hand to the sedimentation of collectively accumulated experience.[8] This growth of institutions also shows the enormity of the ever more complex social structures that determine individual existence.

• The division of labor and the compulsion for decisions concerning the necessary adaptation to changing life conditions lead to the development of decision-making mechanisms and finally to the delegation of the power of decision. Hence, society is also structured according to the concentration in individuals or groups of the possibilities for making decisions affecting many or all of the members of a society. Domination and power as the disposition over others is only one of many forms of the dependence of the individual on society.

• The development of social norms of conduct and their internalization and transmission in different phases of socialization reaches even into the origins of individual consciousness. This makes possible the establishment of a stable ego identity; on the other hand, prior social decisions thus impinge on consciousness and determine it through the entire weight of internalized traditions. Thus, the decisions of the individual always stand in a societal context.

• A society's common consciousness of its social nature is also determined by what general norms, roles, institutions, conditions of labor and domination, and decision-making mechanisms are experienced as naturally given and immutable—removed from one's own disposition—and which will be experienced as mutable and responsive to one's own decision. The mode of transformation of a society, either in the forced adaptation to altered conditions of life or in the free choice of goals and of the necessary means to be utilized, characterize the degree of self-consciousness and the measure of common, free autonomy of decision in the society. The relationship of the individual to the society changes according to this measure.

• Broadly, all this again points to the realm of the "political." Indeed, we are immediately faced here with the question of the status of the social sciences as a whole. On the one hand, they have the task of presenting the above-described phenomena in an intersubjectively confirmable way, making their importance clear and thus contributing to the self-enlightenment of society. On the other hand, the social sciences cannot avoid the question of which theoretical framework and which projection of meaning are the bases of their analyses. It is not accidental that there has arisen in sociology a controversy concerning the methodology, the status of concept formation, and the political character of the fundamental presuppositions of the field. More generally, one could formulate the problem in this way: Do the facts of social development and their sedimentation in social relationships simply force the inquirer to take notice of them, while their facticity requires of him an objectifying attitude, or is the reflective analysis of social facts also the point at which individual and social consciousness become aware both of their conditionedness and of the possibilities of action? If the latter is the case, the concept of society and its construction decides whether inquiry itself also falls under the reification of social processes, or whether it is called upon to overcome the power of facticity precisely by uncovering societal constraints as such and indicating how actually operative projections of meaning are products of social and historical factors and thus compete with other possibilities.

Such a concept of society intends to promote a style of thought that is conscious of its own dependence and conditionedness while at the same time attempting in reflective distantiation to transcend the already attained condition of the totality. For this task a critical theory is necessary, insofar as "critique" signifies the possibility of analyzing one's own horizon of consciousness and, in doing so, of going beyond it.

We can use the term "society" for the constellation of a totality that has the tendency, as such a totality, to determine all the individual elements, so that in the extreme case the private sphere is reapportioned as something reprivatized. Such a conception of totality leads to the crucial question: How can critique be credited with any power for change at all? Even prior to that, how can critique orient itself at all? If we allow the possibility that socially conditioned consciousness can develop into false consciousness, how can it be shown to be false consciousness over and against the social reality of which it is a product?

Thus, the question is whether society can be so totalizing that the suffering apportioned to and inflicted upon certain individuals and entire strata is gratefully accepted. Or could experiences of injustice and suffering be so fundamental as to break through the appearance of false consciousness and expose a utopian presentiment of other possibilities for one's own life and for society as a whole? If such a utopian, fantasizing consciousness exists, what is its function? Does it only mitigate experienced suffering or assuage anger against it, and is it then an "opiate" that numbs the pain and at least makes it bearable? Or is this utopian consciousness the index of a human freedom that can set itself against the power of social relationships and even overcome them?

What is decisive for theology is the question of how it can obtain and justify its own statements in a definite situation in relation to the actual state of social relationships. Even theology must begin with the fact that in these historically realized social relationships there can have been objectified violence, injustice, and oppression. These relationships themselves, however, are not external to the consciousness of the individual or general, publicly articulated consciousness. Social relationships thus become contexts of social illusion.

The first general problem of every critical theory of society is the problem of any theology that is oriented toward society: How can a "false" social consciousness and its illusions be broken through, dissolved, and transformed into "true" consciousness? The theological tradition has always included at least the representation of the possibility and even the reality of false social consciousness and its deceptions. Theology ascribes to the *kerygma* the function of dissolving false social consciousness and thus liberating it to find, communally, the "true life." A society-oriented theology that wants to develop a hermeneutic of its own statements has the task of clarifying exactly the ways in which the hold of false consciousness can be broken.

Does such a theology presuppose an already worked out conception of "correct" social relationships, and hence of true, undistorted consciousness? Or is the primary experience by which theology first orients itself that of suffering within these social relationships and protesting against them? How is it that false consciousness suffers from false relationships if it must first be transformed into true consciousness? What drives this transformation forward? How are we to characterize this transformation from false to true consciousness? How can theology be a theology of this transformation if it cannot simply claim already to be the completion of true consciousness but must first make clear to itself that it shares in the structure of delusions that perpetuate the present reality? The interdependence of theology and society belongs to the methodological consciousness of theology.

Theology and the Theory of History

The attempts to do theology with these presuppositions can first of all be characterized by how they differ from a theology such as Bultmann's. A theology that regards transcending existence in its individualized decision as the only possible horizon of theological statements is in danger of losing sight of concrete history and its future by exclusive concentration on the existential structure of existence. The radicalness of an existential theology fixated on the God-man relationship cannot perceive the fundamental societal conditionedness of existence. The decision of faith remains worldless; it becomes a private event in relation to society. These dangers must now be spelled out in all their acuteness.

This changed problematic can also be discussed and explicated in terms of the theory of science. The hermeneutics of existential interpretation proceeds from the difference between pre-understanding and the thing to be understood. Pre-understanding as projection determines the horizon of interpretation. Even in the empirical sciences, there are proposed hypothetically a theory and a system of categories in terms of which one approaches the object of inquiry. The great scientific revolutions are accomplished at the moment when these fundamental, hypothetical assumptions are changed, as was the case with the theory of relativity and the conceptions of space and time. Reflection on the theory of science achieves the level of consciousness only when it accepts into the methodology of scientific inquiry the reciprocity of projection and object, as well as the constant possibility of correction of this projection. Existential interpretation as a hermeneutic program satisfies these claims insofar as it accounts for its horizon of interpretation, thus making exact statements that may be criticized precisely.

Above all, a new level of reflection is achieved with the insight that the horizon of the interpreter is itself transformed in the understanding of the historical situation; it becomes apparent that this transformation necessarily belongs to the nature of the matter at hand to be interpreted. Theological-hermeneutical consciousness can no longer dare to regress below this level. For theology, it is obviously a matter of illuminating the process of historical experience at this very level of the problematic. One's own historical horizon as pre-understanding has to be brought into the knowledge of the subject matter at hand, first in the analysis of one's given situation and second in the explication of the difference of this situation from that of the historical event. The historical difference in the hermeneutic circle is not to be overcome; rather, it constitutes the circle precisely as the difference between pre-understanding and subject matter. The central hermeneutical question is just how the reality at hand can be grasped out of this difference. The question becomes more acute if one's own situation as interpreter must be characterized as one of alienation and one's consciousness as false consciousness. The hermeneutics of existential interpretation resolved this problem by determining the understanding of the event of redemption, with which theology is concerned, as anticipatory transcending toward the authenticity of existence, and determining this existence as the eschatological moment of the decision of faith. Correspondingly, the event of salvation was understood as the constitution of the eschatological moment, cutting through and across history. Thus, at least formally, the overcoming of the situational difference in understanding as the movement of existence appears fortunate. However, the price of that understanding itself then becomes a stepping out of history and a becoming worldless. Faith and historical understanding are thus completely displaced into the movement of individualized existence. The question must then be put to a hermeneutics of existential interpretation whether, under the conditions of socially determined and alienated existence, the understanding of historical experience and its self-transparency can then be successful if the conditions of one's own understanding and self-realization are radically altered. Is it then not so that the obstructions to self-realization, to relations to other human beings, and thus to social relationships must be changed radically if the process of understanding is to succeed? Is it not necessary to place greater value on the sheer factual weight of concrete history and the dynamics of its antagonisms rather than remove transcending existence from them? Does a hermeneutics that is based on a theory of the historicity of existence not merely withdraw itself from history?[9]

Theological discourse on "the" unified history has its own aporias. Existential hermeneutics could explain the universality of the saving event and of faith in terms of the momentary nature of eschatological existence. If theology does not again want to adopt the absolute standpoint of an observer outside of this existence, then it must make explicit in what sense it can speak of the whole of history with the claim to universality. If theology is a discourse on God that is related to history, it does not seem possible that this universal claim could be surrendered. However, at the same time, theology has to establish that there is no innerworldly subject that could ascribe to itself an absolute knowledge of the totality of history for each point in its course or might possess an unequivocal strategy for the realization of an already known meaning of history. The biblical discourse on God as the Lord and the eschatological Judge retains its hermeneutical significance; we cannot speak at all adequately about God under the present conditions. The Throne of history cannot be occupied by a mythical construct. Adequate discourse on God can only speak of the one who is to come, and, at the same time, point to the transformation of the present conditions of speaking. This hermeneutical insight has manifold significance:

• Discourse on history assumes the primacy of the future. History is not closed but open; "novelty" is thus its central category. Inasmuch as a mode of thought claims to speak of the end of history within the framework of "knowledge" of the whole, it misses not only the situation of its own discourse, and thus its own structure, but also what God can be. Indeed, the movement beyond the present to the future and the uncovering of the novel characterize existence. That nonetheless this future is precisely this novelty (that which is not yet thought or experienced) and as such first gives the past its final significance, that existence can be provoked to this meaning of the whole in terms of its end and yet cannot produce this meaning as the meaning of the whole out of itself, is constitutive of the difference between existence and God. In this difference, God constitutes himself as God.[10]

• An eschatological, hermeneutically reflective theology therefore can only be characterized as a "negative" theology; it protests against the objectification of God precisely in thinking of God strictly as the One who is coming and who leads us to the future. Just in this way does it hold fast to his transcendence, in contrast to a purely constructed future. For this reason, the inner temporality of the discourse about God is shown to be that of negative dialectics. Under present conditions, the totality is not to be grasped as fully comprehended truth. Reaching outward toward an undominated future and protesting against what is historically actual first opens up the very possibility of the discourse about God as Lord and Meaning of history.

• Because discourse about God is aimed at the transformation of the conditions of this very discourse, theology posits a new relation of theory and practice. Discourse about God is directed toward the mediation of the freedom that changes the factually realized and existing conditions, that renews lost freedom. The goal of such discourse is liberating, transforming action. Free action therefore entails a primacy over the thinking that informs it. The quieting of thought in the reflective mirroring of speculative thought comes to its own perversion. In this sense, Kant was indeed right about the primacy of practical reason. This assertion is not a fall from the highest possibilities of human existence, but rather first and foremost points the way to them.

Theology and the Theory of Communicative Action

If history and discourse about God are determined in this way, then the question that arises next for theological hermeneutics is how the historically significant saving event is to be established and understood at all. Theology as existential interpretation understands the significance of the saving event as the opening of the possibility of authentic existence, whose eschatological momentary nature consists in the fact that it leaves history behind for the simultaneity of the moment. Indeed, the significance of the saving kairos of the event is postulated and thought to be grasped in the paradoxical act of faith, and yet its relation to concrete history and its future remain unclear. From what has just been said, however, the historic power of the redemption event would have to consist in making possible the anticipatory grasp [Vorgriff] of the novelty of the future and the possibility of the transformation of the present in the direction of this future.

First, this experience discloses the basic structure of history, insofar as this structure is determined by the future and forces us to think of God as an eschatological God. Second, this experience determines the historical event as something that anticipates this future, marks a breakthrough in history, and expresses a promise that can be fulfilled only in the future. Third, this experience demands that transforming action be directed to this future and makes clear that the understanding of the event comes into view in this action alone. The historical memory of such an event is "dangerous" for existing relationships to the extent that in an anticipatory grasp of the future it leads to the transformation of these relationships and already breaks through in the present to this future act of making this past present. The validity of what is meant in the historical event is realized through the provocative free action of the one whose memory provokes him to act. In this consists its historic power. The statement Bultmann took from Dilthey that historical events show their full meaning only in the future receives a precise meaning in such a conception of history and historical hermeneutics.[11]

The question is whether there are still other explanatory models for the process of this transforming memory. The problem is heightened if one's own capabilities of memory are blocked by one's own history or collectively blocked by sedimented social relationships. In the framework of the critical theory of society, a solution has been sought chiefly in reference to psychoanalysis.[12] The psychotherapist has the task of explaining the genesis of the patient's fixated patterns of behavior in reactions to specific experiences, breaking through these patterns in the process of therapeutic conversation, and achieving insight into and practice of "appropriate" modes of behavior. It is presupposed in all this that the patient suffers because of his false behavior and, at least in this negative form of suffering, has a vague notion of other possible modes of behavior and a desire to change himself in terms of them. Thus, the patient has a kind of negative, suffering pre-knowledge, which of course neither transforms nor heals him by itself. The therapist's advantage lies primarily in his ability to obtain, through his own affective reaction to the behavior of the patient, indications as to the genesis of this suffering and insightful proposals for the interpretation thereof, so that new and more appropriate modes of acting become conscious and graspable for the patient as possibilities in the very process of the explanation of the old ones. The qualification of the therapist lies primarily not in his "mastery" and rendering harmless of his own experiential history through repression but in his recognizing the pathological reactions of the patient by seeing through his own crucial threatening experiences. He thereby creates a situation for learning new modes of behavior in the process of working through the individually and socially conditioned history in clinical conversation.

The healing process is necessarily dialogical, since the patient's illness consists in his inability to remember his own history as such. Filtering it through repressive mechanisms, which fixate behavior at the same time, the patient becomes caught in a vicious circle. Unable to free himself without help from the outside, he holds back his own history and displaces his future. Only as the patient remembers his own life history, and after constant conflict with the therapist (who at every turn must be able to interpret his own life history), are new life possibilities disclosed. What the analytic and therapeutic process sets in motion is this: Other distantiated modes of action, put into play through the advanced knowledge of the therapist, release the creative power of probing and appropriating changed modes of action. In learning the capacity to remember, the patient acquires the productive power of disclosing new life possibilities. The healing of the individual remains particular, and therefore it is immediately threatened again if the social relationships that helped to induce the illness are not changed. Otherwise, there remains only the fatal alternative of sheer adaptation to those relationships presupposed as healthy or "normal," or the illusory postulate of demanding from the patient such a measure of ego strength as to break the power of these relationships. Already in Freud, therefore, the theory of psychoanalysis and psychotherapy surpasses the realm of the purely individual and incorporates the realm of societal institutions.

The reference to psychoanalysis and to the method of ideology critique can have paradigmatic and heuristic significance for theology. First, it can be shown that the relation to one's own history and the capacity for undistorted memory is of a piece with the structure of a sort of communication that does not block such memory but rather permits its occurrence. Second, one can ask what a theological theory of communication that would be attentive to these structures could look like. Then it is a matter of whether theological statements themselves (and, ultimately, those of the Judeo-Christian tradition) have an ideological function in the sense that they merely supply a background of legitimation for the communicative situations distorted by power and injustice in various societies. Or do theological statements and the linguistic communicative actions that have grown out of the Christian tradition possess the innovative and critical power to uncover and break through the injustice and violence of the context of interaction (what the Bible calls "the world") and, as linguistic actions, have a rectifying and therapeutic effect? A theory of rectifying speech belongs, then, to a society-oriented theological hermeneutics. Perhaps a theory of therapeutic dialogue can give suggestions for such a theory of remembering and liberating speech, since such dialogue has recourse to scenic understanding and the narrative introduction of possibilities of action and understanding and is directed as a whole to the reconstitution of the freedom of the individual.[13]

The question is, then, how such a theory can be developed as a theological one and whether in the end it is really necessary that it be theological at all. If a theory of communicative action is central to the essential sciences of man, such a theory could be developed only in an interdisciplinary manner. This only multiplies the problems. The sciences of man, for their part, have stood since the Enlightenment under the pressure of the expectation that theology would be dissolved both metatheoretically and empirically, but they themselves are in turn subject to the hypothesis that they too must be ultimately reducible to the theories of the classical natural sciences. A theory of communicative action that is to have foundational significance for theology must be developed through the controversy surrounding these conflicting claims.

I

Theory of Science and Theory of Action

1

Contesting the Possibility of Theology

The Systematic Significance of Critically Reconstructing the Discussion within the Theory of Science Since Logical Positivism

The opposition between hermeneutically oriented human sciences and empirical sciences oriented toward seeking causal laws with prognostic relevance did not originate in this century. It can be traced throughout the history of Western thought. In our century, however, this opposition has been developed theoretically with a sharpness, a clarity, and a decisiveness as never before, so that the previous arguments are re-formulated and developed on a new level. This step was taken by Wittgenstein in his *Tractatus Logico-Philosophicus* and, in a cruder form, by the Logical Positivists and their antecedents. The positions that developed thereby present the most severe and consistent challenge to the possibility of theology in modern times. The internal difficulties of these positions have already been pointed out—primarily by their own advocates—and pursued to the point of transforming the entire approach.

My starting point, therefore, is that a presentation of this discussion, which understands itself as a critical reconstruction of the decisive arguments, also has systematic significance for theology. I shall explain briefly just what I mean by this before I begin with the various steps of the reconstruction.

My thesis is that this development can and must be interpreted as a turn to "pragmatics," to a more comprehensive concept of rationality resting on a more comprehensive concept of binding intersubjective communicative action, and that this turn entails a radically changed situation in which the question of a fundamental theology has to be posed anew.

The basic thesis of the Vienna Circle is that only the sentences of mathematics and logic and those of the empirical sciences can be meaningful sentences. All statements that go beyond these limits, as in metaphysics and theology, must be considered meaningless. Although Wittgenstein was never a member of the Vienna Circle, his *Tractatus* advances this position in its essential points. According to Wittgenstein in the *Tractatus*, the task of the philosopher as the critic of language is to prove to anyone who formulates a sentence not belonging to logic or the natural sciences that he has not given any meaning to certain signs of that sentence. For Wittgenstein, the sentences of the *Tractatus*, which draw the boundaries within language between sense and nonsense, still have the paradoxical function— through their very meaninglessness—of putting one in the presence of the unsayable. For the Vienna Circle, this function of language was also simply nonsense. Theology was condemned along with traditional philosophy to muteness and to the loss of its language. If one speaks in this context of "semantic atheism" or the "death of God in language," the radical nature of this position has not been made clear; these very phrases are also without any possible meaning and thus nonsensical.

The missionary zeal of the Vienna Circle was guided by two fundamental ideas. The first is that the progress of the natural sciences gives rise to the conviction that the single criterion for the relation of a statement to reality, and thus for its meaning, is what is immediately given in observation and subject to experimental confirmation. Enlightenment appears to have finally found an unambiguous criterion for critique and to have established itself as the culmination of Western thought. The second fundamental idea is that mathematical-logical research has made available an adequately differentiated theoretical apparatus for both the critique of ordinary-language sentences and the transparent construction of scientific theories. The clarity of formal operations that use abstract signs contains evidence of this. The meaning of an operation lies only in its execution and is clear only through it. The formal thought of logical operations is pure thought, as it were— thought that thinks itself. Thus, it seemed as if an unsurpassable clarity was achieved in a thinking that illuminated itself. As the apparatus of this thinking, logic had already demonstrated its efficiency in the empirical sciences. The possibility appeared irrefutable that what was given in experience could be represented unambiguously through formal theoretical constructions.

In this state of the development of the problematic, the fronts between the representatives of the traditional human sciences and the theoreticians of the empirical sciences became even more entrenched. Each side sought to punish the other with disdain. The logicians pointed out the logical fallacies of the humanists, and the humanists in turn affirmed that the logicians knew nothing of the really important questions.

The contemporary state of knowledge no longer corresponds to this image of trench warfare. In a process of unrelenting self-critique, which in its radicality and honesty of questioning is paralleled in theology by almost nothing but the study of the Bible during the last two centuries, fundamental problems have surfaced in the discussion of the theory of science—the very problems worked on in the study of hermeneutics. This critical discussion is concerned above all with research in the foundations of logic and mathematics, in the theory of the empirical sciences, and in individual empirical sciences. As an example, we shall examine the discussion of the methods of linguistics and the social sciences. From such an investigation it can be seen that these problems converge in a theory of communicative action, but in such a way that this theory can be developed only in the dimensions of a theory of society and a theory of history.

It cannot be claimed that every historical development unfolds according to an inner logic that is at the same time systematically relevant. However, the discussion of the theory of science since Wittgenstein's *Tractatus* seems to possess an argumentative core that also has significance for the development of a conception of a fundamental theology. It has this significance for the following reasons:

• The challenge to the possibility of theology is so radical that theology is forced to start over from the absolute beginning and, in a methodologically verifiable manner, to develop anew the possibilities of its language.

• This challenge to the possibility of theology and the discussion that follows from it are not merely arbitrary but rather must be seen as taking up the central questions of modern times. Therefore, it has the character of a paradigm with a systematically significant core.

• This discussion is concerned not only with individual questions but also with problems of foundations, in the sense that the possible approaches to grasping reality, and finally the character of rationality itself, are put into question. All this takes the form of very detailed investigations into the basic concepts, methods, and modes of argumentation and their social and historical context.

• Methodologically, the attempt to reconstruct this development critically can also claim to have a paradigmatic character for theology, inasmuch as the attempt to develop a conception of fundamental theology can be undertaken by first traversing the inner problematic of the foundational theories of other sciences. Such an undertaking must have an interdisciplinary character from the very start.

This chapter presents the approach of Wittgenstein's *Tractatus* and its radicalization by the Vienna Circle as the point of departure and the constant background of the following discussion. The decisive internal critique of this conception occurred in the discussion of the foundations of logic and mathematics (chapter 2) and in the precise examination of the process of theory formation in the empirical sciences (chapter 3). The resulting turn to pragmatics is discussed in terms of Wittgenstein's later philosophy and the development of linguistics (chapter 4) and then investigated more closely in a discussion of the methods of the social sciences (chapter 5). The constructivist theory of science of the Erlangen School (chapter 6) can be understood as an approach that tries to account for the entire problematic and to develop an alternative that includes from the beginning the question of the normative orientation of human action and thus already raises for discussion those consequences that can be drawn from the entire course of the development of the problematic (chapter 7).

Wittgenstein's *Tractatus* as Starting Point

The Position of the *Tractatus*

In the German-speaking world, the fact that the *Tractatus* is considered the most important philosophical book of this century in the Anglo-Saxon world meets with much amazement. We can understand this judgment of the English-speaking world only if we see that the *Tractatus* brings together the lines of development of many problem areas, to the point where all further positions in mathematics and logic, as well as in the theory of the empirical sciences, can be seen as developing various perspectives out of this single work. Thus, its significance does not lie in the fact that in it one can find, "on all essential points, the final solution of the problems"[1]; rather, we find in it the cutting edge of lines of development and the antithetical foil of later positions. The *Tractatus* is an "extreme" book, and we can agree with Karl Otto Apel that it represents the exact counterpoint to the spirit of hermeneutical philosophy.[2]

In the views of the early Wittgenstein, English empiricism's anti-speculative critique of language joins forces with the logicism developed to its highest form in Russell and Frege to radically place in question Western metaphysics as theoretical science.[3] From the vantage point of this "transcendental linguisticism,"[4] one can explain the development of ordinary-language philosophy as well as the development of Logical Positivism and its foundering on the aporias of its own philosophical conception.

For the enterprise of justifying theological statements and thus intelligibly grounding a hermeneutical procedure, the train of thought of the *Tractatus* signifies an extreme challenge. Every utterance that goes beyond empirical and logical statements is declared to be non-sensical; the limits of the sayable are delineated from the inside, and silence before the self-manifestation [*Sich-zeigen*] of the "mystical" becomes the only possible remaining course of action. One cannot simply accuse Wittgenstein of being areligious; against such a view there is much biographical evidence, as well as his comment in the preface to the *Philosophical Remarks* that he would have liked to say that the book was "written for the honor of God" (if he could be sure that this statement would only be understood properly).[5] In any case, the *Tractatus* signifies an implicit condemnation of theology to the loss of its language. Everything it could say participates in the absurdity of Wittgenstein's own assertions. In this way, when one chooses the *Tractatus* as a starting point, even in the investigation of further developments of this view, the possibility or impossibility of theological statements is always in question. Theology must give an account of how it understands its own discourse and how its statements can be distinguished from those shown to be nonsensical.

The basic position of Wittgenstein's *Tractatus* is heavily influenced by Russell's "logical atomism."[6] Objects of experience are seen in the first instance as individual things, nameable by proper names. The possible constellation of objects divide up into states of affairs, which, if they actually exist, can be called facts. Thought is the picturing of facts, and thoughts express themselves in sentences as "sensibly perceivable."[7] The structure of sentences corresponds to the structure of states of affairs—that is, to facts. There exists between sentences and facts an isomorphic relation of "picturing."[8] Wittgenstein's picture theory of meaning cannot be understood in a naive sense as pictorial description, but it can be understood in a strict sense as a structural correlation, and thus in the mathematical sense as an isomorphism. Only then does Wittgenstein's theory receive its pregnant meaning: The relationship of language and the world is a structural correspondence that must be presupposed but cannot be further grounded. The language that can unambiguously express these structures cannot simply be ordinary language, which rather conceals the structure of sentences (4.002). The ideal picturing language can only be a language of signs that obeys "logical syntax" (3.325). The logical scope of this syntax and thus of the ideal language determines the possibilities of meaningful sentences along with the possibilities of experience. Stenius therefore considers the *Tractatus* a sort of "critique of pure language" analogous to Kant's critique.[9] In what sense such a position can be called transcendental is a matter of controversy. Habermas, following Stenius, Apel, and Stegmüller, believes that the concept of the logical syntax of a unified language represents a "transcendental logic in the strict sense."[10] Walter Schulz strongly objects to this interpretation and calls Wittgenstein's position precisely the end of all transcendental reflection in the classical sense and the "negation of philosophy itself,"[11] while H. Fahrenbach has found a mediating position between the two.[12] It is just this question that decides how Wittgenstein's theory of a logical, ideal picturing language is related to the starting point of philosophical and theological hermeneutics.

What is decisive here is what Wittgenstein denies that an ideal language—the only language in which meaningful statements can be made—can accomplish:

• In the ideal language, no statements can be made about its picturing relation to the world. The isomorphism of language and the world—

that language is a mirror image of the world (6.13)—cannot be grounded or justified any further; it simply "makes itself manifest." What makes itself manifest cannot be spoken of; that is, any doubt of the picturing character of language can only be its complete negation. For this reason, "logic must look after itself" (5.473). The insight into the logical syntax of language and its self-illuminating evidence marks it as "transcendental" (6.13), and thus at the same time as the unsurpassable framework of all possible experience. Indeed, Wittgenstein states that "to understand a sentence means to know what is the case if it is true" (4.024). And one can see from his conversations with the members of the Vienna Circle that Wittgenstein came very close to their formulation of the verification principle.[13] But the principle of verification itself is not a meaningful sentence of the ideal language; it can be seen only as a (nonsensical) explanatory sentence about the relationship of language to the world.

• A language that obeys the rules of logical syntax cannot speak about itself. "Propositions can represent the whole of reality, but they cannot represent what they must have in common with reality in order to be able to represent it—logical form. In order to be able to represent logical form, we should have to be able to station ourselves with propositions somewhere outside logic, that is to say outside the world."[14] (4.12) These important sentences implicitly assert the impossibility of philosophical reflection, inasmuch as what is understood by reflection is just this elucidation of the constitutive conditions of human action and speech. Philosophy now can be understood only as the activity that transforms statements into clear propositions of the logical, ideal language (4.112). "Most of the propositions and questions to be found in philosophical works are not false but nonsensical. Consequently we cannot give any answer to questions of this kind but can only point out that they are nonsensical. Most of the propositions and questions of philosophers arise from failing to understand the logic of our language. (They belong to the same class as the question whether the good is more or less identical with the beautiful.)" (4.003) Philosophy is then nothing but a "critique of language" (4.0031). From a mathematical perspective, this theory entails at the same time the rejection of all metalanguages. "A metalanguage would picture not the world but rather the scaffold of the picturing, the logical structure; that is absurd for Wittgenstein, because there is nothing there to picture. Logical structure does not correspond to something objective that could become the content of a new language."[15]

• The transcendental philosophies of Kant and Husserl both return to transcendental subjectivity as a constitutive principle. It is only consistent that Wittgenstein declares this return to be nonsense. "The ego enters into philosophy only in the sense that 'the world is my world.' " (5.632) "The subject does not belong to the world; rather it is a limit of the world." (5.632) The limits of the world, which are the same as the limits of experience and of language (5.62), cannot be surpassed in a sort of Hegelian dialectic of limits and thereby become the point of departure for philosophical reflection. These limits are the unsurpassable horizon of experience and of all meaningful statements. Transcendental experience as constitutive of objective experience cannot exist. "This is connected with the fact that no part of our experience is at the same time *a priori*." (5.634) "Where *in* the world is a metaphysical subject to be found?" (5.633) The limits of experience as the limits of both language and thought forbid any reflection that would go further.

• However, there is in Wittgenstein the category of the "mystical." "There are, indeed, things that cannot be put into words. They *make themselves manifest*. They are what is mystical." (6.522) "Feeling the world as a limited whole — it is this that is mystical." (6.45) The mystical is defined by the impossibility of its expression in language. "What we cannot speak about we must pass over in silence." (7) Every conceivable theology is also thereby deprived of its language.

The Relationship of Wittgenstein's *Tractatus* to Transcendental Philosophy and Hermeneutics

Since Stenius's reconstruction of the train of thought of the *Tractatus* there has been almost unanimous agreement among Wittgenstein scholars that in his analyses of language Wittgenstein wanted to formulate some sort of transcendental philosophy in the Kantian sense, with the aim of specifying the *a priori* form of experience in such a way as to indicate paradoxically what makes itself manifest in language. What was to be achieved through Kant's transcendental deduction is now attributed to the paradoxical sentences of the *Tractatus*. Wittgenstein's analysis can rightly be called "transcendental linguisticism,"[16] and it is of one piece with Kant's transcendental idealism except that Wittgenstein moves the locus of Kant's transcendental idealism from reason to language.[17] Schulz has objected to this interpretation, saying that Wittgenstein negates precisely the most essential elements of transcendental philosophy, insofar as the latter is a philosophy of subjectivity that becomes complete in presenting how and why subjectivity can apply its basic conditions to the given as such and yet does not itself fall under these conditions.[18] An interpretation of Wittgenstein as a transcendental philosopher must interpret his thought as the limit case of transcendental thought. Since transcendental philosophy in Wittgenstein is consciously taken *ad absurdum*, it reaches its limits.[19]

This fundamental difference between Wittgenstein and transcendental philosophy is demonstrated most clearly by Wittgenstein's thesis that solipsism coincides with pure realism: "Here it can be seen that solipsism, when its implications are followed out strictly, coincides with pure realism. The self of solipsism shrinks to a point without extension, and there remains the reality coordinated with it." (5.64) "The philosophical self is not the human being, nor the human body and soul, the subject-matter of psychology, but rather the metaphysical subject, the limits of the world—not part of it." (5.641) "The subject does not belong to the world; rather, it is a limit of the world." (5.632) This attempt to reduce classical transcendental philosophy to an absurd limit position can be formulated in the following theses.

• Talk about a transcendental subject is nonsense. It represents a limit, not a condition, and one can no longer speak of these limits. Wittgenstein refuses to participate in the Hegelian dialectic of limits, which thought always transgresses in its propositions. Thought itself is brought to a standstill insofar as it is dialectical, transcendental reflection.[20]

• The metaphysical subject eliminates itself as subject.[21] The dialectical relation of ego and world as the basic structure of classical transcendental philosophy is eliminated. The ideal unified language becomes the total transcendental subject, a subject from which all subjectivity has disappeared. Thus, Wittgenstein draws a radical conclusion from the basic problem of the transcendental approach (namely, to determine the relationship between concrete and transcendental subjectivity): Concrete, historical-perspectival subjectivity has dissolved itself in the unified language of logical syntax without a subject, in which only the propositions of the natural sciences are permitted as meaningful sentences. With this radical turn the linguistic and objectivist ideal of the modern natural sciences is stylized to its extreme limit. Everything that goes beyond the sentences of the natural sciences is nonsense. This has at the same time the fatal consequence that all sentences concerned with the relation of language and reality, and thus all sentences of logical semantics and sentences such as the verification principle, must be considered nonsensical as well. This conclusion was taken by Wittgenstein to pertain to himself: The sentences of the *Tractatus* as a whole are nonsense (see 6.54).

• This thesis marks a *reductio ad absurdum* of hermeneutics as well.[22] Hermeneutic understanding is necessary only when historical experience is to be understood in the perspective of a specific past language. The dialectic of such perspectival experiences comes to a preliminary halt in an understanding that is itself again historically conditioned. For Wittgenstein, the ideal unified language excludes any historical perspective. The task of the philosopher as the critic of language who would dissolve the need for hermeneutics consists in freeing historical utterances from their guise of ordinary language through logical analysis, thereby tracing them back to the sentences of the ideal unified language. As provocative as this may sound, such a view only takes implicit tendencies of modern science to their logical conclusion. In this way, Wittgenstein's *Tractatus* marks the point of extreme opposition to all hermeneutically oriented inquiry, and thus is an unavoidable "opposing foil"[23] to it, if only as a thought experiment.

• Such a view seems to leave open only the possibility of devoting oneself to the experience of the "mystical" (no longer expressible in language) or to purely practical activity. Quite aware of this, Wittgenstein drew the practical conclusion from his own thought: In the approximately 10 years between finishing the *Tractatus* and taking up philosophical activity again at Cambridge, he worked as an elementary-school teacher, as a gardener in a Benedictine monastery, and as an architect. Only after overcoming his own position in the *Tractatus* with a new starting point for the philosophy of language was Wittgenstein able to resume his position teaching philosophy.

Despite everything, the *Tractatus* remains essential for the analysis of the dialectical development of the modern theory of science; its radical starting point brought modern scientific consciousness up against its own limits.

The Fundamental Question of the *Tractatus* as the Leading Thread of the Debate between Theology and the Theory of Science

If certain tendencies are actually pursued to their extreme conclusions in the *Tractatus*, then this perspective also allows us to bring into sharp focus the problems that persist between theology and the modern theory of science. We could even do this in terms of Wittgenstein's position as described previously, for in the *Tractatus* Wittgenstein took explicit positions on questions at the boundary between science and theology.

Since the meaning of sentences consists in their projective picturing of the world and in this picturing alone, one cannot speak of the "meaning of the world" as given in such sentences. This lies "outside" the world and beyond all possible speech (6.41). The accidental nature of facts inside the world cannot be surpassed by anything in the world. Therefore, the meaning of the world and of life (6.521) can be neither questioned nor expressed. One could say it is strictly transcendent if this statement were not itself meaningless.

This is also true of ethics and of questions of good and evil. The thesis that "ethics cannot be put into words" (6.421) has parallels in the value-free character of the sciences. Psychology can of course be interested in the will as a phenomenon; however, the will cannot be spoken of as ethical, as having good or bad intentions. The assertion that ethics is transcendental reveals much about Wittgenstein's conception of the transcendental: It is not what reflection uncovers as the probable and expressible conditions of knowing and acting but simply that which lies outside any reflection and linguistic communication. The belief that the world could be changed through good or evil intention, that its limits are changed, can no longer be given any ascertainable meaning (see 6.43). The catastrophic consequence of this thesis if it is taken seriously—as it is by many scientists for the entire domain of their statements—are apparent. A rational discussion of goals, values, or political decisions becomes impossible, and every attempt at such a discussion is explained away as nonsense. This is one of the basic aporias of the very conception of modern science.

As a statement, the supposition of the immortality of the soul is nonsensical, not only in the world-picturing language, but also because it does not do what it is supposed to as it is usually understood; temporal persistence would then be equivalent in meaning to eternity. Eternity as nontemporal could mean, at most, the highest life in the present. But nothing is thereby resolved; the question of eternity is simply not a problem for the natural sciences. If one sees it as a question of the riddle of life, then it must be said that the solution to this riddle lies "*outside* of space and time"; however, this statement in turn cancels itself out (6.431).

Talking about God is therefore impossible. "God does not reveal himself *in* the world." (6.431) God is not an object that could be encountered in the world or a state of affairs that could be named or pictured in a sentence. Other forms of meaningful discourse do not exist, according to the *Tractatus*. As in Nietzsche's maxim that metaphysical speculation can only construe a dead object and that this God is in fact meaningless, "dead," so too Wittgenstein's transformation of the aporia of a metaphysics with a transcendental starting point on the level of language results in something like "the death of God in language." The word "God" cannot occur in a language purified through the critique of language (see 4.0031). The methodological agnosticism of the modern sciences is pursued to its conclusion on the level of language—whether this is Wittgenstein's actual intention or not—with the exclusion of words or sentences in which the word appears. Both classical philosophy, with its discourse on the Absolute, and theology are brought to an end.

Admittedly, Wittgenstein insists: "There are, indeed, things that cannot be put into words. *They make themselves manifest*. They are what is mystical." (6.522) But precisely this "making manifest" [*Sich-zeigen*] lies beyond the sayable, and the question of the function of Wittgenstein's own sentences is posed in its most extreme form. He writes: "It is not *how* things are in the world that is mystical, but *that* it exists." (6.45) The experience of the mystical could thus be understood as an experience of the contingent facticity of the world. Indeed, Wittgenstein characterizes this "experience" rather vaguely as an "intuition" or feeling of the world as a finite whole. However, this experience can no longer be expressed linguistically in the strict sense. Whereas it was still possible for classical philosophy and theology to go beyond the experience of that which factually exists to the prehension of an unlimited horizon through the transcending movement of finite spirit, and then to make this movement transparent in the reflective movement of language, this possibility has been cut short by the construction of the ideal, unified, world-picturing language. What can be said falls under the ideal type of the "propositions of the natural sciences"; the task of philosophy informed by the critique of language consists essentially in correction: "whenever someone else wanted to say something metaphysical, to demonstrate to him that he had failed to give a meaning to certain signs in his propositions." (6.53) A discourse that would explicate the act of transcending — as the starting point for metaphysics — must be convinced of its own meaninglessness.

Wittgenstein therefore calls his own propositions "elucidating" on the one hand and "nonsensical" on the other. They are elucidating only insofar as they can be recognized as nonsensical. They function as a ladder upon which one can climb beyond oneself, but they communicate nothing, clarify nothing, and do not articulate any experience. The end result of such propositions is speechlessness. One of the pioneers of Logical Positivism, Otto Neurath, pointed out the ambivalence of even this silence: "The end of the *Tractatus*, 'What we cannot speak about we must pass over in silence,' is at least linguistically misleading; it sounds as if there were something of which we could not speak. But we would say, should one wish to withdraw into any sort of metaphysical mood, one is silent, but not 'about something.' "[24]

Consequences for Theology

Wittgenstein explicitly directs his demarcation of what can still be said or thought against philosophy, specifically against metaphysics. He charges that it makes statements about the relationship between language and the world, about the subject, about time and eternity, and about God. It is of course true that modern theology has tried to scrutinize its connection with metaphysics. To the extent that metaphysics is characterized by speculative thought attempting a construction of the absolute, either as absolute being or according to the model of absolute subjectivity, and to the extent that it understands itself as the thinking of the absolute itself, it falls under a critique that emphasizes the preeminence of freedom over speculation and attempts to destroy all speculative foundation systems that would domesticate this freedom.

Even in relation to such a critical conception of theology, the style of thought articulated in the *Tractatus* still represents an extreme counterposition. The various conceptions of theological hermeneutics presented in this book would lose all possibility of expression in language, according to the *Tractatus*. Problems such as those dealt with under the titles of subjectivity, historicality and history, language and reflection, language and reality, decision, and the political dimension of theology could no longer even arise as problems.

For theology, three basic courses of action are possible in this situation:

• Theology could then understand itself merely as an initiation into pure mysticism. Its propositions would not even be those of a negative theology positing a wordless experience beyond its negative statements; it could no longer even give an account of its negative character.[25]

• Even dialectical theology can be understood as a reaction to the inroads of scientific methods in theology and as a general answer to a modern consciousness so impressed with empirical science. One can at least see liberal theology and its means of dealing with historical-critical methods in this context. Dialectical theology extracts absolute paradox as the basic structure of Christianity; faith is the leap of existence into the absurdity of the Word of God. In this leap, faith also gains its own linguistic realm, one that can give expression to theology. No dialogue with science can attain to the realm and language of faith; its demand for justification of theology has validity only as a sign of unbelief. The special language of belief then excludes any possibility of a conversation with science.

• However, the question is still whether theology can be satisfied with so radical an opposition to the empirical sciences. First, this presupposes that a view like Wittgenstein's in the *Tractatus* finally resolves the problematic and exhausts the propositional possibilities of science. Moreover, theology retreats to a harmless island of truisms, an esoteric language. It would then renounce any claim to formulate its subject matter in a communicable and comprehensible manner, and would even insist on the disparity of all scientific discourse and theological statements, thus eliminating any critical relationship between theology and the sciences. This is the surrender of the fundamental concern of the Enlightenment: to speak in a public, critical, and criticizable way.

Theology must therefore accept its situation in relation to the modern sciences both objectively and methodologically, while at the same time attempting to return to its beginnings, where nothing is taken for granted and the individual steps must all be learned again. Theology must uncover again the fundamental operations of the theological mode of thinking, recreate the fundamental conditions of theological discourse, and introduce its statements so that they are intersubjectively reasonable.

In what follows, we will be dealing not only with the debate surrounding the possibility of science but also, more fundamentally, with the dimensions of experience, the possibility of communicating it in language, the character of language and reflection, the possibility of giving expression to the temporal structure of interaction and death, and the question of meaningfully reconstructing the reality of God.

The Logical Positivism of the Vienna Circle

From the beginning of the 1920s a number of philosophers, mathematicians, and natural scientists gathered around Moritz Schlick in Vienna. They soon formed a group and gave themselves the name Vienna Circle.[26] In a manifesto from the year 1929, "The Scientific Conception of the World—the Vienna Circle," they presented their common views and placed themselves in the tradition of Enlightenment philosophers such as Comte and Mill, theorists of the sciences such as Mach, Duhem, Boltzmann, and Einstein, and logicians such as Leibniz, Frege, Russell, Whitehead, and Wittgenstein. In general, they sided with positivist thinkers such as Hume, Feuerbach, Marx, and Menger. Their views had a special proximity to those of Wittgenstein, although Wittgenstein himself was never a member of the circle; his thoughts and suggestions were always mediated by Schlick and Waismann.[27] Soon there was also contact with the Berlin School around Hans Reichenbach and later Carl Hempel, and with groups in Scandinavia, England, Poland, and the United States. Karl Popper distanced himself from the group but remained in contact with individual members.

The Vienna Circle was dominated by the view that progress came about in the entire history of philosophy only when thinkers oriented themselves by the methods and results of the empirical sciences. Only the verification of all statements without condition in terms of their empirical content could end the fruitless controversies of the philosophical schools and steer effort away from mere pseudo-problems to truly helpful knowledge. The "reawakening of metaphysics" following from Schopenhauer, Nietzsche, Bergson, and Klages that was so widespread after the First World War could only have awakened their deep distrust. Thus, the binding element for the Vienna Circle, besides the orientation to the natural sciences, was the turn against everything that its members could call metaphysics.

In this critique of metaphysics there was a consciousness of standing at a decisive turning point for philosophy.[28] Whereas Mach's positivism of immanance still saw the task of science as the simplest and most exact possible description of the immediate, sensibly given, now the insight that science began when it formulated its knowledge in propositions moved into the foreground. The decisive turn of philosophy initiated by Wittgenstein was the turn to language. The investigation of language first created the distinction between meaningful and meaningless propositions.

Only two sorts of statements are to be considered meaningful: the statements of logic and mathematics (which have no empirical content and which present, according to Wittgenstein, only formal tautologies) and the statements of the sciences (which can be verified in experience). The possibility of verification becomes the criterion of the meaning of sentences. Even though the verification principle is never formulated explicitly in the *Tractatus*, it seems to be traceable back to Wittgenstein.[29] If scientific propositions are formulated in a language in such a way that they satisfy the demands of logic and are subject to strict empirical verification, they are recognized as meaningful by "Logical Positivism" or "Logical Empiricism." Any proposition that goes beyond these limits is nonsensical.

This is meant as a demarcation from the propositions of metaphysics as well. The concept of metaphysics of the Vienna Circle can basically be defined only negatively, and it remains global and indeterminate in its demarcation from logical and empirical propositions. In any case, the sentences of metaphysics are called pseudo-statements. Such statements give the impression that they are meaningful propositions, since meaningful and meaningless sentences appear similar in structure. There are two reasons for calling a statement meaningless: the use of pseudo-concepts such as the absolute, the unconditioned, the being of beings, absolute spirit, and the ego, which have no meaning because no empirical conditions for their verification can be given,[30] and the

combination of concepts or pseudo-concepts in syntactically incorrect ways, as in the sentence "Caesar is a prime number." At best, metaphysics can function as conceptual poetry, giving the impression of the feeling of life as if it were the attempts of unmusical men to express the feeling of life that musicians express more completely.[31]

The denial of metaphysics also includes theology, insofar as metaphysics attempts to formulate theology on the level of systematic formal thought. Carnap writes: "Only in the fields of philosophy (and theology) do ostensible statements occur that have no factual content."[32] Theology becomes subsumed under metaphysics in this sense. What is most important in this critique of theology is not that its statements are false or shown to be uncertain or unfruitful but that they are dismissed from the start as nonsensical and seen as having no expressible meaning.

The concepts of theology are pseudo-concepts, its sentences only pseudo-sentences, its questions only pseudo-questions; the word "God" cannot be distinguished from a senseless, invented word like "bab," for which no criteria of meaning can be given. Even atheism presupposes but rejects some content in a specific concept of God. Agnosticism still asserts the unknowability of this content. From Carnap's standpoint, even the distinction among theism, atheism, and agnosticism is meaningless; he wants to assert that we are finally finished with such alternatives. The characterization of "semantic atheism"[33] is possible only from a position that has not yet left these alternatives behind. Here we have arrived at the point where it is meaningless to call oneself an atheist.[34]

The Vienna Circle dissolved in the 1930s,[35] but the discussion of the theory of science went on, leading to the withdrawal and differentiation of earlier individual theses. The further history of Logical Empiricism may be presented as one of the dramatic phases in the history of philosophy. Above all, there began a "colossal intrigue"[36] around the explication, rejection, or defense of the verification principle. To this extent, Logical Positivism remains a contrasting background for the entire later development; the state of the development at every point can be measured against the early radical theses that provoked the entire discussion.

One cannot enter into a direct debate with Logical Empiricism's critique of theology without giving consideration to further developments in mathematical logic and the theory of science. Only through the uncovering of their internal problems and aporias is a fruitful conversation possible, for only then is it possible to formulate questions that engage both the theory of science and theology, and only then could rules of interdisciplinary research be formulated in which theology participates as a partner with full standing. In what follows we shall examine developments in mathematical logic and in the theory of science, and the concretization of their internal problematic in linguistics and sociology.

The Discovery of the Internal Limits of Formalism

The Crisis of the Foundations of Logic and Mathematics

The fundamental ideas of Wittgenstein and the Vienna Circle would not have been possible without the development of modern logic since the nineteenth century.[1] The exact study of formal operations in symbolic languages led, however, to a foundational crisis for logic and mathematics. The essential results of the study of the foundations of logic and mathematics in the recent decades can also be presented in everyday language, as can the discussion of their consequences.

It has become clearer and clearer in recent years that Frege deserves a key place in this development. His name is invoked by Russell, Wittgenstein, and Carnap.[2]

In the construction of a logical system of language, attention is directed not only toward individual connections within such a language but also toward the system in the broadest sense, in order to come to terms with it as a whole. This tendency was already to be found in Leibniz, who postulated a "characterization of reason by whose power the truths of reason could be attained through a calculus, as in arithmetic and algebra, which could be extended to every other realm, insofar as each can be subsumed under the laws of logical deduction."[3]

A high point was attained by Whitehead and Russell in the *Principia Mathematica*,[4] where they constructed a logical calculus by means of which further parts of mathematics could be deduced.

Gödel's completeness theorem (1930) marked the end of all these efforts at synthesis since Boole.[5] Gödel (a member of the Vienna Circle) demonstrated that in so-called first-order predicate logic all consequences of any arbitrary axiomatic system could be formally derived. In other words, the set of all derivable sentences could be generated (or enumerated).[6]

Toward the end of the nineteenth century, antinomies connected with the concept of infinity appeared in Cantorian set theory. It had been possible to show that one can prove contradictory propositions in set theory. Russell discovered the antinomy that came to be the best-known: Paradoxes arise when one tries to form the set of all those sets that do not contain themselves as members. Such a set cannot belong to its own class, and cannot *per definitionem* belong to the class of sets that have themselves as members. Since both classes form an exhaustive disjunction, there arises a logical paradox. This and other antinomies brought about a crisis in the foundations of mathematics that deprives mathematics of its aura of absolute indisputability and exactness.[7] Various attempts were undertaken to escape this dilemma. Frege tried to avoid the difficulties in the formation of infinite sets through the reduction of arithmetic to a logical model (logicism). Russell later demonstrated that here too the antinomies appear. He and Whitehead tried to formulate a solution through the so-called theory of types, in which sets are divided into an ordered hierarchy of types (a first level of individuals, a second level of sets of individuals, a third set of these sets, and so on), but this solution led to further difficulties.

In this situation, various schools of mathematics were formed, representing various attempts at a solution. Brouwer can be seen as the founder of mathematical intuitionism and constructivism, which drew essentially radical consequences from the crisis. He attempted to build up mathematics from certain, intuitive basic constructions; for example, he surrendered the validity of the axiom of the law of the excluded middle. Hilbert's school tried grounding classical mathematics in another way: The whole of mathematics was to be constructed axiomatically (the axiomatic method) and completely formalized, thus reduced to a pure calculus. This mathematics had then to be grounded in an area of study called metamathematics and shown to be consistent through noncontroversial methods of deduction recognized even by the intuitionists. Hilbert's metamathematical program led to unexpected difficulties, the most important of which for future development was the incompleteness theorem presented by Gödel in his 1931 paper "On the Formally Undecidable Propositions of *Principia Mathematica* and Related Systems."[8]

Gödel investigated arithmetic and the related laws of deduction, a formal system containing both elementary number theory and logic. His basic idea was to transform metatheoretical statements (such as "formula," "theorem," or "provable") by a definite procedure of arithmetization (Gödelization) into arithmetic propositions (about Gödel numbers). What is essential in this procedure is the translation of propositions formulated in the metalanguage M concerning the object language S back into the object language S itself. This procedure gives Gödel's first theorem: Assuming the consistency of S, there is in S a formally undecidable sentence; that is, there necessarily appears in S a sentence that cannot be proved or disproved within the system. Gödel's second theorem is related to the first: Assuming that system S is consistent, the consistency of S cannot be proved in S.[9]

Gödel's results and their subsequent reformulation shocked the mathematical world. Some mathematicians consider these results of metamathematics to be the most characteristic achievement of mathematics in the twentieth century.[10] I will try to indicate their significance in the following.

The most deeply incisive result for mathematics is that there is no decision procedure for any formal system of sufficient complexity. What is most astonishing is that this already holds for first-order predicate logic. In the years following the publication of Gödel's article, more precision was sought in the concepts of decidability and computability. In 1936, Church advanced the thesis that the concept of a computable function is identical with that of a recursive function (Church's thesis).[11] Rosser,[12] Kleene,[13] and other mathematicians studied the area of decidable functions further. The result was almost complete agreement.[14] The question of decidability and computability is related to the concept of the algorithm. An algorithm is usually understood as a general and exactly reproducible procedure of deciding a problem in a finite number of steps. An area of mathematics is undecidable if no algorithm can be provided such that, given a formula of the corresponding system, it can be decided in a finite number of steps whether or not the formula is valid. Elementary group theory, axiomatic set theory, elementary number theory, the elementary algebra of real numbers, and predicate logic have all been shown to be undecidable. As Hermes put it, one could say that "mathematicians have shown with purely mathematical methods that there are mathematical problems which cannot be handled by the apparatus of computational mathematics." He went on to cite Post's mention of natural "limitations of the mathematicizing power of Homo sapiens."[15] The results of metamathematics also had repercussions in the theory of computation machines. Turing developed a theoretical model for any possible computation machine, the so-called Turing machine.[16] This model demonstrates that every function for which there is an algorithm is exactly calculable through a machine. Predicate logic does not belong to this set of functions; it is not "Turing computable."[17] Thus, the limits of the algorithmic decision procedures and those of computation machines coincide. Turing's results meant not merely that the unavailability of technological means made it impossible to build machines that could do more, but rather that the presupposition of the very possibility of such machines involved logical contradictions.

The second important consequence of Gödel's metamathematical results concerns the relation between language and metalanguage. The difference between them was first clearly worked out in the investigation of formalized languages. "Metalanguage" first of all generally signifies a language in which statements are made about the formations of another language and its structures—about an "object language." One could understand a German grammar of Latin as having Latin as its object language and German as its metalanguage. But a language can also be its own metalanguage, as would be the case in a Latin grammar written in Latin. In this case, there arises the famous paradox familiar to the Greeks, as in the example of the Cretan in Epimenides who insists that he is lying while he is lying.[18] In logic, the object language is the calculus. Gödel's procedure consists in translating the propositions of the metalanguage about the object language back into the object language. This leads to the emergence of antinomies having a structure similar to that in the case of the lying Cretan. The formalization of a system thus demands the strict separation of the object language from the metalanguage if the antinomies are to be avoided.

Tarski worked out the significance of this relationship in "The Concept of Truth in Formalized Languages."[19] He showed that the semantic definition[20] of the truth or falsehood of a proposition is not possible in the object language itself but only in the metalanguage.[21] Carnap pointed out that the same holds true for the concepts "analytic" and "contradictory."[22] From this we can draw the following consequences: Logical paradoxes can also be constructed in the metalanguage, so they can be resolved only by a further division between the meta-language and a metametalanguage, and so on *ad infinitum*. Infinite regress is unavoidable and has consequences for mathematics; for example, if one wants a proof of consistency, mathematical theory requires an indeterminate series of ever-richer logical systems.[23] This structure of a transfinite, continuous, and open ordering of a hierarchy of languages was studied from a constructivist standpoint by Lorenzen.[24]

Contemporary debate on the foundations of logic and mathematics is also concerned with how these results are to be interpreted and what consequences are to be drawn from them.[25] As an alternative to previous attempts, the Erlangen School (above all, Paul Lorenzen) proposed a "constructivist" foundation for mathematics and logic. This proposal will be presented more fully later; first I shall try to characterize the results attained so far and to indicate their possible consequences, for this problem situation forms the primary background for any alternative proposal:

• A universal formal system cannot be completely reflective in its basic assumptions, presuppositions, and consequences and in all the move-ments of its reflection itself. A formally closed system that is its own metasystem is self-contradictory.

• The basically given possibilities of concrete, formal operations cannot be exhausted. The closed system as paradigm of all forms of human argumentation and speech, as the highest canon of reason, does not exist. Whatever system one considers, there are always modes of argumentation outside of it, foreign to it. This does not exclude the possibility that these modes of argumentation can be intersubjectively introduced and justified in a convincing manner.

• Every system can be surpassed. There is always something as yet uncomputed, unthought, unplanned, yet to be discovered. There can be something really novel that can be creatively discovered.

• The inner limits of formal systems are presumably closely related to the temporal structure of all operations.[26] In operations that represent at the same time a process of reflection, there is always only a limited segment present; the present is thus withdrawn. Continuity is produced only in the operation itself. Reflective action is thus open; something novel can result from it. Indeed, the "novel" here does not mean simply that a previously determined series is continued (as in the series of the natural numbers) but rather that strange structures could result — something that infringes on the rules, something that puts the whole into question. Thus, the inner limitations of formal systems have to do with a temporal future that can open up to the creatively new.

• Every system of a certain level of differentiation and complexity allows for different interpretations when interpreted in terms of a definite, concrete model, just as, inversely, the metatheoretical pre-suppositions of a system can be altered when realized in a specific interpretation.[27]

• The demonstrated necessity of recourse to ever-richer metalanguages necessarily leads to the use of everyday or ordinary language as the final metalanguage and to the return to an already existing com-municative practice. The constitution of human action and speech cannot be exhausted by objectifiable operations.[28] But in what sense, then, can we speak of a rational foundation of logic and mathematics and of scientific discourse at all? Do not all the aporias of hermeneutics simply reappear?[29] Can we yet again insightfully reconstruct the basis of the practice of understanding? In what sense can this occur? Does it not require discussing all the dimensions of human communicative action and its genesis?

• The return to everyday communicative practice points to subjects who use formal languages, and thus to pragmatics as a foundational realm for a theory of formal operations as well as for a theory of language. How can a pragmatics be developed that is theoretically inclusive of both of these dimensions?

• The use of formal systems as instruments for the construction of empirical theories raises special problems after the discoveries in the foundations of mathematics and logic. First, are formal systems neutral instruments, or does the choice of certain instruments build prejudice into a theory? Second, can all theoretical concepts be excluded from a theory, so that formalism alone is sufficient for the construction of a theory? These are the basic questions of many of Carnap's investigations.

• This problematic arrives at a critical point when formal languages are used in the study of natural languages and in the interpretation of social processes in the action-oriented social sciences. If the limits of formalization refer back to temporal, creative, rule-breaking communicative action of subjects—action that must be called "free" in terms of these limit determinations—then is there not the danger that formalized methods only obscure the basic structure of human action, because of the limits of what they can actually achieve? This seems to be the basic problem of a systems theory applied to society and of what has been called "political cybernetics."[30]

The Limit Problems of Cybernetic Systems Theory

The study of the capabilities of formal systems is the theoretical foundation of cybernetic systems theory, an area of research that has shown the fruitfulness of formal methods in many diverse sciences. *Cybernetics* can be defined as the theory of information-processing systems in abstraction from the form of their realization.[31] A *system* is understood purely formally as a set of elements and a set of relations between these elements which constitute its structure. Cybernetics is concerned primarily with dynamic systems, systems whose elements are active (that is, whose elements influence or are influenced by other elements or systems). These types of relations can be realized in different ways, as material, energetic, or informational couplings. Inasmuch as cybernetic systems regulate themselves, they are able to react to certain environmental influences and eliminate them if they are disturbing the system. Higher types of systems can maintain their stability within certain limits. The relations among the elements of a system and their possibilities of action can be presented abstractly and formally, without consideration of the manner of their realization. Cybernetic systems theory is thus an abstract theory of dynamic, self-regulating systems. Precisely because of this abstractness, it can be applied to various areas: technology, biology, psychology, sociology, economics, and so on. The development of the mathematics of formal systems and of model theory created the presuppositions necessary for cybernetic systems theory.[32]

The concept of *information* proves to be increasingly more fundamental to systems theory, so much so that an unambiguous definition is no more possible for it than for concepts such as mass and energy.

In probability theory, information is a measure of the uncertainty of the appearance of an event within the field of probability of possible events. The appearance of an event has an even greater informational content the more improbable it is. The drawing of a specific lottery number is all the more improbable, and thus has all the more informational content, the greater the number of entries.

To this point, the concept of information is a purely syntactic concept related to the combination of sign elements. The confusion of the concept of information with that of meaning and the reception of information theory from communications technology as a comprehensive theory of communication have often produced great conceptual unclarity. The attempt to broaden information theory to include all dimensions of communication and interactions remains in the incipient stages.[33] Since reports are so often codified in a binary alphabet with two signs, 0 and 1, the quantity of binary numbers (bits) necessary for coding has proved to be a useful measure for information, where information becomes the number of required binary yes-no choices. This unit of codification makes it possible to compute the amount of information in a specific report in relation to the set of signs already available; for example, we can calculate precisely the average amount of information contained in a letter of the alphabet in the German or the English language. Shannon, in his 1949 work *The Mathematical Theory of Communication* (edited with Weaver), developed a general formula for the amount of information in a report in relation to this binary code. This formula can be considered a sort of fundamental principle of information theory. It allows for the average necessary number of bits of a letter to be calculated as a limit, which becomes a lower limit for favorable codings. Because of the analogies to thermodynamics, Shannon called this quantity the *entropy* of a source of information.

Cybernetics is concerned not only with conveying information but also with information-processing (that is, the transformation of specific given reports into other reports according to definite rules through the use of a machine). The study of information-processing machines is a discipline of cybernetics and as such its centerpiece, for the performance capabilities, complexity, and stability of cybernetic systems depends precisely on their capacity for information processing. Since dynamic, self-regulating, information-processing cybernetic systems can be seen as the realization of algorithms, we must look into the significance of the results of metamathematics for cybernetic systems theory. The discussion of the philosophical significance of the cybernetic approach is still in process. Only a few fundamental problems of this discussion can be pointed out here.

The problem of so-called learning machines is of primary importance. In general, this involves machines that are capable of forming internal models of their environment, correcting this model through repeated communication, and modifying its relation to its environment on this basis. These learning automata are also dependent on the realization of algorithms, with all the limitations discussed above. The determination of the optimal relation to the environment usually occurs through a multilayered hierarchy of "optimal value circles," which perform the mathematical function of optimization. A second decisive question arises concerning measures used for the valuation of the model and for the optimization of its relation to the environment. Inasmuch as learning machines themselves are used as models for human learning and social change, in such a theoretical framework can there be a goal beyond the self-stabilization and survival of the system? If so, what does this mean for the modeling of human experience in its totality through such systems?[34]

Cybernetic systems theory has shown explanatory and heuristic value in many different sciences. By means of formal constructions, cybernetic models can formally represent certain interconnections within technical systems, in biological systems and their relation to the environment, and in functional processes in the economy and society as a whole. They can also stimulate the formation of hypotheses regarding other connections, and they are useful in the search for empirical corroboration of these. This leads finally to the well-known question whether all processes, including those of consciousness, can basically be represented in cybernetic models and finally realized in cybernetic machines, so that a cybernetic machine basically performs the same tasks as a human being. In this area, two different kinds of problems must be noted, each with its own specific contexts: questions concerning the range of cybernetic models and theory formation (and thus the range of formal-structural models in all areas of science) and problems concerning the realization of formal-abstract systems in concrete machines. If the explanatory power of a cybernetic model is sufficient and its realization in a machine possible, then the explanatory system itself emerges as a rival self-regulating, dynamic system. It should be clear that this is the point at which important questions emerge for the theory of science and for philosophy in general.

Turing's theories are a classic case of the need to decide whether cybernetic machines perform exactly as humans do. If a human can be put in communication with an information-processing machine, can ask it any question whatsoever, and cannot decide whether he is communicating with a machine, then, according to the theory, one must give fundamentally the same status to both human and machine.[35] Naturally, in this analysis a purely behaviorist understanding of human consciousness is presupposed; that is, processes of consciousness are seen as processes of an input-output machine. Cybernetic methods, of course, allow for no other approach. They can grasp consciousness only as a precisely circumscribed problem-solving behavior.

Under these strictly limiting presuppositions, an attempt was made, relying on Gödel's metamathematical research, to indicate which human performances could not be accomplished by a machine. As mentioned above, Gödel proved that every sufficiently complex system allows for statements that can neither be proved nor disproved in that system. If every cybernetic machine is the realization of a formal system, there must be an undecidable formula for each such realization. It is possible to show that this formula is true through informal reflection, but that is exactly what a machine cannot perform. A variant of this argument is the so-called self-reference problem: Every conceivable information-processing machine (Turing machine) can be characterized as a formal system. There is no algorithm with which a machine could produce its own underlying formal system.[36]

The question whether these arguments point to human performances not achievable by any machine reveals the underlying dilemma of the problematic itself. If we assume that in proving the truth of a formally undecidable sentence or in deriving the formal system that underlies a machine's functioning a human does something no machine can do, then we are implicitly assuming that he is able to do this for himself, and thus that he too can be characterized as a formal system. That is, on the one hand humans may be seen as cybernetic systems; on the other hand they are ascribed an achievement that goes beyond that of any formal system, yet just what this means is not explained. Thus, the decisive problem facing cybernetic theory is to specify human actions that, while not explainable by recourse to an algorithm, can nonetheless be precisely understood and explained.

We can now fix the problem: to indicate modes of human behavior that can be understood without the help of concepts from cybernetics or systems theory. The question now is: Just what sort of theory could do this? Is not human reflection, as temporal action, such that in and through objectifications it always finds itself anew? Formalization as a higher level of objectification would then be necessary from this perspective, but at the same time it always refers back to factual, linguistic reflective performances that go beyond every existing formalization.

Especially in socialist countries, the question of the extent of the explanatory power of cybernetic methods centers on the relationship of cybernetics to the theory of evolution. I have already indicated that the mathematical formula for the lower limit of the informational content of a sign from an alphabet corresponds structurally (even to its mathematical symbol) to a physical formula for the probability of a thermodynamic state in a physical system. The second law of thermodynamics can be understood in such a way that a natural, irreversible process within a closed system proceeds through states of increasing probability, until the process finally ends in equilibrium at the condition of maximal probability. The hypothesis has been put forward that this structural analogy is no accident but rather represents an interrelationship. Whereas the second law of thermodynamics represents the tendency of natural processes toward the condition of highest probability, evolution should be understood as the opposing tendency toward the accumulation of information in ever more complex systems. The opposition of these two directions of development is still disputed.[37] In any case, on the basis of this relationship one could undertake to present a general theory of matter in which information could be equated with thermodynamic diversity and then described formally and mathematically in all complex systems—inorganic ones, organic ones, and finally human ones.[38] This supposition was at first condemned by orthodox Marxism, along with cybernetics as a whole, as bourgeois ideology; it has been received only gradually in socialist countries, after intense debate.[39] On the one hand, there is a tendency to consider cybernetics as simply dialectical-materialist method;[40] on the other hand, the uniqueness of historical dialectics is emphasized over and against cybernetic feedback models.[41]

Thus, the question arises whether cybernetics can provide the theoretical underpinnings for a theory of evolution as well as for a theory of the dialectics of human-historical and social processes. It should be clear that here the question of the structure of scientific theory formation reaches a critical point. Where are we to begin in our understanding of historical processes?

The most important problem complexes requiring some sort of solution are those of the general conception of human language and of the conception of the approach to history. Are their basic structures those of unambiguously describable systems, or does such a conception necessarily break down under its own weight and point toward a concept of open, historical dialectics? How exactly is this concept of dialectical history to be clarified?

The question is then whether man, until now the most complex result of evolution, can indeed be conceived of in the shadow of the evolution of systems and machines that produce transparent and therefore formalizable achievements but cannot supply any orientation for future development. The differentiation of methods of decision making (learning matrices, random-number generators, and methods of approximation) are not enough to overcome these inherent limitations. This is because the structure of human communication is still very much in question, and with it the question of to what extent formal methods can clarify fundamental social decisions. These problems must be resolved if the capabilities of sociological systems theory are to be known. Finally, the question also arises whether the model constructs of a social cybernetic model theory "become hypostasized to quasi-ontological subjects, against whom no critique is possible, but only adaptation,"[42] or whether we must instead return to the actual communication and consensus formation of actual subjects.

Transformations in the Concept of the Theory of the Empirical Sciences

The Destruction of the Reductionist Program

The Problem

While in the *Tractatus* Wittgenstein still considered all discourse on the relation of language and the world to be nonsensical, the Vienna Circle believed that the development of an explicit theory of science was possible through their formulation of the verification principle. However, the radically reductionist conceptions of Logical Positivism soon led to difficulties. The exact investigation of the structure of scientific theories forced substantial changes on all important points of positivist theory. The discussion ignited on the question of the basis of empirical knowledge. Soon the verification principle took the central place in the discussion, however, and with it the emphasis on the relation of scientific theory to its empirical base. Karl Popper's thesis in *Logic of Scientific Discovery* that scientific theories are not verifiable but can only be corroborated by withstanding every attempt at their falsification was a decisive step in the retreat from the verification principle. Further problems resulted from the question of the structure of theoretical language as it is actually used, from the criteria of its selection, from the reduction of theoretical concepts to observation, and finally from the question of the characterization of scientific theory as unequivocal in the framework of the chosen theoretical language itself. In the end, a problematization of almost all essential points of the idea of theory formation reached the point where a self-clarification of the process of scientific knowledge no longer seemed possible without a return to the history of science. The discussion of the theory of science thereby reached a level that allows us to draw many parallels to the hermeneutical discussion in the human sciences. The breakthrough from the natural sciences to the human sciences was discernible in bridge areas such as linguistics and the social sciences.

This entire historical process of the development of the theory of science can aptly be described as "an objective process of reflection,"[1] since in it the radical theses calling for an elimination of the speaking and acting subject turn against themselves, forcing a return to the communicative practice of historically acting subjects. I would like to present the essential steps in this process.

In any such historical reconstruction, a privileged place must be given to the thought of Rudolph Carnap, of whom Wandschneider writes: "Carnap's truly great achievement consists not in the least in that his views were taken to their *radical* conclusions; it thereby becomes clear what is to be disposed of and what is no longer possible in the future."[2]

Carnap's Structuralist Program of "Rational Reconstruction": *The Logical Structure of the World*

The empiricist program of reducing all scientific statements to what is immediately "given" in sensory experience was announced repeatedly by various philosophers in the past but never fully realized. After the progress brought about by Frege, Russell, and Wittgenstein in formal logic, Carnap undertook the "flatly fantastic project"[3] of constituting all the empirical concepts of the natural and human sciences solely on the basis of autopsychological elementary experiences and the relation of remembered similarity. *Logical Structure of the World*[4] is thus a programmatic title for this enterprise of constructing a comprehensive, logically consistent unified science.

As his basis, Carnap chose the "autopsychological" experiences of a subject—indeed the so-called elementary experiences[5]—as the indivisible unity of what is experienced at every moment. (Here Carnap is also referring to "Gestalt theory" as developed by Köhler and Wertheimer in psychology.[6]) As the single basic relation within this stream of experience, Carnap chose the recollection of similarity between temporally separated elementary experiences. Elementary experiences are thus the domain of the set of relations of similarity; through the latter, we can constitute in a purely formal manner similarity circles,[7] quality classes,[8] and finally sense classes[9] and in this way other various senses within these classes. That is, the basic concepts in these realms are reduced to elementary concepts through translation rules. The constitution of autopsychological objects leads finally from physical objects[10] to the constitution of heteropsychological and cultural objects.[11] Thus, the totality of possible objects of science and thus of empirical reality as such is achieved through "rational reconstruction."[12]

Carnap himself emphasized the arbitrary nature of the choice of autopsychological experiences as a basis and the methodological solipsism that results from it. Starting from what is purely physically given would be equally possible, and in fact under Neurath's influence Carnap later chose "protocol sentences" about physical events as the basis for the construction of a universal unified science. Inasmuch as the implementation of his program does not depend on the constitution system chosen, for Carnap the program can be formulated independently as a thesis; all scientific statements can be expressed in formal and structural terms.[13]

One must keep in mind just how radical this program really is. Independent of de Saussure's structuralist approaches in linguistics, Carnap proposes a total structuralism for all empirical reality and formulates a program in which he claims to be able to reconstruct rationally all possible scientific statements about reality without having to materially refer back to the given behind elementary experience. Hence, all this is based on a single relation, by means of which all further complex structures can be constructed. Up to now, none of the structuralists has outdone this radical claim.

The implication of this view is that the basis of constitution and hence the constitution system itself can be chosen freely, with the restriction that within this chosen constitution system only formal and structural statements are still possible. Problems that were traditionally dealt with in philosophy and theology, all of which Carnap brings together under the title "metaphysics," cannot be expressed in a science conceived in this way.[14]

The uncertainty of the presuppositions behind this project were apparent soon after its publication:

• Gödel's and Tarski's results shook radical formalism to the core because they showed that no formal system can be completely specified and that it is necessary to have recourse finally to the linguistic action of subjects in communicative practice if the system is to be grounded at all.

• Silent elementary experience cannot serve as the basis for science, but rather only linguistically mediated experience. Carnap's structuralist thesis that the formal constitution of concepts can be understood as the constitution of reality as a whole and as self-explanatory, as it were, is an assertion for which no proof is possible and which signifies an ultimately decisionist refusal to either assert or ground anything further.[15]

• Subsequent discussion of the theoretical concepts used in scientific theories has shown that not all concepts can be reduced to thing concepts or to concepts of autopsychological experience, nor can statements about things be reduced to statements about sensory data.[16]

The purely formalist and structuralist reduction of science is at the same time its destruction. This result is of fundamental significance for the human sciences.

The Program of Empiricist Reduction: The Thesis of Physicalism

Within the Vienna Circle the underlying difficulty of Carnap's program was thought to be its "methodological solipsism," which calls into question the intersubjective communicability and verifiability of scientific statements. Neurath saw this retreat to the unverifiably and immediately given as a remnant of idealist metaphysics.[17] The postulate of intersubjective verifiability demands that sentences themselves be chosen as the basis for science. The ideals for such sentences are the propositions of physics in which the states of specific space-time coordinates are given quantitatively. Only the statements of physics are verifiable by many observers simultaneously, so only the physicalist language is therefore an intersubjective language.[18]

Carnap acknowledged that Neurath's objections were essentially correct.[19] A consequence of this position, for which Neurath proposed the name "physicalism," was that all statements, insomuch as they claim to be scientific, can be formulated in the language of physics. "The dualism 'natural sciences'—'human science,' the dualism 'philosophy of nature'–'philosophy of culture,' is finally [a] *remnant of the-ology.*"[20] This implies that a science such as sociology must limit itself to the determination of the physical states of human beings and can only make lawlike statements about these states; that is, sociology can only be a kind of "social behaviorism."[21] "Through the fact that physicalist language becomes the foundational language of science, all science becomes physics."[22] We can therefore say that "psychology is a branch of physics."[23]

The thesis that physics is the basis of all other sciences and that on this basis a unified science may be constructed in such a way that all propositions are internally connected can only be grasped through the fact that physics has been the ideal of modern science since its inception. The thesis of physicalism can then be given a positive meaning if we understand physical laws as supplying the conditions of possibility of objectification as such.[24] But even then the status of this assertion itself must be scrutinized. The toppling of this thesis within Carnap's own framework occurred when it was discovered, by Carnap himself, that certain theoretical concepts simply could not be reduced to observational data. This resulted in the problematization of the theoretical constitution of science as a whole.

The thesis of physicalism means first of all that a relation of associative recollection among autopsychological phenomena can no longer form the basis of science but rather must be replaced by the so-called protocol sentences in which physical states are registered.[25] Protocol sentences of the form "N observed object y at time t in space x" already have an idealized form. In principle, however, all observation sentences of any given person in any given language could be translated into sentences of this kind; that is, sentences with empirical content can be translated into the language of the physicalist system.

Carnap and Neurath formulated an important insight in this regard. The thesis of ultimate "elementary sentences," of "atomistic sentences," or of the "immediately given" as the final unshakable basis could no longer be supported. According to Neurath, a protocol sentence can suffer the fate of complete elimination if it conflicts with other protocol sentences or if it is not in agreement with previously confirmed laws.[26]

Thus, on the one hand, a program was proposed that systematized all meaningful statements in a comprehensive unified science, alongside which philosophy and epistemology were no longer possible. To this extent, physicalism is a consequential continuation of Wittgenstein's views and of those of the Vienna Circle. On the other hand, it had become clear that there was no absolute basis for this unified science, but only revisable sentences about individual observations. Popper drew the implications from this in *Logic of Scientific Discovery* (or, to put it in a more historically accurate way, the influence of Popper on Carnap's reflections can be established in Carnap's views on the basis of empirical science).[27]

The Dynamism of an Internal Contradiction

Logical Positivism thought that it had finally put to rest the questions of classical philosophy and the theory of knowledge, and yet at the same time it still had to give an account of the demarcation of meaningful from meaningless speech. The intended renunciation of philosophical reflection made reflection necessary again in its very dismissal. This became clear in the problem of the verification principle, in the problem of the empirical base, and in the relation of this base to general scientific statements and thus to laws or theories. The conception of philosophy as the immanent critique of language turned against itself.

The internal problematic can be seen above all in the development and critique of the verification principle. Along with the tautologies of logic, only empirical propositions are to be considered meaningful. But what of the status of the verification principle itself? It is not a tautological sentence or an empirical proposition about what sentences are seen as meaningful by the speakers of a certain language. Wittgenstein drew the conclusion that such statements as the verification principle must be nonsensical, but this is precisely the step Logical Positivism refused to take. The verification principle also cannot be a metaphysical sentence. Should one interpret it as a recommendation for the use of the terms "meaningful" and "meaningless" the principle no longer has any more force than any other linguistic prescription. If one wants to demarcate logico-mathematical and empirical scientific sentences from the sentences of metaphysics, it is not enough merely to classify the sentences of metaphysics as meaningless; in addition, these boundaries have to be seen as open and susceptible to revision with the progress of scientific inquiry itself. The determination of a criterion for empirical significance or for linguistic significance in general therefore necessarily leads to problems that cannot be solved by the philosophical tools Logical Positivism allowed itself. The question basic to subsequent developments was whether this situation was thought through in all its implications or whether further reflection was simply broken off.[28]

The relationship of the empirical base to theory was also first seen as less unproblematic than it later turned out to be. Hume undermined the principle of induction with his devastating critique, leaving no logically unobjectionable path from individual observations to lawlike statements formulated as general, universal propositions ("all" sentences). Conversely, individual observations do not qualify as the verification of such propositions. Kant attempted to find a way out of this dilemma by grounding the possibility of synthetic *a priori* statements in the constitutive performances of transcendental subjectivity. However, precisely this sort of transcendental reflection seemed "metaphysical" and "meaningless" to Logical Positivism. Since science should and must be more than an arbitrary accumulation of isolated individual observations, the question of the possibility of scientific statements was taken up anew. The question of the structure of scientific rationality and its constitution proved ineluctable.

Theoretical Proposals and Their Falsification: Popper's *Logic of Scientific Discovery*

The Approach of *The Logic of Scientific Discovery*

Although Popper never belonged to the Vienna Circle (he only had close associations with Carnap and Feigel), he saw very early on the significance of these questions and became the circle's most decisive critic. In 1935 he published *The Logic of Scientific Discovery*, wherein he formulated the basic position that he has maintained to the present despite many modifications.[29]

Popper begins with the insight that the development of the sciences in modern times is a dynamic process. The question of human knowledge is most readily answered when one investigates the course of its "discovery" and its inner "logic," and thus the creative process of the inquirer in the formulation and corroboration of new theories. Through this approach Popper hoped to do justice to the character of modern science as an open dynamic process moved forward by mutual criticism and competing proposals. Since the inner logic of this process in many respects closely resembles an agreement on predetermined conventional rules of a game, the investigation of the logic of research could be called the investigation of "the rules of the game of empirical science."[30] Here it is all too clear that Popper is not so much concerned with internal logical problems as with the character of the actual process of knowledge in the empirical sciences.

Theory Formation

For Popper, an unchallengable starting point is that the activity of the scientific inquirer consists in forming hypotheses or systems of hypotheses and then testing them against experience through observation and experiment.[31] But then the question is how a researcher comes to the formation of a theoretical system. For Popper this cannot go the way of induction, not only because individual observations are not sufficient for grounding general theories but also because the principle of induction itself cannot be justified scientifically. If it is conceived as an empirical principle, then it must be grounded by a principle of induction that in turn underlies it, and so on; infinite regress would then be unavoidable.[32] Popper believed that it was no longer possible to return to the Kantian project of grounding synthetic judgments *a priori* in the constitutive performances of the transcendental ego — at least in part because Kant specifically intended to explain the validity of Newtonian physics, the validity of which was precisely challenged by Einstein in our century.[33] There is a chasm between the singular sentences of experience and a hypothesis or theory, a gap that cannot be bridged inductively. Popper gives this view a pointed formulation — "We do not know: we can only guess" — and with reference to Bacon he calls theories "anticipations, rash and premature . . . prejudices."[34] Popper's greatest service is to point persistently to this leap, to the creative act represented by the formation of a theory. That this difference between observation and theory is both ineliminable and constitutive for scientific statements is demonstrated in the whole further development of the theory of science. However, it remains unanswered wherein lies the difference between empirical scientific theories and pure speculation.

Falsifiability as the Criterion of Demarcation

Popper objected against the Vienna Circle that the verification of hypotheses is impossible. If the verification principle is established as the criterion of *meaning* for statements, not only the statements of metaphysics but also the hypotheses of the empirical sciences must be considered meaningless. "Positivists, in their anxiety to annihilate metaphysics, annihilate natural science along with it."[35] Popper's decisive new proposal consists in viewing the empirical testing of a hypothesis as the attempt to disprove or falsify it through the discovery of opposing data from observation.[36] A theory can be called empirical if it can be falsified through observation.

The possibility of falsification of sentences of some generality rests on the fact that these sentences can be contradicted by singular sentences about the existence of certain states of affairs. As a simple example, the sentence "All swans are white" can be refuted by the sentence "At place x, there were black swans at time t." The empirical content of a theory is greater the greater the chance that it can be falsified. So the sentence "All heavenly bodies follow elliptical paths" has greater empirical content then the sentence "All the orbits of the planets are circular," because it is more general and at the same time more specific and thus is subject to greater possibilities of its falsification.[37] From this fact results the requirement that theories be made as general as possible and as specific as possible in order to raise their empirical significance; the risk of their falsification is therefore raised at the same time. One implication of this view is admittedly that certain singular existential sentences must be regarded as nonempirical. The sentence "There are white crows" cannot be contradicted by any particular sentence.[38]

The Problem of Basic Statements
Within the Vienna Circle, Carnap's point of departure from the autopsychologically given was revised and protocol sentences became the empirical basis of theories. Popper subscribed to the view that only sentences containing the results of observations and experiments can be used in corroborating theories, since only sentences can logically refute other sentences. Above all, Popper considered recourse to the person giving the protocol to be superfluous. The self-evidence of perception does not belong to the context of justification of scientific propositions. It is sufficent that they are formulated in an intersubjectively understandable language. Popper therefore rejects the expression "protocol sentences" and speaks of "basic statements."[39]

The same problem that arose for hypotheses arises for basic statements. As in any linguistic representation, general signs or universals must be used in their formulation. " . . . [W]e can utter no scientific statement that does not go far beyond what can be known with 'certainty' on the basis of immediate experience. (This fact may be referred to as the 'transcendence inherent in any description.') . . . every statement has the character of a theory, of a hypothesis."[40] This is the case for such a banal statement as "Here is a glass of water,"[41] since by the word "glass" we denote a physical body that exhibits a certain lawlike behavior.[42]

The turn to language, in the sense there is no basis behind such statements, implies that one must become acquainted with language as the medium for reaching understanding. Popper writes: "If some day it should no longer be possible for scientific observers to reach agreement about basic statements, this would amount to a failure of language as a means of universal communication. It would amount to a 'Babel of Tongues': Scientific discovery would be reduced to absurdity. In this new Babel, the soaring edifice of science would soon lie in ruins."[43]

The hypothetical and theory-specific character of basic statements is strengthened still further by the fact that "observations, and even more so observation statements and statements of experimental results, are always *interpretations* of facts observed, and they are *in the light of theories.*"[44]

Popper clearly sees that the fundamental problem of infinite regress — the regress to ever more fundamental observations — is solvable only through the decision to break the regress off at some point and thereby to accept certain statements as basic. He poses the dilemma that these decisions must be seen logically as "free decisions"[45] that cannot be grounded any further, and he explains this through the example of classical trial procedures. The system of criminal law can be compared to the theoretical system of science, since both direct their questioning to a certain state of affairs. The decision of a jury concerning the facts of a case corresponds to the positing of basic statements. The judgment handed down by the judge, like that of the theoretical inquirer, must then establish logically whether or not the facts of the case (basic statements) are subsumable under a certain law (theory).[46] In both cases, the decision about the facts must be interpreted as an application of theories or of lawlike determinations.

"Thus, the empirical basis of objective science has nothing 'absolute' about it. Science does not rest upon solid bedrock."[47] Popper compares the basis to a swamp into which one drives piles only so far until one may hope that they will carry the weight of the structure; one then decides to accept the firmness of the piles, at least for the time being.

The Corroboration of a Theory

A theory cannot be verified; it can only be corroborated in that it stands up under any attempt to falsify it; that is, the attempts to disprove the theory through conflicting experience themselves fail. If, on the contrary, a theory contradicts a recognized basic statement, then it can be seen as falsified and must then be replaced with another. Popper points out in the first edition of his work that individual basic statements are not yet sufficient to falsify a theory. Falsification occurs, at least in theories of higher generality, only when a reproducible effect is pointed out and formulated in a "falsifiable hypothesis."[48] Here Popper is taking into account research practice, since a theory usually stands in competitive relation to other theories and is abandoned only when it is replaced with a better one.[49] Beyond this, Popper attempted to ascertain the degree of empirical testability of a theory through rules; this means only the degree of their falsifiability.[50] Popper summarized the results of his reflections in the following way: "The old scientific ideal of *epistemē*—absolutely certain demonstrable knowledge—has proved to be an idol. The demand for scientific objectivity makes it inevitable that every scientific statement must remain *tentative forever*."[51]

The Problematic of Popper's Approach

Conventionalism and Critical Rationalism

Popper's *Logic of Scientific Discovery* marked a clear step beyond classical empiricism and the views of the Vienna Circle. For Popper, theories are in the first instance hypothetical, creative proposals that are not inferred inductively from observations but rather must always be freely developed. The distinction between theory and its empirical basis is both lasting and unbridgeable. The empirical base, for its part, can only be captured in sentences. In this process, concepts must be used that are current in ordinary language, by means of which a consensus must be achieved among observers about certain data. Basic statements are thus always interpretations, significations of observations. What is distinguishable as the basic sentence of a theory can only be determined in the context of its interpretation. Popper is quite aware that the interpretative mingling of theory and theory-specific basic statements is in danger of becoming circular.[52]

In fact, anyone who is the least bit acquainted with hermeneutics will recognize here the problem of pre-understanding and interpretation. Popper is also aware that breaking through this circle does not mean that one has broken out of it. He treats this problem under the heading of "conventionalism."[53] A strict form of conventionalism would ground theories and sentences about experience merely in terms of the history of such experience and the agreement found there about certain interpretations. Popper admits that there is no logical way out of conventionalism; the only way out is through methodological conventions [Festsetzungen].[54]

As long as no data are discovered that contradict a theory, conventionalism remains unproblematic. Even such data are eliminated by conventionalism through *ad hoc* hypotheses, changes in definitions, and the cleverness of the practitioners of science. However, in all these maneuvers the progress of discovery is blocked. Popper's chief aim is to ensure this progress through "anti-conventionalist" methodological rules:[55] Auxiliary hypotheses are permitted only when they raise the degree of falsifiability of a theoretical system, and new definitions must be judged as changing or rebuilding a system, not as confirming it.[56] Here Popper exposes all the difficulties of the inner problematic of empiricism. The hermeneutical circle of theories and their basic statements—which are established by agreement in the application of theories—can for Popper be made fruitful in an empirical-scientific sense only through conventions. This raises a twofold question. First: Can this circle be grounded yet again, be made reasonable in its very necessity, and be explained in its structure? Second: Are these conventions, which within this circle govern both the construction of theories and the determination of basic statements and methodological rules, themselves yet again subject to criticism and justification? At this point, the very conception of the empirical sciences as such is put into question. This is also the starting point for the attempt of the constructivist theory of science to develop an alternative proposal for the analysis of the construction of objects and for the achievement of basic statements in the empirical sciences.[57] The answers to these questions also decide whether Popper's claims for the exclusiveness of his methodology are justified, and also whether their extension to all areas of knowledge (thus even to history and society) is valid.[58]

Popper himself insists that the creation of theories and the trustworthiness of fixed basic statements can be traced back to innate dispositions to expect and to react.[59] This biologically grounded horizon of expectations has undergone constant critique in its development "from the amoeba to Einstein,"[60] especially since the arrival of "critical rationality" in Greek philosophy. This does not essentially change the fact that the activity of the empirical scientist is thought of in terms of the biological model of the adaptive behavior of an organism in relation to its environment.[61]

Popper's Concept of Metaphysics

From the start, Popper objected strongly to the Vienna Circle's critique of metaphysics. "The repeated attempts made by Carnap to show that the demarcation between science and metaphysics coincides with that of sense and nonsense have failed."[62] Popper recognized that metaphysical sentences can indeed be fully meaningful, even though they do not belong to the realm of the natural sciences. For this reason, from the beginning Popper defended himself against the view that the criterion of falsifiability must be used as the criterion of meaning as such.[63] Falsifiability is rather a criterion for the demarcation of empirical sentences from other, completely meaningful sentences.[64] Popper even emphasizes that the idea of a unified science is in fact nonsense, and he rests this claim on the results of Gödel, Tarski, and Church, whose full significance was not recognized by the members of the Vienna Circle and was not taken seriously in their philosophical programs. "A unified science is really nonsense, I am sorry to say, and demonstrably so, since it has been proved by Tarski that no consistent language of this kind can exist. Its logic is outside it. Why should not its metaphysics be outside it too?"[65] For Popper, there can be completely meaningful sentences that go beyond the purview of science. At the same time, it is of course significant that the function of metaphysics is then again immediately limited to its relation to scientific statements. Metaphysical theories are understood ultimately as precursors to truly scientific theories; they represent, so to speak, theories of a higher level of generality that gradually find their place in science, where they then become falsifiable.[66] In general, this process succeeds when such a theory is connected from the start to a specific problem in the sciences. Metaphysics can then have, as Schäfer writes, a "generative function for science."[67] Popper acknowledges that there are legitimate and genuine philosophical problems that cannot be explained fully by means of the natural sciences alone. The problems of cosmology are perhaps foremost in this category.[68] But in these reflections the concept of metaphysics remains unclear; it remains a vague heading for possible statements and reflections exceeding the present limits of empirical science. On the one hand, Popper agrees that "nontestable (i.e., irrefutable) metaphysical theories may be rationally arguable."[69] On the other hand, he emphasizes that "those (theories) that are nontestable are of no interest to empirical scientists. They may be described as metaphysical."[70] Thus, Popper's statements remain ambiguous and symptomatic of the ambiguity of his position as a whole. This ambiguity can be made even clearer through Popper's concept of truth and reality.

Popper's Concept of Reality

The falsifiability criterion of demarcation was directed against a theory of induction and verification. Despite this, Popper endeavors to introduce a concept of the corroboration of a theory and to distinguish various degrees of corroboration. This puts him under the suspicion of still trying to sneak in some sort of verificationism. Popper strictly rejects any such attempt. What is most illuminating in this context is his concept of "verisimilitude."[71] Popper is convinced that this concept describes the degree of "similarity to the truth" of a statement, measured against its approximation of "complete," "comprehensive," or "absolute" truth.[72] The exhaustive description of all facts, indeed of all *real* facts, as Popper adds emphatically, would entail absolute truth. Thus Popper establishes a sort of realism in which all his previous insights into the preliminary, rule-governed character of concepts and hypotheses seems to be forgotten. One would have supposed that the theses of the necessity of a presupposed language as a medium of all understanding, the transcendence of representation[73] in both basic statements and in theories, and the contextualization of all theories in experimental activity—all these theses of the arbitrary and pragmatic character of methodological conventions—indicated that Popper had overcome the naive concept of reality and remained firm in his judgment of the problems behind realism. Yet Popper's concept of truth shows that he has regressed behind the level of the problem he himself has already achieved.

As much as Popper recognized the significance of Tarski's work for the critique of the idea of a unified science and an empirical unified language, Popper's interpretation of Tarski's concept of truth is none-theless inadequate.[74] Tarski defined the concept of truth for formalized languages, emphasizing that this concept can only be that of a me-talinguistic relation between sentences. At the same time, Tarski re-jected the idea that this concept made any difference for the debates among naive realists, critical realists, and idealists, or between em-piricists and metaphysicians. His semantic concept of truth was sup-posed to be completely neutral on the questions of these controversies.[75] Popper nonetheless still understood truth as "correspondence with the facts."[76] He interpreted the semantic concept of truth as a realistic concept of truth, as the correspondence between propositions and facts. Here Popper uses this concept of facts quite naively, as if what was just said was forgotten. Wellmer is correct in saying that here Popper transforms a metalogical argument into an ontological one.[77] In these contexts there is hardly a difference between Popper's views and the picture theory of the early Wittgenstein. Apparently Popper did not succeed in interpreting his own insights into the course of knowledge in the sciences in such a way as to overcome the contra-dictions of classical positivism and empiricism. The concept of truth as correspondence becomes for the empirical sciences the ideal of absolute truth (even if only as a limit concept), and this sort of truth can finally be found only in the empirical sciences.

Popper's position on a transcendental mode of argument is note-worthy.[78] He calls an argument transcendental if it rests on the fact that we possess knowledge and infers from this fact that knowledge must be possible. Popper concedes the validity of this argument insofar as it is directed against a theory that would result in the impossibility of knowledge or learning from experience. However, transcendental arguments must be rejected insofar as they overlook the fact that knowledge is won only through the sometimes circuitous route of conjectures and refutations. From this argument it is clear that Popper wants to establish his realism as some sort of transcendental insight while at the same time rejecting the possibility of transcendental ar-guments about the concrete course of scientific knowledge. His realism proves to be opposed to his methodology, and it also raises the claim that this methodology will lead to an ever greater degree of "verisimilitude." Popper's methodological realism proves to be a decisionist conventional decision that has nothing to do with his methodological conventions; indeed, one could say that it stands in opposition to them. The problems raised in the discussion of conventionalism and instrumentalism are pushed aside by this decisionism. The problem of historicity even in the natural-scientific knowledge—a basic problem of the modern theory of knowledge that had already turned up in Popper's reflections—is decisionistically ignored just as it becomes most acute.

This contradiction can be shown at another important point. Popper emphasized in the first edition of his influential *Logic of Scientific Discovery* that changes in definitions should be regarded not as the confirmation of a theory but rather as its restructuring; that is, they are to be understood as replacement by another theory. In his later works, Popper further explicated the moment of competition among theories and their mutual replacement. His basic thesis was again that observations are always made in light of theories. Falsified basic statements can then derive greater probability if new experiments are constructed on the basis of alternative, competing theories.[79] The goal of critical rationality and maximal progress in knowledge can be attained only when competing theories are not only tolerated but even encouraged.[80] Popper thus permits the principle of the maximization of critique through competing theories to enter into his methodology. However, this principle does not hold for his theory of realism, with which Popper absolutizes his own methodology and fortifies it from all attack, despite its conventional character. According to his own principles of critical rationalism, Popper has to admit alternatives to his own methodological conventions. But this is precisely what he refuses to do.

This inner contradiction becomes completely clear only in the application of these methods in the social sciences. When the objects of observation are themselves theory-forming subjects, the application of Popper's methodology reveals its positivist core and the question of alternative methodologies necessarily arises.

The Question of the Theoretical Status of a Theory with Empirical Content

The Background: The Attempt at Reduction to Syntax

The original ideas of Wittgenstein and the Vienna Circle were shaken to the core by the discoveries of Gödel and Tarski and by Popper's critique. Above all, Carnap took up this criticism and tried repeatedly to come to grips with it. This finally led to the distinction of various components in the language of empirical theory (theory language, correspondence rules, observation language). These reflections can be characterized as the most differentiated in the contemporary analytic philosophy of science. The basic problems of the attempt to determine the theoretical status of empirical theory can be discussed in connection with them.

However, in 1934 Carnap again proposed in *The Logical Syntax of Language* to reduce all the problems of philosophy and the theory of science to problems of the syntax of artificial languages. The controversy surrounding the foundations of mathematics provided the background to his work. Carnap alone among the better-known philosophers had actually studied under Frege, and he defended Frege's logicist point of view in various publications. Eventually Carnap also adopted Hilbert's formalist program, and like Hilbert he wanted to incorporate the intuitionist claims of Brouwer and Heyting into the grounding of his own procedures. Now Gödel's important results and Tarski's investigations also had to be taken into account.[81]

Carnap understood logical syntax in the same sense as the construction of calculi. According to Tarski and other Polish logicians (among them Lukasiewicz and Kotarbinski), there has to be a distinction between the calculus of the object language and the metalanguage in which the syntax of the calculus is formulated. Carnap constructed two languages, of which the second and richer language is to be thought of as the representation of classical mathematics. He wanted to show that the syntax of a language can be formulated in that very language. Admittedly, Gödel's results were still valid; a complex language cannot prove its own consistency. Carnap's goal was to sketch a universal syntax for any arbitrary language. The program he had in mind was even more comprehensive than that of Russell. Its basic thesis was that "all philosophical problems that have any meaning belong to syntax."[82] This program goes back, even in its wording, to the *Tractatus*, where Wittgenstein writes:

In everyday language, it very frequently happens that the same word has different modes of signification—and so belongs to different symbols—or that two words that have different modes of signification are employed in propositions in what is superficially the same way.... In this way the most fundamental confusions are easily produced (the whole of philosophy is full of them). In order to avoid such errors, we must make use of a sign language that excludes them ... a sign language that is governed by logical grammar—by logical syntax.[83]

In the same way, Carnap wants to expose many problems of previous philosophy as merely pseudo-problems.

Carnap explains his thesis in terms of "the so-called problem of the foundations of the sciences."[84] The question of the structure of space and time is transformed into the question of the syntax of space-time coordinates. The problem of causality is concerned with the syntactical structure of laws, the determinism controversy only with the specific quality of the completeness of the system of physical laws.[85] The problem of the foundations of biology, psychology, sociology, and finally even the historical sciences has to do primarily with two main questions: whether the concepts of these sciences are reducible to those of physics in the strict sense and whether their *laws* are reducible to those of physics in the strict sense. Both questions are raised by the problem of the translatability of statements in the languages of biology, psychology, and sociology into the language of physics, and indeed in such a way that this language can be shown to be part of a physicalistic language. Problems of the content of the relations among the various sciences can then be formulated only as syntactical problems, and thus as problems of the relationships among various scientific languages. The thesis of a unified science is repeated here in terms of the formalizability and the translatability of individual scientific languages by means of the syntax of a language of science. "Only then will it be possible to replace traditional philosophy with a strict scientific discipline, namely the logic of science as the syntax of the language of science."[86] The problem of a "logic of interdisciplinary discovery" would then be resolved reductionistically.[87] Carnap thereby explicitly betrays the "principle of tolerance": "*It is not our business to set up prohibitions but only to arrive at conventions.... In logic, there are no morals.* Everyone is at liberty to build up his own logic, i.e. his own form of language, if he wishes. All that is required of him is that, if he wishes to discuss it, he must state his methods clearly and give syntactical rules instead of philosophical arguments."[88]

This renewed attempt to save the idea of a unified language of science failed when Carnap ultimately saw that in such a conception of science various levels must be differentiated within the language of science. The steps along this path included a proposal for a semantics[89] as well as the attempt to construct a unified empirical language. I shall discuss briefly the reason for the failure of these attempts.

The Weakening of the Criterion of Empirical Significance

Popper directed his criticism primarily against the principle of verification as the criterion for the meaning of propositions. He saw the connection of theories or laws to their empirical base only as the possibility of falsification through basic statements; falsifiability then decides the empirical content of laws or theories. However, then it must be admitted that universal singular existential statements (such as "There are nonwhite swans") are meaningless. They are not falsifiable for the same reason that *all*-statements (such as "All copper conducts electricity") are not verifiable; in both cases the entire universe has to be searched through for confirmation or disconfirmation.[90]

Ignoring these weaknesses (which hold for the principle of falsification as well, and which Popper was able to overcome only through conventional decisions), Carnap for the most part incorporated Popper's criticism. This led him to a first reformulation of the empiricist criterion of meaning. He gave up the concept of verification and replaced it with that of confirmation.[91] The concept of confirmation seems to correspond to corroboration in Popper, at least insofar as a sentence can be called confirmable if observation sentences or "control sentences," as Carnap now called them, could contribute to the confirmation or refutation of statements. Beyond that, a confirmable sentence is called "testable" if experiments that could lead to its confirmation can be specified and carried out at any given time. Every testable statement is thus confirmable, but not every confirmable statement is testable. Carnap tried to determine the concept of confirmation more precisely through extremely differentiated logical investigations.[92] The concept is explained as the reducibility of a statement to a finite class of control sentences. This reduction can be complete or incomplete, direct or indirect. Accordingly, there would then be different levels of the empirical criterion of meaning in terms of the strictness of the claims. It can be demanded that a statement be completely testable, completely confirmable, testable, or confirmable, according to the claims made for the statement's empirical meaning.[93] The claims of complete testability and complete confirmability would then basically correspond to the principle of verification, whereas for testability a factually realizable method of testing would have to be known for every case. Carnap believed that all these demands were too strong to correspond to the actual course and requirements of the sciences.[94] He therefore proposed that only confirmability be required as the criterion for an empirical statement.

Since the concept of confirmability is concerned with the logical relations between lawlike statements and control sentences, and thus presupposes a language system that has exact syntactic and semantic rules and for which all basic but undefined concepts are exclusively related to something observable, the principle of confirmability can then also be formulated such that a sentence is considered meaningful if it belongs to an empirical language that satisfies these demands. In short: A synthetic statement is meaningful if it belongs to an empiricist language.[95] This formulation of the empiricist criterion of meaning is essentially more tolerant than verifiability or falsifiability. It signifies yet another step along the way to the dissolution of the verification principle. The formulation of an empiricist language again breaks down of its own accord. The further development of ·this process of dissolution is the next topic of discussion.[96]

The Gap Between Theoretical Language and Observation Language

For Carnap the problem of the reducibility of an empirical base exists not only for laws and theories as a whole but even for individual concepts within the empirical language. The assumption that all scientific concepts are ultimately reducible through interlinking definitions to significations of what is immediately given in sensory experience underlies both the constitution system of empirical concepts in Carnap's *Logical Structure of the World* and the various theories of unified science on a physicalist basis.

Carnap discovered that the so-called disposition concepts, such as "fragile," "soluble," or "magnetic," are simply not definable, either through nominal definitions or through so-called "definitions from use."[97] Carnap therefore proposed the procedure of reduction through "reduction sentences." A reduction sentence for the concept "soluble in water" has the following form: "If x is found in water, then the following is true: x is dissolved if and only if x is water-soluble."[98] A reduction sentence for a disposition concept consists in specifying the conditions for an experimental test and determining that the disposition concept is properly attributed if there is a specific empirically ascertainable reaction. However, a disposition concept is then incompletely determined, since all objects that are not part of the given experimental conditions remain outside of its realm of validity; aside from that, its meaning is only approximated by giving these conditions and cannot be completely replaced with fully equivalent, already known concepts. This has the consequence that, unlike a defined concept, a concept introduced through a reduction sentence cannot be eliminated from a text by simple substitutions. This means that in science we have to use concepts that do permit only partial reduction, rather than direct reduction, to their empirical base. Thus, an essential postulate of empiricism must be surrendered: The empirical sciences cannot operate without concepts that have a surplus of meaning over and against their empirical base, a surplus that is irreducible.

The procedure of introducing theoretical concepts into science through reduction sentences can be misunderstood as that of "operational definition." In operationalism[99] the determination of the meaning of a concept consists in giving the method for its empirical determination; the best-known example of this is Einstein's analysis of the concept of "simultaneity." If, for example, one wanted to determine the concept of temperature, one would have to give the method for measuring this concept (for instance, through the expansion of a body such as mercury). But usually there are quite a few methods for the measurement of physical concepts. For example, temperature can also be measured through changes in color or through changes in the intensity of an electric current. In a consistent application of an operational definition, various concepts of temperature must be introduced. For all the significance operationalism has in the sciences, it is incapable of eliminating this surplus of theory in scientific language.

Thereafter it was shown that not only disposition concepts but also many other concepts of the language of science can receive only partial empirical interpretation. Such "theoretical concepts," as distinct from "observation concepts" or "empirical concepts," are indispensable for science, since general theories can be formulated only through such concepts. Certainly one can still distinguish experimental or empirical laws that contain concepts directly related to sensory experience from theoretical laws that contain theoretical concepts. In scientific practice, it has been shown that one cannot do without theories that use these theoretical concepts. One might try to construct a physics solely on the basis of empirical concepts, but the result would not be physics as it is done today. This is because the theoretical statements of physics do not merely represent inductive generalizations of experimental laws; rather, their significance lies in the fact that they possess prognostic relevance—that is, they allow for the derivation of yet-undiscovered laws. Without this heuristic function of theories, science would be quite different from what it has been in modern times.

The difficulties of reducing theoretical statements to their empirical base and of determining an empirical criterion of meaning led Carnap— after discussions with Tarski, Quine, Goodman, Feigl, Hempel, and others—to the thesis that scientific language as a whole must be sub- divided into an observation language and a theory language. The structure of a scientific language could then be represented in its various elements.[100]

The observation language contains observational concepts, which signify observable objects or processes and observable properties and relations of such objects (for example, "Zürich," "cold," or "heavy"). Aside from such concepts, the connectives of propositional logic and elementary semantic rules for the interpretation of observational con- cepts are included in this observation language.

The theory language contains theoretical concepts, which are defined negatively in contrast with observational concepts. In this category belong the classical fundamental concepts of theoretical physics, such as "mass" and "temperature." The theoretical language must also include the totality of classical mathematics. Thus, all the problems of the philosophy of mathematics arise for theory language as a whole: Any formalization results in a hierarchy of logics with an infinite series of domains.[101] This hierarchy of logics requires a syntactic and semantic metalanguage on which one can place strict demands.[102] Carnap admits that in such a hierarchy of logics "the clarity of our thought and thus the certainty of our insights is gradually lost in the transition to higher and higher levels of the hierarchy."[103] As for proofs of the consistency of the entire language system, "new deductive means are necessary, which are themselves more uncertain the more comprehensive the calculus."[104] Despite all that, Carnap believes that the use of formalization is nonetheless meaningful, inasmuch as it "has been shown to be the most successful means of mutual understanding through its use by a large group of people for a long period of time."[105] Only the addition of theoretical concepts to the language of mathematics allows for the emergence of theory language; formalized concepts appear then to be indispensable. "For this very reason," Carnap writes, "it seems to me that the old saying that the book of nature is written in the language of mathematics is genuinely misleading."[106]

Since theoretical concepts and observational concepts still stand unconnected alongside one another, Carnap introduces his own "correspondence postulates" to bind the two sorts of concepts. Such postulates do not represent definitions, but rather more closely approximate certain empirical rules for the use of theoretical concepts. An example of an ordering rule for the concept of temperature could read "If a body is warmer than another, then the temperature of the former is higher than that of the latter."[107] Through these correspondence rules, theoretical concepts entail an empirical meaning which can in principle never be complete. For one thing, not all theoretical concepts are usually connected with observational concepts in this way; some of them receive their meaning chiefly through their interconnection with other theoretical concepts in a theory. For another, even correspondence rules represent only an incomplete interpretation, since they are never explicit definitions but are more like practical rules of use.[108]

Clearly it is much more difficult to find a criterion of empirical significance for theoretical statements. It is as if the concepts of a theory distance themselves more and more from what is immediately observable. The question then is whether there is still an unequivocal boundary between the theoretical concepts of the empirical sciences and so-called metaphysical concepts. In this context, this becomes a question not merely for individual concepts but also for theories as a whole, since to a great extent theoretical concepts can be interpreted only in the context of a theory.

Carnap nonetheless tried to give a criterion for theoretical concepts when he proposed the requirement that such concepts raise the prognostic relevance of a theory; that is, that more empirical laws be derivable from the theory through the use of the concept than without it. But even this formulation of an empiricist criterion remains controversial. In this form the verification principle, which originally demanded the direct verification of all statements, is now generalized to such a degree that many philosophers of science are of the opinion that the problems of the empirical sciences are hardly distinguishable anymore from philosophical problems.[109]

An attempt had been made to demonstrate that theoretical terms are basically superfluous in a theory by providing alternative formulations of theories no longer containing these concepts. These attempts rest on Craig's theorem and on a principle originated by Ramsey.

In the explanation of a change in the state of a specific system that requires the use of both empirical and theoretical concepts, Craig's theorem allows for the substitution of the original theory by another one that has no theoretical concepts.[110] This method is valid only for particular explanations; if one wants to retain the theory in all its generality, one has to have recourse to its theoretical concepts.

Already in 1931 Ramsey had demonstrated that one retains a theory of the same empirical content (that is, one with the same possible inferences) if one replaces theoretical concepts with variables, which then must be placed within existential quantifiers.[111] However, this solution only replaces one difficulty with another. At first glance the problem of the status of theoretical concepts seems to have disappeared, but it reappears in the question of the "ontological presuppositions" of the theory (namely, insofar as it must be decided for which theoretical entities existence is presupposed, so that a proposition containing existential quantifiers can be considered to have any meaning whatsoever).[112] These attempts at substitution thus show yet again just how indispensable theoretical concepts are, despite the fact that they cannot be interpreted completely.

The Question of the Possibility of a Theory of Pragmatics

The question then arises of the criteria by which a specific language system and its underlying theoretical concepts are to be chosen. Carnap treats this question explicitly.[113] The problem of universals had resurfaced in a new form: Are properties, classes, relations, numbers, and the like to be considered abstract entities? Since their emergence is again dependent on the choice of a specific formal language, what status should be attributed to that language as a whole? What criteria are there for the choice of such a language?

Carnap distinguishes two sorts of questions, which he regards as fundamentally different. He calls the choice of a linguistic framework and the questions that concern the reality of this framework "external questions." Questions about the appearance of individual entities in the language system and questions about their place within the structure of the system are called "internal questions."[114] Internal questions concern either the rule system of the language or the connection of concepts or statements with observations. They must therefore be explained either logically or empirically. External questions cannot be formulated simply by means of the chosen language system and therefore cannot be answered within that system; they are formulated in a metalanguage. Therefore, criteria for the choice of a language must be given in a metalanguage. Only then can the question of the reality of the abstract concepts of the language system be posed at all.

Carnap then asserts that the concept of reality is scientifically meaningful only for internal questions. Because the term "real" in the scientific sense can only mean "that which appears as an element in the language system," the question of the reality of the language system itself cannot be posed as a meaningful problem; it is a pseudo-question. Carnap writes: "An alleged statement about the reality of the framework of entities is a pseudo-statement without cognitive content. . . . We take the position that the introduction of new ways of speaking does not need any theoretical justification, since it does not imply any assertion of reality."[115] For Carnap, to say anything more is to be entangled in the meaningless controversy between Platonism and Nominalism.[116]

This does not do justice to all the dimensions of the problem. If only "internal" questions of a language system are recognized as meaningful, then a naive concept of reality is in the end simply presupposed without question. Naturally, what is behind this view is the empiricist criterion of meaning. But it had already been shown that this criterion only became more unclear as it developed. "External" questions would then be concerned with this criterion itself: the concept of what is observable, the problems of induction and deduction, the demarcation of observation language and theory language, and finally the undefined concept of experience itself. These questions are withdrawn from the rationality of scientific explanation. Inasmuch as classical philosophy dealt with similar problems from a different point of view, it too is meaningless. Philosophy as the critique of language can investigate and criticize individual problems in the construction of languages, but cannot deal with the language system as such in a manner surpassing the techniques of formal operations.

However, it can be shown that the choice of a specific mathematical formalism has repercussions for internal questions even in the most formalized of the sciences, such as quantum mechanics. The mathematical formalism of quantum mechanics is disputed in the study of the foundations of mathematics on the grounds that the connection of theoretical statements in this formalism to their empirical base (that is, to specific results of experiments motivated by theoretical reflection) is very indirect. The choice of a different formalism would result in a completely different structure for the whole of quantum mechanics. The controversy among the various interpretations of quantum physics—the Copenhagen intepretation, that of Heisenberg, and attempts (such as that of D. Bohm) concerned with determinism and indeterminism—consists for the most part in the discussion of the interpretation and choice of various formalizations. A significant part of the discussion centers on the concept of the object in modern physics.[117] This is precisely the sort of discussion Carnap wanted to exclude from science.

Carnap does not dispute that the choice of a specific formal language has a definite meaning. "To be sure," he writes, "we have to face at this point an important question; but it is a practical, not a theoretical question; it is the question of whether or not to accept the new linguistic forms. The acceptance cannot be judged as being either true or false, because it is not an assertion. It can only be judged as being more or less expedient, fruitful, conducive to the aim for which the language is intended."[118] For Carnap, a specific linguistic form can be chosen only on the basis of "practical" considerations—that is, according to whether a language system is expedient, useful, easy to handle, and fruitful. In this context, Carnap confirms his principle of tolerence for the choice of languages.[119] Behind this principle there is hidden a return to a criterion of instrumental efficiency that can no longer be grasped theoretically—a return to *convention*.[120]

This reduction to purely practical considerations and convention reveals a characteristic trait of the development of Logical Empiricism. From the start, there was still the idea of a science that pictured the immediately given in a unified language. Popper was the first to dare to break with this conception, but in his theory of methodological conventions he ended up with criteria of usefulness and conventionality similar to those of Carnap.[121] The discussion of the logic of scientific knowledge was in danger of being reduced to the realm of purposive-rational, means-ends choices. This realm of what is practical and of what grows out of conventions still suffers then from the absence of theory.

Now, within general semiotics, pragmatics is supposed to be more comprehensive than syntax or semantics, since it investigates not only the relations between signs and the signified but also the relationship of this relation to the subject of the signifying process itself. To reduce all pragmatic reflection to what is practical in the sense of purposive rationality is a decision, and one that is not justified. Pragmatics in the comprehensive sense cannot allow itself to be restricted in this way. Rather, its task would be precisely to investigate and develop the foundations of science in the historical, communicative practice of subjects. But then the theory of science could not be limited to the inner realm of specialized sciences derived through methodological conventions; it would have to go beyond this inner circle to the historical movements and constellations to which science owes its emergence. Going beyond a historically conditioned limit in this way would mean going beyond the accepted methodology of the modern empirical sciences as well; that is, the concepts of experience and of theory would have to be transformed as well. From this perspective, the relation of practice to the leading type of theoretical reflection in any given period could be analyzed anew in a more comprehensive horizon;[122] that is, such an analysis could produce a comprehensive theory of communicative action in its historical dimension.

That the theory of science is forced by its breakdown through its own inner aporias not only to return to subjects in their concrete actions but also to investigate this action in its historical dimension is shown by the discussion sparked by the work of Thomas Kuhn.

The Reopening of the Theory of Science to the History of Science

The Structure of the Process of Discovery and the Logic of Scientific Revolutions

The self-destruction of the reductionist program of Logical Empiricism, the gradual dissolution within the discussion of the theory of science of an unequivocal criterion for the empirical significance of theories, and the admission of the basic conventionalist characteristics of scientific rationality all raised questions that could no longer be fitted into the framework of the previous discussion. Against that background, the problem of how one of the essential characteristics of modern science (its "progress") could be explained has to be almost irresolvable. Are there still any criteria by which one theory can be considered to be refuted and replaced by another? Is it not necessary that the discussion of the theory of science be opened to the dimension of history? Are the conceptual tools previously worked out adequate for this realm? Do not the very problems that caused the retreat to the crystal clarity of the world-picturing unified language arise again here? Are we not faced again with the problems of hermeneutics and historicism, as a result of internal problems in the theory of science? Are we now better equipped to deal with these problems?

The controversy surrounding these questions ignited in 1962 when Thomas Kuhn published *The Structure of Scientific Revolutions*,[123] which brought about such a change in the accepted canon of questions that there was talk of a "new philosophy of science."[124] Kuhn maintained that incisive new theories arise only through revolutionary transformations in the world view and the scientific consciousness of certain groups of researchers. According to Kuhn, the research activity of "normal science" is dominated by a "paradigm" in which one or several scientific achievements of the past become recognized by the scientific community as the foundation of its furthur work.[125] The most explicit example of such a paradigm is Newtonian mechanics. Newton was able to formulate the results of his predecessors (among them Copernicus and Kepler) in a simpler and more insightful manner. His underlying intuitions on space and time, mass, and the force of gravity completely dominated physics during the period from their formulation to Einstein's Theory of Relativity. The paradigm of Newtonian mechanics formed a complex of intertwining theoretical and methodological convictions. The tasks of a science dominated by these convictions essentially consist in collecting ever more new facts to confirm the underlying theory, deriving from it predictions concerning new phenomena, developing corresponding apparatuses for new experiments to obtain even more new supporting data, and raising the precision and elegance of the mathematical and theoretical instruments of the theory. Newtonian mechanics is an excellent example, in that for more than two centuries it reigned as the undoubted presupposition of all physical research and enjoyed enormous triumphs.[126]

The dissolution of a dominant paradigm is the result of a protracted process. It does not suffice that individual counterobservations are registered. The history of science is full of examples showing that such observations are either interpreted as mistakes in measurement, reinterpreted through additional auxiliary hypotheses, or simply suppressed. Even the discovery of an anomaly and the awareness of a new phenomenon are very complex events,[127] both of which presuppose that the structure of expectations has changed and often even that the means of perception have changed.[128]

The transformation of what is "normal" or even of what is considered a scientific fact usually presupposes that the existing theory as a whole has already experienced a crisis, that the complexity of the necessary auxiliary hypotheses has grown faster than the precision of predicted observations, and that inexplicable anomalies increase and deviant experimental norms begin to prevail, or at least the questions of the compatibility of the existing data with other theories is explored in thought experiments; thus the basic presuppositions of a theory are tested and tentatively changed in thought.[129] Only such a process of ever-intensifying crises prepares the way for the replacement of one paradigm by another, as in the case of the replacement of Newtonian mechanics by relativity theory. This process is neither linear nor culminative; it is revolutionary, in the sense that what can be called institutional intuitions have to decline or be destroyed so that a new theory can prevail. According to Kuhn, scientific progress takes place in revolutions. Not only does a theory change, but the entire world view changes with it;[130] even the data become different.[131]

Such revolutionary transformations cannot be explained merely by the scheme of simple falsificationism. The significance of falsifying data must first be recognized as such if it is to be interpreted in the light of a competing theory and thereby receive the function of confirming it. Neither verification nor falsification is sufficient as an explanatory model for scientific progress. Only the model of the competition of rival paradigms can do justice to the richness of the actual history of science, but even that would not provide a complete grasp of all the moments of a historical transformation.

The Model of Competing Research Programs

Kuhn had to explain the origin of scientific revolutions by returning to the psychology and sociology of scientific groups.[132] There is no simple, straightforward methodology of the research process. The controversy surrounding such a methodology is concerned with whether psychology and sociology can supply anything more than hints for the explanation of the creative process of knowledge.

Popper objected strongly to Kuhn's views.[133] For Popper, what Kuhn calls "normal science" neglects the principle of critical rationality, since it is not willing to constantly put into question and revise its own underlying theoretical presuppositions. In this way, Kuhn's thesis seems to Popper to result in historical relativism and to be ultimately irrational.[134] Popper bitterly remarks that all his arguments against sociologistic and psychologistic tendencies, above all in the historical sciences, have been in vain.[135]

On the basis of similar considerations, Imre Lakatos proposed to go beyond Popper and mediate the two positions.[136] He tried to point out where in Popper's work it is possible to differentiate his theory to a greater degree. According to Lakatos, falsification is not to be understood as the refutation of a theory through an absolutely certain empirical basis of facts. This "dogmatic" or "naive" falsificationism is quite widespread, although Popper criticized it in the first edition of *The Logic of Scientific Discovery* and to an even greater degree in later editions of that work. Various students of Popper, such as Feyerabend, Agassi, and Watkins, have taken this critique farther.[137]

Lakatos sees the weakness of Popper's earlier position chiefly in its monotheoretical model of criticism.[138] Even the experimental techniques of a scientist contain theoretical proposals that need not have anything to do with the theory that is tested by the experiment. Thus, a single theory is never what is in question, but rather always a plurality of theories, of which one in particular is chosen to be tested and against which the attempt at falsification is directed.[139] Starting from an analysis of the concrete activity of scientists, Lakatos holds even this more differentiated version of Popper's model of competing theories to be inadequate. The model of a simple theoretical pluralism cannot explain the continuity of science.[140] Lakatos therefore draws a further distinction between "theories" and "research programs."[141] In a research program there are distinct positive and negative heuristic rules. The negative heuristic functions to forbid us to directly falsify in our own basic statements the "hard core" of the program (its specific underlying postulates). Rather, a protective belt of auxiliary hypotheses, placed around this hard core, must first be adjusted and readjusted or even completely replaced.[142] The positive heuristic of a research program consists in a set of suggestions or hints for developing refutable variants and for differentiating the whole series of hypotheses at the forefront of research.

The refutation of an individual theory does not by any means lead to the abandonment of the entire research program. Its replacement by a competing program is a much more complicated and temporally extended process in which the consideration of long-term fruitfulness comes into play. A research program proves fruitful when it can serve in both the articulation of new theoretical proposals and the prediction and explanation of new empirical phenomena, in that it thereby makes possible theoretical and empirical "progressive problem shifts" in the scientific community. In this way, Newton's theory of gravitation proves fruitful in that through it the existence of further planets could be predicted and phenomena such as tides explained. The opposite of this process occurs when, in the framework of a research program, anomalies are discovered that demand ever more complex auxiliary theories for their explanation; this "degenerating problem shift" then reveals the unfruitfulness of the entire research program.[143] Often another proposal is placed in opposition to the dominant theory only after a long process of "degeneration" of the entire trend of research. Indeed, this occurs only when the new, competing viewpoint proves more fruitful, when the change from one viewpoint to another has a "progressive" character.

First of all, this shows that the criteria for replacing fundamental proposals, research directions, weighty conceptions, and key concepts (research programs in general, in Lakatos's sense) can be given neither strictly nor exactly, as is presupposed in the thesis of falsification. The concept of falsification then becomes historically fluid. As Lakatos writes, "Falsification can thus be said to have a *'historical character.'* "[144] Falsification is not simply the relation of a theory to its empirical base, but rather a multifaceted relation among competing theories, the empirical base as determined by theories, and the growth of empirical knowledge that arises from this competition.[145] The concept of falsification is dissolved into various perspectives, such as "degeneration," "fruitfulness," and "progressiveness." These criteria cannot be put in formal language and cannot be abstracted from the historical process of research and the history of science.

Second, Lakatos shows that a criterion of empirical significance can no longer be given for individual sentences but only for the whole direction of research. What can be called scientific or empirical, according to Lakatos, is decidable neither for individual sentences nor for individual theories, but only for their underlying research programs.[146] The final empirical meaning of a sentence can no longer simply be derived through comparison with "the facts"; its meaning depends on the historical fate of the relevant basic conceptions.

Thus, it is now clear that the theory of science itself, as the theory of the empirical sciences, cannot be developed without reference to the history of those sciences and to a theory of this history. This too marks the overturning of the program of Logical Empiricism. The demarcation and objectification of a specific set of objects through a theoretical approach, and the choices of a linguistic framework and of basic guiding models, all transpire in the historical context of fundamental research programs that overlap with, change, and replace each other. From this it follows that scientific discussion and its progress are located in a space that is transparent neither in itself nor in its relationships, a space that is historically open. The question of the conception of the individual sciences, even the question of the structure of scientific rationality itself, can no longer be answered without a consideration of their history and thus without a theory of history.

The New Attitude Toward "Metaphysics"

For Popper, "metaphysical" proposals can be seen as preliminary stages of scientific theories. Lakatos emphasizes that the underlying conceptions of scientific research programs in a technical sense, as the highest heuristic rules, must be regarded as "metaphysical."[147]

Accordingly, since a naive criterion of either verification or falsification is no longer sufficient for the determination of the meaning of statements, the question of continuing philosophical reflection is once again renewed. The concept of "metaphysics" is, since the beginnings of Logical Positivism, only a shorthand for this problem. Lakatos goes so far as to say that science as a whole can be grasped as an enormous research program whose methodological rules can be formulated as metaphysical principles.[148] In the framework of the model of competing research programs, there arises the task of developing different metaphysical programs; only the development of rival metaphysical theories can lead to the growth of insight. The fate of these theories is decided in exactly the same way as is the fate of empirical research programs: whether or not in the long run they lead to progressive empirical and theoretical problem shifts. If they result in the degeneration and unfruitfulness of scientific programs, they must be dissolved through a rival theory.[149]

Paul Feyerabend has repeatedly emphasized the necessity of a critical metaphysics. "A good empiricist," he writes, "must also be a critical metaphysician."[150] Feyerabend then goes a step farther; he poses the question to Lakatos of what time limit must be imposed for when a degenerating theory is to be dissolved by another.[151] Feyerabend thereby raises the central question whether there are rational criteria for this process of replacement or whether this process resists any rational analysis.[152] More than anything else, Feyerabend insists (in agreement with Kuhn) that there are indeed incommensurable theories; thus, for example, the fact that the concepts of length and mass have a completely different meaning in relativity theory than in Newtonian mechanics makes a comparison of empirical content or verisimilitude in Popper's sense impossible.[153] From this and from the impossibility of direct interpretation of theoretical concepts, Feyerabend concludes that "the realism described here is an impossible doctrine."[154] Popper's assertion that there are rational criteria for proof and critique is therefore "mere 'verbal ornament' "[155] for Feyerabend, who chooses to espouse an epistemological anarchism according to the principle "anything goes."[156] Behind such pointed and sarcastic formulations is the positive side of Feyerabend's interest in human freedom, which may not and cannot be limited by an unequivocal methodology foisted upon it.[157] This is the only way to reach a higher form of consciousness.[158]

Feyerabend's extreme position marks at the same time a new stage
in the problems of the theory of science. After all simple criteria for
the meaning of the statements of the empirical sciences have been
exhausted, and when only long historical processes decide the fate of
basic scientific conceptions, the problem of the direction of historical
development is posed in all its depth. Can there still be criteria for
the judgment of historical development?

Historicism and Neo-Darwinism in the Theory of Science? The Question of the Rationality of the "Scientific Community"

Feyerabend suggests that in this state of the discussion basic problems
of Hegel's thought are imported into the theory of science,[159] —
admittedly in a situation where the insights of Darwin and Marx must
also be part of the discussion (the project called "science" must be
interpreted in the framework of evolution). Feyerabend accuses Lakatos
of not acknowledging his debt to Hegel[160] while criticizing Popper's
all-too-simple understanding of Hegelian dialectics.[161] For Feyerabend,
Hegel made clear once and for all that there cannot be a complete
and unequivocal description of an objective state of affairs. Rather,
the attempt at such a description has the very opposite result and
leads in the end to concepts that contain this dialectical movement.[162]
At the same time, Feyerabend rejects an idealistic interpretation of
the dialectical movement of the concept: "The concept, too, is then
part of the general development of nature, in a materialistic interpretation of Hegel."[163] The history of science is thereby ultimately
placed in the framework of a theory of evolution.

Popper[164] and Kuhn[165] both compare the evolution of scientific ideas
to the evolution of organisms. Stephen Toulmin argues a similar point.[166]
For Toulmin, the acceptance of explanatory paradigms and scientific
theories is also a matter of their "fruitfulness."[167] There are "no black-
and-white questions of truth and falsity."[168] In the succession of phases
of scientific forms of thought, we can only ask what it is about a theory
that makes it capable of survival in the competitive struggle of the
evolutionary process.[169] The further development of science, the
changes of its ideas and goals, can no more be predicted than the
biological future of a species.[170]

There is something ambivalent in the use of Darwinist terminology.
Insofar as those involved are at all aware of the theoretical problems

in the theory of evolution, this terminology seems to serve the metaphorical redescription of a problematic that bursts the previous framework, without whose resolution there is still no adequate vocabulary let alone an adequate conceptual apparatus. This is also true of the first volume of Toulmin's *Human Understanding*. Toulmin characterizes his attempt as "intellectual ecology."[171] In this approach, ideas can be seen as "conceptual populations."[172] As things stand in the contemporary discussion of the theory of science, we are faced with avoiding the dilemma of "quasi-mathematical absolutism" and "historico-cultural relativism."[173] Here we are concerned with the evaluation of fundamental orientations and intellectual strategies in the face of the entire previously comprehensible process of evolution, and thus with the methodology of "transhistorical and cross-cultural comparisons."[174] Decisions then have to be made on just how knowledge and norms are supposed to be justified at all.[175]

We have reached the point where the question becomes one of how we can determine the structure of rational interaction so that it can be the medium for justifying decisions about strategies of knowledge that have an unmistakably normative character. How are we to determine the structure of "rational interaction" at this level of the problematic?[176]

Thus, the final consequence of the development of the theory of science is just this question: What would a theory of rational interaction look like that had as its starting point the recognition of the dependence of scientific discourse on social structures and on the historical dimension—indeed, that began with the dimension of evolution as its fundamental horizon? How can such a theory be developed at all? Must it not consider its own foundations and conceptual development in these dimensions? With this, the basic problem of the theory of science becomes transformed into the basic questions of a theory of communicative action, which must be developed within the dimensions of a theory of society and a theory of history.[177]

4

The Turn to Pragmatics

Wittgenstein's Later Philosophy: The Return to Communicative Practice

It has become a commonplace in the historiography of the development of the theory of science in the recent decades to understand Wittgenstein's transition from the *Tractatus* to his later philosophy as a turn to the question whether a theory of linguistic communicative action can and must claim to be a foundational theory not only for the individual sciences but also for science as a whole. It is also customary to present this turn as logically implied in both mathematical-logical and general research into the theory of science.

This description is certainly historically questionable, since Wittgenstein completed this turn in his later philosophy without having been demonstrably influenced by the discoveries in the foundations of mathematics or in the philosophy of science. Indeed, it has often been pointed out that Wittgenstein interpreted Gödel's results incorrectly.[1] Nevertheless, it seems to be completely objectively justifiable to interpret the development of Wittgenstein's thought and the advance of the discussion of the theory of science as at least parallel processes.

The concern here is not to trace Wittgenstein's development from the *Tractatus* to the *Philosophical Investigations* (the book to which Wittgenstein devoted his energies from 1935 to his death), with the goal of textually interpreting and verifying all the intermediary steps of this development. Most of the necessary material for such an undertaking is now available, and interpretations of the whole of his writings have been undertaken in diverse approaches, none fully successful.[2] Various interpreters have emphasized the continuity of Wittgenstein's thought, but exactly where this continuity is to be located must still be asked.

In any case, it is clear that Wittgenstein's intention was to distance himself forcefully from the ideal of the single, world-picturing unified language. The traditional understanding of logic that Wittgenstein shared in his early works gave the impression that one could speak of logic for an ideal language, as if it were a logic "in a vacuum" (*PI*, 81)[3] or as if it represented an order of "purest crystal." (*PI*, 97) But in view of language as it actually is, this ideal becomes mere empty form. Wittgenstein writes: "The *preconceived idea* of crystalline purity can only be removed by turning our whole examination around. (One might say: the axis of reference must be rotated, but about the fixed point of our real need.)" (*PI*, 108) The search for an ideal language and its logic must be abandoned; another way of examining things must be sought that corresponds to the real needs of the examiner and is guided by these needs. What is this way of looking at things and this need?

If the ideal of the pure language of logic—an ideal that led to the "pursuit of chimeras" (*PI*, 94)—were to be abandoned, one might be left with the impression at first that this new way of looking at things destroys everything "great and important" and leaves only "rubble" in its wake. However, Wittgenstein notes, "what we are destroying is nothing but houses of cards, and we are clearing the ground of language on which we stand." (*PI*, 118) What is this "ground of language" that comes into view through this new way of looking at things?

The ground of language is not something that underlies it, something more fundamental, something to be sought as what is "grounding." Rather, that which is finally given is simply "the practice of the use" of a language. (*PI*, 7) The process of using a language is thus always the totality of a unity of language and the activities with which it is interwoven. This complex whole is what Wittgenstein calls a "language game." (*PI*, 7) It can be spoken of as a game since in it rules are followed.[4] Because a language game in its rule-governedness and its interwovenness with other activities represents life practice itself, the representation of a language is at the same time the representation of a "form of life." (*PI*, 19)

According to Wittgenstein, there is no way to go behind this practice of a form of life, either through explanation or through justification. It is only possible factually to "note" a language game. (*PI*, 655) "Our mistake is to look for an explanation where we ought to look at what happens as a 'proto-phenomenon.' That is, when we ought to have said: *this game is played*." (*PI*, 654) This is simply to be accepted. "What is simply accepted as given, as it were, are the forms of life."[5] Philosophy cannot dispute the actual use of language but can finally only describe it, "for it cannot give it any foundation either." (*PI*, 124) This factual practice cannot be questioned further.

With this, a decisive shift to a new basis is postulated. Wittgenstein's *Investigations* is itself an attempt to effect such a shift. Why does this sort of shift seem so important? What need does it fill? To pursue this question farther, it would be necessary to examine the historical connection with the great Austrian theoreticians and writers on language, including Karl Kraus, Otto Weininger, Adolf Loos, and Robert Musil, and finally even the surprising parallels to Nietzsche.[6] An allusion to these influences can be found in the following passage from the *Investigations*: "The problems arising through a misinterpretation of our forms of language have the character of *depth*. They are deep disquietudes; their roots are as deep in us as the forms of our language and their significance is as great as the importance of our langauge." (*PI*, 111) Forms of language are experienced as elementary forms of life that determine the structure of subjective and intersubjective behavior, speech, and understanding. Disturbances in these forms of life are so elementary that they confuse and destroy what is recognized as self-evident—that which, as self-evident practice, represents the finally given, which is not and cannot be grounded any further. Therefore, the removal of such a disturbance is an elementary need. One of these disturbances was the ideal of a crystal-clear language in the *Tractatus*. Yet another disturbance is the nonordinary, "metaphysical" use of words. (*PI*, 116) Philosophy can thereafter have the function only of showing these metaphysical misuses of language to be the result of the incorrect use of words. "The philosopher's treatment of a question is like the treatment of an illness." (*PI*, 255) "What *we* do is to bring words back from their metaphysical to their everyday use." (*PI*, 116) Philosophy is thus a therapeutic activity, and this is what links the *Investigations* to the *Tractatus*; however, the "normal" state which is the goal of the "philosophy of ordinary language" is no longer the world-picturing, unified language, but the articulated system of language games that constitute a form of life. Philosophy can only "describe" such forms of life. A linguistic activity that is supposed to do more than that necessarily leads to misunderstandings, and thus even to the "deep disquietude" that was to be avoided. It should be clear that this points to the basic problems of both "ordinary-language philosophy" and theory formation in the realm of linguistically mediated action as a whole. It must now briefly be shown why this is so.

The interpretation of Wittgenstein's later philosophy presents great difficulties, in terms of its textual basis and its methods. Whereas the theses of the *Tractatus* were often thoroughly interpreted in content and their implications were brought into direct relation with the discussions in the theory of science, the texts of the later period are much less unified and their implications still quite disputed. Despite all this, I believe a brief characterization of their distinctive features to be possible. Any such interpretation radicalizes Wittgenstein's thought in a certain way in interpreting it as pradigmatic. This radicalization does not necessarily contradict Wittgenstein's intention, but rather throws light on its somewhat strange characteristics and makes understandable the disquieting effects readers of Wittgenstein experience.

Instead of beginning with the logic of the ideal language that "makes itself manifest" in its validity, and thus with a logic that is self-illuminating as transcendentally and structurally pre-given, Wittgenstein returns to the practice of actual language games. In the realm of the theory of science, Carnap (for example) had followed out the starting point of the *Tractatus* in such a way as to extend the "logical syntax of language" from formal and constructive semantics to formal pragmatics. It would then be a misunderstanding of Wittgenstein's new approach to interpret it as a turn to pragmatics in the sense of a pragmatics that would be the basis for a theoretical sociolinguistics. Wittgenstein is much more concerned with the practice of language, and he understands his own texts as just such a practice. Language is that which is finally given, in that it is a factual, practical activity. Wittgenstein's texts are pragmatic in the sense that they are initiations into this practice with the intent of prohibiting any attempt to escape this practice in formulating a purely formal, artificial pragmatics.

Language as practice cannot be explained in terms of the constitutive performances of an individual subject; it is from the beginning both mediator and mediated. This may be seen in Wittgenstein's extended (and at first glance seemingly odd) polemic against the possibility of a private language.[7] Wittgenstein begins with an examination of feelings of pain. In artificial dialogues he explains that only an already public language shared by many others makes possible any meaningful acquaintance with one's own feelings; thus, it is only in this way that the biographical unity of one's own consciousness can be preserved as well. It is clear that here Wittgenstein is also concerned with opposing a philosophy that takes as its starting point the consciousness of the individual.

Since Wittgenstein also analyzes in detail the meaning of verbs like "to mean," "to understand," or "to signify," it seems appropriate to compare his approach with Husserl's transcendental phenomenology.[8] Wittgenstein posits a new universal system of relations that is not oriented to the concept of the subject and seems to avoid the aporias of transcendental phenomenology precisely in its analysis of intersubjectivity and the relationships of any empirical ego, the transcendental ego, and the transcendental observer. It is just as appropriate to compare Wittgenstein's approach with Heidegger's in *Being and Time*, since Heidegger grasps existence, as a linguistically mediated "being with" and this "being with" as "being in the world."[9] What nonetheless distinguishes Wittgenstein from both Heidegger and Husserl is that the problematic of subjectivity seems to be completely bracketed, indeed that in Wittgenstein "the metaphysics of Spirit and subject of modern Idealism is treated as a sickness of language, the very metaphysics which made possible the language of the classical foundations of the 'human sciences' of the nineteenth century."[10] This is significant not only as a controversy in philosophy but also for the foundations of the sciences of action which would draw support from Wittgenstein's reflections. One must ask whether a concept of consciousness or individual identity developed out of interaction in and through all its historical, social, and biographical ruptures is really possible from this perspective.

The practice of language to which we return is always a common practice organized according to certain rules. Both the polemic against the possibility of a private language and the explanation of what it means "to follow a rule" serve to point toward communicative action as "played" according to rules of a game. The following quotation from Wittgenstein is significant for such a view: "It is not possible that there should have been only one occasion on which somebody obeyed a rule. It is not possible that there should have been only one occasion on which a report was made, an order given or understood, and so on. To obey a rule, to make a report, to give an order, to play a game of chess, are *customs* (uses, institutions)." (*PI*, 199) The rules of language games are developed "customs" arising from uses that have been given the status of regulative social facts, of "institutions." The practice of language games is not only a mediating medium of spontaneous activity but also a social practice that is regulative for all such practices.

This poses the problem of the status attributed to language games and the status that can be claimed for the theory of language games. This very question is the subject of the controversy surrounding Peter Winch's Wittgenstein interpretation.[11] For Winch, the rules of language games have a transcendental status. But the term "transcendental" no longer denotes the *a priori* structure of the subject; rather, language games as social forms of life allow the development of those elements that prove to be regulative and *a priori* for the participants of a language game. Hence, a sociology developed on this basis can claim to be more than a purely empirical science; it has the character of a theory of the constitution of objects of knowledge and of the facts of the social life world. This can be explained primarily through Wittgenstein's concept of "grammar." Grammar as exhibiting the valid rules of a language game also indicates the constitutive meaning of these rules for the modes of givenness of objects. "Grammar tells what kind of object anything is."[12] The form of language becomes constitutive of the world. It is clear from this that the meaning of "transcendental" here has nothing to do with the classical use of the term; otherwise we would have to explain why Wittgenstein can say "Here the teaching of language is not explanation, but training." (*PI*, 5) Perhaps the choice of this expression indicates that what claims to have *a priori* validity in a form of life can also be the expression of a coercive context. In any case, it seems as if what is still recognizable in the *Tractatus* from the standpoint of the tradition, namely the dialectical separation of what cannot be said through saying what can be said, now disappears completely. With it come the basic problems that result in the aporias of Wittgenstein's position.

The questions that result from Wittgenstein's later philosophy could be viewed as its internal problems. However, because Wittgenstein's radical claims have paradigmatic relevance, the fundamental problems they articulate have a much broader significance.

First of all, it is hardly clear in Wittgenstein's writings what further discussion, explication, or explanation could mean within a language game.[13] Wittgenstein still disputes the possibility of changing levels in a language game, just as he did in the *Tractatus*. It is hard to see how explaining can be anything more than simply a form of "training."

Second, if the language games of developed ordinary language are their own metalanguage, in the sense that this practice is simply self-evident, then it must be asked how misinterpretation and misuse of language can be recognized at all, and, above all, how such abuses can be treated therapeutically. Therapy in this sense becomes an apparently impossible task; the language game of critique is not even distinguishable as a special language game. Reflection as the critical examination of the genesis and practice of one's own use of language is excluded in such a conception.[14]

This problem becomes all the more acute when one asks about the relations among historically distant language games. This is the basic problem of the methodology of the human sciences, namely the methodologically testable understanding of that which is foreign across historical distances. Historical hermeneutics would then seem to be impossible for Wittgenstein; he himself posed the same problem in his example of the explorer who comes to a distant, unknown land. His instructions are put in this way: "The common behavior of mankind is the system of reference by means of which we interpret an unknown language." (*PI*, 206)[15] If these instructions are to be understood in such a way as to mean that in the first instance one is to ignore verbal expression and take averbal behavior as the basis of understanding, Wittgenstein contradicts his own conception of action and language games. If action is understood to be always interwoven with language, then the sentence quoted above is only the paradoxical formulation of an aporia. The aporia of behaviorism is here extended to the problem of historical hermeneutics.[16]

The problem of the way in which language games are related to each other can also be put in the form of this question: How is it possible to conceive of dialogue between subjects at all if we do not presuppose that the consciousness of an individual is completely reified and publicly externalized for others in general linguistic structures? The way in which subjects enter into relationships with one another in the practice of language games and also maintain their distance from one another is fundamental to a view that does not grasp subjects as totally determined by society.

These problems also are related to the question of the status to be claimed by social-scientific theory as a whole. I have already pointed out the dilemma connected with Winch's thought that arguments can be found in Wittgenstein for both a behaviorist sociolinguistics and a theory of monadic language games claiming *a priori* validity. In the end it is hard to see how we are to distinguish these two views. The very same phenomena which Wittgenstein cannot adequately explain and which arise again in a more insidious form through their radicalization in the theory of language games relate to the central themes of the history of modern philosophy. It must be shown how, on the basis of linguistic practice, not only a descriptive but also a critical theory of history, society, and the subject can be developed, so that theoretical effort is nourished by common self-reflection, thereby opening up the possibility of free action.

The fundamental problem that proves to be the *experimentum crucis* for any theory of the sciences of action and society is whether such a theory can at least explain concrete linguistic performance that, beyond their self-reflective character, could have an innovative and transforming effect on the system of social relationships, thus at least making room for the possibility of historical freedom. This question presents itself on different levels: the level of theoretical linguistics,[17] and the level of a foundation for the social sciences as a whole, whether it be in the realm of a hermeneutic logic or in the realm of a fundamental theology.

The Model of Linguistic Competence (Chomsky)

The Shortcomings of Behaviorist Theories of Language and the General Status of an Empirical Theory of Language

The "linguistic turn" announced by Moritz Schlick in the name of the Vienna Circle led from the failure to find the final ground in an artificial, ideal unified language back to factual, historically realized communicative practice. Wittgenstein's attempt to show how we are to be satisfied with the description of actually played language games also leads to aporias.

The attempt to develop an empirical theory of language in this situation faces many fundamental difficulties. Viewed in terms of the classical theory of knowledge and transcendental philosophy, such an undertaking takes on a paradoxical character. If language is seen as the condition of possibility of intersubjective understanding and of rational communication as such, then such a theory retains the character of transcendental reflection. Apel writes that an empirical theory of language assumes the task of "making the *a priori* presuppositions of knowledge in the sense of traditional epistemology the object of an empirically testable formation of hypotheses in an individual science."[18] What is the status of such a theory? It must attempt to transform the "organization of mental processes,"[19] the transcendental structures of the human mind, into an empirically testable theory of knowledge. This undertaking thereby receives, when viewed formally, the paradoxical character of a self-reflective theory attempting to investigate language and to represent it theoretically by means that are themselves linguistically pre-given. Noam Chomsky understands his work as an attempt to reconstruct in an empirical theory of language the elementary and universal systems of rules that have been formed in a process of evolution. These rule systems function as genetically innate dispositions in the development of the individual; they are activated through interaction and shaped into the concrete, fundamental, regulative structures of the subject. The character of the attempt to link quasi-transcendental reflection on elementary structures of the subject with the theory of evolution and developmental psychology makes it akin to an endeavor with a quite similar structure: Piaget's developmental psychology.[20] The central place of language in the theory of science transforms an empirical theory of language into the cutting edge of the basic problems of the philosophy of science. This gives Chomsky's position and the entire development resulting from it the rank of a paradigm.[21] But how can an empirical theory of language be constructed at all?

In Chomsky's view, the various research programs in linguistics since the nineteenth century could each individually give some order to the voluminous data already collected, each with its own specialized regional theory of a carefully circumscribed domain; however, the modes of investigation and explanation in these theories were not adequate for deriving a comprehensive empirical theory of language. The nineteenth-century theoretical program of a historical linguistics was essentially fulfilled when the comparative study of Indo-Germanic languages had established the genetic interdependence of various languages and the structural laws for the development of sounds, etc. Ferdinand de Saussure saw that a purely diachronic study of language oriented to its development was insufficient since it neglected synchronic considerations of the inner order of language, the inquiry into language as a structured system. Saussure's procedure of segmentation and classification has proved quite fruitful on the levels of sounds, syllables, words, and groups of words. The breakthroughs of Trubetzkojs and Jakobson in phonology gave rise to the hope that the transparency of the structure of sounds would allow the same sort of theory formation for all other linguistic phenomena. This hope was soon to be disappointed. Chomsky's demand that the structuralists' "impoverished and thoroughly inadequate conception of language"[22] be overcome results primarily from the insight that the theoretical methods for the classification of the elements of pre-given linguistic utterances did not yield the means to explain the generation of sentences by a speaker. The level of explanation at which the structuralist theory stops remains close to the surface; "little of any significance remains."[23] The contribution of American linguistics is to be judged in the same way. Though these investigations collected an enormous amount of empirical material in the study of American Indian languages, they suffered from a very low level of abstraction, using a series of almost mechanically applied procedures to derive the grammatical rules of various languages.[24]

Chomsky also sees behaviorist theories of language as completely inadequate. The notion that "language is an essentially adventitious construct, taught by 'conditioning' (as would be maintained, for example, by Skinner or Quine) or by drill and explicit explanation (as was claimed by Wittgenstein), or built up by elementary 'data processing' procedures (as modern linguistics typically maintains)"[25] is completely unacceptable to Chomsky. Thus, Chomsky mounts what Stegmüller calls a "frontal attack on this behaviorist-scientific concept of man."[26] Chomsky's decisive objection to behaviorist learning theory is to its failure to explain how a child can acquire the capability of producing an unlimited number of new and correct sentences merely through contact with limited, fragmentary, and deformed language material. An adequate theory of language would have to explain how a competent speaker is in the position to bring about this creative achievement. A theory of language must therefore uncover the system of rules of which a speaker has command if he understands a language and can make himself understood in it. Where is such a theory to begin?

The Search for a Model of Linguistic Competence

The primary phenomenon to be explained by a theory of language is creativity: the ability to generate an unlimited number of rule-following linguistic forms. A theory of language is thus primarily a theory of linguistic competence: the ability to produce sentences never before heard by the speaker and recognized as correctly formed by other competent native speakers, and to produce them out of a finite repertoire of elements according to a finite number of rules in a finite number of steps.[27]

Chomsky's incisive basic idea was to apply the results of mathematical research on formal systems since the 1930s (specifically the theories of recursive functions and finite automata) to linguistic phenomena. Accordingly, when Chomsky demands that a theory of language as a theory of linguistic competence must be a theory of generative grammar, he is demanding that generative rules for sentences on the levels of syntax, semantics, and phonology be formulated as the rules of a formal system that is able to generate all correct and understandable sentences in a specific language, and only those sentences, it is a requirement of rules of this sort that they can be applied purely mechanically. But one must try to carry out only a small part of such a formalization to see what enormous difficulties such a theoretical program faces in its realization and what a degree of linguistic and mathematical-logical sophistication it demands.

Chomsky and his disciples dedicated themselves for many years to the formal, mathematical-logical problems of a generative theory of grammar.[28] Chomsky himself devised a series of formal systems and investigated their qualities (such as recursiveness and decidability) and their suitability for the construction of the generative grammars of concrete languages. He was able to show that certain formal systems cannot give an account of the complexity of sentence formation and thus cannot furnish a model for the creative linguistic competence of a speaker of a language.[29] For example, finite-state grammars, as models for abstract automata with a finite number of inner states, can indeed represent the constructions of a sentence in such a way that, given a beginning element, a further one can be generated according to specified rules.[30] However, this linear mode of sentence generation is not adequate to the complexity of sentence structures.

This failure led to the development of the "phrase-structure grammar" or "constituent-structure grammar," in which derivation rules can be presented in tree diagrams. In such diagrams the real achievement of this form of grammar, the transformation of elementary deep structure into a surface structure,[31] is represented intuitively. However, it can be shown that certain languages have structures that cannot be grasped by means of these grammars.[32] Derivation as a whole is more easily attained through transformation rules, which change a tree structure entirely and which generate the final surface structure of the sentence through this transformation. This sort of analysis is what is called generative transformational grammar.

Chomsky's theory of generative transformational grammar raises a universal claim: "This inquiry aims to elaborate the formal properties of any possible human language."[33] The basic hypothesis of this endeavor is that the formal properties of various grammars can be stated as formal universals.[34] The grammar of an individual language could be articulated through restriction rules from the general system of language. The question of the innate ability to acquire a concrete language must be treated on this same level. However, the concept of "innate ideas" has meaning for Chomsky only in the framework of a theory of evolution that ascribes the capacity to acquire language and linguistic competence not just to "months (or at most years) of individual experience" but rather to "the millions of years of evolution" or to "the principles of the neural organization that may be even more deeply grounded in physical law."[35]

In the discussion of Chomsky's views that dominated almost a decade of linguistics, many individual problems were discussed and many new proposals elaborated. We shall return to them in a moment. The underlying problem, one with objective implications, is the status of the theory as a whole. As Bierwisch puts it, "Linguistics shows, on one hand, that the essential conditions of concept formation and of logic rest on the innate dispositions of the human organism and finally on its biological structure and the physical laws of the universe. On the other hand, in order to formulate its theoretical assumptions, linguistics needs the laws of logic and mathematics to ground itself."[36]

From this insight, Bierwisch draws the conclusion that "in this apparent paradox, an idiosyncracy of human knowledge is expressed: that it is not constructed on a given foundation, but must as a whole always ground itself in a complex, dialectical process." The question is then one of how this dialectical process can be given a more precise determination. In Chomsky's theory these basic questions are hidden, for instance in the idea that the recognition of the adequacy of a grammar finally depends on the insight of a "native speaker."[37] The testing of formal rules depends on insight into a linguistic norm acquired in interaction. Nevertheless, the question remains whether Chomsky's model in its developed form is not ultimately monological. In any case, one can interpret the subsequent discussion of his theory to the effect that, as a result of the internal problems in semantics (the weakest point of the theory), an expansion of the framework to intersubjective communicative action must be undertaken.

The Problem of a Pragmatics in Linguistics

The Controversy in Semantics

Chomsky's views were soon criticized sharply, chiefly by his own students. His basic idea, which was to reconstruct the generative system of rules of a language according to the model of an abstract automaton by means of categories from the mathematical theory of automata, was called one of "communicative indifference."[38] The dimension of communicative action and interaction was bracketed out completely in Chomsky's theory. One could then attempt to reconstruct the further development of research in linguistics through the problematic of how the communicative indifference of the basic model was increasingly overcome and how linguistic phenomena were grasped as actions within the structure of interaction.[39]

The controversy was ignited through the problem of semantics. Chomsky began in *Syntactic Structures* with purely syntactic formation and transformation rules, and completely excluded meaning components. In *Aspects of the Theory of Syntax* he proposed the introduction of semantic components with their own system of rules operating over the basic syntactic components, which consisted for the most part of formation rules and a lexicon. The semantic interpretation of a sentence must accordingly be grasped as the semantic interpretation of its deep structure. (Deep structure merely represents the grammatical categories of sentences in their relations to each other and their subdivision into formatives, and in the lexical meaning of formatives.) Semantic rules must generate the meaning of a sentence from this syntactic structure and its lexical elements by producing relations of its particular kind between individual elements. Semantic or projection rules can be explained in their function in that they hinder the construction of meaningless sentences, or rather that they allow such sentences to be seen as meaningless through the analysis of their structure.[40]

This conception of "interpretative semantics" within "classical transformational grammar" has been presented often since Chomsky's first attempts, and it even found its way into language textbooks. By 1965 (the same year Chomsky published his *Aspects*) this view was being criticized, above all by Lakoff, McCawly, and Ross.[41] The criticism was directed primarily against Chomsky's conception of a semantically neutral deep structure that simply applies the already produced grammatical categories and which does not allow the unequivocal interpretation of specific semantic structures.[42]

In order to give this interpretation of semantic structures, the critics proposed a new theoretical approach misleadingly called generative semantics.[43] Their important differences with Chomsky's "interpretative semantics" consist primarily in the following.

• Formation rules are introduced as the basic components of the system. These formation rules generate an abstract structure of meaning represented in terms of predicate logic. Therefore, semantic structures are not derived from the interpretation of syntactic structures but are themselves generated as the basis.

• The sharp distinction between syntax and semantics is eliminated; grammatical relations are phenomena of the surface structure derived from the primary "grammatical" relation between predicates and arguments.

• A special deep structure for grammar is rejected; the underlying structure of a sentence coincides with its "logical form."

• The representation of the semantic-grammatical structure of sentences requires another formal-logical descriptive apparatus, which, in contrast with the great number of categories of interpretative semantics, requires only three categories: proposition, argument, and predicate.

• Conceived in terms of elements, this descriptive apparatus is not primarily a sentence grammar but is rather more concerned with the possibility of the analysis of larger text complexes.

This brief description does not yet adequately characterize the significance and the capabilities of this new conception of linguistics, since the decisive impetus for its further development, even of its theoretical apparatus, arises from problems that result from the factual, communicative use of language.

Problems Resulting from Speech-Act Theory

Here we must recall the development that followed from Wittgenstein's later philosophy.[44] J. L. Austin attempted to analyze linguistic utterances as rule-governed actions in a social context, and thus to relate the meanings of sentences to the situation of their use or simply to derive them from these situations. Austin's basic distinctions are among the verbal utterance itself (the locutionary act), the action accomplished by the utterance in a specific situation (the so-called illocutionary, or performative act), and the effect evoked in the listener by the linguistic action (the perlocutionary aspect of the action as a whole).[45] Linguistic utterances are from the start characterized as actions in dialogical situations; the analysis of an isolated aspect, as in pure semantics or in syntactic analysis, necessarily remains incomplete. Searle systematized this sort of analysis further by making more precise the rules according to which linguistic utterances are generated and understood as linguistic actions. In these analyses, the pragmatic dimension that Morris showed to be distinct from syntax and semantics become the explicit theme of linguistic analysis.

What is most important for both Austin and Searle is that linguistic utterances can be analyzed only as interactions, that is, as the reciprocally dependent actions of the speaker and the listener. A model of language that stops with the mechanisms of syntactic and semantic production of sentences could not fulfill the demands prescribed by speech-act theory.

However, this theory raises extraordinarily complex problems:

• If one wishes to explicate the illocutionary force of a speech act, one must refer back to rules that in many ways are not explicitly expressed in linguistic utterances but rather are mutually presupposed by both parties in the communication. Rules of linguistic action have the character of expectations of expectations; that is, the meaning of speech acts can be analyzed only in multilevel, interactive, reflexive models. Perhaps the most important aspect of such models is exactly how they are to represent formally what is meant by "convention."[46]

• Communication in everyday language is in many ways incomplete communication, in which full understanding is nonetheless achieved with what seems to be only fragmentary utterances. Similar phenomena can be seen in the poetic use of language. It seems therefore to be a characteristic of functioning language games that the competence of a speaker and of a listener is not limited to generating and decoding explicit syntactic and semantic information; rather, the comprehensibility of an utterance rests on a great number of presuppositions indirectly expressed in it and made simultaneously by both speaker and listener. This seems to be the basic mechanism of linguistic action. The analysis of an utterance must therefore include the speaker's and the listener's "presuppositions"[47] of an utterance. Only then is it possible to grasp the dimensions of communication at all.

• Linguistic utterances can only be of the sort that do not simply address what is self-evident to the speaker and the hearer but are meant to change conventions, the sedimented meanings of language use, and the presuppositions always made by the participants. How can such a process be presented?

• Text contexts larger than sentences are increasingly recognized as the authentic object of linguistics. In texts whose dimensions exceed the unit of the sentence, many problems arise that are not analyzable on the level of the sentence alone—for example, the problem of employing pronouns, the relation of topic to comment, and the change in the constellation of meanings and presuppositions in a larger text (such as a novel) or in the course of a dialogue. The mechanisms of textualization have to be seen as mechanisms of creative and innovative action.[48]

The problems do not seem to be solvable by means of the theories previously analyzed.

The Semantics of "Possible Worlds" and the Problem of a Logic of Dialogue

A solution to the aforementioned problems seemed to require a new theoretical instrument within foundational research in logic, an instrument that would at least allow the problematic to take a more precise form. Since the 1950s, important progress has been made in logical semantics and model theory.[49] Just as the theoretical instruments oriented to the paradigm of abstract automata used by Chomsky permitted the investigation of syntactic questions, a new theoretical instrument was now developed that at least helped to make the questions of semantics and pragmatics more precise. Contemporary research is, however, still far from integrating into a unified theory the three different directions in the development of semantics and pragmatics. Structuralist-oriented semantics, speech-act theory, and formal-logical and model-theoretical semantics remain separate research trends, all presenting each other with seemingly insoluble problems. Nevertheless, I shall attempt to list certain basic problems and perhaps clarify them a bit further by explaining which can be dealt with by these new instruments and which remain unclear, even in the strategy for their solution, because of considerations from the theory of science.

Within the study of the foundations of logic and semantics, a distinction that has been called by many different names and that goes as far back as the Stoics and has repeatedly played an important role is the distinction between reference and sense (Frege: *Bedeutung* and *Sinn*), denotation and meaning (Russell), reference and meaning (von Kutschera: *Bezug* and *Bedeutung*), or extension and intension (Carnap). Though the exact delineation of this distinction is different in these various authors, one can say that proper names, predicates, and sentences are to be given two semantic functions. In extensional semantics, the reference of a proper name is to the object it names, the reference of a predicate is to the scope of its concept and thus to a class, and the reference of a sentence is considered to be to its truth value. There is general agreement in extensional semantics, and extensional logic has proved extraordinarily fruitful, primarily in mathematics. There is much less agreement within intensional semantics. Carnap, for example, considers the meaning of a proper name an individual concept, the meaning of a predicate an attribute, and the meaning of a sentence a proposition. The primary difficulty in this area is that the meaning of the extensional notions of object, class, and truth value can be described very precisely, whereas what is meant by the notions of intensional semantics (such as individual concept, attribute, and proposition) remains so unclear that intensional semantics is far behind the standards of exactness and precision usually demanded of extensional logic. Even the attempts to formulate all statements in purely extensional language could not be carried out satisfactorily; see Quine's thesis of extensionality.

The underlying idea for further development in intensional semantics can be traced back to Carnap's ground-breaking 1947 study "Meaning and Necessity."[50] The most important aspect of this conception was the attempt to extend or transform semantics through modal logic by introducing the concept of "possible worlds" in the framework of an artificial logical language. Carnap's considerations can be broadly put in this way: If the intension of a predicate (the attribute it expresses) is determined, then, for every possible world, the objects in that world to which this attribute applies are also determined; that is, the extension of a predicate is determined in all possible worlds. Similarly, the truth value or extension of a sentence is determined when its intension (the state of affairs the sentence expresses) is determined. Carnap's proposal for the definition of intensional concepts is simply "to reverse this relation according to which the intension of an expression determines its extension in all possible worlds: if the extension of an expression is determined for all possible worlds, then its intension is unequivocally determined as well."[51] The intension of an expression A is thus the function that associates with every possible world the extension of A in this particular world. By using the concept of possible worlds, it is thus possible to successfully define intensions in extensional terms.

Before commenting on the application of this logical instrument to theoretical linguistics, I should say something about the status of the concept of possible worlds. Leibniz used it in the context of his investigations into modal logic. However, for Leibniz the concept has its significance only within a certain ontology;[52] for Carnap it is strictly related to an artificial language of predicative logic. If a language S has certain individual constants and certain predicate constants, then a possible world related to language S is that "state description in S" in which all individuals are characterized with respect to all predicates available in the language. A possible world as a state description in S is therefore simply a class of sentences such that for any elementary sentence in S either the sentence or its negation is a member of the class. The number of possible worlds thus results from the richness of the language in question and not from an ontology of possible worlds.[53] However, this resolution marked the breakdown of Carnap's immanent-artificial-language approach. Carnap assumed that there is exactly one adequate description of the present state of the world—in other words, that there is a unique actual world—and that this unique actual world can be determined only in relation to a previously selected language. If we recall the problems presented above regarding the status of theoretical concepts in theories and the choice of a corresponding theoretical language—a problem whose solution Carnap sought in criteria of the usefulness of a language—it should be clear that with the thesis of one actual world the entire set of problems connected with the linguistic interpretation of reality only arises again.

Matters are only made worse for the question of the status of theoretical concepts if one brings a specific theoretical language (and hence a logical construct) to bear on the interpretation of ordinary language, specifically for the clarification of the pragmatic problems of ordinary language. This is because in the texts of ordinary language, such as dialogues, the changing perspectives of diverse world views must be characterized, together with the different "worlds" of the various speakers both in their relatedness and in their distinctness.

The further development of modal logic and the construction of a pragmatics based on modal logic both tried to give an account of these problems. For one thing, the attempt was made to include the perspective of a specific context of application by defining a two-place predicate over the set of possible worlds, selecting out of the entire set only those worlds that stood in that defined relation to a specific world. It is, or course, crucial how this relation is defined. This definition remains relatively simple if the relation can be specified simply according to the appearance of specific individuals in the possible worlds. However, it remains unclear how this relation can be determined with respect to predicates and sentences.

The apparatus of Carnap's proposal also cannot adequately capture the complexity of ordinary language. The meaning of a sentence uttered in ordinary speech can be changed by other sentences uttered by the speaker before or after it (its linguistic context) and also by the speech situation in which it is uttered (its nonverbal context).[54] A further development in modal logic attempted to take into account these distinctions. Montague, Lewis, and Petöfi[55] are the leading theorists in this area. The intensional interpretation of certain linguistic utterances now is determined through specific indices, or reference points. An index is fixed by coordinates that can take into account various contextual and cotextual dimensions, for example time of utterance, place of utterance, audience, speaker, and deictically identified objects. Theoretically, the interpretation of an ordinary-language text then consists in the procedure for determining the extension of the elements of the sentence in the possible worlds selected by the reference points chosen. Text interpretation is then the generating of a world-semantic representation of the text in the theoretical language which the interpreter must already have constructed beforehand.[56]

Of course, this approach raises a whole set of questions. It is not my concern here even to mention all the problems posed by the investigations in modal logic and model theory, the problems involved in the construction of a lexicon needed in interpretation, and the problems of integrating the various parts of the theory, for instance. I shall confine myself to pointing out several fundamental methodological questions that already emerge as unresolved problems in the present state of speech-act theory.

The Text-Theoretical Interpretation of Dialogue in a Semantics of Possible Worlds

The basic internal theoretical and methodological problems that arise for a linguistic theory that follows the proposals of Montague, Lewis, Stalnaker, and Petöfi is best discussed through an example. Petöfi chose the section of Saint-Exupéry's *Little Prince* where an echo repeats every utterance.[57] In this text the author apparently intends to communicate to the reader something about existing reality and its possible (and desirable) transformation by picturing someone in a fictive world who protests against a world that is held to be real within this fictive world.

In connection with this text, we can first of all explain how a text as such can be generated according to the text grammar proposed by Petöfi. This type of text grammar is made up of a lexicon, a synthetic algorithm, and an analytic algorithm. The lexicon consists of a core lexicon of nondefined elements and a lexicon of defined elements; definitions are represented as predicate functions. A system of formation rules operates over the lexicon, generating the basic semantic structure of texts. From these textual bases, the system of transformation rules generates the final text—even its phonetic realization. Analyzing the text may be described as simply reversing the process of its production according to a synthetic algorithm. The conception of this sort of grammar presupposes that the formational and transformational rule systems function like automata.[58] These rule systems have the advantage that they can be linked with further operational components, primarily world semantics, which attribute to the text a representation in terms of various world complexes. The theoretical instruments on the basis of which such an "interpretation" is carried out have been discussed above.

The specific sort of problems that result from such a notion of interpretation can be illustrated in the example of the text mentioned above. In interpretations using world semantics, various subworlds must be distinguished: the world of the planet of the Little Prince, the world of the part of the planet Earth known by the Little Prince, and the world as it is represented by the assumptions of the Little Prince about the part of the Earth known to him. Within the semantic representation of the text, the relation among these worlds must be determined. This is usually done in modal logic by specifying what is "attainable from a certain world," "possible," or "necessary in a certain world." Within the text itself, the problem arises of how the relations of the different worlds to each other are to be "evaluated". This means that evaluations or wishes play a role in ordinary-language and poetic-figurative texts. But this approach has this much in its favor: With these theoretical instruments, the problems may be formulated as problems.[59]

A pragmatic study that considers texts as linguistic actions in communicative situations must then investigate what function the text should have for the reader according to the intention of the author. It is clear that this makes our problems even more complex. The simple case is a speaker who wishes to communicate a certain fact to a hearer without demanding from the hearer a change in his basic assumptions about the world or in his attitude toward this world. Much more interesting and complex are cases where the intention is to change these basic assumptions and attitudes. A theory of speech acts, and correspondingly a linguistic pragmatics that intends to explain the phenomena analyzed in speech-act theory, would then have to investigate how such a transformation can be grasped theoretically.

The analysis of a dialogue has the task of explaining the following problem complexes:

the speaker's basic assumptions about and attitudes toward his world, and thus the theoretical reconstruction of the world of the speaker,

the assumptions of the speaker concerning the basic assumptions and attitudes of the audience, and hence the reconstruction of the world of the audience,

the intention that the speaker pursues in expressing his "text," above all insofar as it is directed toward the transformation of the basic assumptions and attitudes of the audience,

the fact that the reconstruction of this intention is possible only if the assumptions of the audience about the basic assumptions and attitudes of the speaker can also be reconstructed as the speaker expects them to be (that is, if his expectations of the expectations of the audience can be reconstructed),

the fact that the intention of a linguistic utterance aimed at changing attitudes (and thus also at disappointing expectations and creating new ones), must then at least be reconstructed on the level of expectation expectation, the fact that the course of dialogue, and thus the utterances exchanged by the speakers, must be analyzed as processes in this complex succession of levels, and

the fact that the achievement of a "consensus" must then be reconstructed as the process in which the basic assumptions and attitudes about the world of the speaker and the world of his dialogue partner come into some sort of agreement such that both can be represented in a unified framework of basic attitudes and assumptions about their common world.

Only a theory of texts based on such an explanation of the dialogue process can give an account of the problems that inevitably arise in speech-act theory.[60] In the example introduced above, this would mean that the formal instruments of linguistics based on model theory must not only analyze what worlds can be distinguished in the text and how their relation to each other can be determined in terms of modal logic; beyond that, this theoretical framework must be able to describe what intention the author is pursuing in the text—that is, the assumptions of the author about the world of the reader, the valuation of such an assumed world within the world of the author, the assumptions of the author about the changes desired in the world of the reader, and the production of these various subworlds in one comprehensive text as an action directed at bringing about this change. Only this sort of complex reconstruction would disclose the pragmatic dimensions of the text. The claim that these are the minimal requirements of a text theory should not be viewed as controversial. Analyses of this sort have been performed by Lewis[61] and others.

Lonergan

The Problem of Innovative Speech Acts

Against the background of this set of problems, the weaknesses of a speech-act theory based on Austin's work also become immediately clear. The central concept of Austin's speech-act theory is the illocutionary act. This concept is supposed to explain the way in which a linguistic utterance represents an action. For Austin, the illocutionary force of an utterance rests on convention. The illocutionary act is a "conventional act," an "act done as conforming to a convention"[62] and "constituted not by intention or by fact essentially, but by *convention* (which is, of course, a fact)."[63] Hence, speech acts draw their force from the conventions, or rules, that Searle calls "constitutive rules."[64] The basic problem of a theory of linguistic action formulated in this way is that speech acts directed at the transformation of conventions cannot at all be understood. Austin presupposes that action is always conventionally and institutionally bound.[65]

The theoretical explanation of innovative, situation-changing, and convention-dissolving speech acts—speech acts that ground something new—raises problems that are linked to almost all the basic problems in the theory of science discussed above. This can be illustrated through the limit problems of semantics based on model theory. The results of Löwenheim and Skolem's attempt to incorporate the consequences of Tarski's theories are concerned with the relationship of models and theoretical language. On their view, in a sufficiently powerful formal language an interpretation in terms of a model is never unique or unequivocal but always allows for several valid interpretations at the same time. Conversely, a specific interpretation also changes the presupposed metalinguistic conditions of the theory language, so that the language system as a whole can change through a speech act. The problem is therefore that a model-theoretical interpretation within the framework of theoretical approaches in linguistics, as outlined above, is in danger of concealing this space for innovation and reducing to unidimensionality a dialectical process in language (that is, a process whose development uncovers the conditions of its very possibility and at the same time changes these conditions). But here we address a whole series of fundamental problems of theory formation in linguistics. These problems have a significant two-sided character: Certain linguistic phenomena are of the sort that in a certain way they put in question the entire process of theory formation as it has heretofore been conceived; also, such phenomena always cut through theories, so to speak, and force a change in their status.

Open Questions

A few of the problems now increasingly occupying research in linguistics should be mentioned.

Chomsky was still able to conceive of the process of learning a language within the framework of a system of rules that, as the universal basis, is supposed to be able to explain all linguistic phenomena in any language. But the acquisition of linguistic competence must presumably be thought of as a transition between various rule systems. It is still unclear whether this transition itself can yet again be explained within a more comprehensive system of rules.[66]

Similarly, it is still not explained precisely how the appropriation of conventions, and, even more so, their transformation, can be understood theoretically.[67]

A linguistics of dialogue processes that is to comprehend innovative phenomena raises the question of how we are to conceive a logic of dialogue that is supposed to be able to explain utterances whose understanding requires a transformation of attitude. How would a logic of questions, for example, be characterized? Are the present theories adequate to explain even this seemingly trivial phenomenon?

A logic of dialogue has to include a logic of argumentation that explains what it means to reach a consensus in innovative conversational processes. Reaching a consensus would then mean establishing in the course of the dialogue a previously unaccepted and even unknown system of rules. The question would then be whether reaching a consensus is not to be characterized as a "dialectical" process, in a sense that is made explicit through this process itself.

The poetic-figurative use of language is innovative in an empowering sense and thus marks the farthest possibility of linguistic competence and the touchstone of such a theory. In it, almost all the previously mentioned problems come together in a new way. How must we characterize the theoretical analysis of poetics?

Speech-act theory and the research in pragmatics that starts from it have determined that an analysis of linguistic action and interaction requires making connections with a sociological theory of interaction that illuminates the social dimension of linguistic action. We may conjecture from the previous discussion that a sociological theory of interaction would also present similar problems if it were concerned with social action in the context of societally sedimented structures. We may further surmise that the touchstone for a sociological theory of action will also be the problem of innovative, structure-changing action, and hence the problem of a dialectic by which action changes the conditions and possibilities of its own theoretical explanation and orientation.

The Requirements for a Linguistic Theory of Communicative Action

The enormous volume of detailed studies undertaken in linguistics in the last decades can hardly be surveyed, and any attempt to determine even the basic lines of development in the contemporary situation is in danger of only adding one more standpoint to the enormous number already articulated. One could say, nonetheless, that one line of development extending at least from Chomsky exhibits a certain coherence. Chomsky's reliance on an approach derived from the theory of automata has to be both changed and expanded if linguistics is to give an account of concrete linguistic processes. This development now reveals two diverging tendencies. Linguistics based on model theory attempts to develop a basis for formal analysis corresponding to the strict claims of research into the foundations of logic. Speech-act theory begins with more intuitive concepts, but better maintains the whole complexity of the phenomena.

An integrating, unified theory is still not in sight. All that has transpired suggests that such a theory is to be found only through a change in the status of the entire theoretical approach to linguistics. This can be explained once again through the circularity that is at the basis of a linguistics that employs mathematical tools. The research into the foundations of mathematics has as one of its results that the final basis of formal operations is to be found only in ordinary language. The approach of operational mathematics only makes matters worse in regard to this result of the formal-axiomatic method; it goes back to elementary communicative practice, which cannot itself be traced back to any further basis but can only be reconstructed. We are supposed to obtain the formal tools with which linguistic practice itself is to be analyzed. It should be clear that this poses a fundamental problem for the theory of science: that of the scientific-communicative eluci-dation of communicative practice, and thus that of a communicatively reflective self-enlightenment itself proceeding through linguistic pro-cesses. A theory that is to give an adequate account of the problems presented here has to satisfy the following requirements.

• It has to be a fundamental theory of linguistic interaction that makes possible theoretical self-clarification of interaction by means of inter-action through elucidating the structure of communication.

• The basic problem, the touchstone for such a theory, remains the question of innovative social action. Innovation in communication poses the problem of dialogical reflection and the problem of reaching con-sensus in reflectively refracted, temporal, dialogical processes. The innovative and temporal dimensions of linguistic action in dialogue mutually condition each other, and any theoretical approach that does not take both into account from the beginning will certainly fail.

• This may be explained through the relationship of such a theory to structuralism. Structuralism as a method of describing relations among elements presupposes a limited body of elements, the possibility of denumerating the possible relations among elements, and the limitation of the variation of relations in terms of a mode of combination pre-determined in this way. Structuralist theory therefore ultimately points to "dead" structures that exclude temporal, innovative processes; its theory is then in principle limited.[68]

• A basic theory of communication must be fundamental. That is, it must elucidate the basic structures of linguistic interaction, in this elucidation it must also make intelligible the possibility of constructing theories about linguistic interaction, and it must be aware of the necessity for the transformation of the theoretical framework of linguistic interaction resulting from the process of interaction itself. Only then can such a foundational theory both ground the possibility of science and be a practical theory at the same time.

The development of linguistics seems to be a paradigm for the way in which the persistent pursuit of objective and methodological problems leads to the development of a basic theory of communicative action. With this result, we have arrived at the basic problems of the sciences of social action and the theory of science as a whole.

5

The Problem of Method in the
Social Sciences

At several points in the development described above it seemed that perhaps the aporetic limit problems of the theory of science become all the more pointed, and even enter a new dimension, when the theory of science has as its theme the realm of subjects and their communicative actions and thus is concerned with the object realm of the social sciences. The decisive transition to that dimension is this: The objects of the social sciences must themselves be understood in the broadest sense as "theory-forming subjects." Thus, social-scientific theories have a reflective character (though here in a banal sense), and a self-reflective character as well, since the social scientist himself belongs to the same social context he is studying.

This touches upon the critical limit problems uncovered in the theory of science. The empirical characters of basic statements in the social sciences cannot simply be achieved in arbitrarily repeated test situations through the measurement of physical magnitudes; they are rather the result of the interaction of subjects, as in an interview. Methodology here has the same basic interactive structure as its realm of objects.

The problem of legitimizing the theoretical concepts by which data are interpreted is especially difficult in the social sciences, since theoretical interpretations of the actions of subjects are at the same time decisions about their self-understanding. Here the problems of instrumentalism, conventionalism, and pragmatic decisionism in theory formation are not simply harmless abstractions. The choices of a theoretical framework and an interpretative paradigm imply the choice of an interpretative framework for the understanding of a historical society.

Objections can be raised against such a dramatization of the problem of method, since what we find at the roots of modern sociology (for instance in Comte and his successor Durkheim) is precisely an insight into the factual character of social relationships—even their thinglike character, whose massive objectivity can crush individuals. "The first and most fundamental rule," Durkheim writes, is *"Consider social facts as things."*[1] For Durkheim, however, the thinglike "fait social" consists precisely of intentional, intersubjective actions. Thus, for him sociology has as its object the constitution of social reality from the actions of subjects and the influence of this constituted reality on the actions of subjects. If the object of investigations into social reality is to be independent of the intentional actions of subjects, then the context of this interrelationship will be absent from theory formation in the social sciences. But exactly how a social-scientific theory that captures this interconnection of action and reification is to proceed is the central question in the controversies surrounding the methodology of the social sciences.

With the insight that a social-scientific theory has to grasp the actions of subjects in reflexive interaction, we still have not appreciated the full gravity of the problem of method in the social sciences. We might do so if our confidence in the ability of any theory to grasp elementary social relations were to be fundamentally shaken. This mistrust of theoretical constructs is exactly what has been constitutive of the social sciences since the emergence of the concept of ideology in the Enlightenment and (more important) since Hegel, Marx, Nietzsche, and Freud. Since then, the sociologist must make it his profession to harbor a suspicion that theoretical interpretations of social reality—especially when they are widely accepted—reflect a false consciousness of that reality and thus falsify it either consciously or unconsciously. Hegelian reflective philosophy, which sees consciousness as both productive and product; the Marxian interpretation of the history of the species, which sees contemporary consciousness as the result of social labor and the relations of production and domination resulting from it; Nietzsche's and Freud's mistrust of naive consciousness that has not yet seen through itself to grasp that it is itself influenced by deeper underlying forces—these conceptions all demand the critical "second glance" of the social scientist, who thus makes his theory formation reflective and mistrusts his own procedures because they could be the result of a distorted or even destructive manner of association among human beings.

The debates concerning the methodology of the social sciences begin at the point where the suspicion originates that accepted scientific methods finally lose their social innocence when they are simply transferred to the realm of social reality. In this situation, sociological methodology is called upon to perform a double function. First, it has to reflect upon the methodical access to social phenomena, in which the traditional differences of "explanation" and "understanding," of natural-scientific and humanistic methods, collide with one another. Second, since Hegel and Marx, it seems unavoidable that sociology be regarded as a methodological foundational theory that is supposed to supply the legitimizing basis for all knowledge.

This situation, which is expressed most sharply in German sociological discussion, calls for especially careful distinctions. In the discussion above, the quasi-transcendental status that might be urged upon the social sciences was illustrated by the theory of language games of the later Wittgenstein and by the epistemological claims of linguistics as understood by Chomsky. In the following, I would like to explain the basic problem of the theory of the social sciences by first taking a brief look back on the "positivism dispute" in German sociology, in which several basic questions were developed.[2] Next, in a somewhat more detailed analysis, I shall discuss certain recent problems of methodology that have fundamental significance for the social sciences. After this short overview of the contemporary state of the discussion of explicitly sociological theory formation, I shall turn to the general consequences of this inquiry for the discussion of the theory of science and for a foundational theory of theology.

A Backward Glance at the Positivism Dispute in German Sociology

The dispute over the basic methodological problems of the social sciences was the center of two great controversies in German sociology. Both have already received historiographical treatment. We are not here so much interested in the dispute surrounding Weber's thesis of the value freedom of science[3] in the first decades of this century as in the dispute between Karl Popper and Theodor Adorno that began in 1961 at the Tübingen sociology conference and continued with further contributions by Hans Albert and Jürgen Habermas.[4]

After his emigration, Popper extended his methodology to the realms of the historical and social sciences without significantly changing its basic tenets.[5] Opposed to the rigid claims of the Vienna Circle, and conscious of having founded a liberal method of rational critique deriving from the critical tradition but possessing universal validity, Popper spoke out with fervor against dogmatic and ultimately totalitarian ideas. He advocated scientific critique and social freedom and felt that he could ground their unity in the principle of radical critique. Adorno took issue with such claims, although only hesitantly.[6] It was Habermas who first attempted to point out the inner problems of Popper's methodology and its questionable consequences for the social sciences.[7] I shall not attempt to go into the details of this dispute; my concern is to show in the case of one particular question what fundamental problems were at stake in the controversy.

We have already seen that Popper gave a central place to the problem of obtaining basic statements within the process of critical inquiry. Basic statements are never simply a questionless picturing of empirical facts; as linguistic formulations, they have the character of judgments in a court of law, agreed upon in a series of testimonies. Habermas is basically in agreement with this characterization through the metaphor borrowed from jurisprudence, but finds this parallelization more illuminating precisely for the internal problematic of Popper's own proposals.[8] Popper and Habermas agree that empirical facts are always interpreted in the light of laws and judged by the consensus of those who give testimony or take part in the process of inquiry. The dispute begins at the point where we are to determine the character of these theoretical proposals—indeed even the character of the language available for such proposals. Habermas sees the example taken from jurisprudence as significant precisely in this regard: In the process of judgment in a court of law, the validity of basic statements (and thus that of judgments) is measured by a system of socially posited norms. These norms are the product of historical growth; they are sediments of the interaction of subjects and have the meaning of generally recognized behavioral expectations made binding by sanctions.[9] Hence, these norms originate in a context of life that must be interpreted as such and that can be fully understood only in terms of its historical emergence. Social norms must be traced back to the action of subjects in their life contexts.

The decisive question to put to Popper is this: Is it not also necessary to trace the theoretical conceptions of the empirical sciences back to the historical dimension of such contexts of social life? Must we not inquire behind scientific activity to its historical-social basis? Is not the practice of the interaction of subjects the final basis of the validity of statements? This is the problematic of Critical Theory as Horkheimer presented it in his 1937 essay "Traditional and Critical Theory":[10] "The social genesis of problems, the real situations in which science is put to use, and the purposes it is made to serve are all regarded by science as external to itself. The critical theory of society, on the other hand, has for its object humans as producers of their own historical way of life in its totality."[11] In this essay Horkheimer regards this procedure of tracing apparently final facts back to the human activity of interactive production as the point of agreement between German Idealism and the Marxist critique of political economy.

Generally speaking, this approach has a number of basic implications:

• The objectivating attitude of the natural sciences, which aims at discovering lawlike regularities, has its origins in a specific form of interaction and thus in a mode of dealing with external nature conditioned by this interaction, namely socially organized labor.

• A precise structure of this approach can be illuminated only in an analysis of its historical-societal origins. Even the natural sciences can thus be studied historically and genetically.

• A transposition of the objectivating attitude originating from the perspective of social labor to human interaction as a whole is basically a category mistake and a reification of interactive processes and interacting subjects. That the methodology of the natural sciences is extended to the social sciences as well signals, then, a certain stage in the development of human society.

• The inadmissible transposition of reified methods to the study of subjects is a sign of the elementary contradictions in this stage of development; a certain form of reified social labor becomes the horizon of the interpretation of human action as such. The ability to see and criticize this development is the beginning of a historical transition beyond a definite stage of society in human evolution.[12]

• From this context the postulate follows that a theory of unreified and unalienated human interaction must be developed, a theory that can be foundational for both the natural sciences and the social sciences in the broadest sense.

How the last-mentioned postulate is finally to be vindicated is a question that results in different viewpoints within Critical Theory itself. For Horkheimer and Adorno, the vindication of this postulate remains utopian with respect to the present condition of society. Its theoretical claim can only be redeemed as a critique of concrete relations, and thus also as the critique of science. The method of this critique cannot be positive but can only be negative dialectics.[13] Habermas, aware of his differences with the classics of Critical Theory,[14] has proposed a theory of the undistorted interaction of subjects as just such a foundational theory. We shall return to the character and dimensions of such an undertaking.

Among Popper's interpreters, Hans Albert has taken the lead in answering Habermas's objections.[15] Albert does not bring any new arguments to bear beyond Popper's own; rather, he follows a strategy of trivialization, complaining that "the trivial fact, disputed by no one, that theories, explanations, and even perceptual facts in the sciences *factually* refer back to communication, and with it to understanding, is pushed so strongly into the foreground that the question of the general *structure* of this activity itself and its eventual *nomological* explanation disappears completely from view."[16] Albert's basic thesis is that interaction must also be capable of fundamental and complete nomological explanation. "A critical theory of science must take care that it does not take such distinctions all too seriously. . . ."[17] The aporia of such an argument becomes clear when the question arises of how critical rationalism can itself be grounded as a method in the face of Popper's assertion that the problem lies "not in the choice between knowledge and faith, but only in the choice between two kinds of faith."[18] We shall return to these problems in the investigation of the problem of a communicative theory of action as a foundational theory for the empirical sciences, and in the discussion of the problem of the justification of ethical discourse.

After this short review, other approaches will be selected for examination here according to whether they have made advances in the problem of method and subject matter in the social sciences. After these considerations, it will be possible to give a systematic treatment of the contemporary state of the problem of the social sciences.

The Problem of the Foundations of the Social Sciences

The Problem Situation

According to our previous reflections, a theory of the social sciences would have to assume a double role. Such a theory would first have to ground the social sciences in three dimensions: a general theory of interaction, a theory of the relation of interacting individuals to what is structurally given in the system of society, and a theory of the historical constitution of both the interaction and the structure of society, as well as their modes of interdependence. As its second task, such a theory would have to answer the question of how to approach the task of developing a wide-ranging theory that incorporates the structure and the means of reflection into the realm of the objects of its inquiry.

It is not the goal here to give a detailed overview of the contemporary conception of sociological research.[19] This is by no means even possible. Rather, the concern is more with reflecting on basic contemporary research strategies and asking in what direction we might look for a contemporary solution to the problems indicated above.

Symbolic Interactionism, Phenomenology, and Ethnomethodology

The prominence of the work of George Herbert Mead for any theory of the foundations of the social sciences has become clear over the years, especially through Mead's historical influence on and interaction with both the phenomenological approach of Alfred Schütz[20] and ethnomethodological research in the United States.

Mead's central concern is the relation between the identity of the individual and the structure of society in the framework of develop-mental processes.[21] Here we shall consider two questions: that of language as the medium of such processes and that of the identity of the self in society.

For Mead, the mediation of self-identity and social reality is bound to symbolically structured linguistic action. As befits his behaviorist background, Mead attempts to derive linguistic action from gestures that, as social acts, exert stimuli on other individuals of a group and lead to reactions that in turn affect the original actor. In such an analysis, gestures are understood—as, for example, in the case of a dog baring his teeth—as "a syncopal, prematurely suspended act, a torso that communicates the emotional content of the act."[22] A privileged place is given to vocal gestures, since they alone are perceived by the gesturing individual in exactly the same way as by the other; hearing one's own sounds has the same effect as a stimulus as hearing the sounds of another. According to Raiser, this unique constitution of vocal gestures gives Mead "the model upon which his entire further theory of the origin of mind and consciousness, of language and identity is built."[23] The vocal gesture opens the possibility of putting oneself unconsciously in the place of another, of anticipating the probable reaction of the other and producing this reaction in oneself, at least partially. Vocal gestures therefore become "significant symbols." "Symbols," Mead writes, "become significant on the basis of the ability to be both oneself and the other at the same time."[24] Words, as significant symbols, are thus symbolic summaries of social acts. It is characteristic of them that they have the identical meaning for everyone. For Mead, language is therefore fundamentally general; as the pregnant expression of general social reality on the one hand and as the ideal-normative medium as the universe of discourse on the other hand, it makes possible interaction among structurally equivalent individuals.[25]

The structure of significant symbols also permits Mead to answer a second question central to his work: that of how the individual achieves and preserves his identity in social interaction. The acquisition of language develops simultaneously along with the differentiation of the social relationships of the individual. Mead saw important steps in this development in the role playing of children and in their playing by the rules of competitive games. In role playing, children assume the place of a certain person in a social act and call forth in themselves the actions they would expect of others in relation to their own behavior. In organized competitive group games, a child must know and be conscious of the function of every individual player in the rule-governed, organized whole, in such a way that he anticipates at all times the behavior of the others toward him, objectifies this attitude toward himself as the "generalized other," views himself from the standpoint of this generalized other, and is able to act within this framework. The acting "I" moves through reflection and objectification from the position of the other to the "me", and thus becomes the self in an interactive process of reflective self-objectification—a self that can become and be a self only in and through interaction with others. Self-identity is therefore for Mead a process of tension, in which the spontaneity of the "I" and its social self-objectification are logically equivalent constitutive elements. Self-identity and the generalized and objectivated reality of society in the individual therefore mutually condition each other.

This analysis of symbolically structured interaction gave Mead the impetus to further develop the concept of role behavior as one of the basic analytic concepts of sociology. It is also true that the behaviorist elements of Mead's theory[26] helped to give this development a specific direction. In Mead's analysis, role behavior can be understood in the first instance in a neutral sense as linguistically mediated interaction of partners who have certain normative expectations of each other in certain situations of social action and who, in acting, are conscious of these normative expectations. This account was sharpened by Parsons, who grasped the interacting partners as a system of interaction and specified in certain postulates the conditions for the stability of the system.[27] According to these postulates, the role behavior that constitutes one action system and maintains it in equilibrium is guaranteed with the highest degree of certainty when the behaviorial expectations collected in the role are unambiguous, are oriented as far as possible to one role, are mutually agreed upon by both partners, correspond to the individual needs of the actors and ensure the satisfaction of those needs, and are so internalized in the partners that they more or less steer their behavior.[28] In this concept of role behavior, elements of Mead's theory of interaction and of a theory of socialization based on Freud[29] are evidently bound together with conceptions from cybernetic systems theory.[30]

Erving Goffman raises the objection against Parsons's brand of role theory that roles in this sense represent pathological limit cases of social relations. Goffman demonstrated this thesis not in theoretical reflections but in clever studies of social formations and situations that actually came close to the requirements of Parsons's role theory. Goffman himself was a participant-observer in these studies.[31] Goffman's studies of inmates in psychiatric clinics, prisons, and concentration camps leads to the conclusion that even in such "total institutions", where one interaction partner has all the power to impose his role expectations completely on the other, the reaction of the weaker partner discloses certain elementary, basic characteristics that are constitutive of all interaction. An individual does not completely break down in such extreme situations if there is at least a minimal chance to distance himself internally from the total expectations, to present himself in his subjectivity to himself (in the extreme case, through silence).[32] From other similarly perceptive studies of daily situations, and particularly from studies of the experiences of handicapped people, Goffman and others—including a whole group of sociologists who have further developed Mead's symbolic interactionism[33]—present the structural conditions that must be fulfilled if interaction is not to hinder the self-determination of subjects in a total system and suppress the presentation of their self-identity and the satisfaction of their elementary needs. Role distance and tolerance of ambiguity and frustration are characteristic of the individual who has a flexible ego identity in correspondence with an interaction system determined by freedom.[34]

It should be clear that this is a research area in which interaction theory and social psychology join together with individual psychological theory and psychoanalytic theories, on the one hand, and with theories of society on the other. In such research, the concept of undistorted communication that is not determined by domination has a key function; while this concept is open to empirical investigation in the framework of various theories, it also has the status of a research paradigm.

Historical-Materialist Theories of Society

Marxism perhaps raises the strongest objection against a social science oriented primarily to symbolic interaction, in that such a conception of social science has insufficent theoretical capabilities[35] for understanding a wide range of social phenomena; it cannot supply explanations in the realms of production, distribution, consumption, and the political steering of the totality of social processes. The fixation of this approach on language allows it to forget that social labor, as the exchange with nature, has primacy over linguistic interaction in more than just one sense. From both an evolutionary and a causal-analytic perspective, the origin of linguistic symbols is to be explained in terms of the necessity for reaching common understanding in the emergence of the division of labor. From the perspective of the logic of interaction, when the reproduction of the species occurs in a process of production with the division of labor, these conditions also determine the framework of communication in general. For the theory of society this means that the relations of production—specifically the relations of domination in the steering of production, distribution, and consumption—are the fundamental and constitutive phenomena which it is the primary task of the theory of society to grasp and thus to which it must be oriented in its structure. As opposed to these phenomena, language is a secondary phenomena whose structure depends on what is more elementary. If a theory of society gives precedence to linguistic interaction in its orientation, it can hardly avoid ignoring domination and suppression in society and losing sight of the fact that linguistic interaction in this situation is always communication systematically distorted through domination.[36]

It is not our concern here to treat each of these objections in detail. Even proponents of research trends oriented toward symbolic interaction admit that the analysis of social-structural features and the domains of steering mechanisms, production, and consumption are either neglected or very difficult to integrate in the present methodological situation.[37] A further index of the fact that these objections at least partially strike home is the completely formal treatment of economic problems and the theoretical isolation of economics from the rest of the social sciences among non-Marxists.[38]

On the other side are those theoreticians who give Marx a central place in the history of science and attempt to study his conception of the relation of work and interaction. Habermas, for example, has tried to show that reified consciousness is the ultimate result of the subordination of interaction to labor in society. This subordination is made theoretically responsible for the ability of bureaucratic and totalitarian tendencies to dominate in socialist states, at least at present. Only a correction of this false view allows for the theoretical possibility of proposing a structure for society necessarily binding together progress in the forces of production with progress in freedom.[39] A still unresolved question of sociological theory formation is how these different dimensions could be grasped in a unified theory.

Sociological Systems Theory on the Model of Cybernetic Systems Theory

In this situation, one strategy that suggests itself is that found in all the various forms of systems theory, paradigmatically perhaps in Parsons and Luhmann. This strategy is supposed to resolve two different problems. First, it attempts to grasp in a unified way the various areas not yet integrated into previous sociological theories. It does so by moving to a high level of abstraction in the conceptual apparatus of the theory, which allows it to be comprehensive of all social phenomena. Second, this process of abstraction is supposed to clarify the question of what theoretical instruments are legitimate in the social sciences as such; it is supposed to lead us to apparently self-evident phenomena which cannot be further questioned and which ground both the realm of objects and the method of the theory.

Parsons and Luhmann both attempt to explain the first problem with reference to a systems theory influenced by cybernetics. The second problem is supposedly clarified through Luhmann's interpretation of the concept of complexity. But Luhmann does not want to limit himself to cybernetic systems theory; indeed, he states explicitly that a sociological systems theory must go beyond cybernetic conceptions.[40] However, the question still remains whether a sociological systems theory surpassing the limitations of cybernetics and claiming to metatheoretically grasp all other theoretical conceptions can be developed at all without internal contradictions, thus without reducing itself to absurdity. In order to test whether this is possible, we must return to several of the basic problems of cybernetic systems theory alluded to above.

Luhmann tries to avoid such contradictions by characterizing the possible relations among system elements established with the modes of combination of a system as complex in their structure. Without any further definition, complexity then becomes the basic concept of Luhmann's theory, a fundamental concept that cannot be gone beyond in any conceivable theory. Accordingly, Luhmann calls both the formation of theories and the action of social units structuring reductions of complexity, so that social action and theoretical interpretation appear to be the same kind of activity. The fascinating appeal of this strategy is that it seems to escape the fundamental aporia of the methodology of the social sciences by attributing analogous structures to theory and object. Moreover, the problem of the suspicion of ideology in sociology seems to be explained through the reduction to a formal metatheory behind which we cannot inquire. But this strategy alone cannot escape the objections raised against cybernetic systems theory. These objections can be formulated most effectively as a demonstration of the self-contradictory nature of the theory.

It is self-evident from the study of the foundations of mathematics that formal systems can be grounded and legitimated only in inter-subjectively performable actions. This is also true of systems theory. If one begins with the process of evolution as a self-regulating process of an overarching system, then a decision is made that cannot be justified: From the start, one assumes an autonomous system operating independent of oneself and everyone else, a system in which the decision-making process is equally autonomous. In the face of all the insights in the theory of science into the problems of cybernetic systems theory, a decision is then made in the theory against any ability to decide, and without any justification. I am not exaggerating when I assert that here a self-contradiction becomes the basis of a theory, and that this theory must then perform a *reductio ad absurdum* of itself. This could be avoided only if this basic aporia of systems theory could be shown to be nonexistent, or if sociological systems theory were to withdraw its claim to universality; such a theory would then be limited in its explanatory power to special areas and dependent on further justification in the theory of science.[41]

The Problem of an Integrative Theory

The previous reflections have ended more or less in aporia; the challenge of the problem of a theory integrating all the various problem areas is as yet unmet. In the contemporary situation, one could be satisfied with simply juxtaposing the various theoretical approaches. However, it is profitable at least to reflect on the direction of the search for a foundational theory of the social sciences.

The Contemporary State of the Discussion in the Foundations of the Social Sciences

Whether explicitly formulated or not, the great classical and contemporary conceptions of sociology seem to have the goal of developing something like a foundational theory of sociology, in two senses. First, such a theory should delineate a certain realm of phenomena that constitute social reality as such, whether it be symbolically mediated interaction, social labor, or the action of system elements in a self-

regulating system. Second, such a theory must explain its methodological access to this realm.

The positivism dispute in German sociology was concerned with
the question of whether problems arise in the theory of science that
cannot be resolved conceptually by a theory of science based on the
model of the natural sciences. The acute analyses of Wittgenstein's
later philosophy already uncovered this same problem. Wittgenstein's
reflections make the point in the naive theory of science where a break
is made with the naive application of an empirical methodology to
linguistically mediated social phenomena, and where actual communicative practice becomes a foundation in its own right that cannot
be further questioned. We already discussed above the aporias that
led Wittgenstein to forgo reflection and finally even theory.[42]

The development of linguistics since Chomsky is still perhaps the
most instructive case study for the full scope of problems to which
empirical theories of social science fall prey when one consistently
pursues the implications of their subject matter. The most decisive
critique of Chomsky is that his model of competence is incomplete,
so that his entire theory must be restructured in terms of the guiding
question of how linguistic utterances can be explained as situated
communicative action directed to partners in interaction. Much as
happened to Austin's and Searle's ordinary-language philosophy under
the influence of Wittgenstein, linguistics took a pragmatic turn of its
own. The necessity of developing new theoretical instruments in modal
logic in order to be able to explain how a linguistic utterance can be
understood in concrete interaction points to the fact that, finally, only
an analysis of the dimensions of the reciprocal reflectivity of linguistic
action comes close to approximating the real degree of complexity
of linguistically structured social reality. This places standards on the
theoretical claims that can be surrendered only at the price of general
regression. But these standards only mark a certain degree of complexity and do not yet develop a foundational theory of the social
sciences as a whole.

In the contemporary state of theoretical discussion and empirical
research, it seems that in the social sciences no theory has yet succeeded
in establishing itself convincingly as such a foundational theory. The
contemporary discussion is characterized to a great extent by the
competition among diverse theoretical proposals.[43] None of these contemporary theories can now be declared the universal theory of social

science. If such a theory were to be formulated through the analysis of communication, it might rest on Mead's important insights, which meanwhile have been further developed in many different directions. In any case, the mechanism of significant symbols grounding the factual and normative structures of intersubjective reciprocity in the framework of a "universe of discourse" marks an important breakthrough in evolution and characterizes something like a foundational structure of social reality. It cannot be denied that both the evolutionary level and the structural ordering of interaction partners in actual interaction is determined by factors from the domains of steering mechanisms, production, distribution, and consumption. The theoretical claim of systems theory becomes clear at this very point, where it tries to supply explanatory models for both the interdependence of modes of communication and the structural properties of society as a whole, as well as for the evolution of societies. The theoretical instruments of systems theory are inadequate for the problem of the evolution of societies hence for the problems of system transformation, and they show themselves to be self-contradictory.[44] The problem of system transformation seems to be resolvable only on the basis of an analysis of innovative, system-transforming communicative action. This marks a basic problem requiring further investigation.

Hence, a foundational theory of the social sciences seems to be conceivable only if it is developed as a theory of interaction, a theory of society, and a theory of history at the same time. In the contemporary discussion, the question of which of these dimensions is to be given priority in terms of the subject matter and the logic and strategy of research cannot be decided within an investigation of the logic of the social sciences. Rather, this seems possible only through a reconsideration of the entire problematic of the discussion of the theory of science with this problem in mind. That does not exclude the possibility that the discussion of the social sciences formulates problems that are also decisive for the foundations of a general theory of science, precisely because the development of the theory of science has led to insights into the social dimension of general questions of method.

6
The Constructivist Conception
of the Theory of Science

Life-World Practice and Normative Reconstruction

Appraising the Situation in the Theory of Science

The results of the research into the foundations of logic and mathematics since the turn of the century and the new level of the discussion of the theory of science since the first programmatic theses of the Vienna Circle both pose the question of whether another sort of grounding of science and mathematics, with a new emphasis, should be attempted. The proposals of the so-called Erlangen School for a "constructivist theory of science"[1] must be seen against this background.

The Erlangen School has produced numerous historical studies in the critical interpretation of the history of science.[2] The underlying agreement in these studies concerning the evaluation of the theory of science can best be shown through the position taken in them on the controversy over the foundations of mathematics. The constructivist proposals are also highly developed in this area, especially by Paul Lorenzen.[3] Hilbert's program of metamathematics foundered on Gödel's proof and the undecidability of complex formal systems. The attempt to construct formal systems through syntax alone, and hence through the interconnection of signs according to a closed system of rules, failed as well, as did the attempt to construct the semantics of a system without recourse to a more powerful metalanguage. The necessity of the hierarchical ordering of metalanguages forced the recourse to the ordinary language developed in life practice as a final metalanguage. The intent of the old program—the idea of providing logic and mathematics with *a priori* validity and thereby ensuring the linguistic foundation of the sciences in such a way that this foundation can bring unequivocal intersubjective recognition on the basis of immediate evidence as a final ground—must be surrendered. Language then proves to be, in its logical structure, an open system that cannot be the basis of the elimination of ambiguity. Hence, a return to the practice of mathematicians and their agreement with each other about their common activity is required. Here again the danger of the circularity of hermeneutical understanding arises—the very problem that was to be avoided through the reductionist programs of the past. Lorenzen speaks of a "coincidence of hermeneutics and logic."[4] It no longer appears possible to secure truth claims, even in mathematics. The formalist approach seems to be forced to "refuse to give justifications."[5]

The formalist and empiricist conception also implied that the relation of science to practical action is reducible to purely instrumental questions, thus condemning ethical and political questions to complete irrationality. The thesis of the value freedom of the sciences, consistently pursued in this view, begins by disqualifying moral argumentation as unscientific and severing any connection between science and ethics.[6] But decisions in the theory of science then prove to be practical-ethical ones concerning the politics of science, and thus decisions of universal political significance in a society determined by science. In contrast with the empiricist position, a view that would introduce both the operations of logic and scientific discourse, as well as ethical statements, through insightful and reconstructible speech would stand in the Western philosophical tradition of a unified rational and practical philosophy. Even in the roots of logic there can be found the will to practical reason in common action.

How is the construction of the formal and empirical sciences at all possible in such a way as to satisfy these demands? One obvious suggestion is to begin with the end point of the process of development that led in the theory of science from formal syntax and semantics back to life-world practice; this leads to the attempt to ground rational speech and action in this practice.

Reconstruction and Construction of Rational Practice

The attempt to reconstruct insightfully the normative foundations of existing communicative practice, however, runs into grave difficulties. Wittgenstein's theory of language games and the philosophy of ordinary language based on it agree with the hermeneutical tradition that it is impossible to "go behind" ordinary language as the final foundation.[7] In the theory of science both Popper and Carnap have shown that conventionalism in some form is finally unavoidable, in mathematics the Dutch mathematician J. Brouwer proposed a grounding of mathematics through intuitively comprehensible actions.[8] The contradictions that arise from set theory in the treatment of infinite sets are the major impetus for allowing into mathematics only those statements about quantities that are achievable in intuitive constructions; validity in logic and mathematics can be claimed only for what can be constructed in basic intuitive actions. Furthermore, H. Dingler formulated an operational conception for the grounding of science as a whole: "Here (i.e., in operationalism) the principal laws of the ideal science (i.e., mathematics and logic) are not laws grounded metaphysically in nature. Rather, they are consequences of our operative measures (whether actually practiced or only planned)."[9] In this same way— that is, through basic intuitive actions—the basis of geometry and physics is to be achieved.[10] Lorenzen more than anyone else has gone back to Dingler's proposals.

The problem of a constructivist grounding of scientific discourse consists in locating the *founding realm of linguistic actions* that precedes the various language games of ordinary language and the theoretical constructions of scientific language. These linguistic actions then have a "synthetic *a priori*" function.[11] They are synthetic in that they do not arise from the analysis of a situation of reaching understanding but represent elementary, practical accomplishments in a dialogical situation; they have an *a priori* function in that, as actions, they first constitute the dialogical situation and hence both open up and at the same time determine the possibility of speech and understanding. Therefore, such fundamental actions cannot simply be the intuitively comprehended constructions of an individual; they are necessarily both dialogical and dialogue-constituting.

The process of *predication* may be understood as an elementary basic action. Within a situation where humans want to come to some sort of understanding with one another, a conversation partner can be directed toward certain objects of discourse; an object can receive its own unique "proper name" or can simply be identified by the action of pointing, and is either attributed or denied a certain "predicator." A predicator is introduced in this way through its attribution or denial in respect to objects given in examples. We do not gain insight into the elementary linguistic schema of predication[12] in *a priori* reflection; rather, it is learned in the practice of examples and counterexamples in the dialogical situation. The starting point is therefore this dialogical action in the "primary dialogical situation."[13] It is "a situation of both learning and teaching."[14] Such acts of linguistic training therefore have the function of creating a situation of mutual understanding and, at the same time, in their role the constitutive elements of the process of being able to make oneself understood, of exhibiting the basic linguistic schemata. This we may call the "transcendental role of predication." Mittelstrass writes

It is predication as linguistic basic action that reflection cannot get behind in the strict sense, because every reflection about predication must already make use of predication itself. That is, predication is actually a *beginning* point in the strict sense; it cannot be grounded and is at the same time the condition of possibility of common, communicatively distinguishable orientations, because these sorts of orientations only occur in differentiated form.[15]

On this view, neither axioms nor formally determined linguistic structures are the starting point, but mutually limiting and mutually explanatory linguistic actions in a dialogical situation. In predicating, two accomplishments of a dialogical sort are given at once: In the speech act that is tied to a present or past action of pointing, the conversation partner is given something to *understand*, while at the same time either his *agreement* or his *disagreement* is solicited. The elementary speech situation is dialogical insofar as it is concerned with reaching a consensus with the conversation partner. On the basis of these elementary speech acts, additional linguistic actions must be introduced in a comprehensible and reconstructible way—as the formation of terms such as definitions, abstractions, and the formation of indicators.[16] Only on this basis can the construction of a scientific language be intersubjectively testable.

Hence, all discourse can finally be traced back to situated linguistic action making use of examples and counterexamples. The implicit rules of such linguistic action must show themselves to be rules of all dialogue as such. They function as both rules and metarules; to put it in a formula, as the rules of conversation they are both practical and constitutive for the emergence of the conversation. They form a practical *a priori*; practice is at the same time transcendentally constitutive.[17]

On the basis of this primary dialogical situation, we can get at the constitutive elementary actions and thus the operative-dialogical foundations for the individual sciences. However, this is not the place to go into the details of such a grounding for the sciences.[18] The discussion of various proposals in individual areas is still in the incipient stages.[19] We must still deal with problems resulting from the foundations of the social sciences, chiefly in their historical dimension.

Life-World *A Prioris*, Normative Reconstruction, and the Question of Acting Subjects

The conception of an operative-dialogical logic and a constructivist theory of science seems to avoid many of the aporias of other theories of language. First, a practical-normative element is incorporated into the basic conception through the starting point of the dialogical situation. Second, the conception of a practical *a priori* avoids the infinite regress of metalinguistic levels of reflection, in that discourse and meaning are seen as constituted all at once in unmediated speech acts. Third, the diversity of arbitrary language games is reduced to elementary linguistic acts and explained genealogically in terms of them. Fourth, the language of the theory describing and explaining these processes need not be presupposed or construed as a foreign medium; rather, it can be insightfully and critically reconstructed on the basis of this reconstructive investigation itself, so that the investigation retains the character of self-enlightenment.

Despite all this, the conception has some underlying problems, even though it gives the impression of imposing closure. Because we still want to investigate this approach more closely in the framework of the theory of communicative action, here I shall only touch upon the question of the relation of the temporal structure of communicative action and of "life-world *a prioris*"[20] to the process of predication. The attributing or denying of a predicator is the result of training through examples and counterexamples; that is, it presupposes "the return of what is the same" ["*Wiederkehr des Gleichen*"][21] and its identification, as well as the distinction of what is not the same. Predicating always occurs, therefore, as the differentiation, as well as the positing, of an open horizon of possible objects and possible predicators. A statement about one of these objects or predicators goes beyond its singularity as concrete act of speech and points to possible statements about another of these objects. In speech, a "world" is in this way always disclosed; or, more precisely, speech begins with a "world always already disclosed in language."[22] Speech therefore always discloses a horizon of possible objects. This becomes particularly clear in the introduction of empirically general sentences. "Such predicators disclose our world, in that they allow objects encountered in the *future* to appear to us as already known and familiar."[23] Although the word *world* is neither a proper name nor a predicator in the sense introduced above, it nonetheless proves indispensable to the analysis of the basic program of predication. Kamlah emphasizes that this word can be learned only "synsemantically"[24] through drill. It seems that unresolved problems are revealed here.[25] In any case, linguistic action that discloses the world and grasps ahead to the future is thus itself to be signified as a temporal, situative act, and at the same time as constitutive of temporality. If the disclosure of a world of possible objects and states of affairs is not to be thought of as the constitution of a Platonic ideal world (a view that is the object of criticism in both Intuitionism and Constructivism), then this disclosure must be interpreted in terms of the open temporality of the dialogical speech act itself.[26] This temporality of speech acts would have to be explained more precisely, or at least delineated over and against other views. It seems that behind the question of the temporal structure of communicative action is hidden the question of the subject of action and its constitution. Then there arises the question whether the concept of action in the constructivist theory of science as previously explicated is not still trapped in a too instrumentalist form of thought. This will have to be shown in the discussion of other positions, such as those of Apel and Habermas, and finally in attempts to reconstruct the "rational core" of theology.[27]

7

Implications of Recent Theory of Science

The Changed Situation of the Conversation

The Question of the Foundation in Communicative Action

In the historical reconstruction of the theory of science, of the formal sciences and the empirical sciences, and particularly of the social sciences, I have attempted a systematic explication of basic problems. Wittgenstein's views in the *Tractatus*, and their even more pointed formulation in the Vienna Circle, were chosen as both a starting point and a constant counterfoil, as a position representing the strictest and most consequential calling into question of the possibility of theology in modern times. Within this development, the inquiry into the foundations of logic and mathematics led to the demonstration of the unattainability of the goal of producing an all-comprehensive formal system as the essence of all possible formal operations. The core of the discoveries of Gödel and Tarski is that even formal operations remain bound to the foundation of the process of practically reaching consensus as formulated in everyday language.

In the realm of the empirical sciences, the ideal of the immediate reduction of all sentences to what is observable proved just as unattainable. Direct verification can be given neither for singular universal sentences nor for the basic concepts of a theory. This is the core of both Carnap's and Popper's results. Empirical theories prove increasingly to be more like risky hypotheses, reducible only in part and only very indirectly to observation. The study of the various dimensions of the structure of a theory—including both the dimension of linguistically articulated data observation and the dimension of the actual theory with its basic concepts, its logical formalism, and its interpretation rules—revealed that an irreducible surplus in theoretical interpretation also holds sway in the empirical sciences. Verification and falsification are valid for statements as such only in a very weak sense. An exact demarcation between philosophical and empirical statements is no longer possible.

With this, the question of the origin of available theoretical instruments returned in a new and sharper form in the dispute between instrumentalism and conventionalism. In the positivism dispute in sociology, the point of disagreement centered on the question of the social mediation of all scientific statements and of the incorporation of ideology-critical methods as the guarantor of scientific rationality.

Beyond that, it has become clear that even empirical inquiry cannot simply escape its own history. Underlying theoretical conceptions do not break down merely through simple observations; their dissolution is much more a complex and in many ways more revolutionary process of intellectual history. This is the core of Kuhn's ideas. In this process, the empirical sciences have, Apel writes, "reproduced almost all the problems of the historical-hermeneutical sciences of man at the turn of the century."[1]

This course of development has been interpreted in many different ways. Its most decisive insight may be that linguistically mediated communicative practice is the basis of scientific rationality too. In any case, it is this insight that marks the turn in Wittgenstein's thought. Following Wittgenstein, Austin has shown that all speech, even as purely representational and conventional, always has the intersubjective character of action. Of special interest are those speech acts that generate what is meant in them only through the linguistic action itself, since here evidently a realm of intersubjective linguistic action is opened up that is foundational for social reality. Problems of the constitution of social norms and of ethical speech could thus become the primary theme of linguistic analysis.

However, the turn to communicative practice as the foundation of scientific rationality can be understood and theoretically grounded in quite a different way. Proposals to this effect have been developed by the representatives of the "Erlangen School," by Apel, and by Habermas.

For representatives of the Erlangen School, a real alternative to the postulate of critique in Critical Rationalism and the phenomenology of ordinary-language philosophy could be found only in a procedure of seeking the grounds of rational argumentation only through the methodological and intersubjectively testable reconstruction of its linguistic means. But the discussion of this conception has revealed several basic, unresolved problems. It is still controversial in what sense a lifeworld a priori[2] must be presupposed, how far such an a priori dimension is retrievable and redeemable through methodological reconstruction of the normative rules of the individual sciences as practical a prioris, and how far the achievements of such reconstructions with a priori claims attain to the realm of social, historical, or even biographical reality. The burden of proof lies on such a proposal to show that it actually succeeds in all the hermeneutical performances claimed by traditional hermeneutics.[3] In this regard, the question of just how the temporal structure of dialogical action is to be characterized has still not received sufficient attention in the previous discussion.

Apel has pointed out repeatedly, in a series of extraordinarily important analyses of the history of the theory of science, that the logic of this discussion necessarily leads us to attribute to the linguistic, communicative actions of concrete subjects a transcendental-constitutive significance. In a penetrating critique of classical and hermeneutically oriented transcendental philosophy, and in an equally radical critique of the scientistic attitude of the theory of science, Apel comes to a "transformation of philosophy" in the direction of "transcendental-pragmatic" thought. He sees the significant achievement of Heidegger's and Gadamer's hermeneutic version of transcendental philosophy in their emphasis on the projecting action character of understanding.[4] In such hermeneutic conceptions Apel does not find any way to resolve the problem of the justification of normative orientations in communication. According to him, however, the objectivating, scientistic attitude of the traditional theory of science prevents us from correctly articulating this problem or even acknowledging its existence. Against the conceptions of both scientism and hermeneutics, a transformed transcendental philosophy returns to the tradition that attributes to the ideal communication community of all human beings, which is always the goal of actual communication, a function in deciding theoretical and practical questions that is both *a priori* and posited concretely as normative.

Habermas argues in a similar fashion. In every linguistic utterance aimed at communicating something to someone, the ideal of an all inclusive communication community is necessarily implied and raised to the status of transcendental validity and, at the same time, posited practically as a goal to be achieved. For Habermas as well, this proposal results from an examination of the previous discussion of the theory of science. It is hard to see how the core of the central arguments for these reconstructive interpretations could be controverted. For this reason, these conceptions will have to be more closely examined in a new situation of dialogue that differs considerably from the situation of confrontation in the first decades of the century over the question of how a new conception of theology is to be grounded.

The Characteristics and Dimensions of the Changed Problematic

In attempting to characterize this changed problem constellation, one must at least point out the following.

• The problem domain of a theory of communicative action can be considered a point of convergence for inquiry into the foundations of logic, mathematics, and the empirical sciences (especially the social sciences) to the degree that one expects such a theory to supply a grounding for scientific rationality as such. The emphasis on communicative action signifies the withdrawal of all the restrictions of a purely formal concept of language. The constitution and transformation of reality in action establishes a relation of theory and practice transcending the traditional dichotomy. But the constitution and transformation of reality occurs in intersubjective action, where the dimension of the relation between subjects cannot be moved from the center even of technical and instrumental action. Such action is intersubjectively *reflexive* action; it is linguistically mediated and thus bound to a medium that can be perverted in its structure when participants in communication refuse to reflect on the expectations of others and how they take them into account in the orientation of their own action. Hence, intersubjective reflexive action has from the start the dimension of reciprocal, normative claims. Language in this sense — and here the expectations and demands of logical positivism are surpassed—could be the possible sphere of a universal, truth-oriented search for mutual understanding and progress in science and in the general realm of communicative action.

If one grants such a characterization of the basic direction in which the theory of science is being pushed by its own problems, then at least two issues can be mentioned that are as yet unresolved within such a theory of communicative action. In all the problems treated thus far, the temporal structure of intersubjective reflexive action enters as a limit problem into all the more specific questions. Moreover, the problem remains of just how creative, innovative, structure-changing, and system-transcending action is to be grasped theoretically. This question seems to me to be the touchstone for any proposed theory of communicative action; in it, the question of the constitution of subjects on the basis of intersubjective freedom is raised.

• The relation of structure or system to action is significant for the dimension of society, for it is to society that every theory of action is opened and only in terms of this dimension can such a theory be fully understood and developed. The full circuit of communicative action— its externalization and reification—cannot be suppressed, despite all its diverse interpretations. The theory of action must at the same time be developed as a theory of society. At this point, it can be shown that a theoretical position encompassing only one of these dimensions misses its very subject matter. This has the theoretical consequence that a theory of action incorporating elements of systems theory must give an account of the relationship of both theoretical dimensions.

• The problem of the relation of action and reification is seen in all its difficulties only when the historical dimension of the relationship is thematized. A theory of action and a theory of society can then be adequate to the claims made on them only if they are opened to the dimensions of a theory of history.

Just what these reflections mean for a grounding of theology through the theory of action must be shown in a new series of analyses.

The Metamorphosis of the Question

One would underestimate the change in the constellation of the problem here if one were only to point to the emergence of new problem areas. What is more significant for the changed situation in the theory of science and its relation to theology is that the questions as such are posed in radically different ways. Whereas for the early Wittgenstein every ethical proposition is excluded as meaningless from the unified picturing language, for an approach that begins with the analysis of communicative, reflexive practice the problem of normative orientation and its legitimation is from the start constitutive of its realm of objects. A new relation of the theory of science and practical philosophy is hereby announced. The legitimation of scientific practice in particular and practice in general can no longer be simply separated. Problems in the theory of science must be treated as practical-philosophical problems; conversely, practical-philosophical problems are fully grasped only when their theory-of-science dimension is taken into account.

A further metamorphosis in the way in which these questions are formulated concerns the genetic-reconstructive character of scientific theories. At least alongside of classical empirical theories, a type of theory emerges with the intent of reconstructing the normative, reciprocally valid claims of intersubjective action in a certain practice. These theories thus have a genetic character and involve the dimensions of a theory of action, society, and history all at the same time. It seems that this type of theory poses important questions for theology and demands that theology give an account of the practice it implies.

II

Theory of Action and Fundamental Theology

8

The Convergence of the Questions of Theology and the Theory of Science upon a Theory of Communicative Action

The Relation of Theological Hermeneutics, Theory of Science, and Fundamental Theology: The Approach and Strategy for the Remainder of the Investigation

In the history of the sciences, there are periods in which, despite all the drama of the discussion, the intellectual development seems to follow an inner logic. Risky positions at the beginning of the process provoke movements that can lead to the transformation of an entire science. It is as if, in reaching its conclusion, this inner logic marks off such phases and makes them epochally significant; that is, such phases mark thresholds of development that may be fallen short of only at the penalty of general regression. At the same time, such developments become systematically relevant; that is, they change the modes of inquiry, the methods of verification, and the strategies for searching out solutions, and hence also the nature of the reality disclosed. In other words, they open up new dimensions of possible experience.

It is no exaggeration to attribute to both the developments in theology traced in the introductory chapter and the two appendixes and the developments in the theory of science traced in part I the characteristics of just such an epochal transformation.

The starting point for theology was distinguished by the problems of historicism and through the dichotomy of the human sciences and the natural sciences—the problems Bultmann sees as involved in the "modern world view." With this set of problems, the structural analysis of human existence seemed to give theology the means of responding to its basic questions and developing a responsible conception of the task of theology. The existential character of existence seemed to mark both the comprehensive horizon and the center of theological discourse. The succeeding theological development initiated its questioning at the center of this conception. The conception that the utmost possibility of existing is the decisive relation to one's own death inevitably hindered a consistent analysis of intersubjectivity in which existence itself could be encountered in the mortality of the existing of others. In the end, it had to be recognized that precisely this subjectivity is determined through intersubjectivity, through social processes and structures, and through historical development, and that theological discourse is responsible only if it includes these dimensions.

The point of departure of the development of the theory of science was the attempt to bring to an end the claims of the "inexact" methods, primarily in the human sciences, through recourse to precisely constructed languages believed to be able to picture the world univocally. The unified world-picturing language as the basis of a comprehensive unified science was a captivating basic idea. The internal aporias of this conception led to the rediscovery of the acting subject and of the community of inquirers behind the exact constructions. At the end of this development is the insight that even the methodological tools of the sciences are bound to the concrete communicative practice of subjects that cannot be fully comprehended if they are detached from social processes and epochal, historical developments.

Viewing the development in both areas, the previous analyses show a convergence in the lines of development of the two originally opposed starting points—the existential character of existence and exactly constructed world-picturing unified language—on the problem of communicative practice.

A theory of this communicative practice would in turn have to withstand questions concerning both the subjectivity of subjects and the constitutive meaning of history and society. A theory of communicative action including the question of the subject would then be defensible only if it were also developed as a critical theory of history and society.

The question underlying this investigation as a whole concerns the approach to fundamental theology. This theology is to be fundamental in both a substantive and a methodological sense; that is, it should at once designate the fundamental structures of the realm of objects of theology and give theology the methodological means to disclose this realm and achieve justified statements about it.

How are we to go about this investigation, with the goal of developing the approach to such a fundamental theology? I would like to make a proposal for the approach to such an investigation, for the foundational strategy of its execution, and, following from this strategy, for the individual steps in which the investigation is to be carried out.

For the approach to the investigation I propose beginning with the basic problems of a theory of communicative action. As its strategy, I propose systematically pursuing this theory in a radicalized reflection insisting on basic problems to the point of its foundational limit problems. This strategy should be pursued in specific steps. Before the start of the actual investigation, I would like to review the proposals made in the previous discussion, primarily in the English-speaking world, in a somewhat sketchy overview. This review will chiefly test whether these new proposals change, confirm, or fall behind the level of the problem already achieved in our investigations.

Additional proposals that attempt to establish a metatheory of theology deserve special attention. After examining them, I would like to pursue the conception of a theory of communicative action in its basic problems and examine what limit problems result for a theory attempting to give its foundation. From this limit reflection, I will undertake to sketch the conception of a fundamental theology through confrontation with the central statements of the Judeo-Christian tradition, indicating the consequences of such a fundamental theology for the procedure of historical interpretation and for the orientation of Christian practice.

A Critical Review of Attempts to Ground Theology in Opposition to the General Theory of Science

The Systematic Significance of the Realization of the State of the Discussion[1]

The categorical challenge to the possibility of ethics, metaphysics, and theology by the early Wittgenstein, and sharp attacks (such as Carnap's) against the very possibility of theology,[2] were without any special resonance in theology in the German-speaking world. The exile or emigration of most of the members of the Vienna Circle and of almost everyone involved in the theory of science, including Karl Popper, led to a situation after the Second World War where there was no debate about either of these trends in the theory of science; theology remained dominated by the discussion of the questions of existential hermeneutics.

In the German-speaking world, after Kant and Schelling the immediate contact of the philosophical conversation partners of theology with the theory of science was all but lost and even the great outsiders — philosophers of language such as Hamann, Herder, von Humboldt, and Nietzsche — had no real influence. However, in the English-speaking world an empiricistically and linguistically oriented tradition, uninterrupted for centuries and traceable from the Nominalism of the Middle Ages to Francis Bacon, David Hume, and John Stuart Mill to Alfred North Whitehead and Bertrand Russell, determined the background and atmosphere of theological inquiry. Since within Anglican theological faculties philosophers of religion had also (for historical reasons) taken over the business of systematic theology, the reaction to the challenges of the discussion of the theory of science of their contemporaries can be seen much more directly in their work.

In recalling here several central points of this discussion, I do so primarily for systematic purposes. Both the reconstruction of the discussion of the theory of science and the description of the corresponding replies in theology, precisely at the point where they begin to face aporias, allow us to recognize a tendency of the sort of questions asked and protect us from too hastily accepting certain theoretical proposals as definitive solutions. The aporias shown here are not simply the embarrassments of theology but can be opportunities for it to remain more rigorously close to the substance of its problems.

I shall try to call to mind the state of this discussion in two ways: through a review of the English-speaking discussion between theology and the theory of science and through a sort of systematic typology of attempts to establish metatheories of the empirical-analytical type.

A Review of the Anglo-Saxon Discussion Between Theology and the Theory of Science

Theology in the Face of the Challenge of Verification and Falsification

Wittgenstein's *Tractatus*, first published in English, attained enormous influence in the Anglo-Saxon world in just a few years. Pitcher writes: ". . . in fact, it occupied something like a position of the Bible of Logical Positivism. In its name, the Positivists waged holy war against the infidels, primarily metaphysicians and next the ethicists, for the greater glory of the gods—science, logic, and mathematics."[3] Explicit attacks against theology reached their height in 1936 in A. J. Ayer's *Language, Truth and Logic*.[4] Advanced aggressively, the theses of the Vienna Circle hardly left open any possibility for a dialogue with theology. Individual contributions to such a conversation were possible only after the moderation of the confrontation through the discussion internal to the theory of science, the effects of which can be recognized in the second edition of Ayer's book (1946).

The discussion, in its full breadth, began when Anthony Flew posed the questions of the falsifiability of religious and theological statements. Flew borrowed Wisdom's parable of the dispute between two investigators about an invisible gardener of a jungle clearing, who is postulated by the one because of the beauty of the clearing but whose existence is denied by the other because of the failure of all attempts at its empirical proof.[5] The entanglement of the example in the aporia of the falsifiability of singular existential statements did not detract from its stimulating effect on the theological discussion. Flew put the following question to theologians: "What then would have to occur or to have occurred to constitute for you a disproof of the love of, or the existence of, God?"[6] Further, he raised the objection that the theological strategy of the mollifying qualification of religious statements destroys their core: "A fine brash hypothesis may thus be killed by inches, the death by a thousand qualifications."[7]

When they did not simply retreat into the incommensurability of Christian discourse in the sense of dialectical theology, theologians and philosophers of religion attempted to disarm these attacks through various strategies. A. M. Crombie does not dispute the paradoxical and anomalous character of religious speech; rather, it becomes for him constitutive of the field of its meaning and characterizes its very significative structure. It is precisely these paradoxes, with the net effect of mutually enforcing each other, that summon the sort of understanding that corresponds to the reality to be communicated.[8] A more precise theory of such discourse admittedly remained only a postulate for Crombie. As opposed to Crombie, J. Hick accepted the requirement of verification and tried to show that theological statements can be verified in the total framework of a theistic interpretation of reality, since it is admitted that this verification is not actually performed, and is not necessarily bound to particular here-and-now situations, but is deferred to an "eschatological verification" transcending time.[9] Precisely these concessions, however, would not be made by the other side. For this reason, other authors, such as W. S. Zuurdeeg, attempted to develop other basic characteristics of religious speech through the theory of conative and expressive function of language: As the communication of an unconditioned engagement, it must have a quite different structure from the discourse of the sciences; it is intended to convince others, and thus it has a primarily appelative character.[10]

Religious Speech as the Communication of an Attitude Toward
Reality Without Cognitive Claims

A whole series of proponents of analytic philosophy, including Hare
in his classic work *The Language of Morals*, were prepared to admit that
religious speech is meaningful. However, since the "meaning" of statements results from their "use" and since basically only two modes of
the use of language can be distinguished (the communication of descriptions and the communication of attitudes), religious speech is
supposed to serve only in the communication of a certain way of
looking at reality (a "blik") and cannot make claims to either truth or
falsity. The declaration of an ethical engagement and the explication
of a scheme of intersubjective behavior—even in narrative texts, like
the Bible, which can be interesting independent of any claims to historical veracity—then constitute the possible horizon of meaning of
religious and theological statements, according to Braithwaite, Hepburn,
and van Buren.[11] The question remained whether theologians such as
van Buren can fully endorse the view that religious and theological
statements are without any cognitive content.[12]

Ramsey's Anchoring of Religious Statements in Experience-
Transcending "Disclosure Situations"

For some theologians, the dichotomy of possible speech acts into the
communication of descriptions or of attitudes and the reduction of
religious discourse to ethical speech as understood by linguistic analysis
no longer seemed to correspond to the more differentiated state of
inquiry into the theory of science. Ferré emphasized, as Max Black
already had shown,[13] that the discourse of science, and especially its
use of models, cannot be described so one-dimensionally.[14]

I. T. Ramsey, the Anglican bishop of Durham, was versed in the
natural sciences as well as in linguistic analysis. In his wide-ranging
work, Ramsey repeatedly pointed out that even the use of the word
"I" in ordinary language expresses an experience that goes beyond
the mere observation of a fact and can be considered a paradigm for
the possibilities of language that surpass empiricist reductionism. The
operative qualification of empirical, intersubjective model situations
in religious speech, as in talk about a "love" that may be qualified as
"infinite," supplies an orientation toward the possibility of new kinds

of experiences that surpass concrete situations but cannot compel the "disclosure" of such experiences.[15] So, too, W. H. Poteat points out that in the attempt to explain the language of creation difficulties arise that are similar to those that arise when one wants to make clear to someone who only has mastery of an empirical thing language that there is such a thing as persons who can say "I" and "Thou."[16] A certain anchoring of religious speech in empirical situations is indeed given in this way, emphasizing its relation to situations and to the performances of speaking and understanding subjects; however, the exact character of the reference to reality and the reality intended in such speech remains unclear.[17]

The Theory of Religious Speech Acts

The conceptual tools supplied by Austin and Searle in the analysis of speech acts seemed to lead at least a step further. Donald Evans[18] tried to show in extremely sophisticated reflections that religious speech represents a linguistic operation that names what *becomes* reality in the performance of these operations for the speaker (and for the listener).[19] At this point, two questions must be asked of this progressive theory.

First: Exactly how are we to conceive of this mode of communication, the acting of the speaker on himself and on the conversation partner? Here practically everything seems to be open. It is all too clear that the theories of religious speech acts are restricted by their analytical tools, which conceive of "self-involvement" in monological terms. For this reason, the results of these theories are quite close to those of existential-analytical theology. The tools of analysis needed to grasp speech acts strictly on the model of reciprocal *inter*action were not yet developed.

Second: How are we to more precisely ascertain the intersubjective assertion of reality contained in such speech acts, assuming that there is one at all? The distinction between the performative and the propositional aspects of any linguistic utterance also seems to be helpful in the analysis of religious utterances. However, the problem for religious utterances, implied in the very expression "self-involvement," is that the referential content of the meaning of what is said is related to the actions accomplished in the very act of the linguistic utterance. The sentence "I believe that God loves me" represents an action in which the actor acts in such a way toward himself that he changes himself; this occurs in that he asserts something about a reality that acts in him and makes this self-transformation possible. This is certainly quite common Biblical theology. Indeed, an example of religious speech more appropriate to the Bible would be "I believe that God loves you." In both cases the problem arises of the way in which a reality is to be "confirmed." The reality here asserted obviously is asserted to be strictly effective in the action itself. How does this sort of assertion of reality compare with the propositional aspect of speech acts in the usual sense? That is one of the central, unclarified questions that will still preoccupy us.

"Wittgensteinian Fideism"

Wittgenstein's theory of language games and his remarks on religion[20] seemed to supply to D. Z. Phillips especially the possibility of analyzing religious speech in the context of the form of life and the mode of behavior of the believer.[21] Wittgenstein's conception of language games was already discussed extensively earlier in this study. Phillips simply transfers Wittgenstein's theses *in toto* to religious language games. According to Phillips, one can only attempt in every case to explain such language games in their structure. The meaning of individual concepts can only then be uncovered in the practical life context of language games; outside of this context they cannot be understood. Even what it means to assert the reality of something is decidable only in the context of the language game involved in it. The illumination of the inner structure of language games is, as it were, the discovery of their grammar; theology becomes the grammar of religious language games. This does not even begin to take into account the fundamental significance of Wittgenstein's insights, so that they then could be incorporated in theology. It must, however, be pointed out that the decisive problems this view is to address now arise again in an even more difficult form, as we shall see.

How does one enter into such a language game at all, if not through the famous conception of "training" or "drill"?[22] Moreover, is there any possibility of critically questioning such a language game, either from within or without? Can we at all reflectively thematize what is "played" in religious language games? There is no recognizable, positive solution to this problem. This implies that the reality that is the concern of this game can no longer be made understandable outside of the participation in the language game itself. Ultimately, the claim to the communicability and universal understandability of religious utterances and of Christianity is surrendered altogether. In agreeing with Winch's position, as presented above, Phillips then assumes all the aporias of his theory. In the ensuing discussion, Kai Nielsen quite appropriately called this view "Wittgensteinian fideism."[23]

Summary

In retrospect, we can say that Anglo-Saxon philosophy of religion and theology completed the turn to pragmatics in a manner parallel to that of the general theory of science. The object of inquiry is no longer simply the syntax of sentences characterized as religious or the semantics of the words used in them. Rather, such questions are now investigated in the horizon of the performance of linguistic utterances or of the linguistic communication between subjects. The theory of performative speech offered the possibility of bringing into play the constitutive significance of the speaking subject for the referential structure of religious speech and of clarifying the character of such speech as the effective action of a listener upon himself and on his conversation partner. The ability (deeply anchored in the capability of speech as such) to open up the communicative situation by parabolic speech to new dimensions and new experiences seems to provide paradigms for the basic structure of religious speech. This would ultimately permit the question of the reality intended in religious speech to be posed in a more precise way. Provisionally, it can be said to reveal the access to the categories of a reality disclosing itself for subjects who enter into commitments in linguistic action.

On the one hand, some of the old questions of existential and personalist theology could thereby receive new articulation by means worked out in linguistic analysis; indeed, perhaps the decisive importance of this development is that in an empiricist-oriented tradition the return to objectivist stages of thinking has been made more difficult.

On the other hand, in this development—again one sees parallels to the general discussion in the theory of science—the unresolved problems of theological hermeneutics and even those of historicism are obviously reproduced.[24] Hence, one could get the impression that the problem of the social constitution of meaning systems, and with it the suspicion of ideology against theology, yet further heightened by empiricist-oriented examination, have not yet been fully recognized in all their radicality.

Thus, the development of the Anglo-Saxon discussion did not lead to any clear results. The same point of development was reached as in hermeneutics, so it may be said to characterize the situation of the inquiry into the general theory of science. This could lead one to the resigned observation that the theory of science is no better than hermeneutics, since both face the same aporias.

Nevertheless, this development has advanced in the meantime in at least two respects. First, it has become clear that the approaches of ordinary-language philosophy can be developed further only if they are again connected with the substantive and methodological questions of the individual empirical sciences. The theory of language games cannot be carried any further without the general discussion of methods in the social sciences; speech-act theory cannot do without general research into pragmatics in linguistics. Second, precisely these research areas have developed theories with a new sort of theoretical status. (We shall investigate more closely a theory of communicative action as an example of this new sort of theory.) Consequently, theology finds itself in a new situation. To clarify this new situation for theology, I would like to preliminarily investigate what types of theory formation can then confront theology and in what direction we can best expect fruitful development.

A Typology of Attempts to Develop a Metatheory of Theology

The basic ideas underlying the history of the modern sciences claim universal status because they rest on the principle of critique. The theory of these sciences therefore claims to develop the criteria for the meaning of all theoretical statements. As a matter of fact, a theory of science emerges with the claim to delineate metatheoretically the framework for theology.

The concern of this section is to investigate specific fundamental possibilities for such attempts to establish a metatheory of theology. As distinct from the previous section, we are not here testing fully developed conceptions, but rather basically possible positions, even if this investigation itself takes its starting point from specific proposals of its own. The function of this section is to exclude insufficient strategies for the solution to these problems by pointing out their inner aporias and so to outline in some detail the solution sought by saying what it is not.

The Conception of Theology on the Traditional Model of an Empirical-Analytical Science

The convincing claim of scientific critique led to the fact that its standard did not remain external to theology itself but, by way of historical-critical inquiry, has even carried the day in theology itself. Modern theology is unthinkable without this solidarity in critique.

However, the question arises whether or not theology as a whole can be conceived on the model of an empirical-critical science as understood by the theory of science in recent decades. It should be clear that everything depends on how one assesses the results of the discussion of the problem of foundations.

This question may be exemplarily explicated in the problem area of a theory of religious speech. The basic problem of any such theory is to indicate precisely what relation to reality religious discourse has and what criteria satisfy its claims to truth. This dovetails into many individual subquestions: Does religious speech have its own semantics, distinct from other modes of speech? If so, in what ways can it be distinguished, and how can this special semantics be formulated? Can religious discourse be differentiated and identified syntactically? Do images, metaphors, and models in religious speech have their own independent function? Is it sufficient merely to investigate particular concepts within religious discourse, or must their meaning be discerned from situationally related texts? Besides a universal pragmatics, is there something like a special pragmatics of religious speech acts and speech situations? All these questions could be asked within a traditional theory of language. If theology is to be understood as a theory of religious discourse, then this raises the question of whether theology merely coincides with this theory of language.

Decisive questions remain, however. If what is characteristic of scientific theory formation is the objectivation of a realm of objects, then the inquirer as subject (or, rather, the community of inquirers) is missing; it emerges only in limit problems, such as those points in inquiry where decisions have to be made about the metatheoretical suppositions of a theory or an entire research program. The place of the subject in these limit problems can be seen to emerge in the development from Wittgenstein to Kuhn and Feyerabend.

What stands out as the characteristic feature of religious discourse, as opposed to scientific theory formation, is that the subjects, or more precisely the parties engaged in speech, are constitutive for the realm of objects of religious discourse. A theory of religious discourse, then, faces the question whether it can be developed as an objectivating construction about speaking subjects, or whether in its basic structure it must have the character of self-reflection, which seeks to clarify one's own actions.

We have seen that such questions are characteristic for the problematic of the foundations of the social sciences. The basic problem that arose there was whether theories about subjects do not at the same time always have to represent enlightening, ideological-critical self-reflection. It need not yet be decided here how theology is to be conceived within such a framework. What now must be debated is whether theology can be thought of in terms of the model of objectivating theoretical constructions. There is obviously something self-contradictory about affirming such a claim. An objectivating theory of subjects would have to exclude theory-forming subjects, along with their metatheoretical decisions, from its theory; however, the very principle of critique would necessarily stand in the way of an uncritical acceptance of such a model.

In an objectivating conception, one regresses behind the state of the problem fought for in the theological discussion of the last two centuries, primarily in theological hermeneutics. Even in theology, regression in not a possible problem-solving behavior. All attempts in which theology simply assumes the principles of "Critical Rationalism" fall under this criticism, especially since such a view does not even do justice to the present state of the theory of science.[25] Theology also may not simply retreat to the stage of an objectivistic scholasticism that does not even understand its own foundations. Similarly, attempts to transform an objectivistically understood linguistics into a metatheory for theology would also have to be criticized. I shall discuss several such proposals later.

Assuming on the one hand that the discussion of foundations in the theory of science from Gödel and Tarski through Popper and Carnap to Kuhn and Feyerabend reaches dimensions traditionally ascribed to hermeneutics and, on the other hand, that hermeneutics can no longer be seen as the single "method" in the classical humanistic disciplines but rather that "understanding" is still possible only by integrating analytic procedures, the question is posed for theology even more stringently as to the status of a theory that, as an empiricial theory, includes reflection on subjects and their performances.

"Cybernetics of Truth" and "Negative Theology" in C. F. von Weizsäcker

At least theoretically, one can attempt to so radicalize the problem of the relation of the objectivating attitude of science and the self-reflection of subjects that the two are ultimately identical. C. F. von Weizsäcker undertook such an attempt.[26] Such an undertaking admittedly has its own difficulties. As having an "empirical basis," such an identity could hold true only under several presuppositions. Theoretically, objectivation must be considered the decisive achievement of human consciousness; physics would then be a theory of this objectivation, "in that the laws of physics are nothing but laws formulating the conditions of possibility of the objectifiability of events."[27]

The ability to objectivate develops in evolution. It would then have to be possible to propose a general theory of evolution, so that both physical and biological facts could be grasped in a theory of the hierarchicalization of ever more complex cybernetic systems related to each other precisely in their irreducible discontinuity. The background of this theory would then be the general assumptions of thermodynamics and cosmology. This conception has as its result that one can explain even the achievements of the consciousness of human subjects in the framework of a cybernetic theory of evolution. This theory ultimately would be a "cybernetics of truth."[28] Such a cybernetic theory of evolution would have the status of an objectivist physical theory that, as an empirical theory, also would transcendentally explain the conditions of the possibility of objectivation by subjects.

In such an attempt the problem arises of how to conceptualize this identity of objectivation and self-reflection—how to conceive the "unity of nature." This task—thinking of reality as a whole, and thus objectivating objectivations yet again—proves ultimately unthinkable. It is the question of the One that points directly into the unthinkable. "The One," writes Weizsäcker, "is the concept of classical philosophy for God."[29] "Physics," he notes, "is possible only against the background of negative theology."[30]

It should be clear that foundational problems are posed here concerning the relationship of cosmology, the theory of evolution, the cybernetic concept of reflection, and theology. Many of the basic presuppositions of such a hypothesis are still purely postulates, and we cannot tell how or whether they can be empirically tested. But theology must at least try to justify its own status in confrontation with such limit reflections, and thus to see whether it is satisfied to be a purely negative theology arising from limit reflection on the possibility of objectivation as thinking about what is unthinkable in the strict sense.[31]

Luhmann's Systems-Theoretic Determination of the Function of Religion and Theology

In many sciences, cybernetic conceptual models have become self-evident methodological tools and have proved quite fruitful. In sociology, the influence of cybernetics led to the reworking of older forms of systems theory and functionalism into approaches oriented to the theory of self-regulating systems. The later Parsons and Luhmann are among the proponents of this type of theory.

At least since Comte, attempts have been made in the history of sociology to bring religion into connection with the problem of the constitution of society. For Comte, religion explicitly symbolized the totality of society; if this symbolization is recognized as a production of myth, society itself takes the place of God, since it is now what is highest. Sociology is then the scientific theory of a "religion of humanity." Sociology hence becomes the demythologizing, ideological-critical metatheory of theology. The problem of the theoretical enlightenment of the function of religion for the whole of society, and thus of the metatheoretical dissolution of theology by sociology, has determined the relation of sociology and theology ever since. This problem necessarily emerges again in a new form wherever a systems-theoretical theory of the totality of society is attempted.

For Luhmann as well, "religion remains bound to the level of the total social system."[32] Luhmann thereby attributes to religion the most extreme function attributable to a total social system. As was said above about his approach, and especially the concept of complexity, the most extreme horizon of a total social system is the horizon of indeterminate complexity. In relation to it, the totality of society cannot retreat into the complexity-reduction performances of its already existing subsystems for its own stabilization. "Therefore," writes Luhmann, "on the last functional level of social systems indeterminate complexity must be transformed into determinate or at least determinable complexity. . . . Cultural structures with precisely this functional relation are those of religion. The function of religion is related to the determinability of the world."[33] The disposition of these final, foundational reductions is yet again institutionalized in religion, in what Luhmann calls "dogmatics"; it is "the ongoing verbal and conceptual equipment of this interpretation function."[34] Such dogmatics must primarily give answers to basic structural problems connected with the evolutionary situation of the total system, thus making contingency formulas available to the system; that is, dogmatics must blunt the finally incalculable risks of human existence and social systems in their accidental nature. According to Luhmann, this usually occurs through the concept of God.[35] Notwithstanding such functions for the total society, dogmatics has a function on "the level of the differentiation and self-steering of religious systems and subsystems of society."[36]

The question that occupies Luhmann is whether the traditional forms of dogmatics, in particular the Christian form traditional in the West, "can still identify and steer a religious system of our society."[37] Luhmann discusses the possibility that religious systems that renounce the concept of God might be better equipped to find solutions to the fundamental problems of the developing world society.[38] However, he objects to any such interpretation on the grounds of the unresolved problem of complexity; interaction systems can constitute the world only with it as its horizon.[39] This world "cannot be transcended," because references to other possibilities "remain in the world, which is to say they are the world."[40] Luhmann sees a chance for theology in "revising the concept of reflection."[41] "Perhaps," he writes, "theology will find possibilities of transforming interpretations of revelation and interpretations of the process of interpreting into functionally conscious reflection of interpreting."[42] Theology then must assume the theoretical position of systems theory, reflect the mode of constitution of the world society as world society, and then on the one hand prepare the final legitimation that explains and makes acceptable the contingency of the world society and on the other hand organize the social subsystem of religion so that it effectively mediates these final legitimations that illuminate only in this system's actual functioning. This is the Church's function: "It has to put to the modern world the prospect of a theology of contingency; it will be able to fulfill that promise only through organization."[43] Put pointedly, the practical implication is that theology has to surrender its task to administrative experts.[44]

I have attempted to point out the inner aporias of Luhmann's position. In the words of W. Schulz: "Luhmann evidently does not want to recognize the dialectic by which human beings are conditioned by the system as much as they condition it, without these relationships being directed by a third quantity. He inserts an overarching *total system*, over all subsystems, as absolute regulator. . . . This overarching system is, however, the entity that bears the weight of the entire project; it is the decisive final mediation."[45] If systems theory is not to be understood as the final metatheory, then one is forced to explain the relation of man and system in terms of an entirely different starting point and to trace Luhmann's hypostatizations arising from a denial of the status of modal-theoretical reflections[46] back to the basis from which they were developed by Parsons—namely, the theory of social action.

Theology then inescapably faces the inquiries of a theory of communicative action.

Reconstructing the Function of Religion in the Theory of Action: Döbert and Habermas

We can see in Luhmann's position the demands placed on a theory in the tradition of Hegel, Comte, Marx, and Darwin as soon as it surpasses mere subregions and is applied to a phenomenon such as the total society. The demands on such a theory are at least threefold: First, it must seek to grasp the object of the theory in its constitution; second, it must make intelligible the interdependence between modes of constitution of the object and of the constitution of the subject, including the subject's capacity to theorize; third, it should make this constitution process understandable in terms of the comprehensive process of evolution. The basic problems of this type of theory have been debated since Hegel; since then, theology has been forced to face the challenges of theories of this type. After all our previous investigations, the discussion of the theory of science seems to have as one of its results that the construction of a comprehensive process in which reflection seeking identity could be explicitly surrendered leads to internal contradictions and absurdities. Even theoretical constructions are referred back again and again to the factual existence of human beings and their communicative action in the service of reaching mutual understanding.

One could undertake the attempt to develop a theory of communicative action that would avoid such hypostatization but would nonetheless fulfill the demands of a theory of the interdependence of the constitution of objects and subjects and their genesis.

Starting with Habermas's reflections, R. Döbert attempts to make plausible the thesis that "religious development can be conceived as a manifestation of communicative competence."[47] According to this view, a process of reflection manifests itself in the entire course of the development of religious consciousness, within which humanity gradually achieves increasing clarity about its own essence and, in the succession of religious systems of meaning, fashions the theoretical and practical means for shaping its life autonomously.[48] In the basic thesis of the theory, it is asserted that religious systems of meaning follow an inner logic in their development that permits their intelligible reconstruction in specific sequences: for example, the expansion of the profane realm in relation to the sacred, the tendency to move from widespread heteronomy to increasing autonomy, the emptying of world views of cognitive content in moving from cosmology to purely moral systems, the tendency to develop from tribal particularity to universalistic and at the same time individualistic orientations, and the increasing reflectivity of the mode of belief.[49] The end point of the development appears to be the competence of subjects to test assertions in linguistically mediated action and behavioral expectations in a process of reciprocal reflectivity, and to make them so intelligible to each other that finally this intelligibility [Einsichtigkeit] implies the transparency [Durchsichtigkeit] of the communication partners to themselves and to each other.

Here we are interested only in the claim that at this stage of evolution both previous religious systems of meaning and explicit theologies are surpassed, so that they can be assigned respective places in evolution. This claim can be explained in the way Habermas characterizes the development of the critique of religion since the nineteenth century. Metaphysics was still in the position to conceptualize the idea of God developed in the religions of civilized cultures by means of the idea of the One or the Absolute, and thus at last to successfully take religion's place. The revelatory character of revelation could be thought of as a process of reflection, and thus as transparent for all thought. "Post-metaphysical thought," writes Habermas, "does not challenge any specific theological assertions; rather it asserts their meaninglessness. It wants to prove that, in the basic conceptual system in which the Judeo-Christian tradition is dogmatized (and hence rationalized), theologically meaningful statements cannot be asserted."[50] Besides this, at least since Marx, "self-reflection limited to the sphere of the history of the species"[51] has taken the place of the final grounding of metaphysics. At the same time, philosophy also appropriated "the utopian content of the religious system"[52] and "an interest in liberation and reconciliation heretofore construed as religious."[53] The emerging primacy of practical philosophy allows it to detach the rational core of the utopian contents from its religious guise and to take over. The linking of practical philosophy with empirically established theories of action supplies the means of interpretation necessary to understand and to appropriate what was "heretofore" meant in a religious sense in its authentic meaning. Finally, such a theory claims to have a meta-theoretical status in relation to the history of religion and theology.

Although in the meantime Habermas may have formulated some of these questions with more restraint,[54] the basic problem is still posed in the same way. Does such a theory of action reach the vantage point from which human history can be deciphered as the history of religion and then reconstructed with a new interpretation, so that every religious interpretation of this history is superseded and hence theology is an anachronism? Or is it possible that (as our previous analysis has shown and our review of Anglo-Saxon developments has verified), since the problematic of theology and the theory of science converge in a theory of communicative action, dimensions may be opened up in the constitutive structure of communicative action? May not precisely these dimensions raise the question of the place of the Judeo-Christian tradition in a new way?

Dimensions, Fundamental Problems, and Aporias of a Theory of Communicative Competence

The Significance of Recourse to a Theory of Communicative Competence for the Strategy of Research and the Theory of Science

The Convergence of the Aporias

The inner logic of the development depicted above in the reflection on foundational theories in theology and in the theory of science does not consist so much in showing clearly demarcated and unambiguously formulated tasks that can be resolved in a methodologically justified series of steps. Rather, it follows the process of internal critique from relatively clear solutions of problems to ever more difficult aporias that were not straightforwardly answerable in all previous accounts. I have tried to show that the pressing problems of these aporias point to a convergence and demarcate the field of problems of communicative action as the cutting edge of developments in theology and the theory of science.

The term "communicative action," of course, denotes more a negatively delineated field than a firmly outlined research program, but precisely this shows the contemporary state of research. This development seems now to demand new solutions to problems with a new sort of theoretical status. In this sense, I shall next attempt to state the formal demands such a solution would have to satisfy.

The Formal Demands on the Theory

The nature of the claims discussed here can be shown by collecting the basic questions of these converging developments.

• The object realm of this theory would have to be grasped in both its empirical and its synthetic *a priori* character. It has been shown that the operations of purely formal theoretical constructions refer back to the practice of elementary communicative action. In this respect, the object realm of theory as such presents on the one hand an empirical practice to be grasped theoretically in its own right. On the other hand, this practice first constitutes the inner possibility of theoretical construction as such, the means by which practice as such is to be grasped. A theory of communicative action therefore has the double character of an empirical theory and of transcendental self-reflection on a constitutive practice. In the terminology of classical philosophy, it is paradoxical that something that is empirical is at the same time supposed to be transcendentally constitutive. We can see in this double character the fundamental relevance of this theory for the theory of science.

• A theory of elementary communicative practice must meet the demand to grasp communicative action as fundamental to the logic of constitution, insofar as the constitution of both things and persons ultimately results from communicative practice. The inquiry into the transcendental logic of constitution from Kant to Husserl and Heidegger must be reinterpreted to its core in terms of the logic of interaction and then fulfill the claim of supplying the means for establishing a foundational theory for the natural and social sciences. From this, we can see the epistemological scope of such a theory.

• The unsolved questions connected with theses on the logic of constitution may be located in the fact that the constitution of the world could not be explained simply by the process of the reciprocal constitution of individuals in interaction (a later achievement in terms of the theory of evolution, though more fundamental from the perspective of the logic of constitution). If a thoroughly objectivating, scientistic attitude is to be avoided, the consequent scope of the logic of interaction must be grasped in its significance for both epistemology and the theory of science.

• A theory of communicative action can fulfill the demands mentioned previously only if it can supply categories for a theory of language.

Language, the cutting edge of interdisciplinary questions, has proved to be the medium of mediation between reified and objectivating constructions and processes of self-reflection in the theory of science. However, this achievement of language has to be seen as still more deeply anchored; as a structurally describable, reified medium, it is rooted in the communicative and reflexive practice of individuals in interaction. This interaction is creative; that is, in the process of linguistic communication it can put itself into question and can unlock and change reified, rigid structures. Language is thus the medium of historical self-enlightenment and of self-transformation in communicative practice.

• Hence, we touch upon a basic problem of the discussion of the theory of science. Theoretical constructions always emerge in a specific practice. If they are, in general, to avoid the suspicion of being mere convention, or (in the social sciences) of being mere ideology maintained by domination, it must be shown how communicative practice makes possible self-reflection and orientation with the character of ideology critique.

• The suspicions of conventionalism and ideology are heightened by the question of the rationality of scientific progress in history. If the history of science is not to be conceived of on the model of Darwinism, according to which theories survive when they find favorable "cognitive-ecological" niches, then it should be asked whether there are also criteria for the rationality of historical developments that can be applied in the communicative practice of scientific inquiry and verified at the same time.

• At least since Darwin, a theory whose object is to explain the behavior of living beings has been required not merely to analyze the capability for this behavior as it is given in its present structure but also to reconstruct this structure genetically in two dimensions: ontogenetically in the dimension of the development of the individual acquiring a distinct ability, and phylogenetically in the dimension of the organism and of a specific species. A theory of reflexive communication cannot forgo the dimension of the reconstructive summation of its own prehistory. Such a theory will have to be verified in relation to the logic of these attempts at reconstruction that are supposed to derive temporal, reflective, and innovative-creative action.

• The whole structure of this theory may be characterized by a certain relationship of theory and practice. A theory that would apprehend the actually reflective self-transformation of subjects in communication is itself rooted in such practice and ultimately represents just such a practice. Such a theory would then be true to its own status, if it is proved to be the initiation into the performance of such communication in open conversational processes.

Looking over this list of claims to be raised for a theory of communicative action in the contemporary state of the discussion of the theory of science leaves the impression that one is asking for the impossible. But it is also clear by now that we cannot fall short of these claims if the entire discussion in the theory of science is not to be simply forgotten again. It is certainly impossible to do justice to such demands without further qualification. It is no less possible to regress to a historical stage where they could not be advanced at all.

It must also be made clear that the most essential of the demands listed above have been on the table not only in the contemporary discussion but at least since the arrival of modern science and modern philosophy, and in a more systematic and reflective form at least since Hegel. It is through Hegel that we can best clarify the ultimate problem of contemporary reflection. The framework and the outermost horizon of such a theory can no longer be—as for Hegel—self-presence in an all-encompassing absolute reflection. Rather, we must withdraw from the illusion that absolute reflection is possible for communicative practice and its reflective self-enlightenment. This is the core of the "transformation of philosophy" (K. O. Apel) impelled by reflection in the theory of science.

The demands of this new constellation of problems also cannot be escaped by theology. If earlier it still seemed possible to do theology based on the classical philosophy of religion, today a theology can only prove itself both practically and theoretically if it does not shun the above-mentioned formal demands on its theoretical conception.

Distinction From Other Approaches

I would like now to attempt to delineate more closely the starting point of this approach from other approaches: classical transcendental philosophy, traditional hermeneutics, a certain form of dialogical thought, and the dialectical theory of history with a claim to a certain priority.

Classical transcendental philosophy is not concerned merely with objects but rather, writes Kant, with "the mode of our knowledge of objects insofar as this mode of knowledge is to be possible *a priori*."[1] It inquires into the structures whose locus is the subject and which make possible both knowing and acting. Insofar as it derives its concepts from the analysis of the subjectivity of the subject, it is broken up into several steps. The first step is completed within the idealist tradition itself, most clearly in Fichte. Fichte analyzes the Ego in its freedom, the Ego which is itself indeterminate in its unlimited grasping outward and in danger of dissolving itself. Only the recognition of the other freedom of the Thou makes possible the self-determination of the ego and its rescue from the intoxication of dreamlike indeterminateness. Only the relation to the other makes possible the achievement of self-formation through the interaction with another reality recognized as ultimately prior. In this interdependence of mutually interacting freedoms and the free formation of reality, Walter Schulz correctly sees posited a dialectical relation of reality and action and thus the development of a concept of reality pointing beyond the traditional one.[2] The second step of the breakdown of classical transcendental philosophy was completed by Hegel, insofar as in his thought the transcendental structure of the subject is dialectically unfolded in its externalization in reality so that the experience of reality becomes the self-apprehension of the subject. Concrete historical and social experience thereby become transcendental-constitutive occurrences. This dialectic is admittedly bound up with a dialectic of knowing, which remains finally trapped in the model of the relationship of subject and object and ultimately falsifies the dialectic of subjects freely acting together. The third step in the breakdown of the traditional conception of transcendental philosophy was accomplished by Marx, for whom the empirical struggle with nature acquires the significance of the constitutive process for the development of subjects. The transcendental structures of subjects must then be reconstructed from natural history and from the history of society—of course, without the guarantee that this dialectic of constitution is able to ground again the freedom of subjects.

No conception of transcendental philosophy has yet been developed that forcefully integrates these new dimensions. The point of the whole development consists in that the transcendental becomes regional and can be determined through its dialectical relationship to empirical occurrences. An approach from communicative action gives a better account of such a concept of the transcendental, since transcendental elements emerge in the very practice of communicative action. This still will have to be made more precise.

If one attempts to distinguish a theory of communicative action from hermeneutics, then one must be wary of minimizing the claims and achievements of hermeneutics. Both for Heidegger and Gadamer and in theological hermeneutics, "understanding" means not simply the empathetic reconstruction of linguistic utterances but the transcending self-actuation of existence. Nevertheless, as could be shown, this conception does not allow for the solution of many different problem areas. First, no hermeneutic conceptions up to now explain how a linguistic utterance as an action can affect a subject to the core. This can be shown in the analysis of death. Second, the dimension of instrumental action as the transformation of elementary, material conditions of existence is not sufficiently related to what stands at its center: purely linguistic communication. Third, the problem of grounding normative orientations of action and the problem of ideology critique (that is, the critique of the authoritative claim of hermeneutically explicated historical worlds of meaning) remain unresolved. This tendency of hermeneutics to allow all claims to retreat back to a fateful, linguistically mediated fundamental occurrence of history, so that they can no longer be intersubjectively criticized, provokes the strongest objections against purely hermeneutical thought.[3] Hence, this critique of a purely hermeneutic approach also raises strong misgivings about an approach that chooses the dialogical relation between the I and the Thou as its starting point. Indeed, it seems possible to extend the understanding of the study of dialogue in such a way that the problems of social and historical determination, and therefore of alienated, ideologically distorted communication, are also included in the analysis. But this would then be far from the classical approaches to dialogical thinking. The basic categories of these conceptions are hardly appropriate for the development of normative criteria for the critique of social processes and the lack of social freedom, because these categories in many respects were developed precisely in order to designate a private realm of retreat for the subject threatened by social developments.[4]

At first glance, it seems possible to avoid all of these difficulties by choosing the most comprehensive approach and then attempting to develop a dialectical theory of history. The first problem then is how one can arrive at its basic categories in any methodologically grounded way if one does not set out from the historical action of subjects and thus from the theory of communicative action. Moreover, such a theory is in danger of being constructed over the heads of subjects in more comprehensive processes, in which subjects can be defined only through these processes and can emerge only as their victims. The inner aporias of such a conception have already been discussed.

In these attempts at distinctions, it should be relatively uncontroversial that all these approaches contain certain elementary problems that must be considered as dimensions of a theory of communicative action. The concern here is to develop the problematic in such a way that it remains central to all these concerns and through which these other dimensions can be reached methodologically and secured.

Preliminary Outline of the Problem Dimensions of a Theory of Communicative Action

Previous reflections make possible at least an outline of the dimensions in which a theory of communicative action must be grasped.

Communicative action here signifies the following:

the intentional acting of subjects related to and oriented toward the acting of others,[5]

that such action is linguistically mediated (that is, the historically and socially given system of symbolic signs and the rules of their use are applied in illuminating the common situation and aimed at changing it),

that action in relation to others constitutes a common world whose reality is related to this action,

that communicative action is temporal action related to a temporal world and produces the identity of subjects through the constitution of biographical contexts,

that the action of partners reciprocally and reflectively related to each other is still further determined by given historical and social orientations internalized in the process of socialization,

that communicative action, as temporally and linguistically mediated, contains the possibility of reflection and the active revision of internalized orientations and of reifications in the dimensions of the individual and of society determined by historical processes,

that the reflexivity and reciprocity of communicative action achieves its utmost possibility in the reciprocal innovative opening of new life possibilities, and

that through reciprocally assumed and granted freedom the actors mutually recognize each other as free subjects in solidarity.

Possible Terminological Misunderstandings

Even if one agrees with the determination of the domain of problems as the convergence of the developments of theology and the theory of science, it does not necessarily follow that the concept of communicative action is the optimal designation of this realm. A likely objection is that the concept "*Handeln*" already etymologically excludes dimensions such as receptivity, passivity, suffering, silence, and aesthetic perception. This may be more true of the English words "to act" and "action." Even in the concept "*kommunikatives Handeln*" the dialogical, reciprocal, and reflective character of such action is not sufficiently clear. It could, moreover, be pointed out that in the English-speaking world "communication" refers more to a technical concept of the conveying of information between a sender and a receiver.

The disadvantages of this conceptual apparatus are not to be disputed. However, the following must also be pointed out:

• In certain approaches to action theory in analytic philosophy,[6] action certainly denotes, at least abstractly, the transformation of the state of a system. In recent discussions of such fundamental concepts as causality, lawlike dependence, and the determinateness of systems, and above all in the question whether the concept of causality can be determined without recourse to the problem of counterfactual statements and finally to the question of the freedom of action, all this discussion and this development make it seem advisable not to simply rule out the search for an interdisciplinary foundational realm inclusive of the natural sciences for terminological reasons.[7]

• In the social sciences, since Weber, "social action" signifies action in terms of meaning orientations of at least two interrelated actors. Action is then from the start communicative action. The action and speech of one actor necessarily imply the capability of perception and the hearing of the other. Sociology, psychology, pedagogy, and linguistics have all in the meantime quite self-evidently incorporated multilevel models of mutual expectations within their theory of action, so that the reproach of simple actionism (to be expected from theologians especially) depends on simple associations from ordinary language that are unrelated to the use of such concepts in the human sciences. Finally, the concept of communication (at least in the German-speaking world) is not limited to the technical dimension. As opposed to the concept of action, communication has the distinct advantage of unifying the natural and human sciences. Even those who would not defend the concept of communicative action at any price can readily see that it indicates problems of the complexity fundamental to interdisciplinary, multidimensional research projects. A theory of communicative action therefore cannot be rejected as the starting point for the search for a fundamental theology solely on terminological grounds.

The Further Course of the Investigation

After this discussion of the significance of the theory of communicative action for the strategy of research, I would like to specify the central core of such a theory. Next I would like to show that the thesis of the egalitarian and solidaristic basic structure of communicative action is at the same time the central thesis of the whole of theology. From this structure results the difference between the factual and ideal communication community and the possibility of the transition from simple communicative action to its problematization in discourse. After that I want to discuss further some basic questions about this approach: the problem of the grounding of action orientations, the relation of such groundings to historical experiences, the question of the revision in ideology critique of historically and socially given orientations, and in this critique the question of the possibility of situation-transforming, innovative speech acts. The questions that result from the logic of unfolding these problems are whether the communicative action of free subjects in solidarity does not ultimately refer back to an absolute freedom and whether death, the experience of the guilt of oneself and others, and finally the experience that in history the innocent are annihilated do not contradict the core structure of egalitarian and solidaristic action, thus bringing the actor himself into a destructive, despairing self-contradiction. This then becomes the occasion to rethink the entire approach to the theory of action.

The Approach to a Theory of Communicative Action: The Theory of Communicative Competence

The Approach to the Problematic

When one recalls the claims of a theory of communicative competence and its comprehensive, interdisciplinary dimensions, the question of the level and point at which the investigation is to begin takes on the utmost significance. How are we then to find an adequate approach?

A theory of communicative action is concerned with the constitution of subjects and of society in interaction; this constitution is understood not as a mere structural analysis of a momentary situation but as a reconstruction in terms of evolution and history. According to our investigation so far, any theory of interaction must have the dimensions of a theory of the subject, history, and society.

The question of the starting point of inquiry is all the more difficult because the general discussion of the theory of science and the positivism dispute concerning methodology in the social sciences no longer permit such naiveté about the neutrality of methodological reflection. Thus, a theory of communicative action is concerned at once with the criteria that are the basis of its critical validity. The intent of our investigation must then be to legitimate once again both the justification of its approach and—by explaining the relevance of the entire problematic as discussed in the previous section—the means to accomplish this justification.

In response to these complex questions, Habermas has proposed beginning with the investigation of "communicative competence." Habermas has presented this proposal in many different ways, each time with a different accent.[8] Whereas Habermas to a great extent began with a systematic conception of speech acts, in his recent work he extends the problematic to the investigation in developmental psychology of the acquisition of communicative competence. This extension has the following advantage: With the presupposition (hardly disputed since Darwin) that certain phylogenetic developments are taken up in ontogenesis and replicated as a model, starting with developmental psychology offers the possibility of systematically connecting the core of the research program with the theory of evolution and with historical questions. At the same time, the question may be posed whether the inner tendencies of evolution and the series of stages by which communicative competence is acquired point toward the normative elements of communicative action. If we link the present investigation with Habermas's proposal, two preliminary remarks must be made. One is concerned with terminology, the other with the processing of the results of research.

• The concept of "competence" was introduced by Chomsky. In the framework of his linguistic theory, it signifies the ability of a speaker to generate grammatically correct sentences according to the mathematically describable system of rules of a language. We have already discussed this model and pointed out its inherent limitations. The discussions in the research into the foundations of mathematics, in analytic philosophy, in the general theory of science, and in linguistics itself all demand a more elementary justification and the development of another basic model for competence. Habermas accounts for the "pragmatic turn" in these disciplines in that he wants to develop a theory of communicative competence as "universal pragmatics," no longer merely concerned with the universally valid structures of the rule-governed generation of sentences but also concerned with the ability of the subject to acquire and preserve identity in interaction.

• Habermas's proposal integrates the results of research in many diverse areas in an extraordinarily creative way, with great systematic power. Directly pertinent here are results from the various forms of developmental psychology, from general sociology, from specialized sociology (such as research into socialization), from interaction research in its various forms (ranging from systems theory and symbolic interactionism to enthnomethodology), and from linguistics (although it is obvious that Habermas hardly considers the significant developments in linguistics in recent years). Any discussion of Habermas's proposal must take into account the research results that are the basis of his program. This means at the same time that the discussion does not simply end with a critique of Habermas, since the problems resulting from the results of research in various disciplines are not yet resolved.

The Distinction and Integration of the Dimensions of
Communicative Competence

If it is necessary both analytically and in terms of the present state
of research to distinguish various dimensions of communicative competence, this must be done in such a way as not to lose sight of the
question of their unity. Indeed, this unity is a matter of the conditions
of possibility of subjectivity and intersubjectivity posited in the practice
of interaction. In terms of both the state of research in various disciplines
and an analysis of communicative practice, it seems necessary to distinguish three dimensions of communicative competence.

• *Cognitive competence* has been investigated for decades by Piaget and
his disciples, with a high degree of theoretical differentiation and an
advanced awareness of the theory of science.

• Chomsky's conception of generative linguistics must still be regarded
as the decisive impetus for a theory of *linguistic competence* and its
development, as well as for investigations in psycholinguistics and
developmental psychology. Even in the resulting development of linguistics, with its extension into pragmatics, elementary realms of linguistic behavior are still explainable through the model of the command
of an abstract system of rules.

• The fact that the individual parts of a theory of *interaction competence*
and its development are still the least developed of all these theories
may be due not only to the complexity of its subject matter but also
to the explanatory burden borne by this theory for the others and to
the fact that the overlap between linguistic and cognitive competence
is usually put in the realm of interaction competence. Here the task
is to integrate the theorems of role theory in their most differentiated
and developed form, the theorems of psychoanalysis, and the theorems
of the study of development of moral consciousness (based on Piaget
and conducted on an extraordinarily sophisticated theoretical level by
Kohlberg and his circle at Harvard).

The problem of the development of moral consciousness points to
the unity of these three dimensions, because the ability to make judgments in situations of ethical conflict refers to insight into principles
that make possible the preservation and achievement of identity for
a subject through the recognition and maintenance of the identity of

the interaction partner. This is doubtless the core problem of a theory of communicative competence, insofar as its concern is the problem of the identity of subjects in interaction determined by social and historical norms. Our next task is to investigate this problem more extensively.

The Appraisal of Contemporary Hypotheses for a Theoretical Framework and Problems of Strategic Importance

It is not possible here to characterize the state of research, or even of a small part of it. I intend only to point out tendencies in the discussion that have significance for our reflections in the theory of foundations.

It is acceptable for analytic reasons to begin with the supposition that the various competences have independent roots in early childhood, from the standpoint of both developmental history and developmental psychology. In this Piaget[9] understands the development of cognitive competence as adaptation—"that is," write Nunner-Winkler and Rolff, as "an equilibrium between assimilation and accommodation." "Assimilation," they continue, "signifies the subsuming of new experience under old schemata, accommodation a simultaneous change and adaptation of schemata."[10] As opposed to behaviorist concepts, schemata are thought of as capable of movement, changeable in the learning process itself. The development of cognitive competence proceeds in phases, in which the formed capacities each represent an independent, unified structure that is completely transformed in the transition to the next phase. In the sequence of these irreversible stages, an inner tendency is exhibited toward ever greater balance between the acting, learning individual and his environment. In the course of this development, the active constitution of matter and the concepts of space and time are learned. The point of the theory lies in the fact that the acquisition of a capability of action constituting the world is explained through active exchange with the environment. As soon as the level of the acquisition of systems of phonetic rules in the theory of the development of linguistic competence is achieved (Jakobson's investigations of language in children are classic[11]), the controversy over the very foundations of linguistics arises. This controversy is also relevant for developmental psychology.[12] Some evidence favors the view that in early childhood certain linguistic rules are learned almost automatically if the rest of a child's development proceeds undisturbed.

This may be true of syntactic rules. If this question is to be clarified, we must give an account of the character of such rules, the neuro-psychological possibility of their anchoring in the structures of the brain, and the degree of universality of an almost automatic development in various age-related stages.[13]

Beyond this point, questions of the development of language involve questions of the development of interactive competence, so that the mutual dependence of the dimensions of linguistic and interactive competence must be decided. The way a child in early development learns to experience himself as the interaction partner of others also (according to all insights of psychoanalysis and psychiatry) influences the way language becomes the medium of self-perception, of self-presentation, of the perception and interpretation of others, and finally of metacommunication (that is, the reflection on interaction that proceeds harmoniously or conflictually).[14]

According to the present state of the field, it seems possible to grasp linguistically mediated communicative practice in its genesis, so that the diverse, independent competences form a systematic unity through the medium of language and, at the same time, are extended to the dimension of the possibility of the reciprocal reflection of interaction partners. This view would be supported by the hypothesis in developmental theory that the behavioral possibilities of animals experience an elementary transformation in crossing the threshold to language. Language would then be confirmed anew as the emergent, unforeseeable, newly appearing achievement of evolution responsible for a new unity at a higher level.

The Basic Tendency of Communicative Action Toward Reciprocal-Egalitarian Solidarity

Our question then is this: How can we determine the unity of cognitive, linguistic, and interactive competence in "communicative competence" in such a way that the interrelationship of truth-related statements, the identity of subjects, and their mutual, free self-determinations becomes intelligible? This would have to be accomplished in such a way that the formal demands on theoretical construction outlined above would be preserved.

The contemporary state of research seems to indicate a convergence of various theoretical approaches to a core structure of interaction that can be seen as elementary. Even from the perspective of a theory of foundations, this convergence seems always to have a mediating function in which empirically gathered facts reveal a normative core.

From this standpoint I would like to mention again these converging approaches, already presented in part, and then to attempt to characterize this common core structure.

The Intersubjective Constitution of Reality in the Cognitive Dimension

Investigations in developmental psychology concerning the constitution of objective reality in the active exchange of the child with his environment have their counterpart in the philosophical tradition in those theories of the constitution of reality that begin with the performances of an empirical or transcendental subject. In Idealism, Kant's transcendental unity of apperception was fragmented by Fichte into intersubjectivity and by Hegel into the dialectical process of history. Husserl vainly attempts to explain the intersubjective constitution of the world. Since Husserl, sociological theories via Schütz and Luckmann up to contemporary proto-sociological theories of interaction influenced by Mead show that the constitution of reality, and thus the constitution of the world, must finally be established as an achievement of interaction. The experience of reality in everyday life—the basis of both experimental action and theory formation—is constituted through reciprocally acknowledged idealizing performances, which make possible a common and at the same time individually experienceable space, a generally shared and individually biographical time, and a generally accepted reality with socially and individually significant structures of relevance. That the construction of reality as experienced rests on reciprocal, idealizing suppositions [Unterstellungen] can be proved on the one hand by investigations in developmental psychology concerning the distortion or absence of the experience of reality through insufficient interaction[15] and, on the other hand, by research on the effects of disasters (in the collapse of all orientations to reality) in ethnomethodology.[16]

The Egalitarian-Reciprocal Structure of the Linguistic and
Significant Symbol

George Herbert Mead sees the decisive transition from the animal to
the human realm in the emergence of the significant symbol. This
thesis can also be supported by general research into evolution.[17] The
important characteristics of the significant symbol can be clarified
through the model of vocal gestures. Vocal gestures have the same
effect on both the speaker and the hearer. The significant symbol thus
makes possible the egalitarian, reciprocally understood, and therefore
common constitution of reality. The significant symbol is therefore
also the decisive mechanism for presenting the reality constituted in
reciprocal interaction in the medium of linguistic symbols. Even though
Mead's theory bears all the marks of behaviorism, it comprehends an
important basic characteristic of human language.

The Constitution of the Self in Interaction

For Mead, it is also possible to explain the emergence of the self in
interaction on the basis of significant symbols. The human being, born
with a, so to speak, purely organic identity, achieves selfhood in
interaction with the significant — and finally generalized — other in the
reciprocal-reflective return to the self, which achieves its biographical
identity[18] and its capacity for communicative action in this very interaction. This elementary mechanism, by which the ego is able to take
the role of the alter ego as its own, constitutes the fundamental possibility of mutual understanding of any interaction partners. Therefore,
the mutual dependence of the achievement of selfhood and the empathetic perception of the other as a partner of equal standing lies at
the root of the possibility of interaction.

The most decisive objection that can be brought against Mead is
that his theory is dangerously near to a one-dimensional explanation
of the genesis of the self from society, and hence threatens to transform
society into a totalitarian entity. This can be shown through the critique
of Mead's behaviorist elements. However, this does not eliminate
Mead's key insight into the egalitarian structure of language and interaction. Important in this context are those theories that take this insight
further, primarily in psychoanalytic approaches and approaches arising
from the further development of symbolic interactionism.

The Acquisition of the Primary Qualifications for the Production of Reciprocity

In psychoanalytic research the transition from early childhood, in which the mother-child dyad has primary significance, is effected chiefly through the expansion of the system of interaction to include the father as the partner of the mother. The achievement demanded of the child in a process marked by crises consists in bringing the behavioral expectations of the second partner into harmony with those of the first in such a way that the differences in expectations can be integrated and responded to in one's own actions, without tensions endangering the stability of the personality. The elementary achievement of the four-to-five-year-old child, then, consists in preserving or newly achieving his identity by conducting himself in a situationally suitable manner in relation to diverse partners of equal standing. The acquisition of the primary qualifications of role actions (namely role distance, tolerance of ambiguity, and empathy) strengthen rather than rupture the basic principles of equality and reciprocity.

Role Action: The Perception and Transformation of Expectations of Expectations

The way in which Parsons's more developed role theory both criticizes and pushes further Mead's original theory was presented above. Achieving personal identity and assisting in the development of the identity of the other in interaction are acts of balance in which the freedom of self-presentation and the attribution of identity to the other are no longer automatic acts of the use of fixed symbols; instead they are constant, active, multifaceted acts of interpretation entering into the expectations of others and one's own expectations, in which one's own identity is bound to the granting of the identity of others. The elementary structure of interaction as the mutual granting of freely shaped and receptive identity then only increases the demand for a basic structure of egality and solidarity.

The Principle of Cooperation as the Basic Structure of the Logic of Interaction of Linguistic Communication

Ever since linguists stopped using individual sentences as the paradigm of their object of inquiry, the inner mechanisms of normal conversation processes have been more closely investigated. The primary phenomenon in need of explanation is exactly how mutual understanding can occur at all despite the extremely fragmentary character of utterances.

Reaching an understanding appears to rest on strategies of suggestion and implicit supplementation learned with and mutually presupposed in language. These implicitly conveyed performances are hardly recognizable in the surface structure of language and become clear in all their dimensions only in cases when the implicit agreements about commonly held perspectives, the common store of knowledge, the congruence of systems of relevance, and the "normalcy" of others and their view of reality break down entirely. H. B. Grice, who perhaps more than anyone investigated the various modes of "conversational implicators," ultimately formulated a general "principle of cooperation" for linguistic understanding, which principle is fundamental for a pragmatic conception of meaning.[19] These investigations are of course still in their incipient stages, but it is not an exaggeration to affirm that they tend toward the view that "the principle of cooperation is a basic structure of the logic of interaction of linguistic communication."[20]

The Logic of the Development of Moral Consciousness and the Principle of Perfect Justice

These suggestions are verified and carried further in the research into the development of moral consciousness, which assumes a central strategic place in terms of methodology and subject matter. These investigations are significant for foundation theory in terms of their object and in terms of their status in the theory of science.

Moral decisions are concerned with the principles by which conflicts between interaction partners are resolved. Kohlberg and his collaborators assert that an unequivocal and irreversible succession of stages may be ascertained in the development of the ways in which conflicts are resolved.[21] Each of the stages corresponds to a certain sort of identity formation and interactive reciprocity and may be designated by the structure of this interdependence. The inner tendency of this development is toward an increase in self-determination and, at the same time, an increase in the reciprocity of the relationship between interaction partners, in such a way that in the final stage reciprocity is thematized as such and raised to the principle of moral decisions. Kohlberg distinguishes six different stages in this development from early childhood to adolescence. At each stage, interactive behavior is oriented toward a certain form of reciprocity. The starting point of the process is the orientation implied in physically turning toward or away from persons who are immediately present. From this purely external orientation, the development leads from the orientation to a sympathetically and hence authoritatively perceived interaction partner to orientation within given rules. At the next stage, principles or rules emerge according to which rules can first be grounded at all; the need to ground principles results in a tendency toward the ultimate principle in which reciprocity in its reflective form becomes the only standard. The only binding mode of discovering norms is that in which all interaction partners are recognized as having equal rights and standing.[22] The inner tendency of the development of moral consciousness advances toward internalization and universalization in an ordered series of stages with increasingly higher forms of reciprocity.[23]

The attempts to reconstruct the various dimensions of communicative action, which have been empirically tested to varying degrees, all point to a convergence in a core structure characterized by the reciprocal mutual recognition of the communication partners in their binding equality of the rights through all the dimensions of communication. The basic structure of significant symbols opens up the possibility of articulating both states of affairs and norms with the same claim to mutual agreement, and, in a normatively reflective turn, of making the basic structure of communication once again the medium and measure of the balancing of disputed claims.

With these reconstructions, normative and ideal conditions of communication are demonstrated. Mead was quite aware of these conditions. The significant symbol, opening up and constituting the "logical universe," posits for the development of human society the goal of "ideal communication," inclusive of everyone. "The universal conversation," Mead writes, "is therefore the formal ideal of communication."[24]

What claim can justifiably be made by such reconstructions? In terms of the theory of science, they have a key function. As empirical theories they uncover a normative core of interaction. Hence, the claim implicit in the reconstruction seems to bridge the gap between "is" and "ought," between statements of fact and statements of value, which pervades the entire tradition of modern philosophy and theory of science. The "naturalistic fallacy" of deriving ethical claims from empirical statements then need not be seen as a simple fallacy in the realm of the analysis of interaction. It is indicative that one of Kohlberg's main works, one that rests on extensive empirical studies, bears the title "From Is to Ought: How to Commit the Naturalistic Fallacy and Get Away With It in the Study of Moral Development."

Nevertheless, as regards the status of such studies we are dealing with empirical theories still operating primarily in the objectivating attitude. How could such theories be justified and, as determinations of contingent facts, become the principle for the grounding of binding orientations for action? This question gives the problematic a decisive focus.

The Systematic Reconstruction of the Normative Core of Communicative Action: The Necessary Supposition of the Ideal Speech Community

The Structure of the Problematic

By now it should be clear that here a decisive point is reached in an investigation that returns to communicative practice as its foundational realm. Here the question is whether a basic normative structure of communication as both medium and criterion for deciding theoretical and practical questions can be found.

The essential aporias of the theory of science inevitably refer back to communicative practice. However, neither the pragmatic principle of tolerance in the situation of competing theories nor the principle of the proliferation of theories has led to criteria of rational decision making. The reference back to ordinary language leads to the problem of a plurality of developed language games and the insoluble limits of conventionalism. Can a procedure and a criterion be found for the process of theoretical decisions in all these dimensions?

As soon as normative questions arise in the realm of empirical theory, the aporias of analytic ethics emerge in just as vicious a form. Ever since Hume's *Enquiry into Human Understanding* the empirically oriented scientist has cast a critical gaze on the thought operations of those who assert the possibility of grounding ethical statements. Analytic ethics generally falls back to the distinction between empirical observations and ethical attitudes and seeks to develop systems of logic for the latter. In this undertaking, enormous progress has been made in the study of deontic logic, which is to say a logic of norms and values and of ethical argumentation.[25] The basic problem, however, still remains the grounding of the validity of normative statements. If this question goes unclarified, moral argumentation remains caught in a questionable circularity.

The same is true for all the various approaches developed up to now. Naive utilitarianism must be able to give an account of the grounding of its conception of the "good life" to be desired, in the same way that its scientifically more ambitious version, derived from game theory, must presuppose certain goals if it is to assign criteria for selecting strategies for achieving them. The attempt to understand evolution as the self-transcendence of systems becoming ever more complex and to show their inner finality fails to specify the inner indeterminacy of such system transcendence. The normative claims of behavioral research cannot simply be derived from the theoretical status of its statements. The program of reconstruction of a normative genesis of needs ultimately only poses in a more radical form the problem of the grounding of this normative status.

The question thus remains one of how ethical statements can be grounded at all. The problem is obviously that every attempt to provide the foundations for ethics arrives on the scene too late if it does not begin with the most elementary practice in which theoretical and practical claims are inseparably bound together and mutually ground each other. How can we demonstrate the interdependence of "is" and "ought"?

Suspicions may be raised that the claims of theoretical assertions and proposals for practical orientations that they serve the interests of certain groups legitimate their domination in certain societies and distort the situation in which claims are supposed to be grounded or rejected. How can such a suspicion of ideology be refuted, if it is so comprehensive? Is it possible to achieve in the structure of communicative practice itself the possibility of grounding theoretical and practical statements, as well as the refutation of the suspicion of ideology?

The question of the possibility of grounding the claims implicitly raised in communicative practice in this practice itself brings to mind the problem of classical transcendental philosophy. However, for Kant such a transcendental demonstration was thinkable only as the demonstration of *a priori* principles of the rational will in a "metaphysics of morals," free of all empirical, anthropological constraints.[26] After the critical turn to language, philosophy objected to this sort of transcendental thinking on the grounds that it naively overlooks the linguistic conditionedness of reflection upon the structure of subjectivity. Could these aporias be overcome in a transformed version of transcendental thought? Can a definite form of communicative practice be shown to be "transcendental"?

The Systematic Reconstruction of the Normative Core of Communicative Action: The Ideal Speech Situation

The above-summarized attempts to derive from empirical theories the "universal conversation" as "the formal ideal of communication"[27] and hence the possibility of grounding intersubjective claims in the logic of development and constitution must be taken up once again in systematic analysis of the most extreme possibilities of self-reflective communication. Such analysis has been undertaken in many different ways, most extensively by members of the Erlangen School, by Apel, and by Habermas. In the various analyses different vocabularies have been developed, most of which serve to distinguish the various attempts at analysis rather than to make substantive distinctions. We shall investigate Habermas's proposal first, since it comes closest to reaching the dimensions most appropriate to the problem at hand. Thus, we shall adopt Habermas's terminology and shall also note at important junctures how this approach differs from others.[28]

Habermas has tried to develop the basic structure of communication as a system of speech acts.[29] However, the different classes of speech acts can be grounded relatively clearly in terms of the dimensions of communicative action and competence presented above—something Habermas did not accomplish in his first essay on communicative competence. "Communicative" speech acts are related to communicative competence and hence to the opening of an always intersubjectively accessible realm of mutual understanding [Verständigung]. In such speech acts, the claim is made to the "understandability" of what is uttered. "Constative" speech acts are related to cognitive competence and to the possibility of the transformation of experiences into statements with truth claims; they make the claim to the "truth" of statements. "Regulative" and "representative" speech acts are related to two dimensions of interaction competence. On one hand, they articulate norms to guide action and thereby make the claim to "correctness" for the proffered or demanded norms; on the other hand, as representative speech acts they refer to mutual self-presentation of the interaction partners[30] and make the claim to "truthfulness," which is to say the claim that an interaction partner deceives neither himself nor the other but rather truthfully presents his intentions.[31]

In everyday communication, the validity claims of truth, correctness, and truthfulness are all raised and understood as such without necessarily being explicitly articulated. On the level of the metacommunicative relation of communicative action, there is usually agreement as to what counts as asserting a state of affairs or disputing an unacceptable demand. This sort of metacommunicative, reciprocal reflectivity of mutual suppositions in everyday interaction offers the possibility of explicitly thematizing these mostly implicit validity claims on the level of direct interaction (which is of course reflexively stratified in this way) in an act something like "Now let's see just what's going on here." The structure of everyday interaction thus offers the possibility of passing over, so to speak, into a self-reflective form of communicative action. The possibility of this transition is built into the very core structure of communication. Habermas calls "discourse"[32] just this form of communication in which validity claims are thematized as they become controversial in interaction. The goal of this recourse to an explicitly reflective form of communicative action is to bring about agreement concerning claims that have become controversial. Discourse aims at the consensus of its participants.

Claims to understandability can evidently be explained only through the acquisition of the specific language in use. (This will not be pursued here.) The claim to deceive neither oneself nor one's partner can be decided only in the course of a longer-lasting communicative experience, or the transition must be made into therapeutic or ideological-critical-oriented modes of communicative action. According to Habermas, the validity claim to "truth" is thematized in "theoretical discourse" and the validity claim to "correctness" in "practical discourse." Our interest here is in both of these forms of the thematization of validity claims. We shall turn later to the question of the logic of argumentation in discourse.

Our primary interest is in the following questions: With what right can the result of, say, a theoretical discourse claim to be "true"? By what criteria can it be decided that a consensus is a true consensus?

To begin with, one could call to mind various kinds of criteria. But even a criterion such as "the reliability of observations" or "the adequate interpretation of the results of experiments" must in turn be decided upon in a discourse. Even if one's intent were to refer back to the truthfulness of the partner or to the correctness of methodological rules, one is still obligated to explain such claims discursively.[33] However, if the claim of a discourse to call "true" a statement about which one has reached an agreement could only then in turn be decided again in a discourse about this discourse, infinite regress is unavoidable. On the other hand, it would be absurd to hold that any given factually attained agreement is valid as a legitimation for the truth or the correctness of statements. This would entail giving up the search for any grounding of validity claims.

Here we have arrived at a decisive point in our inquiry. It is not possible here to introduce criteria for this grounding external to reflective communicative action. Without disputing the very possibility of the human capacity to raise truth claims, there is no alternative but to seek the criteria for the legitimation of validity claims in the structure of reciprocal-reflective communication. This means showing just how in the course of elementary communicative action mutual, normative suppositions are proffered and accepted as binding the communication partners from the moment they enter into communication.

What is the nature of these normative suppositions? According to our previous analysis, the core structure of communicative action consists in that the communication partners mutually accept each other as having equal standing and rights in all the dimensions of communicative action and recognize the obligatory character of their mutual claims. This structure is then at the same time the distinguishing feature of an ideal speech situation presupposed in entering into communicative action. It is also the distinction of forms of discourses that decide the correctness of validity claims.

With such a transcendental presupposition of an ideal speech situation, each of the communication partners must in principle have and grant to others the same possibility for acting in the various dimensions of communication and of choosing from the different classes of speech acts: to open up the conversation as such, to raise or to dispute assertion with truth claims without excluding certain presuppositions for possible disputes, to explain or to reject as regards their normative character the correctness of behavioral norms without the threat of sanctions against arguments, and to enter subjectively into the conversation or to withdraw from it without deception.

The idealizing supposition of such a situation in the practice of communication has yet another dimension. The conversation in which validity claims are decided upon argumentatively cannot in principle be limited. Anyone who brings forth arguments, anyone who in any way enters with the intention of entering into communication, must be accepted as a partner. The supposition of the ideal speech situation thus implies an unlimited communication community. Hence, in principle, in any communicative act the entire human species is implied as the final horizon of the communication community. Communicative action is thus bound to normative, ideal criteria. In it we receive insight into what should be. But how can the character of this insight be more closely determined? This insight is at the same time an acceptance. What is the character of this insightful acceptance? Is it a process of constitution of an act through an unavoidably posited condition of its possibility? Or is it simply one factually occurring resolve among others? Obviously, all the traditional distinctions are inadequate here. There has also been intensive controversy over the status of this insight.

The Controversy Over the Status of the Ideal Speech Situation

The origins of this controversy extend back to the question of the proper status of the return to ordinary language as the final metalanguage behind which reflection cannot go, as opposed to the constructivist attempt to "go behind" ordinary language in first attempting to attain the linguistic means of ordinary language through paradigmatic introduction in elementary dialogical situations.[34] Four views may be distinguished in the contemporary discussion.

• In his first essay on communicative competence, Habermas emphasized that an ideal speech situation is inevitably presupposed in all communicative action: "Upon the two counterfactual suppositions that participants in communication follow intentional norms, about which they could at any time furnish discursive justification, rests the humanity of intercourse among human beings who are still human, that is, who, as subjects, have not yet become completely estranged in their own self-objectivations."[35] The very possibility of communicative action rests on the supposition of this model of pure communicative action.[36] The demonstration of the necessity of the anticipatory grasp toward the ideal speech situation is, however, accomplished in an analysis of discourse.[37] This procedure has been the source of the sharpest criticisms of Habermas's view. Wunderlich, for example, writes that this model is not only idealized in respect to actual communication but is utopian in every respect.[38] Discourse here is regarded as the normative model of interaction, not as a possibility built into communication of a transition to reflective forms of conversation. Against this misunderstanding, Habermas explicitly emphasized that one must understand "the communication community *in the first instance* as a community of interaction and not of argumentation, as action and not as discourse."[39] Its basis is communicative action, for the possibility of discourse is built in "the transcendental character of ordinary language"[40] and rests upon the necessity of presupposing the ideal speech situation: Inasmuch as I act communicatively I suppose this situation as "always already" (*immer schon*) realized in the suppositions of the partners. Habermas explicitly defends himself against the notion that this supposition must be accepted through "voluntaristic affirmation."[41]

• Very early on, Paul Lorenzen raised strong objections against any interpretation of Gödel's metamathematical results that did not allow for any methodological starting point for thought. Nevertheless, Lorenzen explicitly emphasizes that the beginning of argumentation requires an "act of faith," a first fundamental decision for reason. As opposed to Popper, whose "two modes of belief" are alluded to here, this "act of faith" is to be understood as "the acceptance of something that is not justified,"[42] or, more precisely, as "ventured quite preliminarily."[43] The decision made here initially consists in transcending subjectivity. The demand "Let us transcend our subjectivity!" is the norm that makes possible the justification of all other norms. Transsubjectivity is thus the "supernorm," and for this reason it has the status of "the moral principle as such."[44] However, the question is whether this "act of faith" finally represents a form of "decisionism."[45]

• Friedrich Kambartel suggests a middle way: that a "transcendental" mode of argument can be maintained only insofar as one can convince the person who is asking for the justification of an argumentatively grasped rational principle that merely asking such a question places him on the ground of this principle. That this principle of reason must then be carefully and methodologically reconstructed makes this initial recognition of rational argumentation only something "ventured initially,"[46] a point of agreement between Kambartel and Lorenzen.[47]

• Apel makes this view more precise in two respects. First, he establishes that in the return to the mutual recognition of the members of the community of argumentation their mere recognition as subjects of logical argumentation is not sufficient; rather, we can speak of reaching the basis of all possible argumentation (and hence of an "ethics of logic") only when the subjects of argumentation are recognized as *persons* who are possible discussion partners in *all* actions and utterances and whose possible contributions to any discussion are indispensable.[48] Such an investigation must go beyond the logical subject of argumentation to the real subject of communicative action. Otherwise the significance of the pragmatic turn of language-critical philosophy would be lost. Moreover, Apel understands the argument that the inquirer who seeks reasons has "always already" accepted the basic principle of transsubjective argumentation as well as the significance of a methodological reconstruction and grounding of the principle of transsubjectivity in the return to Kant and Fichte, as a "self-reconstruction of reason" that becomes transparent in its genesis.[49] This self-reconstruction of reason even leads to the point where the philosopher "must *voluntaristically affirm* in every moment of his life"[50] the insight into his participation in the transcendental language game. Hence, for Apel transcendental reconstruction leads to the freedom of intersubjectivity.

We must then investigate, independent of these disputes, the sort of meaning the word "transcendental" can have in this context. In relation to his analysis of the cognitive interests, Habermas at one time established that they could claim a "transcendental" status, in that they are achieved in reflection on the logic of process of inquiry, but they nonetheless also have "empirical" status, in that they may be conceived as the result of natural history.[51] This is also true in an analogous way for the status of the presupposition of the ideal speech situation. A phylogenetic, ontogenetic, and action-theoretical reconstruction of communicative competence leads to hypotheses to the effect that the core structure of communicative competence consists in the reciprocal recognition of communication partners of equal standing. A systematic reconstruction of the logic of interaction in communicative competence leads to the conclusion that the communication partners within the framework of an unlimited communication community must "always already" be recognized as having equal standing if communication is to succeed at all in all its dimensions and if (here we touch upon the most clearly and systematically reconstructed paradigm) argumentation is to be possible. Hence, one could put it in this way: This transcendental adverb, "always already," has the character of indicating a presupposed, free decision. This presupposition is not transcendentally necessary in the classical sense, like the Kantian categories, as the condition of possibility of the constitution of objectivity. Instead, the condition of possibility of subjectivity and intersubjectivity is precisely this free mutual recognition. What is transcendental in the realm of practical reason is shown as a transcendental necessity only in free practice and as the necessary reference to this free practice.

This has significance for any conception whose intent is to connect empirically reconstructive theories of evolution with the systematic reconstruction of a critical anthropology, theory of interaction, or theory of society. At the same time, as these terminological difficulties make clear, many important unresolved problems remain. This can be clarified as follows: The concept of "emergence" used by Mead at key points in his later works[52] signifies the emergence (surfacing) of something new in evolution that is both system-transcending and system-transforming. The emergence of the phenomenon of human communication, with its core structure of reciprocity freely accepted and yet constitutive for communication, is obviously the most important achievement at the forefront of evolution, in terms of which and on the strength of which all other phenomena can be explained as derivative and surpassed. However, this phenomenon can illuminate itself by manifesting its emerging free necessity and necessary freedom. For this reason we can here justifiably ask whether the distinction between "contingency" and "necessity" still makes sense in this context.[53] This is the same point at which theology has had its starting point since nominalism.

It remains to be established that the condition of possibility of the identity of subjects in intersubjectivity is this basic structure of free mutual recognition emergent in evolution. Freedom in intersubjectivity is then not a property to be granted or denied a human being but rather is simply revealed as the condition of possibility of being human at all. In this sense, the supposition of the ideal speech situation has "transcendental" status.

The Supposition of the Ideal Speech Situation as "Anticipation"

The insight that communication partners necessarily implicitly acknowledge ideal suppositions about each other and hence about an ideal speech situation may be gained from analysis of immediate interaction. This insight becomes evident in the degree to which reification and strategic manipulation of one's partner as a basic attitude necessarily destroys one's own humanity. The normative core of communicative action, and thus the postulate to act impartially, without force and deception, is directed in its normativity against reified domination, deception, and self-deception. What is implicitly supposed in communication as ideal may not simply be reduced to what is realized in history. This supposition has the character of "anticipation" in the direction of something yet to be realized in the course of communication; it is a "formal anticipation of the correct life."[54] Therefore, it has a temporal character, it transcends the contemporary situation, and it points beyond itself to what is to be brought about—to the future. The situation that is anticipated shows itself as that which ought to come about, as what is "always already" normatively effective. The status of this necessary anticipation is therefore paradoxical: As a historical anticipation, it is a factual performance of free subjects and is at the same time transcendentally constitutive.[55]

The Difference Between the Real and the Ideal Communication Community

The supposition of the ideal communication situation must be discussed in yet another dimension. This supposition is in the first instance already anticipated in direct interaction; it is also binding for those participating in the interaction. Every argument, indeed every human word, and (precisely speaking) every action that is supposed to be understandable[56] makes the claim of being understandable by anyone, even beyond the actual situation in which it arises; in this way, the community of those who are immediately in interaction expands to the "ideal communication community" of all those who could participate in communication or have participated at any time. Apel has

researched the history of this idea of the ideal communication community in American social philosophy and in the empirically oriented
social psychology of the nineteenth and twentieth centuries.[57] For
C. S. Peirce this postulate takes the form of the "indefinite community
of investigators," which now represents—in a conscious transformation
of Kant—the transcendental subject of the process of inquiry. For
Josiah Royce, it is the "community of interpretation," which can ultimately only be understood religiously as the community of interpretation of all human beings. G. H. Mead, who studied with Royce
at Harvard, sees the "community of universal discourse" built into
the mechanism of the significant symbol, a community which is the
normative guiding conception for any idea of democracy.[58] It is possible
to demonstrate the historical interrelationship of Peirce and Royce
with the basic ideas of German Idealism. Mead was increasingly skep-
tical of precisely these idealistic elements in the work of his mentor
Royce at Harvard.[59] Nonetheless, this historical context cannot be
ignored; it must be accepted as a challenge that the unresolved problems
of Idealism again come to light via a detour through American social
psychology.

Mead proceeds from the idea that the universal, ideal community
is posited in every use of a significant symbol. As such, it is both the
utopian goal and the already concretely effective norm of communicative action, which for Mead is already opened up toward society
and constituted by it in acquiring the capacity to act. Inasmuch as it
has been developed from a theory of communicative action, therefore,
the idea of an ideal communication community shows itself to be the
basic normative concept of a critical theory of society in a double
sense. First, on the level of a theory of the foundations of the social
sciences, it is possible to develop the concept of society in terms of
the analysis of communicative action, as had already been attempted
by Durkheim and Parsons; indeed, this can be done in such a way
that the normative implications of this context are also shown at the
same time. This in turn makes possible the development of the analytic
tools necessary for the study and judgment of distorted communication
and, in general, for functional analyses of society.[60] Second, it is also
possible to view the evolution of society from the viewpoint of the
dialectic of the real and the ideal communication community. Communicative action is always played out in a concrete society, with all
its contradictions and reifying mechanisms. In its factual implications,

concrete communicative action already points to the ideal communication community, if such action is not to become self-contradictory. The ideal implications of any socially constitutive action are the concrete impulses to change the currently existing situation and to transform human society as a whole. For this reason, "the critical theory of society" here has its starting point[61] in the normative implications of communicative action. For Apel, the dialectic between the real and the ideal communication community contains in it the possibility of mediating between historical materialism and idealism.[62] However, two important questions result: How can orientations for action be concretely grounded in an existing society, so that they can claim to be binding? How can the history of the current situation of action be reconstructed so that the reconstruction contributes to the judging of the contemporary situation and the gaining of orientations for action directed toward the future? In both these questions we can find further concretization of a theory of communicative action. We must next explain the basic characteristics of such a concretization.[63]

The Justification of Orientations of Action within the Framework of a Critical Theory of Society and History

Toward the Ethical Legitimation of Action Orientations

In the framework of the discussion of analytic ethics, the requirements for a theory of the justification of orientations of action have been well articulated.[64] In Logical Positivism, ethical utterances could only be understood as expressions of feelings and attitudes, whose expressiveness was supposed to influence the feelings and attitudes of others. This is the core of the long-dominant trend of emotivism in ethics.[65] R. M. Hare, *especially*, promoted the discussion of these issues. For Hare, both a theory of meaning of moral words and moral judgments and a theory of the grounding of moral judgments belong to a theory of ethics.[66] In such a theory, it seems, almost all meta-ethicists have reached one point of common agreement: A moral judgment can be viewed as justified when it has universal validity, that is, when it is acceptable in principle to everyone.

"To justify means to universalize."[67] Precisely these conditions are fulfilled in an ethics grounded in a theory of action. First, it can characterize ethical judgments as linguistic actions which are related back to such (universal) claims in the context of action constituted by reciprocal claims; second, it can show that ethical speech always occurs in the horizon of a community which is universal and within which claims upon actions and orientations of actions must be tested and established.[68]

Perhaps the most genuinely interesting case for a theory of ethical argumentation is a conflict in which various interests are represented and it cannot be easily decided which of them could be acceptable to all participants. Only two alternatives are then open: An attempt can be made to come to some sort of agreement through argument, or the dialogue can simply be terminated and the transition be made to the strategic action of political struggle. If the second possibility is chosen, the question remains how such action can be morally justified. In terms of the presuppositions developed up to this point, this is possible only if one who chooses to enter into strategic action tests beforehand, in a simulated discourse, whether the interests he represents can be the interests of all and whether his own arguments stand up to the critical objections of all possible conversation partners. Strategic action must then undergo the test of representative, advocatory argumentation and counterargumentation. Even a theory of conflicts, therefore, has its normative implications. If advocatory argumentation is not to remain completely naive in this context, then it must naturally take into account the consequences of the transition to strategic action for the total structure of communicative action in a specific situation. Here we find the fundamental ethical problems of a theory of strategic political action.

Nonetheless, we must pursue further the possibility of the argumentative clarification of conflict. We cannot avoid at least broadly outlining the structure of an ethical argument.

Ethically relevant conflicts arise in situations of action in which certain actions are to be judged in terms of their correctness. The logic of argumentation in such situations should be investigated.[69] In any situation of human action, specific information and data are available about the situation (including possible courses of action within it). We are looking for a way to evaluate these various actions, and thus for an orientation or concrete instructions for action. Such an evaluation can be found only if certain generally formulated norms of action and value, or (on a level yet farther removed) principles for the evaluation of norms, are available. The decisive question is then how such norms or principles can themselves be grounded. As has been described above, this usually occurs in such a way that there emerge certain needs already appearing as interpreted needs, or, in other words, as direct or indirect consequences of action which are already desired or undesired and now judged as to whether they are universally acceptable—that is, these needs become universalized. Universal norms of action rest on the process of universalization for their validity. It should be clear that problems arise for universalization that are similar to those associated with induction.

An argument about orientations of action free from conflict can be achieved if the general norm of action is recognized as universalizable and if it is agreed that, in terms of the available information about the situation, a certain action can be interpreted in such a way as to be subsumed under this norm. The evaluation of an action is still only a question of a deductive logic of norms.

According to these suppositions, ethical conflicts arise when the interpretation of the situation is controversial or when it is disputed whether a given norm of action can be grounded through universalization. The meaning of the converse of this statement must also be clarified: Consensus about an orientation for action rests on the fact that, on the one hand, in the language available to us, universal, normative interpretations of needs, actions, and consequences of action have been found, and that, on the other hand, in this same language a commonly acceptable interpretation of the actual situations of action can be found, and indeed in such a way that once again in this same language these interpretations can be interpreted by norms of action. In other words, it must be presupposed that in the previous development of the human species and of any specific society a linguistic system has been formed with certain normative schemes of interpretation which permit agreement concerning interpretation of different situations of action and thus of the orientation of action. In turn, this confidence in the existing language system is acceptable only if it is also presupposed that this development is not simply unconscious but rather is already under the watchful eye of ethical dialogue. Habermas writes that "the force of an argument with the goal of consensus rests on an achievement of cognitive development guaranteed by the adequacy of the system of description which precedes any individual argument."[70] This presupposition means that revisions of the entire system of language and interpretation have been undertaken in history and must now also be possible in principle.[71]

The result of all this is a succession of stages in the radicalization of ethical discourse. Along with the discussion of individual needs, the interpretation of situations, norms, and principles (that is, norms for the justification of norms) has to be able to thematize the revision of the previous language system and at the same time the establishment of a new one. The nature of this new language system must then be decided; that is, we must again give criteria for the adequacy of what has never previously been used, for the novel.

We have now come to one of the most interesting and important points in the development of the theory of action. The question of a rationally justifiable revision of systems of interpretation is a consequence of the development of the basic approach of the theory of action. With this question we have now reached the historical dimension of the theory of action. This question of how changes in systems of interpretation can be grounded contains the basic questions of historical hermeneutics and thus also of historicism, although naturally in a transformed form. The proponents of the various forms of the theory of action are quite aware of this. Habermas tries from this perspective to develop the outline of a logic of the sequence of world views or normative interpretations of reality. The proponents of the Erlangen School try to develop the foundations of a normative theory of history through their distinction between "factual" and "critical" or "normative" genesis.[72]

The problem with such theories lies primarily in that proposals for normative orientations developed historically have always been present and have drawn their normative power primarily from general social recognition. But how can what has come to be factually be shown to be rational or rejected as irrational? Even the starting point of the attempt to analyze the contemporary situation of conflict leads to the necessity of explaining its emergence from prior action and, if our concern is with justification or critique, of reconstructing it in such a way that at the decisive points in its genesis those actions advancing the development can be tested as to whether they may be justified in a simulated discourse of all those affected by them. From the agreement of the "factual genesis" with the "critical genesis" reconstructed in simulated discourse, or from its deviation therefrom, emerge criteria for the judgment of possibilities of action in the contemporary situation. Since the consequences of an action are never fully foreseeable at the transition points of its development, there must be a constant return from discursively justified practice initiating factual development to ever-renewed testing of its validity. In this process the proponents of the Erlangen School see the "dialectic" between factual and critical genesis. This dialectic is understood as the necessary structure of a rational treatment of history.

In the controversy between Kambartel and Lorenzen about whether there must be established as the principle of rational action an independent "principle of dialectics" alongside the principle of transsubjectivity, one must certainly agree with Kambartel: If one agrees with the principle of transsubjectivity as a basic principle, it is naive not to establish this transsubjectivity in its historical dimension from the start.[73] My intent is not to investigate this thesis in its entirety, or even the total structure of such a reconstruction, but rather to analyze more precisely the decisive point of the proposed procedure in its microstructure. The decisive point seems to lie in the question of how, in a situation of conflict or in a period of historical transition, a revision of the previous language and system of norms may be found that heretofore did not exist but nonetheless should be rationally justified. It should also be shown by this investigation that this question is not only a core problem of practical discourse but one of theoretical discourse as well.

The Mutual Limitations of Theoretical and Normative-Practical Questions

The catch phrase "the revision of language systems and normative orientations" immediately brings to mind one of the most important problems of the discussion of the theory of science: Kuhn's thesis that scientific revolutions arise from the replacement of one dominant paradigm as the guide of all research by another. How this process of replacement of paradigms is to be rationally conceived remained unclear. The review of this discussion conducted here has contributed no convincing candidate proposal for the unequivocal clarification of this question.[74] "Intertheoretical rationality" must indeed consist in reducing theories to each other and embedding them in more expanded theoretical structures, but how these operations are to be conceived is still an open question. Returning to dialectical forms of thought has been proposed by Feyerabend and demanded repeatedly more recently.[75] The history of science can no longer be relegated to a mere preliminary stage to contemporary reflections on the theory of science; conversely, the theory of science must increasingly be pursued as the history of science. In any case, this insight stands out in this development. In this respect, parallel problems exist for the theory of science and for a theory of practical orientations of action.

With respect to the development of certain questions, this parallel becomes a limitation. In earlier discussions, quantum physics was considered the most theoretically advanced and methodologically reflective science; it was treated as an example of the no longer dispensable mutual influence of subject and object in the process of scientific knowledge. Since then, the problematic has been expanded and sharpened and has ultimately lost its purely theoretical character. This can be shown in certain sets of issues. For example, in ecology one must begin with the fact that humans form a "system" with nature. This system cannot be grasped in terms of the reductionist models of systems theory. Rather, the task of thought consists in conceptualizing the relationship of possible internal goals of the development of nature with the goals of the development of society so that a balanced equilibrium may be formed between newly introduced social developments and current and newly introduced reproduction cycles in nature. Such a view theoretically demands, Diederich writes, both "a concept of the total process of science as part of the development of society in mutual influence with nature" and "an integration of natural-scientific-nomological and social-scientific-normative treatments" of problems.[76] The decision about what is possible for society must then take into consideration the framework of the development of nature, while insight into the future development of nature is to be achieved only from the apprehension of its mutual influence with social development.[77] The problem of conceptualizing the unit of history and nature demands a transformation of the type of theories currently available, and becomes at the same time a practical task as theoretical discourse passes over into practical discourse.

Innovative Speech Acts and the Logic of Discourse

Thus the question of how the revision of existing orientations for action and of theoretical interpretations can be justified achieves still further significance. How are we to grasp innovative, situation-changing and system-changing speech actions that make a new consensus possible? What kind of theory can give an account of this phenomenon?

It seems that this question has in the past been vastly underestimated in its practical significance and its importance for the theory of science. Recall that the question of the completeness and the fundamental openness and surpassability of formal systems had underlying significance for inquiry into the foundations of mathematics and logic.[78] In a linguistics based on model theory, and especially in a theory of the text based on the logic of interaction, the question arises of how we can theoretically comprehend linguistic actions that transform a specific communication situation, surpass previously existing rules and so suspend previously established conventions, and open up the possibility of agreement about new rules. A basic problem of the philosophy of the later Wittgenstein and the approaches in the social sciences that are built on it is the surpassing of given language games, as well as the understanding of strange language games. Thus, it is the problem of accounting for the possibility of creative change and transformation in the rules of the game as such. A theory of art, and above all a poetics, would have to clarify how creative action opens new dimensions and how metaphorical speech can become the medium of a substantive critique of language, without which a transformation of concrete situations and a coming to agreement about new orientations would not be possible.[79] How are we to characterize a theory of linguistic action and a theory of discourse that account for such processes?

The Ideological-Critical Intensification of the Question: Consciousness as Lie

The question of the disclosure of new possibilities of consensus in situations of evolutionary crisis and conflict is intensified if the possibilities of deception and deceitful self-deception are taken into account. At least since Hegel's analysis of the dialectic of consciousness, this question cannot be avoided methodologically; it is concentrated in the suspicion that consciousness is false consciousness and in the presumption that consciousness itself is a lie. The major thresholds of the development of this view are marked by the names of Marx, Nietzsche, and Freud.

For Marx, consciousness presents itself as a function of social development, measured by the state of the unfolding of the forces of production in their relationship to the development of social relations of domination; these are the relations of production for Marx. A consciousness that has not succeeded in grasping this development and its own place in it is a false consciousness. It is deceived, and it deceives itself and others. A theory of this dialectical development tries to lift the veil of this deception in the anticipation of the totality and of a possible end state of this development and to give to the individual an orientation for socially relevant communicative behavior. The decisive question for this theory, of course, is whether it grasps all the important dimensions of communicative action.

For Freud, both conscious and linguistically mediated communicative action are only the symbolic expressions of a deeper, significant activity explainable in a theory of the unconscious. The theory of the unconscious remains abstract if it is not grasped as the predecessor of therapeutic action, in which the therapist understands his own symbolic, depth actions, present to him in consciousness, as a reactive instrument of measurement, a reflective reprojection of the distorted consciousness and action of the patient. Therapy is possible and conceivable only in such a way that, in the interaction of the therapist and the patient, the disturbances in the depth structure of his symbolic productions become clear to the patient and thus correctable in the practice of communicative action. In principle, psychoanalysis is thus, on the one hand, a theory that expands the concept of consciousness to the symbolically self-expressive depth structures of consciousness; on the other hand, it is a theory related to a model of communicative action inclusive of this symbolically productive depth dimension, from which instructions can be derived for rectifying, therapeutic action. Here the question is again whether this theory grasps all the dimensions of communication and can thus produce an adequate theory and adequate guidance for therapeutic action.[80]

A more radical suspicion against human consciousness is to be found in Nietzsche. The "will to power"—to self-creation—is the reason for the emergence of life-affirming, common orientations, although they may give the appearance of claiming moral obligation and truth. A kind of thinking that depicts this "genealogy of morals" and raises the suspicion that consciousness as such is a life-affirming lie tries to return to simpler, more elementary, more sensible modes of mutual attentiveness and consciousness. The question is then how we are to conceive a human solidarity after the ordeal of this disenchantment.

The questions we are concerned with here are not of the sort that have simple answers. The inner tendencies contained in the views of Marx, Freud, and Nietzsche, and the solutions proposed in the discussion of their views, leave no alternative but to see that human beings who live in contact with each other experience the dimensions of their own existing through experiencing the existence of others; they thereby realize a solidarity that alone offers the warranty that self-deception does not become the destructive deception of others.

Creative Communicative Action in the Dimensions of History and Society

We can thus distinguish those elementary determinations of communicative action exercised in the dimensions of history and society. Communicative action is not simply blind reaction to the instinctually guided behavior of others. As intentional action, it is always related to the intentions of others affected by one's own action; it is always subject to claims and it always makes its own claims. These claims can be articulated in the medium of language and thematized in conversation. The basic tendency of linguistically mediated action is a movement toward reflective reciprocity in equal standing and solidarity. In this structure of action the opening up of immediate interaction to an unlimited community is built in, and it is posited and accepted as normative for one's own action. This also gives us exigencies and criteria for the overcoming of untruth, injustice, deception, and self-deception.

If this claim is to be maintained in situations of conflict, that is, in situations where there is the danger that possibilities of action will be truncated and the capability of action itself finally destroyed, a basic structural possibility of human action must be confirmed. Human action in all its dimensions, including language, cannot ultimately be determined through unequivocal definitions of the situation of action or through a system of unambiguous rules of action. Rather, human action has the possibility of viewing itself innovatively in the creation of other situations (or, to put it in linguistic terms, of other worlds)— the possibility of treating the existing situation in a distanced manner in terms of other possibilities, and thereby changing them. It has the possibility of surpassing the rules of action in action and thus disclosing new dimensions of action, about which agreement can be reached.

The character of these innovative actions must be more precisely determined. Their meaning is not predetermined by existing rules or systems of meaning. Innovative actions are constitutive performances. They disclose possibilities for others and for the actor himself. They represent a reciprocal constitution of meaning. In this case, one's action is a disclosive provocation for others; it is the making possible and the realization of freedom.

This action is accomplished in the horizon of an unlimited communication community. In freedom, it is demanded of everyone and is at the same time binding for everyone. Consequently, it is determined by universal solidarity. The community disclosed in this universal solidarity that elaborates its possible self-understanding throughout history is the utmost horizon of action and the condition of possibility that action can contain in this horizon a moment of the unconditioned.

The Unrestricted Communication Community and the Aporia of Anamnestic Solidarity

The Universal Communication Community as the Utmost Idea Achievable

It seems, then, that the just-outlined structure of communicative action formulates the utmost ideal achievable in modern times. It is the binding anticipation of a humanity in communicative practice that, in conflict with nature and in ever further pursued reflection on its situation and its possibilities, grasps that in its free historical movement it projects for itself at every moment that horizon within which all questions must be decided. In reflection on the historical movement proper to it, humanity becomes aware of itself as summoned to freedom, to determine itself in mutually claimed and proffered freedom. Freedom in universal solidarity, to be realized in history, seems to designate the utmost limit of the thinkable. Even so, the question still must be asked whether in the very heart of this conception there exists an elementary aporia. This aporia becomes visible if one unfolds the conception of the unlimited communication community and its elementary determinations of reciprocity and universal solidarity in their historical dimensions.

The Relation of a Theory of Communicative Action to Dialectical-Reconstructive Theories of History

The ideal of freedom in universal solidarity exhibited in a theory of communicative action has implications for the theory of history. It entails on the one hand hypotheses about the direction and the basic tendency of the factual course of history and, on the other hand, methodological hypotheses for the treatment of history. These aspects are interdependent.

It has been shown that the insight into the communicative-practical character of historical action has shown that the purely positivist mode of understanding historical data is inadequate. Historical action can be grasped only if the methodology of its interpretation is determined by the normative implications of communicative action. This implies, then, that the factual state of history at any given time is studied in terms of the degree to which, despite its contradictions, it may be made intelligible as a development in the direction of this normative ideal. This interdependence of the reconstruction of history and the methodology of its reconstruction is unavoidable. The double character of this reconstruction, as both empirical and normative, holds true for all reconstructive theories of history since Hegel.

Recalling Hegel at this point is in no way arbitrary, since it is he who must be seen as the first to formulate and recognize all the dimensions of the problem indicated here. Because he rejects Kant's departure from an autonomous subject, the problem of the ethical order [Sittlichkeit] can emerge for Hegel only if a subject is constituted in his self-consciousness by another by being recognized by this other and recognizes the other as recognizing it.[81] This mutual constitution of subjects through mutually recognized free recognition of one by another is for Hegel the point of origin of the dialectic of Spirit and at the same time of the dialectic of historical development.

Hegel described the process in which this mutual recognition is reached as a life-and-death struggle, and in doing so he developed the categories by which Marx thought he was able to reconstruct the history of the human species.[82] Emerging first in the immediacy of its will to self-assertion as desire, self-consciousness has to be negated in its immediacy if it wants to recognize the other self-consciousness as of equal standing. It risks itself, as does the other, in order to achieve itself anew as mediated through the recognition of the other.

The achievement of self-consciousness thus occurs in the passage through one's own death and through the death of the other.[83] If this passage is successful, the self achieves the status in which it is both "free particularity" and "universal and objective."[84] However, so long as the "reflection in unity"[85] of mutual recognition has not been performed, the one self-consciousness is the master and the other is the slave.

The dialectic of master and slave consists in that the slave, in his "fear of death,"[86] externalizes himself for the master in work on the reality of things; however, in work as the reshaping of reality the slave can nonetheless find himself in relation to the master, who is still trapped in the assertion of his being for itself, and show his superiority over the master. The consciousness of the slave "becomes aware, through this rediscovery of himself by himself, of having and being a 'mind of its own' [eigener Sinn], precisely in labor, where it seemed to be merely some 'outsider's mind' [fremder Sinn]."[87]

Here we can see both historically and objectively the point from which the further development of the Hegelian system and the development of Marxian thought can be made understandable.

The great question remaining for the interpretation of Hegelian thought is whether the model of the mutual recognition of subjects — what was called "love" in Hegel's early religious writings — remains the basic model of thought, or whether the attempt has to be undertaken yet again in an abstract dialectic of reflection to surpass and abolish at one and the same time the factual finitude of subjects and the moment of the unconditionedness of their mutual recognition; that is to say, whether the other self-consciousness simply becomes "the other" which can be superseded. The conflict over Hegel's thought is the conflict about just how far this reflection may go. Also at stake here is what "death" and "the death of the other" mean for Hegel.

In Marx's attempt to grasp human labor as the transformation of nature and precisely in this way as self-transformation and to see in the dynamism of this dialectic the forces permitting a necessary revolutionizing of the social relations of production through the further development of the forces of production, it remains an open question whether the original goal of Hegel's entire analysis, namely the freedom of the mutual recognition of subjects, is not completely lost sight of as the normative foundation of such a conception. Were the answer to this question affirmative, then here would lie the roots of the hidden positivism of Marx's view.[88] Our concern here is not to do more exegesis of the central texts of Hegel and Marx; it should only be pointed out here that in a reconstruction of both Hegelian and Marxian thought in their historical dimension what is at issue is the basic normative structure of communicative action. The entire weight of this problem is concentrated in the question of whether the elementary postulates of reciprocity and solidarity are also valid in a dialectical-reconstructive theory of history.

Even a theory of communicative action has as its point of departure that the factual development of the human species from material need and from suffering under the compulsions of an uncomprehended nature on the one side and from a condition of social violence, exploitation, and oppression on the other side tends toward a condition in which the uncoerced, communicative agreement of subjects makes it possible to explain the emergence of suffering from material need, as well as from mechanisms of social violence, and to overcome it through common practice.[89]

However, if mutual recognition and universal solidarity are posited as the normative core of communicative action and, at the same time, as those dimensions of human action to be achieved in historical development, then the question is raised in a more pernicious form of how this solidarity is to be realized in history and how its claim can be resolved in the methodology of such reconstructions.

The past that is supposed to be reconstructed in a theory of history is certainly primarily the historical, communicative practice of subjects who in concretely coming to terms with nature and with the contradictions of their own society have also disclosed new orientations for their own action and for their progeny. This achievement of new orientations does not simply have the character of a theoretical debate; rather, it consists in the effective action of concrete subjects on themselves and others; that is, they may freely settle in mutual dependence what they want to be and finally what they can be. In this concrete action they disclose their possibilities for action and existence. This action expends the energy and time needed for living; the historical effort to transform existing relationships demands its victims. In what sense, however, can there then be a reconstruction of the past? In such reconstruction, is the central core of the past merely "grasped" conceptually, so that what can be used is prepared from the practice of subjects, so to speak, insofar as it points to the present and can be evaluated in it?

Are subjects themselves then only the refuse of a historical process that determines all that is of value? Do we not then surrender the concept of unconditioned and universal solidarity, which is supposed to be the condition of being oneself? Are subjects simply overwhelmed by the historical process and ignored in the reconstruction of history? The importance of this question shall be illustrated in the example of the debate between Walter Benjamin and Max Horkheimer and then in a more systematic reflection.

The Controversy over the Closed or Unclosed Past (Horkheimer vs. Benjamin)

In this context, one controversy could be of decisive significance: the controversy between Walter Benjamin and Max Horkheimer, which can be considered one of the most theologically significant controversies of our century.[90]

Early in 1937, Benjamin wrote an essay about Eduard Fuchs for Horkheimer's *Zeitschrift für Sozial Forschung* that he believed contained "a number of important reflections on dialectical materialism."[91] In the essay, Benjamin contended that even if the very concept of culture were problematic for the historical materialist, the notion that culture could completely decline into mere exchange commodities, to become mere objects of property, still remains for the historical materialist utterly unintelligible. "The work of the past is not closed for the historical materialist. He cannot see the work of an epoch, or any part of it, as reified, as literally placed in one's lap."[92]

Horkheimer later wrote to Benjamin about the passage that he had reflected for a long time on what it meant to say that the work of the past is closed. "The supposition of the unclosed past is idealistic, if a certain closedness has not been incorporated in it. Past injustice has occurred and is closed. Those who were slain in it were truly slain."[93] Horkheimer here expresses a basic conviction he often advanced in those years. "What happened to those human beings who have perished does not have any part in the future. They will never be called forth to be blessed in eternity. Nature and society have done their work on them, and the idea of the Last Judgment in which the infinite yearning of the oppressed and the dead is taken up once again is only a remnant from primitive thought which denied the negligible role of the human species in natural history and humanized the universe."[94] Horkheimer is indeed emphatic; "All these desires for eternity and above all for the entry of universal justice and goodness are what is common between the materialist thinker and the religious point of view, as opposed to the indifference of the positivist view. However, while the religious thinker is comforted by the thought that this desire is fulfilled all the same, the materialist is permeated with the feeling of the limitless abandonment of humanity, the single true answer to the hope for the impossible."[95]

Benjamin at first softens his view in response to Horkheimer's letter, but nonetheless says: "For me, your excursus on the closed or open work of the past is very significant."[96] It is conceivable that Benjamin only became aware of the explosiveness of the idea of the unclosed past in his debate with Horkheimer.[97] In any case, a straight line leads from this essay to Benjamin's last completed work, "Theses on the Concept of History" (usually referred to as "Theses on the Philosophy of History").[98] There Benjamin no longer talks about "objects of culture" or "the work of the past," but about "what is past" [*Vergangenen*], "what has been" [*Gewesenen*], "enslaved ancestors," "the generations of the downtrodden,"[99] and finally simply "the dead."[100] In these theses Benjamin's position in response to Horkheimer is expressed more clearly, especially with respect to a dimension that Horkheimer alluded to in his letter but that was not explicitly addressed by Benjamin himself. Horkheimer wrote: "In the end, your statements are *theological*."[101] Even in the proposal for his *Arcades* project Benjamin comments on Horkheimer's position: "The corrective for this sort of thinking lies in the reflection that history is not simply a science but a form of empathetic memory [*Eingedenken*]. What science has "settled," empathetic memory can modify. It can transform the unclosed (happiness) into something closed and the closed (suffering) into something unclosed. That is theology, certainly, but in empathetic memory we have an experience that prohibits us from conceiving history completely nontheologically, as little as we may want to try to write about history in immediately theological concepts."[102] Here Benjamin is obviously concerned about discovering a way of treating history without renouncing the elementary solidarity with the generations of the oppressed and the downtrodden, and about retaining this solidarity even while attempting to develop a theory of the writing of history. Any historical hermeneutics with the intent of constructing a "universal history"[103] has to make empathy with the victor[104] its methodological principle and becomes incapable of grasping "history as the history of the suffering (or Passion) of the world."[105] Such a hermeneutics also misses the task of theology. It abandons the "realm of truly historical, i.e., pragmatic-religious considerations."[106]

Benjamin's thought must be understood as the attempt, writ large (and here his dialogue with Horkheimer is further proof), to bring together historical materialism and theology, and to do so in such a way that historical materialism returns to elementary problems resulting from dealing with history and attempts then to indicate a common depth structure, which perhaps could be most clearly designated as "anamnestic solidarity"[107]—as solidarity confirmed in an empathetic memory, in the recollection of the dead and the downtrodden.

The Paradox of Anamnestic Solidarity

Next I would like to try to clarify the basic problem of the controversy between Horkheimer and Benjamin in its relevance to the above investigation. Christian Lenhardt has proposed a sort of thought experiment in this regard.[108] In a perhaps somewhat simplified typology of generations, the distinction can be made among a generation of oppressed, enslaved, unhappy ancestors (called the pre-world [Vor-welt] on the model of Alfred Schütz's terminology); a living, oppressed generation that, within the scheme of historical materialism, struggles for liberation (the co-world [Mit-welt]); and a future generation that achieves this liberation (the post-world [Nach-welt]).

When the concepts of universal solidarity and the unlimited communication community are tested in respect to this simplified typology, unanticipated difficulties and even contradictions arise for these concepts. In this typology, which fits any emancipatory theory of history and even any conception that the labor of historical action is for the greater happiness of others, the place of the oppressed ancestors is at first glance the least problematic. They do not owe anyone anything, but work for the better future of others. The fruits of their labor are received by the next generation, which struggles for its own liberation (and thus for the freedom of its progeny) conscious of the historical dimension of its task. This co-world can satisfy its debt to the pre-world by working for the happiness of the post-world. But what of the fate of the post-world? By definition, this generation is liberated; it has achieved the end state of happiness; its members can live with each other in perfect solidarity. But how is their relation to previous generations to be determined? They must live with the consciousness that they owe everything to the oppressed, the downtrodden, the victims of the prior process of liberation. This generation has inherited everything from the past generations and lives on what they have paid for. The exploited are no longer living among them, but are in the past, those who have gone before them. The happiness of the living exists in the expropriation of the dead. Is happiness at all conceivable under these presuppositions? Is it not the presupposition of happiness that the unhappiness of those who went before is simply forgotten? Is amnesia, the utter loss of historical memory, the presupposition of happy consciousness?

If the unconsciousness of world history is the presupposition of living happily, then is not the life of these human beings in this future inhuman? According to our previous analysis, unconditioned and universal solidarity with others was seen as the constitutive condition of one's own being human. How can one retain the memory of the conclusive, irretrievable loss of the victims of the historical process, to whom one owes one's entire happiness, and still be happy, still find one's identity? If for the sake of one's own happiness and one's own identity this memory is banished from consciousness, is this not tantamount to the betrayal of the very solidarity by which alone one is able to discover oneself?

Anamnestic solidarity marks, then, the most extreme paradox of a historically and communicatively acting entity; one's own existence becomes a self-contradiction by means of the solidarity to which it is indebted. The condition of its very possibility becomes its destruction. The idea of "perfect justice"[109] can only then become a nightmare. But does not this nightmare first shed light on the real situation? Horkheimer writes:

The thought is monstrous that the prayers of the persecuted in their hour of greatest need, that the innocent who must die without explanation of their situation, that the last hopes of a supernatural court of appeals, fall on deaf ears and that the night unilluminated by any human light is also not penetrated by any divine one. The eternal truth without God has as little ground and footing as infinite love; indeed, it becomes an unthinkable concept. But is the monstrousness of an idea any more a cogent argument against the assertion or denial of a state of affairs than does logic contain a law which says that a judgment is simply false that has despair as its consequence?[110]

Here the most extreme point of despair is reached, and, if despair does not kill, the point of inconsolable grief. The paradox of an existence that refuses to extinguish the memory of the victims of history in order to be happy is nonetheless the point at which the Jewish tradition most explicitly penetrates into this sort of thought. Horkheimer wrote, concerning Benjamin's refusal to declare the past to be finally closed, "Your statements are ultimately theological."[111] What sort of theology is this?

The Conception and the Status
of a Fundamental Theology

The Project of a Fundamental Theology

Where We Are in Our Investigation

The point we have reached in our investigation is not an arbitrary one. The question of a theory of communicative action proved to be the point of convergence of the methodological questions of theology and the theory of science. In the framework of this theory, we have inquired into the normative foundations of the sciences and practical action. The utmost limit of what is conceivable—the limit idea implied in communicative action itself—was shown to be the unlimited, universal communication community, the realization of freedom in solidarity through historical action. More precise analysis of these normative implications led, however, to the questions whether communicative action ends in a despairing self-contradiction, in absurdity, and whether a theory of this action is not itself self-contradictory. It is the experience that humans who have tried to act out of solidarity, those to whom we owe our own life possibilities, have been annihilated. The whole impact of this experience first becomes clear when it is viewed in its historical dimension. The normative implications of a theory of communicative action for the identity of subjects, as well as for the structure of society, end in aporia at the point where the attempt is made to conceive of the historical constitution of humanity united in solidarity.

We have attempted to explain the systematic significance of this problem. It is not the sort of problem that, like other aporetic questions, could be resolved once and for all by a wider, even more comprehensive theory at the same level, since it emerges within the concept of communicative practice (supposedly itself the condition of possibility of the clarification of theoretical and practical questions). If this practice becomes self-contradictory, must not the question of the basis of the common search for truth or of the orientation of action be posed all over again?[1]

For the most part, when faced with the annihilation of the innocent, thinkers in the Jewish tradition have decided for a factual surrender of solidarity, if theological discourse remains untouched by this experience. For Adorno, the Old Testament's prohibition of images not only forbids the mention of God's name; ". . . even just to think of hope is sacrilege and undermines it."[2] Theology is then itself precisely what ought not to be thought. But must one simply be mute in the face of the death of the other? Does not one in this way declare the other to be ultimately and irrevocably dead?[3]

The Return to Historical Experience and the Limit Questions of a Theory of Communicative Action

The attempt to live in solidarity despite the experience that others have been annihilated in this attempt clearly assumes the character of a paradigmatic, most extreme limit situation through the fact that in this situation we no longer have recourse to insights and principles outside of the situation itself; rather, in this situation it is only possible to indicate a communicative practice that has been risked and continues to be risked, as temporal, finite action in solidarity. Such an action can be referred only toward the sort of reality that is disclosed in it and made experienceable in communicative action. Only out of this practice and out of what is experienced in it may this activity and the reality it discloses be thematized.

Reflection then would be directed toward a practice not in any way derivable from a more comprehensive theory surpassing its limits. This practice would not be delineated theoretically; rather, as communicative practice, it would itself be the limit and the edge of every theoretical proposal. Theoretical reflection itself thus demands at this point a return to the most extreme forms of historical experience and practice.

To give a formal designation to the sort of thinking that stands up to this experience, one would have to point to the following context: Such thought can only be concerned with exhibiting the experience of a definite reality corresponding to a certain way of acting. The assertation of this reality then occurs in action. If the thinking of theology is to be situated in this limit realm, the theoretical task of theology consists in explaining this correlation of experienced reality and action.

If we start from the fact that the tradition of Judaism and Christianity is concerned with a dimension of experience indicated in the analysis of the paradox of anamnestic solidarity, then the claims of attempts oriented toward the theory of action to achieve a reconstruction of the rational core of the history of religion, and thus to establish the theory of action simply as a metatheory of religious consciousness, fails (at least in respect to this experience), for the systematic relevance of this paradox consists precisely in the failure of any theory that attempts to explain it.[4] But then it must be asked whether the conception of the theory of action would not then have to be formulated even more radically. It seems that an investigation of the elementary postulates of interaction—unconditional equality, reciprocity, and solidarity—run up against the limits of any previously analyzed theory in three ways:

• The unconditional recognition of the equal standing of the communication partner excludes any attempts at force, deception, or manipulation. The other is accepted as one who, in anticipating the future in an unmanipulable, free, innovative way, is capable of actively disclosing new possibilities of action for others. The refusal to revert to force and manipulation is the recognition of an indisposable freedom, reciprocally demanded and granted in such a way that both partners enter into the event of intersubjective, historical freedom. At this point, can we ever afford to exclude the classical question of any theory of freedom, that of the source whence this freedom is provoked? Can we simply leave aside the question of an absolute freedom as the presupposition of finite historical freedom?

• In the previous analyses, the temporal structure of communicative action was hardly touched upon. However, this is one of the basic problems of both the theory of science and the theory of communicative action, and a possible source of important impetus for new approaches in research. The detemporalization of action is thus dependent on the fact that the analytic tools of the empirical sciences do not yet contain a fully developed logic of time.[5] If this were to be developed, it would permit the theoretical representation of speech as temporal action in connection with the tools of modal logic, i.e., a logic of possible worlds, which has already proved fruitful in linguistics. Communication could then be more precisely investigated in its structure as the action of subjects related to each other in dialogue processes: as the process of the constitution of a common world through the action of subjects reciprocally related to each other, each from his own perspective; as innovative transformation of common reality and of self-consciousness.[6] But this does not yet enter upon a problem area that up to now could only be explicated through a set of problems from the history of philosophy. Relying on Kierkegaard, Heidegger's analyses of the temporal structure of existence and action culminated in showing that authentic existence represents an anticipation of one's own death. However, as I have tried to show, the analysis of authentic intersubjectivity nonetheless fails precisely because death is only seen as individualized. A theory of temporal, communicative action in which one's own death and the death of another are both incorporated as the farthest horizon of consciousness is yet to be developed.

• The question of the possibility of historical freedom in the framework of a theory of communicative action is made even more acute in the attempt to exist in universal solidarity, when solidarity is extended to those who have been destroyed and annihilated as victims of historical processes. Can we simply exclude the question of a reality to which communicative action in solidarity is directed? Precisely at this point, does not the theory of communicative action pose the question of the reality that is the subject matter of theology, the question of a reality witnessed for the other in the face of his death by acting in solidarity with him?

The Question of a Possible Conception of Theology

The demonstration of the aporetic limit problems of the theory of science, of the theory of action that was to found the former on a new basis, and of the recourse to experience and to practice does not condemn theology to sheer arbitrariness. Instead, in the new situation of conversation it is challenged to give an account of its basic conception, i.e., its understanding of reality and its access to it, as well as of the possibility of speaking intelligibly about it.

Inasmuch as the critique of theology in modern times does not dispute the very possibility of theology, its intent is to uncover the ideological or illusory character of specific theological constructions and in this way force theology to come to its authentic subject matter.[7]

The awareness of being capable of missing the mark of the very subject matter is integral to theology as well, and compels it to thematize its own point of departure. We have interpreted essential stages of the history of theology in this century as a sequence of attempts to demarcate the basic conceptual framework of a kind of foundational theory of theology in such a way that the reality that is the subject of its discourse is determined and at the same time disclosed in its basic structure; indeed, this is true for a theology starting from a finite freedom that transcends toward an absolute freedom as liberating reality, or for a theology that can only conceive of the relationship of finite and absolute freedom in intersubjectivity, or for a theology that can only conceive of the transcending freedom of subjects as the attempt to realize freedom in society.

I would like to advance two theses in response to this situation. First, I want to assert that the Judeo-Christian tradition is concerned with the reality experienced in the foundational and limit experiences of communicative action and with the modes of communicative action still possible in response to these experiences. Second, I want to assert that a fundamental theology can and must be developed as a theory of this communicative action of approaching death in anamnestic solidarity and of the reality experienced and disclosed in it. This theology is fundamental in the sense that it denotes the originary access to the reality intended in theology, it assigns the basic structure of this reality and possible experiences and action in light of it (indeed, in such a way that a theory of the subject, of society, and of history can also be achieved through this theory of communicative action), and it elucidates the possibility of the reflective theoretical presentation of this reality in terms of these modes of access and basic structures.

Anyone who is aware of the complexity of contemporary research in exegesis and systematic theology will readily admit that the task of a complete elaboration and grounding of these theses cannot be accomplished by one individual alone. To this extent, the following reflections should be treated only as preliminary analyses.[8]

Experiences of the Foundations and Limits of Communicative Action in the Judeo-Christian Tradition

Preliminary Remarks on Methodology

The contemporary state of Old and New Testament research seems to be characterized by a profusion of individual investigations, executed with highly differentiated methods, to which there corresponds no generally acknowledged hermeneutic conception of the whole that would allow the texts to be disclosed in their depth structure and in their basic statements.

The hermeneutic approach of existential interpretation marked the breakdown of the positivist procedures of historicism and joined together systematic and historical-critical interpretation. (The classic example of this is still Bultmann's *Commentary on the Gospel of John.*) The critical destruction of this approach and the extension of the problematic into the dimensions of intersubjectivity, society, and history have not yet produced a conception that could even remotely claim a similar systematic coherence. There is, rather, a tendency toward a relapse into objectivistic historicism. The reception of questions and conceptions from linguistics has not yet brought about a decisive turn; on its own terms, this is indeed hardly possible. We shall return to this point later.

The following fragmentary remarks are also the result of this situation of hermeneutical embarrassment. Their claims are limited for that reason, but they have two primary functions for our investigation. First, they are supposed to point out the dimensions of experience and the structures of communicative action with regard to which the hermeneutic power of previous reconstructions of the history of religion within the framework of a theory of action has broken down up to now. Moreover, they are supposed to identify those phenomena in relation to which the categories of a fundamental theology, which for the most part are yet to be developed, must prove their worth. The following remarks are therefore not to be understood as exactly grounded historical theses, but rather as heuristic hypotheses to guide further inquiry.

The formal organization of these remarks is oriented toward the limit questions uncovered in a theory of communicative action, namely the question of the normative structure of intersubjective, reciprocally oriented communicative action in unconditional solidarity and its relation to an absolute freedom; the question of the crisis befalling communicative action and the understanding of the reality of God as absolute freedom, when those who attempt to act in correspondence with this basic normative structure are annihilated; and the question of what sort of conception of communicative action we can still hold good after we have undergone this crisis, i.e., if the past is not going to be simply extinguished from consciousness, and if action is sustained in a universal horizon.

I shall assume that these questions correspond to the basic experiences of the Judeo-Christian tradition, and that the experiences witnessed in the New Testament further radicalize Old Testament experience and questions.

Remarks on the Tradition of Judaism and Israel

The Basic Experience and Its Inner Law

The most basic fact of Jewish consciousness is the experience of the liberation from slavery. This experience is remembered, in ever renewed actualizations, as the Exodus of a group of conscripted laborers, held captive in Egypt as a cheap labor force, who began to trust in a reality that showed itself to them as a saving, bestowing power of absolute freedom ("I shall be the one who shall be there for you always"[9]).

The experience of liberation remains fundamental. However, it is grasped only if it is understood as a liberation to a freedom which has to be reciprocally granted in changing social constellations. It excludes the oppression of human beings by each other, and it contradicts the unfreedom into which human beings bring each other. The basic historical experience of liberation from the house of slavery of the great world power of Egypt lays claim to normative status even for later generations; such an experience demands to be remembered and to have its claim socially realized in an ongoing way. This is not merely a matter of private relationships. The touchstone of justice is to be found in specific socially neglected groups, such as widows, orphans, the poor, or foreigners—"You shall not pervert the justice due to the sojourner or to the fatherless, or take a widow's garment on pledge; but you shall remember that you were a slave in Egypt and the Lord your God redeemed you from there; therefore I command you to do this."[10]

The prophets radically proclaim the normative weight of this basic experience. Their elementary demand is the intersubjective action demanded and made possible through absolute liberating freedom in unconditional solidarity and equality. The "social" dimension of the prophetic proclamation is not secondary. Criticism of culture and criticism of society are correlative here.[11] The cultic attempt to approach God the redeemer from slavery becomes a perversion and cries out for condemnation so long as others are enslaved.

The claim of this basic relationship, in which the recognition of the unconditional equality of the other is the condition of access to and acceptance of God, loses its former merely national limitations in prophetic proclamation. (See for example Lev. 25:44–46a to 26:46b ff.) It becomes universal. From Amos to the book of Jonah, an ethnocentric conception of divine election, insofar as it is supposed to legitimate the refusal to extend solidarity beyond one's own people and does not make obligatory the commitment to this unlimited solidarity, is attacked.

The basic experience of the Old Testament has as its inner "law" that unconditional, unrestricted solidarity with the other is possible only through the experience of the turning toward us of the reality of God as absolute, liberating freedom. The relation to God is then possible only in the turning to [Zuwendung] the other in solidarity; the turning to the other is only possible in the turning to God as liberating freedom.

The Crisis of the Basic Experience: The Lamenter, the Persecuted Prophet, the Suffering Servant of the Lord
The basic experience of liberation through Yahweh, with its normative claim, is called into question at the point where someone is destroyed precisely because he allows this claim to enter into his actions.

The experience of the failure of the just is in the first instance a prophetic experience. However, it also enters into the traditions as a general experience given cultic formulation in the texts of prayers of lamentation and accusation. The believer calls for deliverance not only from the oppression of physical need, threats, or sickness but also from the experience of being persecuted *because* he tries to live in justice. The desperate struggle to be heard by a higher authority is a struggle concerning the reality of God. The end of the Psalms of Lamentation speaks about being raised up or saved in a way that is hardly understandable. Indeed, this sort of speech occurs in precisely those psalms that cannot be read as text formulas for institutionalized procedures for the absolution of guilt.[12] In these texts, God is affirmed for the one praying as the reality who saves those who are threatened with death because of their attempts to live a just life, the reality that saves those who cry for help from these threats. (See, for example, Ps. 21.)

The question of the reality that can be called God is radicalized in two ways in the prophetic tradition. First, it becomes a matter of the real death of those who try to live in solidarity. Second, by recognizing previous history as the inheritance of guilt, the prophet achieves solidarity not only with the oppressed but also with the guilty; the question of the reality of God originates from his fate.

Most explicitly in the Deuteronomic tradition,[13] the prophet is presented almost according to a fixed scheme. He protests against perversions of the relation to Yahweh—against equating Yahweh to a god to be manipulated in cult—and at the same time against perversions of the relation to the other, and for this he is persecuted and destroyed. This surpasses the situation of Job. Indeed, the book of Job is also concerned with the question of what reality in general may properly be called God. Viewed formally, the book of Job has the character of a trial. Job strains to obtain a guilty verdict against God. He appeals to a higher authority to condemn God, who has allowed him, the innocent one, to suffer. The prophet goes beyond this, since the prophet is pursued and destroyed on account of his solidarity with others. The paradigm for this is Jeremiah: he rails against the day of his birth because of his fate (Jer. 20:14–18). What finally happens to this prophet remains obscure; he is simply swallowed up. But the influence of this figure on the later tradition is fundamental and unmistakable. The question of the fate of the prophets and of the reality which may be called God becomes the central question of the tradition.

The question whether one who lives in unconditional solidarity to the point of annihilation is simply and finally annihilated is especially characteristic of Deutero-Isaiah's *Songs of the Suffering Servant*. Here a figure is depicted who suffers for the guilt of others and is destroyed for it. (Isa. 52:13–53:12) At this point—as the multiplicity of disparate interpretations shows—not only are the boundaries of the extent of mere semantic analysis reached, but evidently even the analysis of the communicative structure of the text, and thus of what is supposed to be communicated at all, reach a limit.

In a form that switches between direct discourse by God and a funeral dirge, it is said of the servant of the Lord, who cannot be further identified, he has been murdered in solidarity with the guilty, in a suffering intercession for them, for the "multitude." It is said of this figure that God saves him and lifts him up in his downfall. This assertion is put in the mouth of God himself. By letting God himself speak in this way, the text affirms God as the reality for the other, for one who suffers in solidarity; the reality of God proves itself as a reality, inasmuch as God saves those who live in solidarity unto death in death. This reaches the limits of what can be said. At the same time, possibilities of understanding and action are opened up, to be taken up again by Jesus or at any rate by the Christian tradition.

Solidarity with the Dead and the Question of a Just God
From a historical perspective, we could advance the hypothesis that the prophetic tradition was chiefly responsible for the survival and regeneration of Judaism in the Babylonian exile after the destruction of all its important institutions (the temple, the royal palace, etc.). This may itself be due to the fact that the destruction threatened by the prophets actually took place. But surely more important in this context was the fact that knowledge of one's own guilt and its historical consequences could be withstood only in a trusting relation to some reality, to what according to the prophetic witness is shown to be redeeming in this very destruction, indeed redeeming even in death.

Ezekiel's vision of the valley of the dead bones (Ezek. 37:1–14) may be placed in this tradition. In a situation where the very existence of Israel was threatened, the prophet, who had taken upon himself the burden of the guilt of Israel and Judah as its representative in his vicarious, physical, symbolic act of laying himself upon the ground, utters the life-renewing word to those who are hopeless and lost: "Thus says the Lord God: Behold I will open your graves, O my people, and I will bring you home unto the land of Israel and you shall know that I am the Lord, when I open your graves and raise you from your graves, O my people." (Ezek. 37:12 ff.)

The historical rebirth of Israel after the Exile is thus mediated through the experience of the prophets, who, in all the ambivalence of prophetic visionary speech, proclaim Yahweh as the one who shows himself in the moment of annihilation, who opens the graves of the dead.

The general hope in God as the reality who saves the dead has various origins in concrete religious history, of course. What may be most important here is the return to the old traditions that Yahweh's power and his unconditional will to justice are not limited, even by death. The wicked do not escape from Yahweh: "Though they dig into the underworld, from there shall my hand take them." (Amos 9:2; cf. Ps. 139:8) This unconditional will to justice is obviously also the underlying motive of the apocalyptic tradition. Its development is not at all clear, especially in its relationship to social history.[14]

During the persecution by the Syrian kings (above all by Antiochus IV, around 160 B.C.), Judaism was confronted with the fact that innocent and just people had to suffer violent and premature deaths. This posed the question whether justice would ever be done to those murdered despite their innocence. At first, this was restricted to the particularistic hope that the innocent dead of Israel would be resurrected to participate in the future salvation at the end time.[15] Later this idea was extended universally to the expectation of the resurrection to Judgment and to the addressing of the balance of justice for all. This hope distinguishes much of later Judaism.[16]

In the explosive development of the apocalyptic tradition, hope is placed in a God who will make the dead live again, who will transform the entire existing order of the world in a cataclysm and thereby inaugurate a kingdom of justice.

Remarks on the New Testament Tradition

The Action and Proclamation of Jesus

From the perspective of the Old Testament tradition, the proclamation of Jesus presents itself as concentration and radicalization; from the viewpoint of a theory of communicative action, it may appear as a paradigm for elementary structures of human interaction as such. The formulation of the two laws that are generally considered to be the core of Christianity speaks for itself: "You shall love the Lord your God with all your heart and with all your soul and with all your mind. This is the first and greatest commandment. And the second is like it, you shall love your neighbor as yourself. On these two command-ments depend all the law and the prophets." (Matt. 22:37–40) Never-theless, the importance and the precise meaning of this statement must still be seen in its historical context.

It may be said that in the study of the New Testament there is a general methodological consensus that the proclamation of Jesus can be reconstructed only in correspondence with his speech and actions. Proclamation and action mutually interpret each other and cannot be separated.[17] Even his proclamation is not objectivating doctrine but rather linguistic action; it uncovers and changes the existing situation through the Beatitudes, the prophetic call, the threat, the contrasting comparisons, through illumination in the style of Wisdom literature, through the telling of parables. The hermeneutics of this state of affairs demands a comprehensive concept of communicative action. However, the activity of Jesus has one central theme: the imminence of the Kingdom of God. Although for any such historical reconstruction the apocalyptic movements[18] of the time must be seen as a general back-ground, the proclamation of Jesus differs significantly from them.

In apocalyptic literature the concept of the "Kingdom of God" plays almost no role,[19] whereas Jesus took this concept out of the hidden reaches of the religious-theological language of his time and made it the "central concept" or "framework concept" of his proclamation.[20] In it, the dualistic motifs and speculation about the end of the world and the breakthrough of the coming age through a destructive catas-trophe fall into the background. Yet a further difference from the apocalyptic tradition consists in the fact that Jesus incorporates not only eschatological traditions but also Wisdom traditions concerning God's action in creation: Divine creation only now is established; the damaged, exploited, distorted creation is now to be restored.[21]

Jesus must certainly be seen in close historical proximity with the prophetic proclamation of John the Baptist. However, for the Baptist the motif of Judgment was totally dominant, even though he makes scarcely any use of apocalyptic ideas, whereas for Jesus the promise of salvation in the urgent situation of the present time of decision has unequivocal precedence.[22] The coming of the Kingdom is a last, decisive offer of salvation [Heilsgebot], and Jesus understands himself as one element in this event. He claims to realize already in his actions an anticipation of the eschatological Lordship of God. Other groups also thought such an anticipation was possible. The Zealots wanted to bring about the irruption of the kingdom through holy war against the Romans. For the people of Qumran, eschatological salvation could be made present through the strict observation of the law in a closed community. In the Talmudic literature, there is a notion of deeds that, as it were, help bring about redemption. For Jesus, however, those acts that anticipate the completion of the Kingdom and make its imminence experienceable are not to be found in holy war, in strict observance of the law, or in penitential exercises, but rather in an immediate turning to others that even surpasses the Law itself. This turning to others extends precisely to the poor, the sick, the oppressed, the guilty, the outcasts of society.

The Kingdom of God can be made present for others because it has drawn near on its own. When Jesus exorcizes demons, heals the sick, and sits at table with social outcasts, the future Kingdom of God is already being realized.[23] From these beginnings provided in the actions of Jesus, it prevails irresistibly "by itself." (Mark 4:28) This awareness may be illustrated in the parables of contrast.

Jesus understands his own actions as believing anticipation.[24] He "dares" to enter into the urgent nearness of God's reign. [25] He anticipates the completion of the Kingdom of God, which yearns for its fulfillment, by asserting the reality of God and his salvation for others. However, Jesus makes such an assertion not merely in theory but in his preaching and acting, in the performance of his existence as communicative practice. He *is* this assertion for others.

In this way Jesus exists radically for God, by asserting this God for others practically and by making this God experienceable in his action as a healing, forgiving, saving reality. By acting in solidarity for others, he asserts God as the saving reality distinct from himself.

It must be assumed that Jesus understands himself precisely in terms of this reality, which he asserts and makes present for others in his actions—that is, he understands himself in terms of others.[26]

In the study of the New Testament, this context of action, proclamation, the determination of the reality of God, and Jesus' self-understanding is treated in the analysis of the parables of Jesus more than anywhere else. The different aspects of Jesus' talking in parables have been investigated quite intensively in recent years.[27]

Jesus' debate with his opponents about the claim to make present the Kingdom of God for others in his own actions can be seen as the original "speech situation" of the parables. Thus, as speech actions related to specific situations, the parables are attempts to overcome this conflict through disclosing insights into the reality that can rightly be called God, and they thereby also reveal new possibilities of understanding reality, of self-understanding, and of common action.

The basic conflict in the attacks on Jesus centers on his siding with "tax collectors and sinners"—socially and religiously stigmatized groups—in his actions, as for example by eating with them.[28] The dispute about the legitimacy of this partisanship has thereby all the characteristics of a dispute about the principles of the "social construction of reality" (Berger, Luckmann), and as such it is a dispute over how the reality of God and his Lordship must be understood. Thus the dispute about a specific mode of communicative action is at the same time a dispute about the reality of God. The telling of parables becomes a means to resolve this conflict.

The parables propose an alternative world, with other things taken for granted. The specific connection with the situation of conflict is achieved through the distantiated mode of linguistic expression of certain models of behavior through the medium of the parable. In this way, models of action are uncovered and put into question. At the same time, other possibilities of action are disclosed in the narrative. The intentions of speech action of telling parables are to surpass the present situation in the distantiated mode of the narrative, to shake the given understanding of reality, and to disclose new possibilities of action and new ways of understanding reality.

Primarily through the narrating of unexpected events (the patriarchal father begins to run, the vineyard owner gives away a day's wages, the banker forgives debts, etc.), the operation of fictive distantiated speech points to another reality that can only be understood as unconditionally good but that, as the unconditional good, is self-evident and disrupts all previous orientations of action. In the speech act of the parable a new possibility of action is opened up; a reality is referred to that makes room for this new possibility of action in the current situation of conflict and distorted communication.

Jesus does not simply legitimize his own actions and the actions of others now made possible by means of reference to his own person. Rather, the distantiating representation of the parable points to a reality that is not simply identical with himself, but which he makes experienceable as reality in his action, a reality which completely determines his communicative practice and which demands and makes possible a new sort of behavior. "So shall it be in the reign of God." Talk about God and his lordship is thus strictly introduced and substantiated action in a specific situation. The determination of the reality of God is bound to a specific mode of communicative practice and occurs in action directed toward others. With his existence and in his actions, Jesus asserts God as the saving reality for others.

It is certainly probable that Jesus went to his death with the awareness of making present eschatological salvation in his action and in his existence and that he understood his surrender in death as the most extreme consequence and fulfillment of this surrender.[29]

The Experience of the Death of Jesus and the Question of the Reality of God
Jesus asserted in his speech and action—in the manner of his factual existence—that God is the saving reality for the poor, the outcast, the lost. His execution must have forced an elementary question on his disciples: Did not this assertion hold for Jesus himself in his own death? The death of Jesus brings with it a change in perspective: Jesus had asserted the reality of God for others. Can one assert the saving reality of God for him in his own death?

The change in perspective entering into the experience of the death of Jesus also radicalizes the question of the reality of God. The Passion narratives intend to make clear that here the most extreme experiences of the Old Testament are attained and surpassed. It is possible that the idea of the fate of the persecuted prophet determined not only the presentation of the way of Jesus to the cross but also his own self-understanding.[30] The texts explicitly hark back to the Psalms of Lamentation and to the Songs of the Suffering Servant.[31] The Gospel of Mark represents Jesus as the just man crying to God in his death throes, dying with the question of why God has forsaken him.

The Passion narratives show Jesus as one who took his stand for God, was delivered over to his enemies in a relentless trial, and was put to death. In this presentation, the question of the reality of God is posed. If the one who in his existence asserts God for others is himself annihilated, is this assertion then not refuted? How can we still talk about God at all? Does not the attempt at an existence that asserts an unconditional reality for others lead to absurdity? If one does not simply extinguish this fate from consciousness, how can one still exist without despair?

The Gospels and the entire Christian proclamation are unequivocal about these questions. They profess that God resurrected Jesus from the dead and showed him to be saved, living, and not annihilated.

The interpretation of the resurrection of Jesus admittedly raises complex hermeneutical questions about the possible basic concepts of theology as a whole.[32] However, it is clear what dimensions are included in the experience and the proclamation of the resurrection of Jesus. The divinity of God is revealed; that is, God shows himself as the power that saves a man in death.[33] Jesus is finally saved and confirmed as the one who existed for others unto death and the one who actualized the saving reality of God for them. The experience of the resurrection of Jesus signifies for others the opening of the possibility of existing in solidarity oriented toward God by having recourse to his death and his resurrection.

An adequate interpretation of this experience would, however, require an adequately developed conception of existing unto death, precisely as an experience in the dimension of intersubjectivity. The temporality of communicative action would have to be developed in its relation to the death of others and its relation to God as the reality who saves others in death.[34]

Making Possible an Anamnestic Existence in Universal Solidarity
In the understanding of the New Testament, the act of the resurrection of Jesus makes possible faith in this resurrection and thus makes possible an existence that hopefully anticipates the completion of salvation for all. God's act of resurrection makes possible an existence that asserts God as the unconditionally saving reality for Jesus and—in anticipation of completion—for everyone. Faith is a remembering assertion of the saving reality for Jesus and at the same time the assertion of the reality of God for all others.

Faith is itself a practice that, as a practice, asserts God for others in communicative action and attempts to confirm this assertion in action. Faith in the resurrection of Jesus is faith as communicative action factually anticipating salvation for others and thus for one's own existence. As practical solidarity with others, it signifies the assertion of the reality of God for them and for one's own existence.

The resurrection of Jesus can be understood as the empowerment to live such an existence and to witness it for others—that is, to manifest the possibility of such an existence through the manner of one's own existence, through one's own communicative action. The experience of the resurrection is always understood by its New Testament witnesses as the enablement to believe and at the same time as the mission to bear witness to this faith, which is the anamnesis of his death and of his being saved in death. As anamnestic solidarity with Jesus made possible through his life and the action of God in and toward him, faith in the resurrection of Jesus is at once solidarity with all others. And as anamnestic solidarity, it is universal solidarity in the horizon of all humanity and of one unified history; it constitutes one humanity in the unconditional solidarity of communicative action that anticipates the completion of salvation for all.

This universal solidarity must be realized in concrete actions of individuals in relation to each other. Interacting in terms of the experience of possible solidarity with the crucified Jesus means asserting God as the reality that unconditionally stands on the side of the other. The radicality with which the other is affirmed is the basic practical demand in terms of which the structure of any society is to be measured; the affirming of the other in the manner of asserting God as absolute reality for the other in death excludes oppression. Jesus' assertion that God is there for the other as unconditional goodness and love is confirmed conclusively in his resurrection. It becomes the normative core of communicative action in the dimensions of society and thus implies the demand of social freedom and solidarity.

A theology of resurrection that takes seriously the assertions of Jesus in his communicative action and conceives them as at once the empowering ground and the standard of one's actions can ultimately only be developed as a theory of history and a theory of society. A foundational theory of theology therefore would have to be developed in this context as a theory of the possible identity of subjects, as a theory of communicative action, as a theory of society, and as a theory of history.

Conception and Status of a Fundamental Theology

The Question of the Foundations of Theology as Theory and the Question of the Status of This Theory

This glance at the Judeo-Christian tradition suggests that it is concerned with the most extreme experiences of communicative action and thus with the communicability of these experiences. Can there be something like a theory of this action and these limit experiences? Can theology be understood as science? As a science, can theology be grounded in a sort of foundational theory, precisely a fundamental theology?

The foundation theory of any science would be concerned first with the disclosure of a realm of reality, second with its linguistic apprehension, differentiation and identification, and third with its reflective communication in language.

In the first part of this investigation we reviewed various conceptions of theology that can claim to be fundamental theologies in this sense. We cannot regress behind their insights. Bultmann began with transcending human existence and made clear that discourse about God can be had only at the price of achieving discourse about one's own existence; that is, theology is the reference to possibilities of existence, and its theoretical status is the indication of a possibility of existence grounded in the dialectic of existence itself. Rahner made it clear that any theological discourse that in its structure is not determined by the experience of the absolute mystery and not understood as an indirect mediation of such experience loses sight of its proper object. The emphasis of Metz and Moltmann on the eschatological and social-critical dimension of theology does not simply try to demonstrate the liberating power of the substance of theology against ideological distortions but rather intends to ground theological discourse itself as ideological-critical discourse pointing ahead to an eschatological fulfillment. Metz writes: "Eschatology is not simply a region of Christian theology; it must be understood radically: as the form of *all* theological statements."[35] The question of a foundational theory is therefore not foreign to theology.[36]

In relation to the discussion of the theory of science in the human sciences, and above all in relation to the extensive debate about a theory of the foundations of the social sciences, a fundamental theology must give an account of the way in which theoretical reflection in theology is linked methodologically to basic communicative actions, or to the foundational actions of subjects themselves. Even this need not be foreign to theology, since its subject matter is related to the elementary accomplishments of human existence as possessing a communicative and reciprocal-reflective character.

Insofar as theology is supposed to be done in a methodologically verifiable manner and wants to prove itself in this sense in relation to other scientific disciplines, its position within the contemporary discussion of the theory of science is all the more peculiar. We have seen that the question of grounding the individual sciences, like the question of the grounding of scientific rationality as a whole, refers back to a theory of communicative action. But such a theory becomes problematic in the limit experiences of communicative action. We could show that at least the traditions of Judaism and Christianity are concerned with experiences in dimensions that show the failure of previously developed theories of action as metatheories. Even before this we saw that, for example, a theory of science in the classical sense or a theory of evolution developed from systems theory is not sufficient for the clarification of the theoretical foundations of theology.

In this situation the attempt could of course be made to ground theology in terms of theories starting from the concept of human freedom, either by trying to gain the concept of absolute freedom from the concept of human freedom as its implicit presupposition or by conceiving of the historical process itself as a history of emancipation, that is, as the ever-increasing realization of human freedom. The first way would be essentially identical with classical Idealism. We must not fall behind its insights; the development of a concept of God demands the development of categories of freedom.[37] Precisely in the late forms of Idealism, however, the factual experience of evil forces a problem of self-legitimation.[38] The transcendental idea of an absolute freedom cannot evade the classical question of theodicy. In the contemporary situation, we must begin with the fact that the question of God is already concretely derived from the disappointment in a conception of God as absolute being, or as absolute freedom. The question of theodicy cannot be a mere afterthought to the development of the question of God; it is at its very root.[39] The second way mentioned above consists in the attempt to think of freedom as the historical result of the forward-directed process of emancipatory action. This attempt then falls into aporia if freedom is understood as real in intersubjectivity and if the naiveté of the concept of a unified humanity aware of solidarity only in the future is penetrated. We analyzed this aporia as the paradox of anamnestic solidarity and showed it to be the basic problem of a theory of intersubjectivity.

It seems that the unresolved problems of a theory of the subject, as well as those of a theory of society and of history, thus converge in the basic problem of communicative action, namely the problem of the possibility of solidarity with those who are innocently annihilated. This problem too denotes the basic experience preoccupying the Jewish and Christian traditions.

What does this say about the possibility of theology as a theory? We could simply propose the usual procedure of the day-to-day business of science, namely, to treat certain basic aporias as "limit questions" and finally marginal questions that cannot hinder what goes on in the limited realm where one can unequivocally ask limited questions and get unequivocal answers. This procedure is indeed legitimate inasmuch as the theoretical claim raised in it remains limited and as long as the charge of an "unscientific attitude" is not leveled against those who pose the question of the foundations and the possibility of science as such. But theology can have no part in such a procedure, at least where it is understood as fundamental or systematic theology; that is, insofar as it makes the claim of being able to account for the problem of its own foundation as theology and for the basic experiences of the Judeo-Christian tradition.

According to our entire previous discussion, no other possibility exists for the foundations of theology than to try to analyze communicative action in its basic experiences yet another time, as they may be paradigmatically reconstructed in the potential for experience in the Judeo-Christian tradition and thereby indicate the possibility of a responsible discourse about God from these basic experiences. This is what shall be attempted in these last pages.

I shall first attempt to analyze systematically the question of the reality of God in terms of the basic experience of the paradox of universal solidarity, and thus I shall discuss and more closely describe the introduction of the discourse about the reality of God. Accordingly, I would like to characterize the conception of a fundamental theology as a theory of communicative action in universal solidarity, account for the theoretical status of this conception, and outline the dimensions of this theory.

If the following hints often have the character of open questions, this is due in part to the contemporary state of the theological discussion as a whole. This state is, of course, not the responsibility of theology alone. The question of the theory of communicative action is the problem at the foundations of the theory of science as a whole. If theology poses these problems for itself, it therefore has as its central concern the meaning of knowledge and action itself, the temporality of this sort of action, its construction and reconstruction, and what it means for any statement to be related to reality. This concerns not only theology but also the basic questions of the other sciences. This corresponds to the insight that theology can be done only by passing through the methodologically controlled processes of knowledge in the other sciences.

Systematic Reconstruction of the Question of the Reality of God

In accordance with the preceding, we shall attempt to unfold the question of the reality of God, and thus the questions of how the reality intended in this question may be determined, identified, and ultimately named in language, in such a way that we shall once more analyze the most extreme limit situation of communicative action, its inner contradiction, and the experience of reality, as well as the assertion of a reality, implicit in enduring communicative action.

Communicative action is, as has been indicated, directed in its very structure toward the mutual recognition of the equal standing and unconditional solidarity of the partners. The possibility of the partner's finding identity depends on this reciprocal solidarity, which is comprehensive of basically all dimensions of existence in intersubjectivity and which, in principle, also incorporates all possible subjects of communicative action. This solidarity is accomplished in temporal, innovative communicative action disclosing and opening up possibilities of action for others. The basic *a priori* law posited in this action is thus universal solidarity in historical freedom.

There are basic experiences that radically call into question this normative structure of action and the possibility of its theoretical comprehension. The most extreme of these counterexperiences can be characterized in the following way: It is a fact that those human beings who have sought to act in solidarity, to whom we owe the very possibilities of our own lives, have been annihilated without blame or guilt. This experience is analytically significant, since it contains and surpasses the other aporetic experiences. It contains the experience that one person can give to or take away from another the very possibilities of life and that one is thereby indebted to the other and owes this person something. It contains the experience of pain, sickness, and the factual contingency of existence. Finally, it contains the experience of death, in such a way that the other is irrevocably taken from us, so that there is no more possibility of making good his suffering. The possibility of reciprocal presence in action is destroyed. This experience is also heuristically significant, in that, as a negative experience, it uncovers dimensions of action that remain hidden in everyday interaction. This experience is also systematically significant, in that the basic normative structure of interaction, namely reciprocity and solidarity, is destroyed as a possibility of action. However, the same structure assured the possibility of the identity of subjects. The actor is hence threatened with destruction at the very core of his being.[40]

What possibilities of action are still available at all in and after such an experience? One could imagine the attempt to completely exclude the memory of the other; this would finally be identical with the attempt to deny reality. Moreover, one could cynically conclude from the experience of the annihilation of anyone who acts in solidarity that everyone should simply use all possibilities of action optimally for oneself alone; solidarity too would then be surrender as the basic principle of the achievement of one's own identity; communicative action would then degenerate into purely strategic action in one's own interest. Even more naive or resigned, ultimately, would be the attempt to allow oneself to retreat to the conception of oneself as a limited natural being in a gruesome struggle of mutual destruction and thus to again regress behind the threshold of the achievement of a basic norm of communication.

Is nonetheless an action conceivable that holds onto the principle of unconditional solidarity in action and yet does not repress from awareness the fate of the innocently annihilated, but rather preserves it by remembering it? How is such a memory even thinkable? If the other is viewed as a reciprocally recognized and recognizing partner in action, his death can no longer simply be ascertained as a matter of fact. The memory of the other as the one who acted for the benefit of the one who is now remembering is only possible in such a way that one returns to the possibilities of action opened up by the one who has gone to his death; hence, he is present, remembered and affirmed as an actor in the other's practice of communicative action. However, opposed to this presence and affirmation is the well-established fact that the other has ultimately been annihilated in his innocence and that one benefits from his annihilation. To simply direct one's solidarity to others and finally to the future generations does not resolve this inner contradiction.

The analysis of this aporetic situation now demands insights into the structure of interaction related to death. In this area the first rough sketches of a more precise analysis are hardly evident. Even in the natural sciences, there is much that could be of significance for understanding discourse on death, such as theories about the temporality and the interdependence of events and about the variations in the meaning of temporality in the different stages of biological evolution, in the ongoing dependency of a complex system that is self-organizing and self-maintaining yet is open-ended and transforms itself into higher stages.[41]

In existentialist philosophy, the anticipation of one's own death has been analyzed as the possibility of authentic existence. The "moment" characterizes this mode of existence; death as the farthest horizon of authentic self-existence refers back to the facticity of free existing and to the necessity of concrete decision. As ec-static, the moment of decision is outside of time and is at the same time the origin of the concretion of existence.[42] Such a moment is historically potent only if it opens up the possibilities and horizons of one's own existence.

However, the temporality of intersubjectivity has not yet come into view, since in this analysis death is also the cause of the radical individualization of subjects. But biographical time of an existence temporalizes itself precisely in interaction. Communicative action that conceives of others as actors who autonomously and innovatively anticipate the future opens the possibility that communicative, reciprocal, reflective temporal interaction appears and becomes present in its temporal genesis as genesis for the partners involved. In communication, finite freedoms experience themselves in time, are provoked to ever greater reciprocally granted and received freedom, and become transparent to each other in the presence of the moment. The becoming present for one another in the moment has, as the becoming present of the reciprocal-reflective genesis of communicative action, the character of surpassing time; the moment of free mutual recognition becomes the origin of the temporalizing of time and disrupts its continuum. The moment therefore can become epochally significant both biographically and historically. In this way, the momentary ec-stasis unto the finality of death can also be grasped intersubjectively.

The death of the other, however, takes away from one's own existence its reciprocal reflectivity and creates asymmetry; the other is withdrawn from one and annihilated. But can the relation to the other in his death be thought of in such a way that his annihilation is simply registered in a proposition? Does this not contradict the basic structure of human interaction? How then is an action to be structured that does not exclude the memory of the victims of history and nonetheless attempts to abide by unconditional, universal solidarity in concrete action? Does the practice of someone acting communicatively, who makes the unconditional recognition of the other in the future the condition of possibility of his own identity, not entail the factual refusal to accept the annihilation of the other? Is not the fate of the annihilation of the other viewed simply as superseded, or at least superable in principle, in such practice? How is such an assertion in practice conceivable at all?

From the perspective of the Judeo-Christian tradition, I would like to advance this thesis: Temporal, communicative action in solidarity unto death anticipates a reality about which it is asserted first of all by one's own practical performance that it can and does actually save others. The performance of one's own existence in communicative action is then factually the assertion, in this action itself, of a reality that does not simply allow others to become an already superseded fact of the past. However, this has to be explained.

The basic suspicion of the modern critique of religion is directed against the assertion of reality by religious consciousness as illusory projections that are merely supposed to secure and stabilize the factual performance of one's own existence and are thus finally directed only at one's own realization of existence. However, within the previously analyzed practice, how much is a reality truly asserted that is not simply a component in the performance of communicative action itself but is rather truly shown to be an independent, "effective" reality? This would have to be shown through the very structure of this practice itself. The death of the other has the character of a fact. His physical annihilation is precisely the paradigm of an irreversible process in the realm of accessible experience. The assertion maintained by means of continued action in solidarity of a reality that does not allow that the other is simply annihilated must be measured in its intention against this facticity of the death of the other. In its very structure it aims beyond one's own communicative action. If the possibility of the memory of the other had resided in one's own factual conscious performance, then sooner or later one would have come to the conclusion that the one who is remembering too irrevocably goes to his death, annihilating the experience of the indestructible presence of the other in interaction. However, the analysis of the temporal structure of interaction points precisely to the possibility of this experience.

The analysis of death from Kierkegaard to Heidegger had affirmed that the experience of the death of the other is secondary to the existential accomplishment of the anticipation of one's own death.[43] This assertion can now be shown to be false. The anticipation of one's own death discloses in the dialectic of existence "the possibility of the impossibility of existence";[44] what is aimed at in this anticipation discloses itself *as* a reality in the experience of solidarity in the death of the other.

Communicative action in remembering solidarity with the innocent victim seems then to be the assertion of a reality which saves the other who acts in history from annihilation. Only in this sort of interaction and in terms of the reality disclosed in it do I obtain the possibility of my own identity in an existence approaching unto death.

This reality disclosed in communicative action, asserted as the saving reality for others and at the same time as the reality that through this salvation of the other makes possible one's own temporal existence unto death, must be called *"God."* Within a situation of communicative action, which is ultimately inevitable, the reality of God becomes *identifiable* and *nameable* through the communicative action itself. In this way, the basic situation of the disclosure of the reality of God and its identifiability, and hence at the same time the origin of possible discourse about God, are given.[45]

Such an analysis of communicative action and its experiences is hardly conceivable without the Old Testament tradition and the appearance of Jesus of Nazareth. Discourse about freedom is not possible without recourse to historically experienced and realized freedom. The paradoxical limit situation that has been our point of departure led at the same time to the thesis that, at this limit of human experience, theoretical proposals alone can no longer make up the forefront of what is experienced and understood. The innovative character of such experiences and modes of action is the real reason why narrative is in the first instance the original mode of its mediation and presence; this has been pointed out most forcefully by J. B. Metz.[46] Nevertheless, the attempt can be made to reconstruct and to systematically and theoretically grasp such experiences in their inner logic. Then the question would have to be asked how our previous reflections on the reconstruction of the question of God (and thus the question of a fundamental theology) are related to Christology.

Our previous reflections can first of all shed light on a fact so often perceived as an embarrassment or an unresolvable dilemma in theology, namely that both the New Testament reports concerning the death of Jesus and the witness of the disciples and the early community of their experience of the resurrected Jesus are historically comprehensible. On this basis the various alternative proposals have been constructed for its interpretation, as to whether the resurrection of Jesus is merely an interpretation of his claims or a real experience. On the basis of our previous reflections, which can also be read as a contribution to a hermeneutics of the reality of the resurrection, such alternatives must seem wrongheaded from the start, since they are separate from an analysis of an interaction approaching death. Only this analysis can disclose the dimension in which the death of the other and his salvation in death can be constitutive for the possibility of one's own life. Hence, contemporary proposals for a hermeneutics of the reality of the resurrection would then have to be tested in terms of how much they can bring into view the intersubjective dimension of the experience of death.[47] Only reflections on an ontology of the reality of the resurrection set out strictly from an analysis of interaction as it approaches death could contribute to the clarification of the meaning of the New Testament texts. As a test case for the understanding of theology, approaches to the hermeneutics of the resurrection would then have to be put to the test of whether they break out of the horizon of the analysis of dialogue and in this way take an objectivating attitude toward the object of theology.[48]

Karl Rahner proposed locating the conception of Christology as a whole in a theology of the resurrection of Jesus. According to Rahner, the theology of the resurrection in turn must be unfolded in terms of "what is authentically experienced, witnessed, and believed in the resurrection of this Jesus"; we experience that Jesus with his concrete claim that in him a new, insurpassable, conclusive nearness of God is given that will come about by itself, is inseparable from him, and is accepted by God as having enduring validity.[49] Rahner sees in this the basis that makes central the experience that "this man who has been saved has a claim on us, and thus puts in experiential terms what classical Christology can only put in objective-metaphysical propositions." "This approach," Rahner writes, "shows that the dilemma between a 'functional' and an 'essential' Christology is overcome from the start as a mere pseudo-problem."[50]

The hermeneutical point of departure from an analysis of communicative action opens up therefore the possibility of explaining precisely the nature of the eschatological intensification involved in the experience of the death of Jesus and the witness to his resurrection: Through the assertion of the reality of God for others practically posed in his existence, Jesus has provoked and opened up the possibility of asserting God as the one acting to save in his death, even for himself.

The assertion of the presence of God for others can then no longer be limited. The experience of the Kingdom of God, the reality of God for all, can no longer be historically separated in its universality from this specific person. Only as practiced solidarity with all others is the assertion of the resurrection of Jesus real. J. B. Metz set forth this inseparable connection between the hope in the resurrection and universal solidarity, which is to say the eschatological dimension of solidarity. The word of the resurrection of the dead "is a word of justice, a word of resistance against any attempt simply to truncate the ever-renewed desire and search for the meaning of human life and to reserve this meaning for those who are ever to come, who have already somehow managed through it all, to a certain extent for those lucky ones who are the final winners and who enjoy the benefits of our history."[51] The confrontation with the Judeo-Christian tradition forces a theory of communicative action in universal solidarity to give an account of the reality presupposed and experienced in this action. The reality of God can be determined through this action. Here we seem to have reached the point where the possible characteristics of fundamental theology should be elucidated.

The Approach: Fundamental Theology as a Theory of
Communicative Action and of the Reality of God Disclosed and
Experienced in Action

Discourse on God has here been introduced as discourse on the reality
to which communicative action in solidarity even with the dead is
directed, in such a way that it asserts this reality for others and thereby
also for the actor. The assertion of this reality is entailed in communicative practice and remains bound to it. Thus, discourse on God
is derived from this dimension of action and refers back to this action.
Theology is then the theory of this action and of the reality disclosed
and experienced in it. This is also the meaning of the statement that
theology is based on the experience of faith. It is the explication of
a performance of existence which, as performance, reaches beyond
itself and asserts a reality, that is asserted as freely effective in such
a way that it is plainly distinct from one's own existence; it is asserted
as that reality which saves others in death. But this reality is only
disclosed in the movement of intersubjective action toward it. Thus,
it can also only be expressed in language as the reality experienced
in this practice. Theology is then theology precisely as a theory of this
action, and a theory of this action becomes theology if it opens itself
to this experience.

The significance of the determination of theology as a theory of
this communicative action is that it cannot simply leap beyond the
dimension of this action without leaving behind its own subject matter.
Hence, dialectical theories of reflection that pretend to encompass the
whole of history and thereby leave behind concrete experience cannot
become the basis for a basic conception of theology; the discovery of
the aporias of naive discourse about the whole of humanity or about
the whole of history leads back to those elementary actions in which
the victims of the historical process are saved from mere anonymity.
The conception of theology also cannot then be determined in terms
of the transcendentally conceived genesis of the isolated subject,[52] or
in terms of a general theory of the surpassing of finite experience in
"revelatory" experiences.[53] Such a conception of theology ultimately
cannot forget the insights of existential hermeneutics and again become
a purely objectivistic scholasticism.

Fundamental theology is thus a theory of communicative action and
the reality disclosed in this action.[54] Theology as a whole is to be
unfolded in terms of the fundamental structure of this action.

The procedure of determining the reality of God in terms of a specific performance and so introducing discourse about the reality of God does not have to be seen as foreign to theology. The "five ways" of Thomas Aquinas must be understood as the attempt to point in a transcending movement from intercourse with material, finite reality to something unconditional as a reality: "Et hoc dicimus deum" ("And this we call God").[55] That all this presupposes a general consensus about the possible experience, determination, and naming of this reality can be seen in another formulation at the end of the "third way": "Quod omnes dicunt deum" ("This is what men call God"). Recent interpretations of Thomas emphasize the transcending movement of human existence toward God as absolute being and the correspondence of free self-actuation and the disclosure of a free absolute as the true Thomistic approach.[56] Rahner also defined the conception of his theology in exactly this way, in terms of the transcending movement of existence toward the reality of the absolute, sacred mystery: "The attribute of 'holy mystery' does not belong accidentally to God like a qualification that could just as well be applied to any other reality. We can grasp what is meant by God only when whatever is meant by holy mystery is conceived to belong to God solely and primarily, according to which He is there as the whither of transcendence."[57]

We have attempted to determine what is meant by the reality of God in terms of intersubjective, communicative action that faces the experience of the annihilation of the innocent and in remembering solidarity anticipates a reality that saves those annihilated in the historical process and, as such, first makes possible a remembering existence in practiced solidarity directed to the future.

In this sense, the "memoria passionis" is for Metz the process by which the reality of God can be determined. "In memory of this suffering, God appears in his eschatological freedom as the subject and the meaning of history as a whole."[58] Such a memory, which anticipates God as saving reality and which is thus "anticipatory memory,"[59] cannot usurp the role of the reality of God. As hope in solidarity with others, it is the determination of a reality that remains free and at no one's disposal and in this sense remains a subject in its eschatological freedom in relation to all. The possible experience of God is therefore the experience of a liberating freedom. A fundamental theology starting from the paradox of anamnestic solidarity is for this reason necessarily a theology of free self-communication and thus a theology of grace.

Such a conception of theology can be considered fundamental, insofar as in it are clarified the access to this reality from the performance of communicative action, the original determination and identification and thus the linguistic nameability of the reality of God, and consequently the possible reaching of an understanding about this reality in linguistic communicative action. This conception of theology is hence fundamental in both a substantive and a methodological sense. Both aspects are not to be separated from the very structure of this conception: The intended reality determines the manner of its possible intersubjective communication, and conversely it must be determined by the process of communication itself. From this perspective the hermeneutical procedures involved here can be more precisely determined.

To what extent can such a conception of theology be defined as "theory"? One could object that in every case the concern of this communicative action is to break through the previous horizon of experience in the hopeful anticipation of something over which one does not have any power; that therefore the apprehension of coherent interpretation of all the data of this realm of experience is not made possible by an all-encompassing theory; that in terms of the character of action in anamnestic solidarity in anticipation of the future the reality of God becomes utterly incommensurable and is first circumscribable only by way of the negativity of experience; that the data to be interpreted in such a theory are only present in narrative presentation, because it always has to do with breaking through horizons of experience.[60]

If one nonetheless insists that theology can be put in the language of theory and then that a fundamental theology can be developed as a foundational theory of communicative action, then one must admittedly leave behind a conception of theory already rejected in the discussion of the theory of science itself. Accordingly, one has to return to the founding process in which the performances of subjects in intersubjectivity first open up the realm of objects of the human sciences and ultimately even of the natural sciences. The fundamental concepts introduced here must refer to intersubjective actions on the basis of which they can be intelligibly applied to any state of affairs and can be used for intersubjective agreement. One is forced to introduce basic concepts in a paradigmatic and narrative fashion.[61] Even the science of history, a psychology oriented to life histories, the theory of evolution, and cosmology all have as their subject matter specific, unique, nonreversible, nonrepeatable processes which continually break through structures to new experiences, and yet all of these disciplines claim to be theoretical. The discussion of the theory of science in recent decades ultimately showed that temporal action and the historicity and unclosed character of the systems of interpretation are characteristic of all theories. It can therefore not be excluded that even communicative action that faces the experience of one's own death and the death of others can be grasped "theoretically."[62]

Dimensions of a Fundamental Theology

We have shown that the theory of communicative action presented above is the point of convergence of the basic problems of the theory of science and theology. A foundational theory of theology, developed as a theory of communicative action, must in turn be able to be unfolded in the dimensions of its central problem constellations. A fundamental theology therefore would have to be explicated in the dimensions of a theory of the subject, a theory of society, and a theory of history all at the same time; indeed, it can only be done in these dimensions.

The Theological Theory of Communicative Action

The central realm of a fundamental theology consists of a mode of interaction in which the interaction partners mutually recognize each other as unconditioned and in which they do so in temporal interaction, approaching death. This mode of interaction is at the same time experienced as being summoned by an absolute freedom which makes it possible. Temporal existence unto one's death in interaction asserts the absolute affirmation of the other through this reality of an absolute freedom precisely in the approaching of one's own death. The recognition of the unconditional affirmation of the other is the condition of self-existence; only through the recognition of the other as unconditioned is a consciousness of the unconditionedness of one's own existence achieved. Communications in which the recognition of the other occurs and in which the other is at the same time defended against humiliation and destruction would then be the primary objective field of a theological theory of interaction. A fundamental theology of this sort can be further unfolded in its basic structure only in interdisciplinary dialogue. Such a theory is in this way on the cutting edge of linguistics, general communication theory, social psychology, and a sociological theory of action.

The Theological Theory of the Subject

In interaction the unconditionedness of the individual, his affirmation in death, is experienced and actuated. From the perspective of social psychology, the identity of the individual has to be grasped as the active capacity to overcome crises that threaten to destroy the personality system. Nevertheless, the question here is to what extent the development of this capacity is dependent on a mode of socialization permitting the experience that one's own freedom is first made possible through an absolute freedom. The capacity to establish an identity is in itself paradoxical; as the overcoming of internalized structures toward the final horizon of dissolution in death, it is the capacity for an ever newly achieved self-presence and presence for others. This capacity makes possible the recognition of others as unconditioned and the achievement of one's own identity from interaction in a free-floating equilibrium and in the granting of this same identity to others as well. Interaction as a temporal, creative, innovative process, surpassing limitations and defining one's own world and a common world, would then be shown to be the condition of possibility of the identity of subjects.

The Theory of Society

Thus, we have named the standard by which the structure of a society must be evaluated. Relations of domination, thus the organization of production, distribution, and consumption, and the accepted rules of the active constitution of reality simultaneously regulate the mode of interaction of subjects, thereby deciding the very possibility of achieving identity for the subjects who take part in and constitute them.

A theory of interaction that approaches the process of mutual unconditional recognition of subjects not merely in an isolated sphere but understands it as a normative core structure that can claim validity in all dimensions of social action becomes simultaneously a foundational theory of any theory of society.

Insofar as one comes to the realization that this interaction can only be grasped as the approaching of an absolute freedom and as the unconditional recognition of others, such a theory of society is also fundamentally a theological theory. The converse is also true: A fundamental theology is to be approached as a theory of society, because the possible identity of subjects depends on the basic structure of socially constitutive interaction.

Theology would remain abstract if it were not to attend to the social repression of freedom and the destruction of possibilities of identity for subjects. Inasmuch as political decisions ultimately decide the basic structure of the processes of social constitution, a theology that is a theory of this process cannot be confronted with the false alternative of developing it as either a theory of the subject or a theory of society. The starting point of a fundamental theology in a theory of communicative action proves to be fundamental and fruitful in that it makes the interdependence of these dimensions so apparent that they can no longer be played off against each other. Thus, the fundamental theology developed here must be understood as "political theology."

The Theory of History
Our decisive argument for the necessity of ultimately developing a theory of communicative action as a theological theory was derived from the insight that intersubjective action shuns reality if it does not face the experiences of the death of the other, of one's own death, and of the annihilation of the innocent. The experience of the death of the other is the original experience of history. The mode of the affirmation of the other in interaction must then at the same time be seen as a mode of presence in history. An analysis of these phenomena admittedly faces grave difficulties, on the level of a methodology for historiography as well as on the level of the analysis of temporal and historical consciousness. This can be elucidated in an example. The Platonic concept of recollection refers to the lightning flash of illumination of the Idea. The Idea has always eternally existed. Upon death, it will stand before us as the eternal past, what has always been.[63] Existential analysis understands the moment as the projection of the utmost possibilities of existence toward the horizon of its no longer being, a horizon that remains empty and therefore refers back

to the appropriating retrieval of one's own history in the moment of factual existence.[64] As opposed to both these views, Benjamin fashioned the conception of the *Jetztzeit* (time of the presence of the now).[65] It signifies the phenomenon that disrupts the continuum of time, an event that can be present for another time insofar as like lightning it "lights up" as that which was and at the same time as that which can be the point of entry for messianic redemption. The structure of this *Jetztzeit* is for Benjamin the condition of possibility of grasping back to the past in remembering, communicative action, so that this past can break through into the present as what is not definitively fixed and finished. At the same time, conversely, we can say that only in the uncovering of this eschatological now in the past, and thus in the uncovering of its shattered possibilities and of its transformation and salvation, does the possibility exist for Benjamin of historiography that does not simply represent "empathy with the victors."[66] The angel of history would like to "awaken the dead, and gather together what has been smashed."[67] "Only *that* historian will have the gift of fanning the spark of hope in the past who is firmly convinced that *even the dead* will not be safe from the enemy if he wins."[68] For Benjamin, a theory of history cannot simply contain a methodology for establishing what really happened. Anamnestic solidarity that affirms the other in annihilation anticipates redemption and lights up the vision of the rubble of history, as a presentiment.

Habermas has disputed the view that such an experience permits the achievement of an orientation for social action.[69] He is indeed correct, to the extent that a theory of historical experience of this sort must be related to an empirical and at the same time normative theory of communicative action, to a theory of the subject and a theory of society that have as their intent to grasp the intrinsic relationship of these realms and their specific historical genesis. But only an unconditional solidarity, inclusive of even those who are annihilated, will derive from the past the potential for resisting the totalitarian claims of social systems that simply overrun the subject. The concept of history in the future will take on an ever greater significance for the orientation of political action.

From this perspective, a fundamental theology developed as a theory of communicative action through the paradox of anamnestic solidarity is faced with the task of developing a hermeneutics of the history of religion in connection with a theory of the development of human consciousness and action as a whole.[70]

An elementary experience seems to lie at the root of modern attempts to develop theories of intersubjectivity, society, and history. To speak unreservedly, it is the constitutive experience of a humanity that sees itself as emerging from evolution to consciousness and reflectivity. The universal communication community of these beings emerging from evolution and seeking mutual understanding demands its own sort of solidarity. This solidarity proves to be the condition of possibility of one's own identity. The insight in the theory of science into the convergence of various questions in the theory of communicative action thus also entails the insight that one can break with this solidarity of all finite beings only at the price of the loss of one's own identity. This is also true for theologians. In the face of the Biblical tradition, the question of this solidarity must be put even more radically. Then it becomes the question of a reality that makes this solidarity possible, even in the face of the annihilation of the other in death.

Appendixes
Conceptions of Fundamental Theology

1

Theology as Existential Interpretation: Rudolf Bultmann

Fundamental Theology and Theological Hermeneutics

If a fundamental theology is supposed to provide the methodological foundation of theology, and to do so in such a way that along with the subject matter of theology it determines both the horizon and the inner structure of theological discourse, then it is within a domain that is far from being unambiguously defined in either Protestant or Catholic theology. One could, however, find general agreement that since Schleiermacher this task can most appropriately be called "theological hermeneutics,"[1] insofar as hermeneutics is understood not merely as a technique in philology but, in its broadest sense, as methodological instruction about the process of understanding the vital utterances of others and thus the texts of earlier cultures as well. This process is understood in such a way that the texts release their practical meaning in a concrete situation, determined by specific societal conditions, even for the individual. Hence, the dimensions of the hermeneutic effort can be designated history, society, intersubjective communication, and the individual. The controversy within the field of hermeneutics, however, is concerned with the relationships among these dimensions and with the basic structure of theological discourse.

In these appendixes, as in the introduction, I want to investigate three conceptions[2] of "fundamental theology" understood in this way. While choosing the approaches of Bultmann and Rahner and the "political theology" worked out by (above all) Metz, I am well aware that any such selection could be accused of a certain arbitrariness. But I would like to show that these three conceptions have a certain paradigmatic significance for the development of a fundamental theology. Moreover, I want to show here that, for all their differences, these conceptions have a basic problem in common, as yet unsatisfactorily clarified—namely, that of intersubjective communication, or, in other words, communicative action. This problem has a sort of steering function for fundamental theology and thus for the determination of a fundamental conception of theology as a whole.

The theology of Rudolf Bultmann may be said to represent one of the most penetrating and complete theological programs of a foundational character in our century. How can the systematic context of this theology be explained?

One could interpret Bultmann's theology as representing a theological anthropology that makes statements intelligible through their reduction to the dialectical structure of eschatological existence in its presuppositions and its actualization. This has often been done.[3] But in many ways the question of a theological hermeneutics seems to have priority over any such interpretation. This question focuses all the varied approaches on one point. In the first instance, the approach appears especially suitable because it corresponds to the central interests of all Bultmann's theological works. Bultmann himself emphasized this above all against Karl Jaspers: "The real problem is the hermeneutic one, that is, the problem of interpreting the Bible in *the* way and the teachings of the Church in *the* way so that they can be understood as a summons to man."[4] Hermeneutic reflection is precisely the place where the universal understandability of theological discourse is in question; thus, within the Western tradition, it is the locus of the relationship between philosophy and theology. Bultmann's philosophical dialogue partner was Martin Heidegger. The constellation of Bultmann and Heidegger[5] has itself a paradigmatic significance, because in it many of the themes of philosophy and theology during the last two centuries find new interpretation.

I would like to try to explain Bultmann's basic conception of Bultmann's theology in terms of this relationship to Heidegger by proceeding in four distinct steps. As a point of departure, I would like to sketch briefly the theological situation in which Heidegger's thought held such promise for Bultmann. Since Bultmann relies almost entirely on the early period of Heidegger's thought (and in that almost exclusively on *Being and Time*), we must next discuss the basic tenets of Heidegger's early views. We then can see more clearly how this thought is applied in Bultmann's theology and what fundamental, unresolved questions result from its use.

The Hermeneutic Situation of the Exegete

Bultmann stands in the great tradition of those exegetes who, using unconditional higher criticism, investigated the New Testament primarily as a historical source.

The history of the historical-critical exploration of the New Testament has shown that exegetes were guided by the intention of uncovering in radical criticism a genuine picture of the true Jesus beneath the dogmatic accretions of orthodoxy and even beneath the New Testament itself. This true picture would either support faith or deprive it of its basis altogether (as Reimarus, the originator of this exegetical enterprise, had intended). The contradictions of the different pictures of the "historical Jesus" that were discovered showed the lack of reflection on the nature of the methods applied and often betrayed the biases of the putatively presuppositionless investigators.

Such a development, among the most dramatic in the history of theology, showed that the consciousness of method and the complexity of the subject matter first needed clarification.

The strongest impulse to reflect on just what the historical critical method really could accomplish, and just what concept of history was presupposed, was provided by the New Testament itself. The fact of the matter was all too obvious: The Gospels were not meant to be a biography of Jesus; their primary intention was not to give a historical-critical report of the facts but rather to give witness to the experience of belief as the summons to believe. One uncovered the *kerygma* in the New Testament, a present, liberating demand providing the horizon of meaning for all statements. What is discoverable about the "historical Jesus" as factual knowledge can only be reached through a methodological screening process involving a critical destruction of the witness character of the texts, reducing them to their mere "historical" basis. The expression "historical Jesus" [*historischer Jesus*], as opposed to the "Biblical," "historical" [*geschichtlichen*], "kerygmatic Christ,"[6] thus became the title for a methodological problem in theology.

Thus the hermeneutic problematic developed from this problem of historical method, the very problem Bultmann faced at the beginning of his theological work.

As a historian, the exegete basically has three tasks: (1) He must attempt to extract from the text the historically attainable knowledge of Jesus of Nazareth through the critical testing of the character and value of the sources of New Testament texts. In his book *Jesus* (1926), Bultmann attempted to do just this on the basis of his *History of the Synoptic Tradition* (1921). (2) Besides this, the kerygma of the New Testament must be historically [*historisch*] discovered in its motifs, in its structures, and in the various perspectives of its statements as the testimony of the faith of the early Church. This is the way Bultmann understood his *Theology of the New Testament* (1953). (3) It also still falls within the realm of historical research to investigate the relationship between the claims Jesus made in his preaching and the statements of the New Testament proclamation, in order to establish the prevailing form of continuity or explication in the texts.[7]

However, even after such historical research is completed, one question still remains completely unsettled: How can the claim of Jesus, the claim of the New Testament kerygma, be perceived by the hearer as a call to decision, so that in his believing acceptance or his unbelieving rejection his salvation is realized or forfeited? More theoretically: In what horizon must the believer's existence and the historical event that unconditionally concerns him be conceived if we are to understand the way in which he encounters his salvation in history [*Geschichte*]? To what end is the kerygma of the New Testament to be interpreted? With his strict consciousness of methods, Bultmann, the critical-historical exegete, saw this as the decisive hermeneutical question.

What is meant here can be illustrated in two areas of New Testament study to which Bultmann especially dedicated himself. Bultmann is one of the founders of the so-called "form-criticism." Fundamentally, it attempts to present the history of the primitive Christian tradition, and thus to analyze the process of interpretation and explication in the New Testament itself and even prior to it. As early as 1921, Bultmann saw the decisive tendency of the Gospel according to Mark in that it interpreted the traditions about Jesus through Hellenistic myth.[8]

In studying the history of religion, Bultmann and his followers further pursued how certain images, especially out of the realm of Gnosticism, were used in the formulation of the kerygma. The result of this work is *Primitive Christianity in its Contemporary Setting* (1949).

The exegete views the New Testament as a product of a process of interpretation which is itself not at all unified, a process he must reinterpret with respect to what is ultimately meant in the text. Already in 1922, in his review of the second edition of Karl Barth's *Römerbrief*, Bultmann demands that the text be understood in terms of its subject matter. This implies criticism—a program which in 1941 received the name demythologization. However, the question is still this: Which critical, methodologically verifiable criteria are available to the exegete in order to bring to light what is meant behind its various interpretations. Which hermeneutic principles are required for the interpretation of an event that is itself historically embedded in various interpretations, themselves conditioned by religious-historical influences?

For Bultmann, the hermeneutical problematic was further radicalized through dialectical theology. Insofar as dialectical theology (in opposition to liberal theology) wants to retain the absolute claim and the transcendence of the Word of God, Bultmann was of one mind with Barth. He also agreed, at first, that "God's being other than the world, God's being beyond the world, means the complete abrogation of the whole of man, of his whole history."[9] However, for Bultmann, revelation must not simply annihilate its addressee if it is to encounter him in his essence. It must rather call him into question in such a way that he can explicitly know and acknowledge it but can also reject it. Revelation must open a new possibility for one and the same human being. If the dilemma of an absolutely dialectical theology that "threatens to turn into a purely transcendental philosophy"[10] is to be avoided, just how man can grasp the Word of revelation that grasps him must be clarified. How should the hearing and the hearer of a revelation that is ongoing in history be understood? What does it mean to be a "hearer of the Word"?

For Bultmann, the problem of dialectical theology also issues in the question of how the hearer can understand the historical [*geschichtlich*] Word of revelation, now explicitly sharpened to the question of the conditions in the hearer of this Word himself.

In his 1927 essay "The Significance of 'Dialectical Theology' for the Scientific Study of the New Testament,"[11] Bultmann saw the essence of dialectical theology as the insight into the historicity of human existence. In 1927 the first edition of *Being and Time* appeared. Bultmann had met Heidegger in the meantime and derived from him the means of clarifying his own theological situation as an exegete.

I shall attempt to elucidate the position of Heidegger in *Being and Time* both historically and systematically, in order to see how Heidegger's thought appeared to Bultmann as precisely what he needed.

Hermeneutics and Historicity in Heidegger's *Being and Time*

It may be objected against most of the studies of the relationship of Bultmann's theology to Heidegger's thought that they lose themselves in the analysis (however necessary) of individual terms such as "existence," "world," "authenticity," and "fallenness." What is lost is the context and tendency of the whole, which first gives the individual distinctions their full meaning.

In the lectures Heidegger held after the First World War, the outline for a new point of departure for philosophy became apparent. At its center stands the accomplishment of actual life in its very facticity. If the question of the meaning of Being is to be properly asked, this accomplishment must be thought as such, that is, in terms of its temporality. This ultimately leads to the elaboration of *Being and Time*.[12]

"Still," writes Pöggeler, "Heidegger's early lectures show that the primitive Christian faith guided his thought to its decisive questions."[13] Two of these lectures are of primary importance in our context.[14] In the winter semester of 1920–21, Heidegger presented an "Introduction to the Phenomenology of Religion" in which he made reference to the "factual life experience" expressed in the letters of Paul. In 1 Thessalonians 4:13 ff. Paul rejects any calculation of the Second Coming of Christ and demands of Christians that they lead a life under the threat of an open future that does not allow objectification, and in 2 Corinthians 12:1–10 Heidegger considers Paul's command not to flee to visions and apocalyptic reports but to come to self-acceptance and to attend to the weakness of the facticity of life.[15] In a lecture entitled "Augustine and Neo-Platonism," given in the summer semester of 1921, Heidegger points out the danger in Augustine's thought of falsifying this factual actuality of life determined by restlessness, suffering, and the Cross into a timeless, nonhistorical *fruitio Dei* under the influence of Neo-Platonism. And in Luther, this actuality of life, which does not escape from angst and the relation to one's death, is experienced and expressed in its primordial character.[16]

Fundamentally, representational thinking which thinks Being as present-at-hand misses this temporal-historical accomplishment, which alone temporalizes time and therefore cannot pose the Being question adequately.

Thus, the decisive step on the way to *Being and Time* is taken. This work is to show that "the central problematic of all ontology is rooted in the phenomenon of time, if rightly seen and rightly explained, and we must show how this is the case."[17] "In the exposition of the problematic of temporality, the question of the meaning of Being will first be concretely answered."[18] At the same time, these analyses were to help derive the essence of a hermeneutics of history, as the method for the sciences of man,[19] thus fulfilling the intentions of Dilthey's program.

The question of the meaning of Being for Heidegger can therefore only be adequately asked and answered on the basis of the movement of factual human being, the movement of Dasein. This movement can be exhibited phenomenologically. Among other examples, Heidegger shows this movement in the phenomenon of angst.[20]

In angst, one is no longer merely afraid of an isolated being. A being can at most be the occasion for the outburst of elementary fear. In angst, one actually is afraid of "nothing." The "clear night of the nothingness of angst"[21] reigns, in which everything objective is left behind and overcome. However, in angst it becomes evident that Dasein cannot flee from itself, but inescapably must be itself and is thrown back to itself and to the totality of beings. It is disclosed as finite transcendence.[22] Transcendence here means the transcending movement of Dasein in which it goes beyond other beings and itself; but precisely in this transcendence Dasein shows its finite facticity and its directedness to beings. Transcendence both makes possible and compels this relationship to oneself and to other beings. For this structure of finite Dasein, which in transcending necessarily relates to itself, Heidegger, drawing on Kierkegaard, chooses the title "existence." "The 'essence' of Dasein," he writes, "lies in its existence."[23]

Heidegger calls the formal description of this structure "existential" analysis, as distinguished from the factual "existentiell" actualization of existing. Nevertheless, existential analysis is of course only possible on the basis of the factual movement of existence. It does not presuppose any objective determination of the content of "existence," but only this transcending, self-relating movement of Dasein itself. The significance of this conception can only be adequately understood in terms of the history of modern philosophy.[24] At least two indications of the significance of the concept "world" must be given in order to show in what way Heidegger takes up classical problems of philosophy.

For Kant, the unity and totality of the world represented in the idea of the world cannot be adequately objectified in empirical intuition; to this extent, this idea has only "transcendental" validity.[25] For Kant, the idea of the world is the "essence of all appearances"[26] or "the absolute totality of the synthesis of appearances."[27] Similarly, for Heidegger "world" becomes the "title for finite knowledge in its totality."[28] The decisive and (for Kant) unresolved question of the "transcendental validity" of this totality is clarified by Heidegger in terms of this transcending movement of Dasein, which always already discloses the totality of beings. That is, existence always understands itself in terms of a totality, and interprets itself in this way. "That toward which Dasein transcends we call the *world*, and we can now define transcendence as Being-in-the-world. World goes to make up the unified structure of transcendence; the concept of world is called transcendental because it is part of this structure."[29]

Thus, the understanding of the world and self-understanding are inextricably bound together; the modification of one conditions the modification of the other.

For Husserl the world of the "natural attitude," the thesis of an *a priori* accomplished world belief within an ever-fluctuating stream of self-apperception, has no apodictic evidence. The world is a phenomenon of validity whose claim is questioned when recognized as ungroundable by the natural attitude and therefore put out of play and no longer considered valid in the transcendental-phenomenological reduction. The phenomenological reduction discloses the sphere of transcendental subjectivity as the original ground of being. This movement of the phenomenological reduction cannot be performed in the natural, mundane attitude, since it presupposes itself and is achieved only in its performance (a process comparable to Hegel's notion of thought's being grasped by absolute Spirit). The ground of the "world" of the natural attitude is abandoned in the reduction; however, at the same time the question of the being of the world is asked, in that this being is traced back to the intentional performances of the transcendental Ego. The absolutely concrete stream of life of intentionality permits the phenomenon of the world to appear as the correlate of the transcendental self-apperception of the transcendental Ego; it is unattainable in ordinary psychological research.[30]

For Husserl, therefore, the question of the "world" is concerned with the question of transcendental origin, which is to be clarified by reflecting on transcendental subjectivity (the problem that is the focus of Husserl's thought even to the end). With it, however, there arise aporias that are never satisfactorily resolved. The question of the relationship of the three different egos especially poses difficulties, namely the relationship among the mundane "psychological" ego of the natural world belief, the transcendental ego and its constitutive intentional performances, and the ego of the "transcendental observer" who views the naive world belief and does not bring it to validity but attempts to clarify it in transcendental analysis.[31] Heidegger attempts to solve these aporias by returning to factual Dasein. The being of Dasein is in itself the occurrence of the constitution of the world, because Dasein as transcending existence itself is factually the difference between the *a priori* and the factual. Husserl therefore reproached Heidegger: "Heidegger transports or transvests the constitutive phenomenological clarification of all regions of beings and universals, of the total region 'world' into the realm of anthropology. The entire problematic is only one of transposition; the Ego corresponds to Dasein, etc. Thus, everything becomes deeply muddled and loses all its philosophic value."[32] A fundamental problem for both Husserl and Heidegger is the *intersubjective* constitution of the world. Husserl has difficulties simply arriving at the full dimension of intersubjectivity.[33] These unsettled problems have had their effect even in the reception of Husserl in American sociology (mediated through Alfred Schütz) and up to N. Luhmann.

For Heidegger, Being in the world is, almost trivially, always already Being with. However, the actual execution of the analysis of death basically retracts this conception. We shall return to this point shortly.

Being and Time explicates in more detail the basic structure of Being in the world as transcending existence. Heidegger carries out this analysis in two parts. In the first ("The Preparatory Fundamental Analysis of Dasein"), the structural elements of existence are provisionally unfolded. "State-of-mind" (or "disposition") [Befindlichkeit] is one existential determination of Dasein, insofar as it finds itself always already in the world in a determined place and mood. "Understanding" [Verstehen] signifies the transcending movement of Dasein that projects a horizon of meaning. What is disclosed in understanding is not just objectively apprehended matters of fact but the directions of the movement of Dasein, the "possibilities" of existing. Insofar as existence is disclosed to itself in this way, it can express itself as "discourse" [Rede] and bring the basic event of transcendence to speech. At the same time, Heidegger indicates that this uniform structure is modifiable, and thus that existence, as concrete Being in the world, can either cling to disclosed objectivity and be interpreted as "fallen" [Verfallen] or face the factual finitude of transcending existence.

Another section of Being and Time inquires into the "meaning" of this structure of existence itself. Meaning denotes generally the horizon in which a being is understood in such a way that it becomes understandable from this horizon. Since this concerns the understanding of existence itself, meaning now signifies that horizon within which existence can understand itself and beings not inauthentically—in terms of objects—but rather in its totality. And since understanding is to be conceived not as any arbitrary activity but as the basic projecting-transcending movement of existence itself, it is a matter of the determination of the farthest possible horizon of existing itself. How can this horizon be determined?

Heidegger's fundamental idea is to undertake the radicalization of existential analysis as the analysis of death.[34] An objective consideration of death is not appropriate to the structure of existence. Death is only grasped if it is apprehended and accepted as the end before which existence inescapably stands. Only then does existence conceive itself as finite and temporal.

The temporality of Dasein is therefore only a radical interpretation of the event of the transcendence of existence in its farthest projectable horizon, namely the horizon of "no longer able to be." Existence is actualized in such a way that, in understanding, the open possibility of existing—the future of existence itself—is disclosed. Precisely in projecting a future, however, existence is turned back to its mortal, finite facticity. Dasein returns to itself out of its future and finds itself the "there" of Being [*Da-sein*], as having already been. Only in this movement can existence be present to itself, *in* the actualization of its temporal existing. "This phenomenon," Heidegger writes, "has the unity of a future which makes present in the process of having been; we designate it as 'temporality.' "[35] Only from this original temporality can it be determined exactly what time means in physical processes and in everyday understanding.[36]

For Heidegger, only from the structure of original temporality can it be shown how existence can have a relationship to history. If existence exists temporally then it is fundamentally historical,[37] for by finding itself in the present, from the future, as already having been, it discloses to itself the possibilities of history as possibilities of its own existing. "Only an entity which, as futural, is equiprimordially in the process of *having been*, can, by handing down to itself the possibilities it has inherited, take over its thrownness [*Geworfenheit*] and be *in the moment* of vision for 'its own time.' "[38]

The moment [*Augenblick*] of authentic temporality is thus the origin of the relation to history. In this moment, existence sums itself up with all its possibilities; it runs before itself unto *death* as the ultimate possibility of its Being and in it accepts its mortal finitude as its own. In this earnestness, existence accepts a history as its own and does not flee to noncommitment. It recognizes that it is here and now qualified by the past and by history. Only in this way can it really be encountered by history.

With this it becomes clear that there are two modes of relating to history—the authentic and the inauthentic—by which existence as a whole is modifiable. The inauthentic relation to history considers it a mere succession of happenings along the endless line of flowing time. In such an "objective" treatment, existence cannot be fundamentally encountered in history. Authentic historical relatedness, however, allows existence to make history its concern on the basis of its own finite, temporal existence. Of course, the question remains whether history can really be conceived of at all from such a point of view.

In his analysis of authentic historicity, Heidegger thinks he has fulfilled the intentions of Dilthey as well, since (Heidegger writes) a methodology of historical inquiry is concerned with the "elaboration of the hermeneutical situation, which—with the resolution of Dasein existing in history—is opened up to the retrieving disclosure of what has been there."[39] "Hermeneutics," Heidegger continues, "is the way this understanding enlightens itself; it is also the methodology of historiology, although only in a derivative form."[40] This is the starting point for Bultmann's attempt to bring Heidegger's insights to fruition for his theological work.[41]

Theological Hermeneutics as Existential Interpretation

When Bultmann as a theologian considers Heidegger's analyses, he is primarily concerned with the process of understanding. He emphasizes again and again that certain of Heidegger's concepts are capable of explaining what is meant in the New Testament, if only because they are themselves stamped with theology. According to Bultmann, Heidegger "never made any secret that he had been particularly influenced by the New Testament (especially Paul), and by Augustine and perhaps most especially by Luther." Bultmann goes on to say: "If one wants to understand Heidegger's influence on my theology, then one must take just that into consideration."[42] More important than this historically explainable affinity of Biblical and existential categories is the basic theological-hermeneutical question of how historical revelation can be conceived in such a way that it becomes intelligible how it can make "salvation" possible and that one can speak about this process in an understandable way. Again and again, above all in his essay on hermeneutics, Bultmann emphasizes that Heidegger brought a new, decisive clarity to this problem through his analyses of understanding and interpretation.[43]

Bultmann begins with an analysis of the hermeneutic circle, which holds sway over every interpretation. Before Heidegger, Schleiermacher and Dilthey investigated the structure of this circle; in all of them, one can trace the influence of German Idealism.[44] According to Bultmann, all understanding and interpretation is possible only if the interpreter has a certain pre-understanding of the subject matter that informs the direction (*woraufhin*) of his interpretation of what is meant.[45] This thesis has been variously misunderstood. Even though Bultmann is not entirely clear in every passage, his concept of pre-understanding ultimately is meant to refer to an existential structure, "the existential *fore-structure* of Dasein itself."[46] Dasein in its being as understanding is, in projecting itself, already ahead of itself (*vor-weg*). The formal structure of existence is precisely the capacity to make something [*eine Sache*] one's own in the transcending projection of a horizon through explicit "interpretation."[47]

Theological hermeneutics has the task of investigating the structure of this circle. An intellectually responsible theology must understand its own pre-understanding if it is not to fall prey to unreflected prejudice.[48]

Each discipline has its own realm of objects and its own specific project and horizon of inquiry within which it sets forth its interpretive discourse. For theology, this horizon, this leading direction (*Woraufhin*)[49] of all its questions and discourse can only be the *question of God* by which every human being is moved.[50]

A question can be more or less precisely articulated. Theological discourse must ask, as precisely as is possible: How is the question of God structured? Bultmann's statements on the structure of the question can be summarized as follows:

• First, it is important to insist that pre-understanding be seen strictly as the *question* of God, not as an already possessed prior knowledge. A question *qua* question is asked in the open horizon of the movement of questioning and expects only to be limited by the answer.

• The question of God is a movement of existence itself, not merely a question of the intellect [*Verstand*].[51] Because understanding is always already the movement of transcending existence, the question of God is existence itself in its questioning movement toward God.

• The farthest possible question for man is not, therefore, that of the questioning intellect which seeks the causal relations between things or the first cause of beings. The farthest possibility and farthest horizon of transcending existence, and thus of all questioning, is the possibility of this existence in its radicality as finite transcendence. The searching movement of questioning seeks as its ultimate end that which makes possible finite, mortal existence itself. The question of God the creator is tantamount to the question of the possibility of authentic existence. Inasmuch as existence is temporal and historical, the movement of questioning is possible only in the horizon of historicity.

• The question of God therefore does not simply ask about the illumination of existence of its correct analysis, but rather about the *communication of existence*—the original event which makes existing possible, which "bestows existence."[52]

• Existential-ontological analysis as the elucidation of existence can provide only a tentative projection of the direction of questioning, a structural analysis of the questioning and its possible resolution, but it cannot mediate the event of authentic existence itself.

In such an understanding of theology, God cannot be spoken of as something purely "objective," "in itself," but rather only as the one to whom a questioning existence projects itself, or as the one who liberates and makes possible an authentic existence. The last horizon of possible discourse is the event of the liberating encounter itself. God can only be spoken of by talking about this movement of human existence and this concrete, liberating encounter as well.[53]

Philosophical, existential analysis, even when and precisely when it does not speak of God, has its validity in that it develops a formal projection of authentic existing without deciding upon the concrete accomplishment of this existing and without confusing the elucidation of existence with the communication of existence. We still must ask ourselves if this theological interpretation of Heidegger is justified and even possible in terms of Heidegger's own thought.

How does the believing understanding of the historical event of salvation, which makes salvation possible, take place? The horizon of this understanding cannot be the objective treatment of history. This would only establish a leveled time of historical facts. Even if it is asserted that this or that fact is my concern, the mode in which it becomes of concern and the sort of claim it makes remain unclear.

History becomes my concern only when I find myself at stake in my relation to it and when at the same time my own life is made possible by my encounter with it. My own ability to be, my own future, must itself be opened in it, and in virtue of this opening of my future I must be set free from the burden of the past which always already displaces my freedom. This demands the collecting of my scattered life into the present of the liberating encounter with history. The horizon of this encounter is authentic temporality, which becomes temporal in the moment of decision.[54] In the moment of decision, I decide both my past and my future life.

The liberation of myself unto myself, however, cannot come about through myself alone, according to Bultmann. By my own powers, I

can only become what I already am, qualified by my past.[55] My
freedom, and with it my future, can only be bestowed upon me in
the encounter with the liberating act of God. This act of God encounters
me in the kerygma of Jesus Christ as the act of the liberating love of
God.[56] How is this process intelligible?

God's act of salvation in Jesus of Nazareth is the "eschatological"
act of salvation, insofar as it calls me into the "now" of its occurrence,
which is the utmost possibility of history, the "fullness of time," which
gives me my freedom of liberated being myself in the "now" of my
decision to believe. The eschatological event of God's revelation thus
occurs in the horizon of authentic temporality, bestowed through God's
act. In it, the "now" of the death of Jesus, which sums up his existence,
corresponds to the "now" of my decision to believe.[57] The eschatological
event of God's revelation consists therefore in the empowering of
authentic, "momentary" temporality, bestowed through God's act.
For this reason, this act cannot be confirmed as a mere fact by historical-
critical distantiation; rather, God's love, having acted in Jesus Christ,
made manifest that in the kerygma I myself have been called into its
sphere of influence, to the historically empowering *kairos* of this act
itself; and that in this act the moment of my authentic self-realization
is made possible. Here we have arrived at the basic structure of Bultmann's theology.

Formally, this concept of eschatological historicity corresponds to
historicity in Heidegger. Heidegger writes: "Only an entity which is
in its Being pertains essentially to the *future* so that it is free for its
death and can let itself be thrown back upon to its factual 'there' by
shattering itself against death—that is to say, merely an entity which,
as pertaining to the future, is equiprimordially in the process of having
been—can, in transmitting to itself the inherited possibility, take its
own thrownness upon itself and momentarily be for 'its time.' "[58] The
possibility of historical existence, for Heidegger, lies in mortality. "Authentic Being toward death, that is to say the finitude of temporality,
is the hidden basis of Dasein's historicity."[59] We must now examine
more closely exactly what this structural parallel means, despite all
the differences, for the fundamental conception of Bultmann's theology.

Theological hermeneutics therefore has the tasks of initiating all
theological discourse into the horizon of this event and speaking from
within this horizon. Theology as hermeneutic theology in Bultmann's

sense distinguishes itself from the *existentiell* experience and discourse of faith insofar as it only points toward and initiates one into this horizon and the structure of authentic believing existence. This means theology as existential interpretation.

To speak of God's activity is not to go beyond theology as existential interpretation, insofar as it is strictly related to the event of authentic existence in its temporality and to God as the liberator of the horizon of theological discourse. What Bultmann means in saying that any discourse on God's activity is "analogical discourse"[60] is that the essence of the analogy is strictly determined by this event itself. This also shows exactly what christology can mean. When Bultmann appeals to Malanchthon's principle "Christum cognoscere est beneficia eius cognoscere,"[61] this means that christology is only possible as soteriology, and vice versa; that is, both are possible only within the framework of the eschatological saving event and its "soteriological," "existential" interpretation. All dogmatic-christological propositions must be interpreted in these terms.

Bultmann's program of *demythologization*, as well, only becomes possible in the framework of this existential interpretation. The propositions of the New Testament can only claim validity for Bultmann within this event of salvation, understood by existential interpretation. Any presentation of it "must interpret theological ideas as an explication of the self-understanding brought about through the kerygma."[62] For Bultmann, the actual difference between today's understanding and that of the New Testament lies in the different world view of the New Testament. The return to the eschatological, momentary historicity of authentic existence makes it possible for Bultmann to expound as the core of the propositions of the New Testament the mere "that" [*Dass*] of the empowering to liberated existence, independent of any differences in world view. The question then is whether the confrontation with modern consciousness, formed by the natural sciences, did not force Bultmann to retreat to a position wherein ultimately only factual existence as such can be asserted monologically. This must be investigated further.

Limit Problems of Bultmann's Conception of Theology

The limits of the basic conception of theology Bultmann developed in discussion with Heidegger in order to be able to use a responsible theological language in a society determined by scientific and technical rationality have in the meantime become obvious. We can now see the consequences of the retreat from history to the historicity of existence and thus to the momentariness of the decision to believe. Theology is threatened with the loss of its relation to concrete history and to concrete society, with all their contradictions, their horrors, and to possibilities for acting in them. The momentariness of the decision to believe can come into contradiction neither with the concrete structures of a society nor with the statements of the sciences. Is not this incontestability too high a price to pay? I need not repeat here the sort of argument that has often been brought to bear against both Heidegger and Bultmann.

In judging the value of Bultmann's theology, one nonetheless is left in an ambiguous position. Some of Bultmann's insights can be abandoned only at the price of a general regression in theological consciousness; these insights are threatened now.[63] In a word, Bultmann ought to have heightened our awareness that discourse about God is not to be had by sacrificing discourse about one's own existence.

In the following I would like to point out a strategic point in Bultmann's and Heidegger's thought that seems to me to cast light on further limit problems. I see this point in the relation of the analysis of death to the concept of intersubjectivity. In this regard, I would like to again take up the question of exactly how the relationship of Bultmann and Heidegger can be fundamentally determined.

The theological relevance of Heidegger's existential-ontological analysis is dependent on Bultmann's decisive thesis: that Heidegger adequately worked out the question of authentic self-existence.[64] Philosophy nevertheless cannot answer the question of where God concretely encounters man. Its achievement lies in developing in a formal and existential way a "neutral" analysis of the possibility of authentic understanding and so of existing, without indicating the direction or goal for which existence decides concretely, that is, from an *existentiell* point of view. Thus, writes Bultmann, "the believing understanding of the movement of existence by the question of God is not obstructed through the formal analysis of Dasein, but is rather clarified."[65] Bultmann can invoke the fact that for Heidegger, too, existential analysis does not predecide anything existentiell: "Existential interpretation never intends to take over any authoritarian pronouncement as to those things which, from an existentiell point of view, are possible and binding."⁶⁶ "In existential analysis, we cannot, in principle, discuss what Dasein *factually* resolves in any particular case."⁶⁷ The concrete possibilities of existing are disclosed to Dasein from its history. "The resoluteness in which Dasein comes back to itself discloses the current factual possibilities of authentic existing *in terms of a heritage* which that resoluteness, as thrown, *takes over*."⁶⁸

The decisive question, however, is whether existence can be concerned at all by revelation. Bultmann, in any case, objects that an analysis of existence that seems to imply that authentic existence could be made possible by human existence itself is "the radical self-assertion of man,"⁶⁹ which is, in itself, despair. Existence can interpret itself only in questioning openness.

It is clear that here it is decided how existential analysis is open to theology, on the one hand, and how on the other hand theology defines itself in the face of philosophy.

I have already noted that *Being and Time* is a fragment and that, at the end, the question of how the temporalization of time [*Zeitigung der Zeit*] is to be grasped remains. One must admit that on the whole the analyses of *Being and Time* are ambiguous. Existence becomes transparent for itself in the powerless power of its finite, mortal ability to be and need to be, which finds its empowering to be in the finite event of itself, over which it has no power. This vacillating self-elucidation allows two quite different modifications: Dasein can grasp itself as a powerless power, asserted itself in the predominance of beings, and resolve only to be itself. (In his later writings Heidegger explicates this self-understanding as metaphysics, which in its inner nature is nihilism.) But Dasein can also choose another self-understanding, and this is the possibility—explicated ever anew after the so-called "turn" [*Kehre*]—to understand itself from the relation to Being itself, from the truth of Being, which is an ongoing "mittence" to finite Dasein. Temporality remains the ontologically basic event, so that Being illuminates itself in the temporally ec-static, open differentiation of Dasein. Existence is ec-sistence into the openness of Being, which provisionally maintains a relation to Da-sein as there-being. Temporality temporalizes itself in the event of the uniting of Being and Dasein. A thinking that has undergone the "turn" has to think Dasein through the mystery of Being uncovering itself *as* an event and to bring this occurrence to speech, keeping in mind that language and interpretation—and thus hermeneutics—are only possible in terms of this event, and that this event therefore is itself originally hermeneutic.

The approach of *Being and Time* is thereby superseded, but in such a way that the analyses elaborated in it must now be thought of as based on a provisional event. In this reinterpretation they are proved true and basically confirmed, not simply negated. Temporality and historicity, their origins now considered more deeply, remain the horizon of all existing.

The question of God in Heidegger's thought cannot be treated in detail here.[70] Basically it is a matter of whether historical, finite existence can be absolutely encountered and whether existence can be not only elucidated in its structure but itself communicated and bestowed; *or*, whether the horizon of existentiell possibilities is limited to what existence already can be on its own on the basis of its facticity. Bultmann's acceptance of the analysis of *Being and Time* in a specific interpretation should not simply be disqualified as unjustified, as much as one may disagree with individual aspects of it. The ambiguity of *Being and Time* allows Bultmann to give his specific interpretation, taken from dialectical theology, of the paradoxical identity of the historical event and the event of salvation, of the word of proclamation and the Word of God, of the authentic moment and the eschatological moment, an identity that finally is the dialogical paradox of the judging, freely encountering occurrence of revelation.

The limits of Bultmann's theological conception can be made explicit through a problem that is also fundamental for Heidegger: the analytic of death. This analytic has an explicit function as a hermeneutic key in *Being and Time*, inasmuch as it makes accessible the entire structure of existence and enables it to retrieve the preliminary analysis of the structures of existence on the level of authenticity.[71] The aporia of Heidegger's analysis of death consists in the fact that, on the level of authentic existence, authentic Being with [*Mit-sein*] cannot be further analyzed: Being unto death is a completely individualized existence; authenticity as the anticipatory running before unto death constitutes authenticity as individuality. Heidegger writes: "The nonrelational character of death, as understood in anticipation, individualizes Dasein down to itself. This individualizing . . . makes manifest that all Being-present-to the things with which we concern ourselves, and all Being-with others, will fail us when our ownmost ability-to-be is at stake."[72]

This "existential solipsism"[73] has been analyzed expecially by Michael Theunissen.[74] Authentic existence is not concerned with others; authentic Being-with-others is only indirect; "in it the authentic self is not constituted."[75] W. Schulz further radicalized this analysis. Schulz writes that Heidegger's ontological transcendental philosophy "begins with finitude as the absolute, in that it calls mankind back out of its totally accidental and uncertain reality of externality and refers back to itself as Dasein, which has already *essentially* internalized that which is external."[76] It is the ideal of an existence unto one's own death "that is no longer affected by the real world."[77] In this view lies the elementary limit of the conception of *Being and Time*.[78]

The aporias of Heidegger's analysis also determine Bultmann's conception of theology, as can be shown especially in the specification of the relationship of eschatological existence to the eschatological event of revelation in the existence of Jesus. The fundamental problem of Bultmann's christology lies in his inability to show in the framework of his concept of eschatological temporality how one human being could at all be constitutively affected by the event of the death of another.

The relation of authentic existence (as the anticipatory running before unto death) to the constitution of the subject in intersubjectivity cannot be explained with the conceptual apparatus of Heidegger's existential analytic. Thus, it remains equally unclear how one could speak of God in the context of a soteriological christology. Eschatological temporality is the temporality of an isolated subject, not the temporality of the interaction of subjects who are able to be affected in their own existence by the death of the other.

The result of this problematic is the postulate of a theory of intersubjectivity for both theology and philosophy, from which the dimension of concrete society and history could be won anew.

Transcendental-Theological Hermeneutics

Transcendental Experience, Intersubjectivity, and History: Remarks on the Theology of Karl Rahner

The Hermeneutical Implications of the Modern Concept of the Subject

Whereas in Protestant theology the basic problems of the Enlightenment and of German Idealism entered into the basic conception of theological hermeneutics, either in the form of the horizon of inquiry or through the historical influence of Schleiermacher and Kierkegaard, Catholic theology was stultified in the formalism of Neo-Scholasticism. Attempts such as those of the Catholic Tübingen School to incorporate the concerns of Idealism were once again suppressed in the course of the conflicts surrounding modernism and even entirely forgotten. Rahner writes:

Certainly [Catholic theologians] were more or less adequately aware of modern and nonscholastic philosophy since the time of Descartes down to the present day, and also of Protestant theology from the Reformation down to the present, although for the most part their knowledge of this was oversimplified and they availed themselves of it only to the extent that it helped them justify their own personal standpoint in terms of scholastic usage and apologetics. Nevertheless, both these areas of thought were, after all, simply things that were alien and that had to be contested. In no sense did they constitute, in the very doubts and questions they raised and in their questionability (in the original sense of the term), something that was itself present and intrinsic to their own proper "system" itself as the seeds of a greater future that involved threats and promises. One could put it this way: As little as thirty years ago [in the pre-war period of the 1930s] Catholic theology was a system closed in upon itself.[1]

The danger of this situation lay not only in the alienation of theology from the fundamental modern experience of the transcending freedom of the subject but also in the self-alienation of religious consciousness, fostered by theology itself. In the face of this situation, [Catholic] theology saw its task as twofold. First, it had to take up the challenges of modern thought since the Enlightenment and give them a theological and creative interpretation; second, in this endeavor it had to indicate the original possibilities of Christian existence. Karl Rahner posed for himself this task of a "transformation of theology" in the service of practical Christian existence. In the following remarks, I would therefore like to indicate a perspective from which his work can be considered.[2] One could call this perspective a hermeneutic one, to highlight the parallels to Bultmann, inasmuch as this theology is concerned with the question of the condition of possibility of understanding what is handed down in the Judeo-Christian tradition in light of the claim that it is of constitutive meaning for the subject. Insofar as a transcendental problematic is given only "when and to the extent that it raises the question of the conditions in which knowledge of a specific object is possible in the knowing subject himself," the inquiry into "the mutual interconnection and mutual interconditioning process between the knowing subject and the object known . . . the object of transcendental inquiry,"[3] Rahner's project is in fact concerned with a kind of transcendental-hermeneutic transformation of theology as a whole. The basic problems of such an undertaking must be discussed in several points.

The Problem of a Transcendental Problematic in Theology

A theological enterprise that is "occupied not so much with objects as with the mode of our knowledge insofar as this mode of knowledge is to be possible *a priori*"[4] faces the same difficulties which Kant formulated and which result basically from the relation of the modern concept of the subject to the concept of God.[5] In knowing, the subject surpasses the merely individual and limited, brings it before itself precisely as that which is objective, and posits itself in the constitution of objects as a transcendental subject that has always already surpassed any limitation imposed by objectivity and can be what it is only in the act of transcending the objective realm. Knowledge of objects and transcending subjectivity mutually condition each other. From this, Kant drew the conclusion that God cannot be a possible object of knowledge, because God, in whose very concept the idea of the absolute and the unconditioned is implied, would then be subsumed under the conditions of possibility of objective experience and would be reduced to a mere object among other objects. I will not here go into the various attempts in German Idealism to resolve this fundamental problem of the modern philosophy of religion. In Catholic theology in this century, J. Maréchal's attempt to formulate a new Kant interpretation has proved to be rich in consequences.[6] Maréchal sees the basic structure of all knowing in the dynamism of the transcending movement of the subject beyond every limitation. The transcending of the subject tends toward the unlimited horizon of being; there is here a new "point de départ" for a new metaphysics and a new approach to the question of God, both of which critically overcome Kant's position and are confirmed in the interpretation of the philosophical-theological tradition. Since the 1930s a whole series of reinterpretations of Thomas Aquinas have appeared: those of Siewerth, Lotz, Müller, Welte, and Rahner.[7] The question of God can no longer be posed as a question of an isolated object of knowledge. Rather, the transcending movement of the subject to that which is unlimited, to the ungraspable, shows itself to be the condition of possibility of objective knowledge.

The Concept of the Absolute Mystery and its Self-Communication

What is decisive here is how this transcending movement and its goals are to be interpreted. Is this transcending of the subject only a formal anticipatory grasp [Vorgriff][8] of an empty horizon that exhausts its function in the disclosure of objects of empirical knowledge? Or does it point, if only unthematically, to something all-comprehensive and limitless toward which this horizon is directed as unconditionally constitutive, only evoked and made possible in this transcending movement?

The transcending movement of the subject characterizes this subject in its freedom and its possibilities of self-existence. The accomplishment of this transcending allows for various interpretations. Existence can grasp itself from this unlimited openness as empowered to be itself and want to be itself in despair. It can also simply refuse to accept this unlimited openness and cling to the merely objective. The subject who returns from its transcending to its finite facticity can, however, grasp this facticity, and its free self-realization along with it, as the "achievement of a free absolute positing of something non-necessary,"[9] and can thereby actuate its own freedom as posited by an absolute freedom.[10] Such a metaphysics of knowledge is thus a metaphysics of freedom and of dialogical existence. The indication that human existence is directed toward an incomprehensible reality, toward an absolute mystery,"[11] becomes most poignant in the experience of human freedom as posited by an absolute freedom. However, then the decisive and basic theological question is whether this incomprehensibility, which sets the subject free in his subjectivity, remains a mere *a priori* construct, or whether it, as absolute freedom, proves to be absolute love, and so makes the transcending movement of the subject and his return to his own facticity for self-discovery an occurrence out of an experience of absolute love. For Rahner, the foundational experience of Christianity consists in the identity of the absolute mystery toward which finite existence transcends with absolute love which gives itself to be experienced historically.

Transcendental Experience and Intersubjectivity in History

For Rahner this experience has the structure of a "transcendental experience."[12] Such a concept of transcendental experience admittedly appears somewhat paradoxical when viewed in terms of the original Kantian understanding of the term "transcendental," for a problematic could be termed transcendental if it inquired into the conditions of possibility of experience. In the strict sense, a transcendental experience would then be an experience that changes the conditions of possibility of experience itself; this would then imply a rigorously dialectical concept of experience. Such a use of the term raises problems that demand further clarification; however, we can immediately see a two-fold significance in this concept. On the one hand, the self-communication of the absolute mystery results in a change in the horizon of knowledge and thus in a change in the self-awareness of the subject. The nearness of the absolute mystery as the presence of absolute love is then what can generally be termed "revelation"; "it follows that the totality of the message of the Christian faith is in a real sense already given in transcendental experience."[13] On the other hand, this change in the horizon of knowledge is a free event, experienced as the liberation of freedom by an absolute freedom.

This alone does not fully explain the dialectical character of the concept of transcendental experience. To exist means to externalize oneself in another and to return to oneself out of the experience of the other. The experience of the other is constitutive of self-existence. Even revelation, as transcendental experience which alters the conditions of possibility of objective experience and so alters the horizon of objective experience, can only become a real experience if it is mediated through the experience of the other to its own immediacy. But the question then becomes: What sort of experience is the experience of this other? Since Hegel there has been at least a formal proposal of a dialectical concept of experience, according to which the fact of the experience of an "in itself" makes it already something for consciousness; that it is for consciousness means it is expressed as "in itself"; the condition and content of the given coincide in the dialectical movement of consciousness as experience.[14] On the other hand, since Hegel it has also been disputed whether the mediation of the self to itself could come about through *an* objective *other* (thing), or, within the framework of a dialectical theory of experience as well, it could come about only through *others* (selves). If the mediated movement to self-existence is thinkable only through another person, then a theory of transcendental experience that indeed implies a dialectical concept of experience necessarily becomes a theory of intersubjectivity and of communication. This is the meaning of Rahner's thesis on the unity of the love of neighbor and the love of God.[15]

Objective experience is, then, always already mediated by interpersonal experience, so that "the world of things is of significance only as a possible object for human beings as a moment within the world of persons."[16] Thus, only "the known personal Thou" is "the mediation of the subject's being-with-itself."[17] If this is the case, however, "the essential *a priori* openedness to the other human being which must be taken freely belongs as such to the *a priori* basic constitution of man."[18] Conversely, one must also say that the originary experience of God is present only in a worldly experience; "this, however, is only present originally and totally in the communication with a 'Thou.' "[19] "The act of love of neighbor is, therefore, the single categorial and primordial act in which man attains the whole of reality given to us in categories, with regard to which he properly fulfills himself perfectly and *in which* he always already has transcendental and direct experience of God by grace."[20] The "transcendental experience of God" is necessarily mediated through the "human Thou,"[21] inasmuch as precisely in the experience of the Thou the transcendence toward the absolute mystery is realized and its nearness is experienced as absolute love. It is with this in mind that Rahner grounds his thesis of the unity of the love of God and the love of neighbor: "The categorially explicit love of neighbor is the primary act of the love of God, which in the love of neighbor as such really and always intends God in supernatural transcendentality in an unthematic way, and even the explicit love of God is still borne by that opening in trusting love to the whole of reality which takes place in the love of neighbor."[22]

Our concern here is not with the details of the arguments Rahner uses to support his basic thesis. It is still clear enough that a theological theory of interaction developed from the aporias of the modern concept of the subject can be fundamental for the whole of theology insofar as it assures access to its central statements and makes their context apparent.[23]

The affirmation of the other in interaction is achieved through the experience of the nearness of the absolute mystery, toward which human existence transcends in turning concretely to the other. The determination of the reality of God thus becomes possible in the process of transcending in interaction and in the reality experienced and disclosed within this process.

The experience of the reality of God is mediated through others. From this fact, there arises a possible starting point for a christology that from the start overcomes the false alternatives of a static determination of essence and a soteriological determination of function. The foundational question of christology is then that of the possibility of the unconditional affirmative self-manifestation of God in one man for all others.[24]

Interaction as a temporal process is in itself the anticipatory grasp [apprehension; *Vorgriff*] of an open future in which something radically new can be disclosed. This anticipatory grasp of an open future does not occur monologically; rather, the anticipatory grasp of an absolute future can be achieved only as the opening of a concrete life possibility for others, through which one's own existence in turn first receives a perspective. In this way, it comes about that "the concrete future of another is the mediation for the absolute future, which is both one's own and that of all others."[25]

Rahner has attempted to develop an approach to a theology of the Trinity[26] through the structural unity of these three moments: the transcending to the absolute mystery, the possible experience of the absolute mystery in another, and the anticipatory grasp of an absolute future accomplished in intersubjectivity. A theory of human inter-subjective interaction in history becomes the hermeneutical basis for a theology of the Trinity that, even as discourse on God himself, remains a theory of experience.

Notes

Translator's Introduction

1. See Habermas, *Knowledge and Human Interests* (Boston, 1971); Habermas, *Communication and the Evolution of Society* (Boston, 1979); T. McCarthy, *The Critical Theory of Jürgen Habermas* (Boston, 1978), chapters 3 and 4. For Peukert's views of the relationship of Habermas to critical theory see his "Kritische Theorie und Pädagogik," *Zeitschrift für Pädogogik* 30 (1983): 195–217. For Habermas's response to Peukert's criticism, see Habermas, "A Reply to My Critics," in *Habermas: Critical Debates*, ed. J. B. Thompson and D. Held (Cambridge, Mass., 1982), pp. 246–247. Although Habermas agrees that the "ethics of compassion and solidarity" are limit problems for communicative ethics, he thinks Peukert does not sufficiently take into account the counterfactual and discursive nature of universalist ethical claims.

2. For example, see K. O. Apel's discussion of the phases of transcendental philosophy in "Sprechakttheorie und transcendentale Sprachpragmatik zur Frage ethischer Normen," in *Sprachpragmatik und Philosophie*, ed. Apel (Frankfurt, 1976).

3. J. B. Metz, "Erlösung und Emancipation," in *Erlösung und Emancipation*, ed. L. Scheffczyk (Freiburg, 1973), p. 137.

4. Ibid.

5. J. B. Metz, *Faith in History and Society* (New York, 1979), p. 12.

6. *Diskussion zur politischen Theologie*, ed. H. Peukert (Mainz, 1969).

7. H. Peukert, "Zur formalen Systemtheorie und zur hermeneutischen Problematik einer politischen Theologie," *Diskussion zur politischen Theologie*, 82–95. See also Peukert's and Metz's contributions to *Theologie in der interdisziplinären Forschung* (Düsseldorf, 1971) and Peukert, "Was ist eine praktische Wissenschaft?" in *Rettung des Feuers*, ed. Christen für den Sozialismus (Münster, 1981).

8. See especially H. Peukert, "Sprache und Freiheit: Zur Pragmatik ethischer Rede," in *Ethische Predigt und Alltagsverhalten*, ed. M. Kamphaus und K. Zerfass (München and Mainz, 1977), pp. 44–75; Peukert, "Pädagogik-Ethik-Politik," *Zeitschrift für Pädagogik, Beiheft* 17 (1981): 61–70; also Peukert, "Universal Solidarity as Goal of Communication," *Media Development* 28 (1981): 10–12.

9. K. Rahner, *Theological Investigations*, vol. 6 (New York, 1974), pp. 231–249.

10. C. Lenhardt, "Anamnestic Solidarity: The Proletariat and its *Manes*," *Telos* 25 (1975): 133–155 (see p. 134). Peukert has recently generalized the discussion of historical limit experiences under

the title *Kontingenzerfahrungen* (experiences of contingency). See Peukert, "Kontingenzerfahrungen und Identitätsfindung," in *Erfahrung, Glaube und Moral*, ed. E. Blank and L. Hassenhüttl (Düsseldorf, 1982).

11. W. Benjamin, *Illuminations* (New York, 1969), p. 257.

12. Another example is Nadine Gordimer's novel on generations of activism in South Africa, *Burger's Daughter* (London, 1979). See also M. Lamb, *Solidarity with Victims: Toward a Theology of Social Transformation* (New York, 1982).

Author's Preface

1. K. Rahner, *Theological Investigations*, vol. 6 (New York, 1974), pp. 231–249. This work is hereafter cited as *Investigations*.

2. K. Rahner, "Formale und fundamentale Theologie," in *Lexikon für Theologie und Kirche*, vol. 4 (Freiburg, 1957), pp. 205 ff.

3. See J. B. Metz, "Erlösung und Emancipation," in *Erlösung und Emancipation*, ed. L. Scheffczyk (Freiburg, 1973).

4. See H. Peukert, "Bemerkungen zur Theorie der Übersetzung," in *Fachsprache-Umgangssprache*, ed. J. S. Petöfi, A. Podlech, and E. Savigny (Kronberg, 1975).

5. Also see N. Mette, Theorie der Praxis (Düsseldorf, 1978).

6. See H. Peukert, "Zur Frage einer 'Logik der interdisziplinären Forschung,' " in *Die Theologie der interdisziplinären Forschung*, ed. Metz and Rendtorff (Düsseldorf, 1971).

Introduction: On Political Theology

1. P. Berger, *A Rumor of Angels* (New York, 1970), p. 29.

2. Ibid., p. 31.

3. See W.-D. Narr, "Logik der Politikwissenschaften—Eine propädeutische Skizze," in *Politikwissenschaften*, ed. Kress and Senghaas (Frankfurt, 1971), pp. 22 ff. The concept of the political must be more closely defined with reference to the contemporary discussion within political science.

4. See J. B. Metz's *Theology of the World* and its programmatic essay "Church and World in Light of a Political Theology," which was the impetus to the controversy connected with the book. The first phase of this discussion was documented by me in *Diskussion zur politischen Theologie* and later by Lehmann and Ganoczy.

5. As in Hans Maier's *Kritik der politischen Theologie* (Einsiedeln, 1970).

6. See my introduction to *Diskussion zur politischen Theologie*, p. ix.

7. See P. Berger and T. Luckman, *Social Construction of Reality*.

8. From a theological perspective, see L. Dullart, *Kirche und Ekklesiologie: Die Institutionslehre Arnold Gehlens als Frage an den Kirschenbegriff in ger gegenwärtigen systematischen Theologie* (Munchen and Mainz, 1975).

9. For earlier forms of such questioning see W. Pannenberg, *Revelation as History* (New York, 1968); J. Moltmann, *Theology of Hope* (New York, 1967); J. B. Metz, *Theology of the World* (New York, 1969).

10. This also marks a point of difference from Pannenberg's concept of the totality and its anticipation. [Cf. Pannenberg, *Theology and the Philosophy of Science* (Philadelphia, 1976).] Ebeling formulated his "reservations" in this way: "If the anticipated completeness of meaning is fulfilled in the totality of the course of history, then I see no satisfactory safeguard against a kind of evolutionary thinking that historicizes eschatology and so makes history ideological." See "Correspondence," *Zeitschrift für Theologie und Kirche* 70: 468.

11. See J. B. Metz, "Politische Theologie in der Diskussion," *Diskussion zur politischen Theologie*, pp. 267–301; Metz, "Zukunft aus dem Gedächtnis des Leidens" and "Erinnerung," essentially reproduced in *Faith in History and Society* (New York, 1979).

12. The appropriation of psychoanalytic categories by Adorno and Marcuse was caused at least in part by fascism, for which no sufficient explanatory theories were available. For discussion of these categories see J. Habermas, "Die Universalitätsanspruch der Hermeneutik," in *Hermeneutik und Ideologiekritik*, ed. Apel (Frankfurt, 1971); see the entirety of this volume as well. See also K. O. Apel, *Transformation der Philosophie* (Frankfurt, 1971), vol. 1, pp. 67 ff. [selections from this are available in English as *Transformations of Philosophy* (London, 1980)].

13. See Peukert, "Theorie der Übersetzung."

Chapter 1

1. Even within strictly analytic theory of science, Kuhn's views have given rise to new directions in the investigation of the history of science. However, the methodology of such research remains in dispute. If one wanted to investigate the history of the relationship of more empirically oriented thinking to more exegetical-interpretative thinking, one would have to write a history of different views of language. This still has not been accomplished. [By way of introduction, see E. Coseriu, *Geschichte der Sprachphilosophie* I (Stuttgart, 1969); E. Cassirer, *Philosophy of Symbolic Forms* (New Haven, 1953–1956); J. Stenzel, *Philosophie der Sprache* (Munich, 1934); P. A. Verburg, *Taal en functionaliteit* (Wageningen, 1952); M. Black, *Language and Philosophy* (Ithaca, 1952); B. Liebrucks, *Sprache und Bewusstsein* (Frankfurt, 1964–1974).] The history of this opposition could be studied in the history of the reception of Aristotle by the extent to which Aristotle's threefold distinction of *logos semantikos*, thus of language itself, is received as a whole or only in a reduced form (language as *logos apophantikos* in the *Analytic*, as *logos pragmatikos* in the rhetoric, and as *logos poietikos* in the *Poetics*). The history of medieval philosophy and theology of language is still murky, because the more exact individual studies have had a limited perspective and because the tradition itself is unclear (especially in the development of individual theories). [See I. M. Bocheński, *Formale Logik* (Freiburg, 1956); C. Thurot, *Extraits des divers manuscrits latins pour servir a la histoire des doctrines grammaticales au Moyen-Age* (Paris, 1969); M. Grabmann, "Die Entwicklung der mittelalterlichen Sprachlogik," in *Mittelalterliches Geistesleben*, vol. 1 (Munich, 1926); Grabmann, "Die geschichtliche Entwicklung der mittelalterlichen Sprach-philosophie und Sprachlogik," ibid., vol. 3; F. Manthey, *Die Sprachphilosophie des hlg. Thomas von Aquin* (Paderborn, 1938); J. Pinborg, *Die Entwicklung der Sprachtheorie im Mittelalter* (Münster, 1967); *Logik und Semantik im Mittelalter* (Stuttgart, 1972). The distinction and reciprocal relation of *modi essendi, modi intelligendi*, and *modi significandi* function within a speculative grammar to mediate grammar, logic, and ontology. Nominalism broke the unity of the logic of language and ontology. Behind the epistemological position regarding universal concepts and the emphasis on the individual is a theological interest in a concept of God focusing on his freedom in history. It is decisive for the development of modern empricism that these nominalist conceptions proved fruitful for the origin of modern natural science. [See A. Maier's five-volume *Studien zur Naturphilosophie der Spätscholastik* (Rome, 1949).] In the English-speaking world we can see a

direct relationship of Ockham to Bacon, Locke, Berkeley, Mill, and finally Russell. Hume gave a classic formulation to the heightened suspicion of the meaninglessness of all metaphysical and theological statements in the last sentences of his *Enquiry into Human Understanding*: "When we run over libraries, persuaded by these principles, what havoc must we make? If we take in our hand any volume, of divinity or school metaphysics, for instance; let us ask, Does it contain any abstract reasoning concerning matters of fact and existence. No—Does it contain any experimental reasoning concerning matters of fact and existence. No—Commit it to the flames: for it can contain nothing but sophistry and illusion." (Oxford, 1951, p. 165) This passage contains many of the themes of Logical Positivism. By contrast, hermeneutic conceptions of language can be traced back to the transcendental themes of German logos mysticism (Meister Eckhart's "unwordly eternal Word"), which was further strengthened by the theology of the word in the Reformation, and to the philological-historical sensibility of Italian humanism [see K. O. Apel's *Idee der Sprache in der Tradition des Humanismus von Dante bis Vico* (Bonn, 1963]. Even within this tradition, those thinkers for whom language was the center of attention (Hamann, Herder, and von Humboldt) remain isolated from the great tradition of philosophy. To conect these two forms of thought remains an uncompleted task.

2. From the preface to the *Tractatus* (London, 1961), p. 5.

3. Apel, *Transformation* 1, p. 343. On the central importance of the *Tractatus* see K. Lorenz, *Elemente der Sprachkritik* (Frankfurt, 1970), pp. 35 ff.

4. See E. Stenius, *Wittgenstein's Tractatus* (Ithaca, 1960), p. 220.

5. L. Wittgenstein, *Philosophical Remarks* (Chicago, 1975), p. 8.

6. See B. Russell, "Logical Atomism," in *Logical Positivism*, ed. A. J. Ayer (New York, 1959); A. Kenny, *Wittgenstein* (Cambridge, 1973), pp. 89 ff.

7. See *Tractatus*, 3.1. The numbers in the text refer to the paragraph numbers used by Wittgenstein.

8. See Stegmüller, *Hauptströmungen der Gegenwartsphilosophie* 1 (Stuttgart, 1975), pp. 539 ff.

9. Stenius, *Wittgenstein's Tractatus*, pp. 220 ff.

10. Habermas, *Zur Logik der Sozialwissenschaften* (Frankfurt, 1967), p. 128. English translation forthcoming (MIT Press, 1984).

11. W. Schulz, *Wittgenstein: Die Negation der Philosophie* (Pfullingen, 1967), p. 108, n. 4.

12. H. Fahrenbach, "Die logisch-hermeneutische Problemstellung in Wittgensteins Tractatus," in *Hermeneutik und Dialektik*, ed. R. Bubner, K. Cramer, and R. Wiehl (Tübingen, 1970), p. 54.

13. Cf. Wittgenstein, *Philosophical Remarks*, ed. R. Rhees (Oxford, 1964), p. 6.

14. See Habermas, *Zur Logik der Sozialwissenschaften*, p. 128; K. Wuchterl, *Struktur und Sprachspiel bei Wittgenstein* (Frankfurt, 1969), p. 42; Apel, *Transformation* 1, pp. 339 ff., n. 8.

15. Wuchterl, p. 62; K. Lorenz, *Elemente*, pp. 75 ff.

16. Stenius, pp. 220 ff.

17. See Stegmüller, *Hauptströmungen* 1, pp. 553 ff.; Apel, *Transformation* 1, pp. 339 ff., n. 8; Habermas, *Logik*, pp. 128 ff.

18. See Schulz, *Wittgenstein*, p. 15.

19. Wittgenstein expressed this intention in the foreword to the *Tractatus*: ". . . the aim of the book is to draw a limit to thought, or rather not to thought but to the expression of thoughts; for in order to be able to draw a limit to thought, we should have to find both sides of the limit thinkable (i.e. we should have to be able to think what cannot be thought). It will therefore only be in language that the limit can be drawn and what lies on the other side of the limit will simply be nonsense." (p. 3)

20. See Schulz, *Wittgenstein*, pp. 35 ff.; Habermas, *Logik*, p. 129.

21. See Schulz, *Wittgenstein*, pp. 47 and 32.

22. Apel, *Transformation* 1, p. 348.

23. Ibid.; see also Wittgenstein's own remarks on the *Tractatus* in the foreword to the *Philosophical Investigations*.

24. O. Neurath, "Sociology and Physicalism," in *Logical Positivism*, ed. Ayer (New York, 1959), p. 284. There could scarcely be a statement that similarly reduces Wittgenstein's attempt to make manifest the presence of the unsayable through negation to simple positivism.

25. Both Stenius and Malcolm indicate that Wittgenstein himself did not go any farther in this direction. If one wishes to pursue this theme, the question of the communicability of mystical experience is unavoidable. Here one must also consider non-Christian mysticism. The closest parallel is perhaps the phase of completion in the Vedanta. See the Kena-Upanishad: "Only he who does not know, knows it; he who knows knows it not—not known by the knower, known by the non-knower! The one for whom it is awakened knows it and finds eternity." See also the Taittiriya-Upanishad: "For if one finds peace, a home in the unseeable, the unreal, the inexpressible, the ungroundable, it is as if he has succeeded in finding peace."

26. The circle consisted of Rudolf Carnap, Otto Neurath, Herbert Feigl, Friedrich Waismann, Victor Kraft, Phillip Frank, Karl Menger, Kurt Gödel, and Hans Hahn.

27. Wittgenstein seemed alarmed by the exclusion of the mystical element from the *Tractatus* in the interpretation of the Vienna Circle, leaving only the theory of science. See G. Patzig's introduction to R. Carnap's *Scheinprobleme der Philosophie* (Frankfurt, 1966), pp. 103 ff.

28. See Schlick's programmatic article in the inaugural issue of the circle's jointly edited journal *Erkenntnis*, "The Turning Point in Philosophy" (in *Logical Positivism*, ed. Ayer).

29. Waismann's reports of conversations with Wittgenstein are most informative here: "The meaning of a sentence is its method of verification." (*Schriften* III, p. 79; remark of January 2, 1930.) Also see ibid., pp. 227, 244; *Philosophical Remarks*, nos. 43, 44, 148, 166.

30. See R. Carnap, "The Elimination of Metaphysics Through Logical Analysis of Language," in *Logical Positivism*, ed. Ayer, p. 80. In this essay Carnap singles out Heidegger's 1929 inaugural lecture in Freiburg "What is Metaphysics?" as the target of his criticism—especially sentences like "Das Nichts selbst nichtet."

31. Carnap, "Elimination," p. 67. Patzig (p. 100) suggests that this understanding of metaphysics as the expression of life feeling is traceable to Carnap's impressions during his studies with Hermann Nohl, a student of Dilthey. To this extent, Carnap's view would also be directed against the knowledge claims of a specific philosophical hermeneutics.

32. R. Carnap, *Pseudoproblems in Philosophy* (Berkeley, 1967), p. 328.

33. See D. Antiseri, *Filosofia analitica e semantica del linguaggio religioso* (Brescia, 1969), p. 27.

34. Also see A. J. Ayer, *Language, Truth and Logic* (London, 1936), pp. 115 ff.

35. Schlick was shot in 1936 at the University of Vienna by a mentally ill student. The event was reported quite maliciously in the press friendly to the existing government. The remaining members of the circle either had already emigrated or had to leave with the occupation in 1938.

36.

37. Patzig, p. 111.

Chapter 2

1. On the following, see H. Peukert, "Zur formalen Systemtheorie und zur hermeneutischen Problematik einer 'politischen Theologie,' " in *Diskussion zur politischen Theologie*.

2. See G. Frege, "Begriffsschrift," in *From Frege to Gödel*, ed. Heijenoort (Cambridge, 1967); *The Basic Laws of Arithmetic* (Berkeley, 1965); M. Dummet, *Frege* (London, 1972).

3. Leibniz, *Schriften* VII, pp. 32 ff. In his reflections, Leibniz explicitly relies on Raimundus Lullus, who in his *Ars Magna* tried to develop a system for the discovery of all truths based on Arab mathematics. [See H. Hermes, *Aufzählbarkeit—Entscheidbarkeit—Berechnenbarkeit* (Berlin, 1961), pp. 28–29.] For Leibniz, it was certain that such a procedure would then also be realized in a machine.

4. B. Russell and A. N. Whitehead, *Principia Mathematica* (London, 1925–1927).

5. K. Gödel, "The Completeness of Axioms of the Functional Calculus of Logic," in *From Frege to Gödel*.

6. Hermes, *Aufzählbarkeit*, p. 30. First-order predicate logic permits rules for propositional logic and quantification only for elements of basic sets—that is, for individual variables and not yet for predicates. Sets of elements and systems of sets are excluded. Second-order predicate logic permits the quantification of predicates, propositions about predicates, or predicates of predicates.

7. Stegmüller, *Hauptströmungen* I, pp. 334 ff.

8. To be found in *From Frege to Gödel*.

9. On this entire problematic see Hermes, *Aufzählbarkeit*, pp. 165 ff.; W. Stegmüller, *Unvollständigkeit und Unentscheidbarkeit* (Vienna, 1959); F. von Kutschera, *Die Antinomien der Logik* (Freiburg, 1964); J. Ladrière, *Les limitations internes des formalismes* (Louvain, 1957).

10. See Hermes, *Aufzählbarkeit*, chapter 6.

11. See A. Church, "An Unsolvable Problem of Elementary Number Theory," *American Journal of Mathematics* 58 (1936): 345–363. In this essay Church demonstrated the undecidability of first-order predicate logic.

12. See B. Rosser, "Extensions of Some Theorems of Gödel and Church," *Journal of Symbolic Logic* 1 (1936): 87–91.

13. See S. Kleene, "General Recursive Functions of Natural Numbers," *Mathematische Annalen* 112 (1936): 727–742.

14. See Hermes, *Aufzählbarkeit*, chapters 5 and 6.

15. Ibid., chapter 6. On the significance of the theorems of Gödel and Church for the theory of the deductive sciences, see A. Tarski, *Introduction to Logic and to the Methodology of the Deductive Sciences* (London, 1941).

16. See A. M. Turing, "On Computable Numbers," *Proceedings of the London Mathematical Society* 42 (1936): 230 ff.; corrections, 43 (1937): 544–546.

17. On the concept of Turing machines and Turing computability see Hermes, *Aufzählbarkeit*, pp. 33 ff., 95 ff.

18. For the history of the problem of antinomies in the Middle Ages and antiquity see Bochénski, *Formale Logik*, sections 23 and 25.

19. See A. Tarski, "The Concept of Truth in Formal Languages," in *Logic, Semantics, Metamathematics* (Oxford, 1956); W. Stegmüller, *Das Wahrheitsproblem und die Idee der Semantik* (Vienna, 1957).

20. By way of clarification of some of the concepts used here, the general investigation of systems of language is usually called *semiotics*. Pure semiotics is concerned with logical calculi, empirical semiotics with natural languages. Semiotics has three subdisciplines: Pragmatics is concerned with the relation of language and the speaker, syntactics with the relations of the signs of a language to each other, and semantics with the relationship of signs and the signified. Therefore, concepts such as meaning, truth, and falsity are semantic concepts. See Stegmüller, *Wahrheitsproblem*, p. 41; A. Menne, *Einführung in die Logik* (Bern and Munich, 1966).

21. See Stegmüller, *Wahrheitsproblem*, pp. 31 ff; K. Füssell, Die sprachanalytische und wissenschaftstheoretische Diskussion um den Begriff der Wahrheit in ihrer Relevanz für eine systematische Theologie, dissertation, Münster, 1975.

22. See R. Carnap, *Logical Syntax of Language* (London, 1934).

23. See H. Steiner, *Grundlagenforschung*.

24. P. Lorenzen, *Einführung in die operative Logik und Mathematik* (Berlin, 1955).

25. Tarski complained that his results were not given the philosophical consideration they deserved: "Although my investigations concern concepts dealt with in classical philosophy, they seem to be comparatively little known in philosophical circles, perhaps because of their strictly technical character." ["The Semantic Conception of Truth," in *Semantics*, ed. Linsky (Urbana, 1952)] For the state of the art here, see R. Klinbansky, *Contemporary Philosophy* II (Florence, 1968); Stegmüller, *Hauptströmungen* II; for an interpretation of Gödel similar to that of this chapter, see Ladriere, "Suggestions philosophiques," in *Limitations*.

26. See Ladrière, in *Limitations*, p. 438: "Chaque opération nouvelle quitte à son tour le champ de la présence pour aller rejoindre, dans l'objectivation réflexive, toutes celles qui appartiennent déjà à ce qui n'est plus. Il y a donc bien ici, dans le dédoublement ininterrompu de soi d'avec soi qui caractérise le mouvement de la temporalisation (et qui caractérise du même coup le mouvement de la réflexion), la source de cette possibilité toujours ouverte d'un *après* qui caractérise les opérations constructives." On the relationship of time and mathematics in Kant see F. Kambartel, *Erfahrung und Struktur* (Frankfurt, 1968), pp. 177 ff.

27. We can distinguish two different conceptions of models. Usually a model is understood as the representation of the general structure of concrete things or processes. In mathematical logic, and especially in semantics, the relation is reversed; the model is the particular as opposed to the general system, so that it is an "*interpretation*" of the system. See Ladrière, in *Limitations*, pp. 55 ff., 414 ff.; H. Hermes, *Einführung in die mathematische Logik* (Berlin, 1961), pp. 21, 71–81. The result of research into models mentioned above is the so-called Löwenheim-Skolem theorem.

28. See C. F. von Weizsäcker, *Die Einheit der Natur* (Munich, 1971), pp. 39-60.

29. In fact, Lorenzen [*Methodisches Denken* (Frankfurt, 1968), p. 27] accuses an axiomatically based foundation theory of the "circularity" common to all hermeneutical thinking, to the extent that Lorenzen asserts "the coincidence of hermeneutical and logical thinking" (pp. 28 and 48), thereby allowing us to forgo constructing thought methodologically. On this entire argument, see Thiel, "Das Begründungsproblem der Mathematik und die Philosophie," in *Zum normativen Fundament der Wissenschaft*, ed. F. Kambartel and J. Mittelstrass (Frankfurt, 1973).

30. See K. W. Deutsch, *Politische Kybernetik* (Freiburg, 1964).

31. One of the best introductions to this field is still R. Ashby's *Introduction to Cybernetics* (New York, 1956). See also G. Klaus, *Wörterbuch der Kybernetik* (Berlin, 1968).

32. See M. D. Mesarovic et al., *Theory of Hierarchical Multi-level Systems* (New York, 1970).

33. See Böhme, "Information und Verständigung," in *Offene Systeme* I, ed. Weizsäcker (Stuttgart, 1974).

34. See W. Stegmüller, *Probleme und Resultate der Wissenschafts- und analytischen Philosophie* I (Berlin, 1973), pp. 612-623. In pedagogical research, this problematic is given the names "programmed learning" and "cybernetic didactics." See H. Blankertz, *Theorien und Modelle der Didaktik* (Munich, 1969).

35. See A. M. Turing, "Computing Machinery and Intelligence," *Methodos* 6 (1954): 23 ff.

36. See J. R. Lucas, "Minds, Machines and Gödel," *Philosophy* 36 (1961): 112-126; J. J. Smart, *Philosophy and Scientific Realism* (New York, 1963); K. Gunderson, "Cybernetics," in *Encyclopedia of Philosophy*, vol. II (New York, 1967), pp. 280-284.

37. On the proposed solutions to the determination of this relationship, see Weizsäcker, *Einheit*, pp. 342 ff.; see also his "Evolution und Entropiewachstum," in *Offene Systeme* I, pp. 200-211. Weizsäcker is of the opinion that the increase in entropy and the decrease in information cannot be considered the same process. Absolute zero would not necessarily lead to the destruction of complicated structures, but might lead to complex structures no longer capable of orderly change; "Assuming a sufficiently low temperature, absolute zero would not be a purée, but rather a collection of complicated skeletons." (ibid., p. 203)

38. See H. Schäfer et al., "Kybernetik," in *Sowjetsystem und demokratische Gesellschaft*, vol. III (Freiburg, 1969), p. 1293.

39. Ibid., p. 1294.

40. See G. Klaus, "Kybernetik," in *Wörterbuch der Kybernetik*, pp. 324-329; Klaus, *Kybernetik und Erkenntnistheorie* (Berlin, 1972).

41. See *Philosophisches Wörterbuch*, ed. Klaus and Buhn (Berlin, 1969), p. 643.

42. Schulz, *Philosophie in der veränderten Welt*, p. 245.

Chapter 3

1. H. Schädelbach, *Erfahrung, Begründung und Reflexion* (Frankfurt, 1971), p. 9.

2. Wandschneider, *Formale Sprache und Erfahrung* (Stuttgart, 1974), p. 5.

3. Stegmüller, *Hauptströmungen* I, p. 387.

4. R. Carnap, *Logical Structure of the World* (Berkeley, 1967). The first edition (1928) was based on a 1925 version; the second edition (1961) had a new foreword by Carnap. For the literature on this work see Goodman, *The Structure of Appearance* (Cambridge, 1951); Stegmüller, *Hauptströmungen* I, pp. 387–392; Kraft, *Der Wiener Kreis* (Vienna, 1968); Kambartel, *Erfahrung und Struktur* (Frankfurt, 1968), pp. 149–198; Krauth, *Die Philosophie Carnaps* (Vienna, 1970), pp. 12–14; Wandschneider, *Formale Sprache*, pp. 30–38.

5. Carnap, *Logical Structure of the World*, p. 108.

6. Ibid., p. 106.

7. Ibid., p. 113.

8. Ibid., p. 132.

9. Ibid., p. 138.

10. Ibid., pp. 191 ff.

11. Ibid., p. 214.

12. Ibid., p. 157.

13. See Kambartel, *Erfahrung*, p. 188. Carnap (*Logical Structure*, p. 27) writes of "the general possibility of structural description" and states that "all scientific statements are structure statements." (p. 28) "The result," Carnap writes, "is that each scientific statement can be so transformed that it is nothing but a structure statement." (p. 29) Therefore, Carnap asserts that "for science it is possible and at the same time necessary to restrict itself to structure statements." (p. 30)

14. "Now what about 'nonrational knowledge,' for example the content of a mystical, ineffable view of God? It does not come into a relation with any knowledge within the limits that we have so far staked out; it can neither be confirmed nor disconfirmed by any of it; there is no road from the continent of rational knowledge to the island of intuition, while there is a road from the country of empirical knowledge to the country of formal knowledge, which thus shows that they belong to the same continent. Thus, it follows that, if our suggested compromise is accepted, then nonrational intuition and religious faith (to the extent to which they are not only a believing the truth of certain propositions, but are ineffable) cannot be called *knowledge*." (*Logical Structure*, p. 294) Carnap did not assert the meaninglessness of religious beliefs but proposed a treaty for "the peaceful relationship between the various spheres of life." (p. 295)

15. See Kambartel, *Erfahrung*, pp. 192 ff.; "the proof that each rational scientific problem may be reduced to a formal, syntactic, or structural-theoretical problem has, according to our analysis, not succeeded, nor does there seem to be any hope of success for further efforts in this direction." (ibid., p. 196)

16. Carnap later was to admit his error here: see the foreword to the second edition of the *Aufbau* (*Logical Structure*).

17. Neurath, "Sociology and Physicalism," p. 305.

18. Carnap, "Die physikalische Sprache als Universalsprache der Wissenschaft," *Erkenntnis* (1931): 432–465; see p. 441. [Revised English translation: *The Unity of Science* (London, 1934).]

19. Ibid., p. 452.

20. Neurath, "Physicalism," p. 295.

21. Ibid., pp. 408 ff.

22. Carnap, "Die physikalische Sprache," p. 463.

23. Carnap, "Psychology in Physical Language," in *Logical Positivism*, ed. Ayer; see p. 197.

24. Weizsäcker, *Einheit*, p. 288.

25. See Neurath, "Protocol Sentences," in *Logical Positivism*, ed. Ayer, pp. 199–208; Carnap, "Über Protokollsätze," *Erkenntnis* (1932–33): 215–228.

26. Neurath, "Protocol Sentences," pp. 204 ff.; Carnap, "Über Protokollsätze," p. 228.

27. Carnap, ibid.

28. See Ayer's introduction to *Logical Positivism*, pp. 10 ff.; C. Hempel, "Problems and Changes in the Empiricist Criteria of Meaning," in *Logical Postivism*, pp. 108–129; Patzig, *Scheinprobleme*, pp. 111 ff.

29. K. Popper, *The Logic of Scientific Discovery* (London, 1959).

30. Ibid., p. 53.

31. Ibid., p. 28.

32. Ibid., p. 29.

33. See the foreword to the second German edition: *Logik der Forschung* (Tübingen, 1973), p. xxvi.

34. Ibid., p. 278.

35. Ibid., p. 36. (This view was already contained in the "Preliminary Report" Popper sent to the editors of *Erkenntnis* in 1933.)

36. Ibid., p. 78.

37. Ibid., pp. 119 ff.

38. Ibid., p. 68.

39. Ibid., p. 100.

40. Ibid., p. 94.

41. Ibid., p. 95.

42. Popper is here directly criticizing Carnap's system for constituting empirical concepts: "Universals cannot be reduced to classes of experiences: they cannot be constituted." (p. 95) A footnote added in the second edition explains that " 'Constituted' is Carnap's term." In place of Carnap's constitution terminology, Popper used "indefinable universal names which are established only by linguistic usage." (p. 84) Thus, Popper emphasizes the necessity of the return to "linguistic usage."

43. Ibid., p. 104.

44. Ibid., p. 107. See also p. 59. For Popper, a more precise theory of experiment could show that theoretical considerations control experimental work from its planning to "the finishing touches in the laboratory." (p. 107) "Experiment is planned action in which every step is guided by theory." (p. 280) Theory alone makes possible a precise statement of the problem under study, allowing other definitions of it to be rejected and other sources of error excluded. Observations then receive the status of meanings derived from theoretical proposals; indeed, they only come about through theory.

45. Ibid., p. 109.

46. Ibid., p. 110.

47. Ibid., p. 111.

48. Ibid., p. 75.

49. Lakatos calls the view that individual contradictory basic statements refute a theory "naive falsificationism." He insists that Popper did not hold such a view, and he attempts to further specify Popper's position. See I. Lakatos, "Criticism and the Methodology of Scientific Research Programmes," *Proceedings of the Aristotelean Society* 69 (1968): 148-186; "Falsification and the Methodology of Scientific Research Programmes," in *Criticism and the Growth of Knowledge*, ed. Lakatos and Musgrave (Cambridge, 1970). Also see L. Schäfer, *Erfahrung und Konvention* (Stuttgart, 1974).

50. See Popper, *Logic of Scientific Discovery*, chapters VI, VIII, X, and the postscript to the second edition.

51. Ibid., p. 280.

52. Ibid., p. 107.

53. Ibid., pp. 78 ff., 108 ff., and the preface to the second German edition, p. xxvi.

54. Ibid., pp. 81-84.

55. Ibid., p. 82.

56. Ibid., pp. 82-83.

57. See H. Oetjens, *Sprache, Logik, Wirklichkeit* (Stuttgart, 1975).

58. On this extension of his thought see K. Popper, *Open Society and its Enemies* (Princeton, 1950); *The Poverty of Historicism* (Boston, 1957). For earlier forms of these views see the bibliography in M. Bunge, *The Critical Approach to Science and Philosophy* (London, 1964), pp. 473 ff.

59. Popper, *Conjectures and Refutations* (London, 1963), p. 47. This is already the view in *Logic*, p. 72.

60. Popper, "Naturgesetze und theoretische Systeme," in *Theorie und Realität*, ed. Albert (Tübingen, 1964), p. 92.

61. On the "Darwinist" passages in Popper see Schäfer, *Erfahrung*, p. 67. This question can only be discussed in connection with the problem of "progress" in the sciences. Popper himself further stressed the evolutionary character of the growth of knowledge; see especially *Objective Knowledge*.

62. Popper, "The Demarcation of Science and Metaphysics," in *The Philosophy of Rudolf Carnap*, ed. P. Schilpp (LaSalle, 1963), p. 183. Also see Schäfer, *Erfahrung*, pp. 81–105.

63. *Logic*, p. 311.

64. Ibid., pp. 31 ff., 49, 54, 69, 190, 204, 278 ff., 425 ff.

65. Popper, "Demarcation," p. 201; on Gödel and Church see p. 202.

66. Popper, *Logic*, p. 277.

67. Schäfer, *Erfahrung*, p. 81; Popper, *Logic*, p. 206.

68. See Popper, *Logic*, chapter XVI; *Conjectures*, pp. 70, 73.

69. Popper, *Objective Knowledge*, p. 40.

70. Popper, *Conjectures*, p. 257.

71. Ibid., pp. 228 ff., 401 ff.

72. "Verisimilitude is so defined that maximum verisimilitude would be achieved only by a theory which is not only true, but completely comprehensively true: if it corresponds to *all* facts, as it were, and, of course, only to *real* facts. (ibid., p. 234)

73. Popper, *Logic*, p. 423.

74. See Popper, *Conjectures*, pp. 223–228, 401 ff. See also A. Wellmer, *Methodologie als Erkenntnistheorie* (Frankfurt, 1967), pp. 227 ff.

75. See Tarski, "The Semantic Conception of Truth," p. 362.

76. Popper, *Conjectures*, p. 224.

77. See Wellmer, *Methodologie*, p. 233.

78. See Popper, *Logic*, p. 368.

79. Ibid., p. 87.

80. On the consequences of this thesis, see the discussion of the Kuhn-Popper-Lakatos controversy presented later in this chapter.

81. Carnap met Tarski in Vienna as early as 1930, and they had further contact during Carnap's stay in Prague. (See Carnap's "Intellectual Autobiography," in *The Philosophy of R. Carnap.*) Carnap was thus able to make use of Tarski's results in his *Logical Syntax of Language* before their publication in German.

82. Carnap, *The Logical Syntax of Language* (London, 1937), p. 280.

83. *Tractatus*, 3.323–3.325.

84. Carnap, *Logical Syntax*, p. 322.

85. Ibid., p. 323.

86. Ibid., p. 332.

87. See Peukert, "Logik der interdisziplinären Forschung."

88. Carnap, *Logical Syntax*, p. 52.

89. See the presentation of Carnap's semantics elsewhere in this volume.

90. See Stegmüller, *Probleme und Resultate* II, pp. 189 ff.; W. Lenzen, *Theorien der Bestätigung wissenschaftlicher Hypothesen* (Stuttgart, 1974), pp. 127 ff.

91. See Carnap, "Truth and Confirmation," in *Readings in Philosophical Analysis*, ed. Feigl and Sellars (New York, 1949). With reference to Popper, Carnap speaks of *Bewährung*; however, he also uses *Bestätigung*. Both are rendered in English as "confirmation."

92. See Krauth, *Philosophie*, pp. 88-98; Stegmüller, *Hauptströmungen* I, pp. 402-411.

93. See Carnap, *Testability and Meaning* (New Haven, 1950), pp. 33 ff.

94. Ibid., p. 35.

95. See Krauth, *Philosophie*, p. 98; Stegmüller, *Hauptströmungen* I, p. 410; Stegmüller, *Probleme* I, pp. 199-212; Wandschneider, *Formale Sprache*, pp. 52-58.

96. Carnap distinguishes the concept of confirmation from that of truth; see "Truth and Confirmation," p. 119. For Carnap, the concept of truth belongs to semantics and is as such a purely logical concept. The concept of confirmation refers to the empirical significance of scientific statements. Such statements are designated as confirmed or confirmable, but nevertheless not as true in any sense greater than a logical one. In the language of science it is therefore meaningless to speak of truth in any other than a logical sense. The question of the truth of a language system cannot be meaningfully posed or decided.

97. On this distinction see Stegmüller, *Hauptströmungen* I, pp. 368 ff.; *Probleme* II, pp. 224 ff.

98. See Krauth, *Philosophie*, p. 64.

99. See P. W. Bridgman, *The Logics of Modern Physics* (New York, 1962); J. Klüver, *Operationalismus* (Stuttgart, 1971), pp. 114 ff.

100. See, above all, Carnap, "Beobachtungssprache und theoretische Sprache," in *Logica: Studia Paul Bernays dedicata* (Neuchatel, 1959), pp. 32-44. Also see Stegmüller, *Probleme* II (Stegmüller provides a detailed analysis of Carnap's theses).

101. Carnap, *Logica*, p. 237.

102. Ibid., p. 238.

103. Ibid., p. 239.

104. Ibid., p. 240.

105. Ibid., p. 239.

106. Ibid., p. 240.

107. Ibid., p. 241.

108. See Krauth, *Philosophie*, p. 120; Stegmüller, *Hauptströmungen* I, p. 464; *Probleme* II, pp. 340 ff.

109. See Stegmüller, "Einige skeptische Schlussbetrachtungen: Der Zusammeubrach der Signifikanzidee," in *Probleme* II, p. 361.

110. See W. Craig, "On Axiomatizability within a System," *Journal of Symbolic Logic* 18 (1953): 30–32; "Replacement of Auxiliary Expressions," *Philosophical Review* 65 (1956): 38–55; Stegmüller, *Probleme* II, pp. 375–400.

111. See F. P. Ramsey, "Theories," in *The Foundations of Mathematics* (London, 1931); Stegmüller, *Probleme* II, pp. 401–437.

112. See J. Ladrière, *Rede der Wissenschaft — Wort des Glaubens* (Munich, 1972), p. 37; Stegmüller, *Probleme* II, p. 435.

113. Carnap, "Empiricism, Semantics, and Ontology," *Revue internationale de Philosophie* 11 (1950): 20–40.

114. Ibid., p. 21.

115. Ibid., p. 31.

116. The controversy between "Nominalism" and "Platonism" can be traced throughout the discussion of the foundations of mathematics and logic. See W. V. Quine, "Logic and the Reification of Universals," in *From a Logical Point of View* (New York, 1953); Quine, *Word and Object* (New York, 1960); Stegmüller, *Hauptströmungen* I, pp. 487–493; Stegmüller, *Universalenproblem* (Darmstadt, 1965).

117. See D. Bohm, "A Suggested Interpretation of the Quantum Theory in Terms of 'Hidden Variables,'" *Physical Review* 85 (1952): 166–179; Bohm, "Classical and Non-Classical Concepts in Quantum Theory," *Journal of the British Philosophical Society* 12 (1962): 265–280; E. Scheibe, "Zum Problem der Sprachabhangigkeit in der Physik," in *Das Problem der Sprache*, ed. H.-G. Gadamer (Munich, 1967); Scheibe, *Die kontingente Aussagen der Physik* (Frankfurt, 1964); R. Mittelstaedt, *Philosophische Probleme der modernen Physik* (Mannheim, 1972).

118. Carnap, "Empiricism, Semantics and Ontology," p. 31. A further criterion for the choice of language forms, for Carnap, is their "efficiency as instruments" (ibid., p. 40).

119. Carnap, "Intellectual Autobiography," in *The Philosophy of Rudolf Carnap* (LaSalle, 1963).

120. "This I called the 'principle of tolerance': it might perhaps be called more exactly the 'principle of conventionality of language forms.'" ("Intellectual Biography," p. 55) See W. Diederich, *Konventionalität der Physik* (Berlin, 1974).

121. See Schäfer, *Erfahrung*.

122. See Schnädelbach, *Erhfahrung*, pp. 185 ff.

123. T. Kuhn, *Structure of Scientific Revolutions* (Chicago, 1970).

124. On the status of the contemporary problematic, see the introduction by Diedrich to *Theorien der Wissenschaftsgeschichte* (Frankfurt, 1974).

125. M. Masterman has tried to show that there are at least 21 different meanings to the world "paradigm" in Kuhn. See Masterman, "The Nature of a Paradigm," in *Criticism and the Growth of Knowledge*. Kuhn now prefers to speak of a "disciplinary matrix" or "exemplar"; see Kuhn, "Reflections on my Critics," ibid., pp. 271 ff.

126. The function of underlying paradigms could also be explained through the Ptolemaic world view, through the phlogiston theory, through the conception of electricity as a liquid, or even through the belief in witches.

127. Kuhn, *Structure*, p. 64.

128. Ibid., p. 112.

129. Ibid., p. 88.

130. Ibid., p. 111.

131. Ibid., p. 135.

132. Ibid., p. 177.

133. See Popper, "Normal Science and its Dangers," in *Criticism*, pp. 51–58.

134. Ibid., p. 55.

135. Ibid., p. 58.

136. See Lakatos, "Criticism and the Methodology of Scientific Research Programmes," *Proceedings of the Aristotelian Society* 69 (1968): 149–186; "Falsification and the Methodology of Scientific Research Programmes," in *Criticism*; "History of Science and its Rational Reconstructions," in *Boston Studies* VIII (Dordrecht, 1971).

137. P. Feyerabend, "Reply to Criticism," *Boston Studies* II, pp. 223–261. See also Feyerabend, "Problems of Empiricism," in *Beyond the Edge of Certainty*, ed. R. Colodny (Englewood Cliffs, 1965); "Problems of Empiricism II," in *The Nature and the Function of Scientific Theories*, ed. R. Colodny (Pittsburgh, 1970); J. Agassi, "Scientific Problems and Their Roots in Metaphysics," in *The Critical Approach to Science and Philosophy* (London, 1964); Agassi, "Sensationalism," *Mind* 75 (1966): 1–24; J. W. N. Watkins, "Influential and Confirmable Metaphysics," *Mind* 67 (1958): 344–365; "Hume, Carnap and Popper," in *The Problem of Inductive Logic*, ed. I. Lakatos (Amsterdam, 1968).

138. See Lakatos, *Criticism*, pp. 155 ff.

139. For example, a scientist who investigates the orbits of the planets in the framework of the theory of gravitation explains the deviating orbit of a planet first in terms of an auxiliary hypothesis of the existence of a previously unknown planet and does not think to call gravitation theory into question. Even if a planet were not to be discovered at the predicted spot with optical instruments, the scientist might advance the hypothesis of the existence of a cloud of cosmic dust rather than doubt the underlying theory. Even then, he would still have the option of doubting the theory behind the observation of astronomical objects; with the emergence of anomalies, he could change the theoretical basis of the experimental techniques. If even that did not lead to any satisfying conclusion, the theory of gravity would probably still not be excluded from scientific discussion. This is more likely to happen when another theory is at hand that can explain both the confirmable results of the previous theory and the new anomaly. Just such a long process was involved in the giving up of Newtonian mechanics, as the theory of relativity was developed and could prove its explanatory power through the discovered anomalies and at the same time could predict new phenomena which could be experimentally confirmed.

140. See Lakatos, *Criticism*, p. 166.

141. Ibid., pp. 167 ff.

142. In the example given in note 139, this would be the hypotheses concerning the number of planets and the techniques of observation. See Lakatos, *Criticism*, p. 169.

143. Lakatos, *Criticism*, p. 164.

144. Lakatos, *methodology*, p. 120.

145. Ibid.

146. "I have shown that the application of 'scientificness' or 'empiricalness' to theories, instead of to 'research programmes,' was a category mistake." Lakatos, *Criticism*, p. 179.

147. Ibid., pp. 173, 177.

148. Ibid., p. 168. Lakatos gives as an example the anticonventionalist rule against neglecting exceptions, a rule that could be formulated as a metaphysical principle: "Nature permits no exceptions."

149. Ibid., pp. 177 ff.

150. P. Feyerabend, "Wie wird man ein braver Empirist?" in *Erkenntnisprobleme der Naturwissenschaften* (Cologne, 1970), p. 325; also see pp. 305 and 322 ff.

151. P. Feyerabend, "Against Method," *Minnesota Studies in the Philosophy of Science* IV (1970), see pp. 77 ff.

152. Ibid., p. 79.

153. Ibid., p. 84.

154. Ibid., p. 85.

155. Ibid., p. 79; on the critique of the Popper School, see pp. 77 ff.

156. Ibid., p. 26.

157. Ibid., p. 92.

158. Ibid., p. 87.

159. Ibid., pp. 27 ff.

160. "Had Lakatos been as careful with acknowledgments as he is when the Spiritual Property of the Popperian Church is concerned, he would have pointed out that his liberalization, which sees knowledge as a *process*, is indebted to Hegel." Ibid., p. 125. See also "Wie wird man ein braver Empiricist?" Ibid., p. 125.

161. Ibid., p. 113, note 54.

162. Ibid., p. 34.

163. Ibid., p. 35.

164. As Popper put it in the English edition of *Logic of Scientific Discovery*, "Its aim is not to save the lives of untenable systems but, on the contrary, to select the one which is by comparison the fittest, by exposing them to the fiercest struggle for survival."

165. See Kuhn, *Structure*, p. 172.

166. See S. Toulmin, *Foresight and Understanding* (Bloomington, 1961); "The Evolutionary Development of Natural Science," *American Scientist* 55 (1967): 456–471.

167. Toulmin, *Foresight*, p. 57.

168. Ibid., p. 84.

169. Ibid., p. 111.

170. Ibid., pp. 111–112.

171. Toulmin, *Human Understanding* (Princeton, 1972), p. 488.

172. Ibid., p. 486.

173. Ibid., p. 485. On this dilemma and on historicism in the history of science, see Kambartel, "Wie abhängig ist die Physik von Erfahrung and Geschichte? in *Natur und Geschichte*, ed. Hübner and Menne (Hamburg, 1973).

174. Toulmin, *Human Understanding*, p. 497.

175. Decisions about epistemological strategies then take on a character similar to that of decisions in jurisprudence. On the problem of the radicalization of discourse, see J. Habermas, "Wahrheitstheorien," in *Wirklichkeit und Reflexion*, ed. Fahrenbach (Pfullingen, 1973).

176. Toulmin, *Human Understanding*, p. 503. Kuhn also admits that one must return to the structure of the "scientific community" in order to be able to answer the question of the rationality of the sciences; see the postscript to *Structure*.

177. See J. Mittelstrass, "Prolegomena zu einer konstruktiven Theorie der Wissenschaftsgeschichte," in *Möglichkeit von Wissenschaft* (Frankfurt, 1974). The writing of the history of science would then have "the character of a historical social science," in which practical reason is confirmed as historical reason (pp. 133, 137). On the question of the relevance of Hegel to the state of the problem in the philosophy of science, see R. Bubner, "Dialektische Elemente einer Forschungslogik," in *Hermeneutik und Dialektik*. In this framework the significance of Stegmüller's proposals must be investigated (see *Probleme* II, section 2; *Hauptströmangen* II, 484–534), especially his use of a reinterpretation of Sneed to attain a new understanding of theory. [See J. D. Sneed, *The Logical Structure of Mathematical Physics* (Dordrecht, 1971).]

Chapter 4

1. See, for example, K. Wuchterl, *Struktur und Sprachspiel bei Wittgenstein* (Frankfurt, 1969), pp. 187.

2. A few examples of the enormous volume of literature: A. Kenny, *Wittgenstein* (Cambridge, 1973); D. Pears, *Wittgenstein* (London, 1971); K. T. Fann, *Wittgenstein's Conception of Philosophy* (Oxford, 1969); J. Zimmermann, *Wittgensteins sprachphilosophische Hermeneutik* (Frankfurt, 1975).

3. The numbers in the text refer to the sections of *Philosophical Investigations* (New York, 1958).

4. On the development of this concept and its relation to the concept of a "calculus," see Kenny, *Wittgenstein*, pp. 186 ff.

5. Wittgenstein, *Schriften* I, p. 539.

6. See E. Heller, "Wittgenstein: Unphilosophical Notes," in *Wittgenstein*, ed. K. T. Fann (Sussex, 1967).

7. See Wittgenstein, *The Blue Book* (New York, 1958), pp. 42 ff.; *Investigations*, pp. 243–315, 348–412; Apel, *Transformation* II, pp. 78 ff.

8. See E. Tugendhat, "Phenomenology and Linguistic Analysis," in *Husserl*, ed. Elliston and McCormick (Notre Dame, 1977).

9. See Apel, *Transformation* II, p. 83.

10. Ibid., p. 69; Zimmermann, *Hermeneutik*.

11. P. Winch, *The Idea of Social Science* (London, 1958). See also Winch, "Understanding a Primitive Society," in *Rationality*, ed. Wilson (Oxford, 1970), pp. 78 ff.; Habermas, *Logik*, pp. 134 ff.; Apel, *Transformation* II, pp. 72 ff.

12. *Investigations*, p. 373. This is the only passage in the *Investigations* where Wittgenstein points out the consequences of his approach for theology, when he adds parenthetically to the above quotation "theology as grammar." Theology would then consist of the investigation of the rules for the use of certain words and modes of speech and would then implicitly determine the sort of reality meant in such speech.

13. Habermas, *Logik*, p. 140.

14. See Apel, *Transformation* II, p. 91; Zimmermann, *Hermeneutik*, pp. 148 ff. The insistence on therapy as practice only makes the dilemma worse. Therapy concerns those speech actions that lead out of a distorted communication situation.

15. See Wittgenstein, *Remarks on Frazer's "Golden Bough"* (Nottinghamshire, 1929).

16. See Apel, *Transformation* II, p. 87; Wiggerhaus, *Sprachanalyse* (Frankfurt, 1976), pp. 8 ff.

17. The consequences drawn from Wittgenstein's conception by J. Austin and J. Searle shall be discussed below in the framework of reflections on pragmatics in linguistics.

18. Apel, *Transformation* II, p. 274.

19. N. Chomsky, *Language and Mind* (New York, 1968), p. 81.

20. See J. Piaget, *Introduction a la épistemologie génétique* (Paris, 1958).

21. The research oriented to Chomsky's conceptions also has the character of a "case study in the theory of science" (Apel, *Transformation* II, p. 364).

22. Chomsky, *Language and Mind*, p. 18.

23. Ibid., p. 75.

24. See for example Z. S. Harris, *Methods in Structural Linguistics* (Chicago, 1951); N. Chomsky, *Syntactic Structures* (The Hague, 1957), p. 52.

25. N. Chomsky, *Aspects of the Theory of Syntax* (Cambridge, Mass., 1965), p. 51. Also see Chomsky's famous review of Skinner's *Verbal Behavior* [*Language* 35 (1957): 16–58].

26. Stegmüller, *Hauptströmungen* II, p. 17.

27. See Chomsky, *Aspects*, pp. 61 ff.

28. See N. Chomsky and G. A. Miller, "Finitary Models of Language Users," in *Handbook of Mathematical Psychology*, ed. Luce, Bush, and Galanter (New York, 1963); J. Lyons, *Noam Chomsky*, p. 58. On Chomsky's hierarchy of grammars see H. Maurer, *Theoretische Grundlagen der Programmierung Sprache* (Mannheim, 1969), pp. 23 ff.; F. v. Kutschera, *Sprachphilosophie* (Munich, 1971), pp. 89 ff. On the problematic as a whole, see H. Hermes, *Aufzählbarkeit*.

29. Chomsky's understanding of creativity rests on von Humboldt; see E. Coseriu, *Synchronie, Diachronie, Geschichte* (Munich, 1971), pp. 143 ff. See also Coseriu's *Strukturelle Linguistik* (Stuttgart, 1968) and *Transformationelle Grammatik* (Stuttgart, 1968).

30. See Chomsky, *Structures*, pp. 21–24.

31. This presupposes the classical categories of grammar, which are now disputed; see U. Weinrich, *Kritik der linguistischen Kompetenz* (Tübingen, 1970).

32. See P. Postal, "Limitations of Phrase Structure Grammars," in *The Structure of Language*, ed. J. Fodor and J. Katz (Englewood Cliffs, 1964).

33. Chomsky, *Language and Mind*, p. 63.

34. The question must certainly be asked whether such a theory is universal precisely at the point where it coincides with the theory of the Turing machine. (See Chomsky, *Aspects*, pp. 60–62.)

35. Chomsky, *Aspects*, p. 59.

36. M. Bierwisch, "Strukturalismus," *Kursbuch* 5 (1966), p. 150.

37. See Apel, *Transformation* II, pp. 285 ff.

38. J. S. Petöfi, *Transformationsgrammatiken und eine kontextuelle Texttheorie* (Frankfurt, 1971), p. 252.

39. On this development, see Petöfi, *Transformationsgrammatiken*; S. J. Schmidt, *Texttheorie* (München, 1973); D. Wunderlich, *Grundlagen der Linguistik* (Reinbek, 1974); H. Schnelle, *Sprachphilosophie und Linguistik* (Reinbek, 1973).

40. Sentences such as "Equilateral triangles are lazy" are not permissible because they are anomalous. It is possible to uncover rules governing the incompatibility of entries in the lexicon of a language (as, for example, organic-inorganic); see Chomsky, *Aspects*, pp. 166 ff.; J. J. Katz, *The Philosophy of Language* (New York, 1966), p. 157; U. Weinrich, *Erkundungen zur Theorie der Semantik* (Tübingen, 1970); M. Bierwisch, "Semantics," in *New Horizons in Linguistics*, ed. Lyons (Harmondsworth, 1970).

41. See G. S. Lakoff, "Instrumental Adverbs and the Concept of Deep Structure," *Foundations of Language* 4 (1968): 4–29; G. S. Lakoff and J. R. Ross, Is Deep Structure Necessary? (unpublished); J. O. McCawley, "The Role of Semantics in Grammar," in *Universals in Linguistic Theory*, ed. Bach and Harms (New York, 1968).

42. For example, verbs of change or effect together with graduated adjectives (the matter became harder), reflexive pronouns used for entire nominal phrases, and the identification of paraphrases with different syntactic structures (x followed y, y preceded x).

43. See Petöfi, *Transformationsgrammatiken*, pp. 105–125; Lakoff, "Linguistics and Natural Logic," in *Semantics and Natural Language*, ed. Davidson and Harman (Dordrecht, 1972).

44. The basic theses of speech-act theory have been presented in quite accessible form by various authors. See E. V. Savigny, *Die Philosophie der normalen Sprache* (Frankfurt, 1969); Stegmüller, *Hauptströmungen* II, pp. 64–85.

45. J. Searle, *Speech Acts* (London, 1969). See also Searle, "What is a Speech Act?" in *Philosophy of Language*, ed. Searle (London, 1971); J. Austin, *How To Do Things with Words* (Cambridge, 1962).

46. See D. Lewis, *Conventions* (Cambridge, 1969); S. Schiffer, *Meaning* (Oxford, 1972).

47. See Petöfi and Franck, *Präsuppositionen in Philosophie und Linguistik* (Hamburg, 1973); Lakoff, "Linguistics," pp. 38–66; Schmidt, *Texttheorie*, pp. 88–206.

48. On the step from sentence to text grammars, see Schmidt, *Texttheorie*, pp. 9 ff.

49. On the ground-breaking proposals that Saul Kripke developed as a 16-year-old student, see Stegmüller, *Hauptströmungen* II, pp. 221 ff. See also ibid., pp. 35–64; S Kripke, "A Completeness Theorem in Modal Logic," *Journal of Symbolic Logic* 24 (1959): 1–14; R. Montague, "Pragmatics," in *Contemporary Philosophy*, ed. Klinbansky (Florence, 1969); von Kutschera, "Intensionale Logik und theoretische Linguistik," in *Aspekte und Probleme der Sprachphilosophie* (Freiburg, 1974).

50. See Wandschneider, *Sprache*, pp. 70–79.

51. von Kutschera, "Intentionale Logik," p. 119.

52. See, for example, K. Jacobi, "Möglichkeit," in *Handbuch philosophischer Grundbegriffe*, pp. 940 ff.

53. See Wunderlich, *Grundlagen*, p. 248.

54. See Schnelle, *Sprachphilosophie*, pp. 193–264; Wunderlich, *Grundlagen*, pp. 238–273.

55. Petöfi makes a conceptual distinction between cotext and context.

56. See J. S. Petöfi and H. Rieser, *Probleme der modelltheoretische Interpretation von Texten* (Hamburg, 1974).

57. Petöfi, "Grammatische Beschreibung, Interpretation, Intersubjektivität," in *Probleme*, ed. Petöfi and Rieser.

58. Ibid., p. 57.

59. See Petöfi, "Thematisierung der Rezeption metaphorischer Texte in einer Texttheorie," and Rieser, "Textgrammatik und Interpretation," in *Probleme*.

60. This has many implications for the further development of symbolic interactionism and for ethnomethodology.

61. See H. P. Grice, "Meaning," *Philosophical Review* 66 (1957): 377–388; "Utterer's-Meaning, Sentence-Meaning and Word-Meaning," *Foundations of Language* 4 (1968): 1–18; "Utterer's Meaning and Intentions," *Philosophical Review* 78 (1968): 147–177; Lewis, "General Semantics," in *Semantics of Natural Language*.

62. J. Austin, *How To Do Things With Words* (Cambridge, 1962), p. 105.

63. Ibid., p. 127.

64. Searle, *Speech Acts*, p. 33.

65. This can also be seen in the fact that Austin was influenced by Hart's philosophy of law. Parallels to Austin's theory of speech acts can be found in classical consensus theory of marriage law, primarily in Church law; such a theory is concerned with the constitution of institutions and conventions through what are themselves institutionally established conventions. A theory of speech acts must also be investigated from the point of view of jurisprudence; conversely, a juridical theory of consensus could be investigated from the vantage point of the basic problems in an extended theory of speech acts.

66. See Schnelle, *Sprachphilosophie*, pp. 305 ff.

67. Wunderlich, *Grundlagen*, pp. 335 ff.

68. Ricoeur, "Structure and Hermeneutics," in *Conflict of Interpretations* (Evanston, 1974).

Chapter 5

1. E. Durkheim, *The Rules of Sociological Method* (New York, 1938), p. 14.

2. The presentation of Wittgenstein's later philosophy and of linguistics (the discipline in which formal methods have penetrated furthest into the realm of a classical humanity) marks the point of transition to the realm of the social sciences.

3. See *Werturteilstreit*, ed. H. Albert and E. Topitsch (Darmstadt, 1971); Ferber, "Der Werturteilstreit (1909–1959," in *Logik der Sozialwissenschaften*, ed. E. Topitsch (Cologne, 1965).

4. See the documentation in T. W. Adorno et al., *The Positivism Dispute* (New York, 1976). See also H. Baier, "Soziale Technologie oder soziale Emancipation?" in *Thesen zur Kritik der Soziologie*, ed. Schäfers (Frankfurt, 1969); J. Matthes, *Einführung in das Studium der Soziologie* (Reinbek, 1973).

5. See K. Popper, *The Poverty of Historicism* and *Open Society and Its Enemies*.

6. Dahrendorf, "Remarks on the Discussion," in *Positivist Dispute*.

7. See Habermas's contributions to *The Positivism Dispute in German Sociology* (London, 1978): "The Analytical Theory of Science and Dialectics: A Postscript to the Controversy Between Popper and Adorno" and "A Positivistically Bisected Rationalism: A Reply to a Pamphlet."

8. See Habermas, in *Positivism Dispute*, pp. 149–158, 204–209.

9. Ibid., p. 155.

10. In M. Horkheimer, *Critical Theory* (New York, 1972).

11. Ibid., p. 244.

12. Also see Habermas, "Technik und Wissenschaft als 'Ideologie,' " in *Technik und Wissenschaft als Ideologie* (Frankfurt, 1968). In the same volume see Habermas, "Arbeit und Interaktion" [translated in *Toward a Rational Society* (Boston, 1970)].

13. See T. W. Adorno, *Negative Dialectics* (New York, 1973).

14. See Habermas, "Urgeschichte der Subjektivität und verwilderte Selbstbehauptung," in *Philosophisch-politische Profile* (Frankfurt, 1971) [translated in *Philosophical-Political Profiles* (Cambridge, Mass, 1983).

15. Besides Albert's contribution to *Positivist Dispute*, see especially his *Traktat über kritische Vernunft* (Tübingen, 1968), *Plädoyer für kritischen Rationalismus* (Munich, 1971), and *Konstruktion und Kritik* (Hamburg, 1972).

16. Albert, *Plädoyer*, p. 131.

17. Ibid., pp. 126 and 94. It should be clear that the basic problems of Popper's methodology are not really resolved but only arise again in a more pernicious form in the consideration of a new realm of objects. In this context, it is of interest that Albert simply designates all questions leading beyond the contemporary conception of methodology as "remnants of theological problematics," or simply as theological, where "theological" becomes an insult to one's opponent. There is perhaps something correct in this designation of theoretical conceptions which are not satisfied with the contemporary state of the philosophy of science.

18. Popper, *Open Society*, p. 431.

19. For such a survey see Matthes, *Einführung*.

20. See G. H. Mead, *Movements of Thought in the Nineteenth Century* (Chicago, 1936); *The Philosophy of the Act* (Chicago, 1938); *Selected Writings* (Indianapolis, 1964); *On Social Psychology* (Chicago, 1964); *Mind, Self and Society* (Chicago, 1934); A. Schütz, *The Phenomenology of the Social World* (Chicago, 1967); *Collected Papers* (The Hague, 1962); *Reflections on the Problem of Relevance* (New York, 1970); Berger and Luckmann, *Social Construction of Reality*.

21. See K. Raiser, *Identität und Sozialität* (Munich, 1971).

22. Mead, *Selected Writings*, p. 102.

23. Raiser, *Identität*, p. 115.

24. Mead, *Selected Writings*, p. 244.

25. See Raiser, *Identität*, pp. 118 ff.

26. Despite his critique of Watson, Mead ultimately remained trapped in the behaviorist position; this can be shown through a more precise analysis of his conception of "social behaviorism" (Mead, *Mind, Self and Society*, pp. 22–125). The value of language is found in its function in the control of the organization of action, in contradiction to the ideal of a universal communication community. This ambivalence in Mead's conception allows for it to be further developed both in the direction of systems theory and in that of action theory.

27. See T. Parsons, *The Social System* (New York, 1951); Parsons and Shils, eds., *Toward a General Theory of Action* (Cambridge, 1951).

28. See L. Krappmann, *Soziologische Dimensionen der Identität* (Stuttgart, 1969); "Neuere Rollen-konzepte als Erklärungsmöglichkeit fur Sozialisationsprozesse," in *Familienerziehung, Sozialschicht und Schulerflog* (Weinheim, 1972); J. Habermas, "Notizen zum Begriff der Rollenkompetenz," in *Kultur und Kritik* (Frankfurt, 1973); "Stichworte zur Theorie der Sozialisation," in *Kultur und Kritik*.

29. See H. Nolte, *Psychoanalyse und Soziologie* (Bern, 1970).

30. Parsons, *Action Theory and the Human Condition* (New York, 1978).

31. See especially E. Goffman, *Stigma* (Englewood Cliffs, 1963); *Asylums* (Garden City, 1961).

32. See especially *Asylums*.

33. See E. Goffman, *The Presentation of Self in Everyday Life* (Garden City, 1959); *Interaction Ritual* (Chicago, 1967); *Behavior in Public Places* (New York, 1963); Arbeitsgruppe Bielefelder Soziologen, eds., *Alltagswissen, Interaktion und gesellshaftliche Wirklichkeit* I (Reinbek, 1973) (especially H. Blumer, "Der methodologische Standort des Symbolischen Interaktionismus") R. C. Coser, "Role Distance, Sociological Ambivalence, and Transitional Status," *American Journal of Sociology* 72 (1966): 173-187; W. Coutu, "Role-Playing versus Role Taking," *American Sociological Review* 16 (1951): 182-187; N. K. Denzin, "Symbolic Interactionism and Ethnomethodology," *American Sociological Review* 34 (1966): 922-934; Steinhart, ed., *Symbolische Interaktion* (Stuttgart; 1973); E. Stevens, "Sociality and Act in George Herbert Mead," *Social Research* 34 (1967): 613-631; H. Joas, *Die gegenwäritge Lage der soziologischen Rollentheorie* (Frankfurt, 1973).

34. Besides Krappmann's *Soziologische Dimensionen*, see C. Gordon and J. K. Gergen, eds., *Self in Social Interaction* (New York, 1968); G. McCall and J. C. Simmons, *Identities and Interactions* (New York, 1978).

35. See for example F. Haug, *Kritik der Rollentheorie und ihrer Anwendung in der bürgerlichen deutschen Soziologie* (Frankfurt, 1972).

36. This is the general problem of sociolinguistics. A good introduction can be found in the following: F. Hager et al., *Soziologie und Linguistik* (Stuttgart, 1973); W. Niepold, *Sprache und soziale Schicht* (Berlin, 1971); Ehlich et al., "Spätkapitalismus—Soziolinguistik—Kompensatorische Spracherziehung," *Kursbuch* 24 (1971): 33-60.

37. See Arbeitsgruppe Bielefelder Soziologen, eds., *Alltagswissen* II, pp. 454 ff.

38. See Matthes, *Einführung*, p. 208.

39. See J. Habermas, *Knowledge and Human Interests* (Boston, 1975), pp. 25-42; A. Wellmer, *Critical Theory of Society* (New York, 1971), chapter 3.

40. See N. Luhmann, "Sinn als Grundbegriff der Soziologie," in *Theorie der Gesellschaft* (Frankfurt, 1971), especially pp. 75 ff.

41. See H. Peukert, "Systemtheorie." For critique and evaluation of systems theory in sociology, see K.-H. Tjaden, *Soziales System und sozialer Wandel* (Stuttgart, 1972); R. Prewo et al., *Systemtheorische Ansätze in der Soziologie* (Reinbek, 1973).

42. See R. Wiggerhaus, ed., *Sprachanalyse und Soziologie* (Frankfurt, 1975). On Wittgenstein's renunciation of theory, see J. Habermas, "Sprachspiel, Intention und Bedeutung," in *Sprachanalyse*, especially p. 337.

43. This situation was documented symptomatically at the Seventeenth Conference of German Sociologists in Kassel in November 1974. The single panel discussion in the conference was entitled "Comparison of Theories," in which communication-theoretic (Habermas), system-theoretic (Luhmann), action-theoretic-sociology-of-knowledge (Matthes), behaviorist (Opp), and Marxist (Tjaden) approaches were presented.

44. R. Döbert, *Systemtheorie und die Entwicklung religoser Deutungssysteme* (Frankfurt, 1973).

Chapter 6

1. P. Lorenzen, *Konstruktive Wissenschaftstheorie* (Frankfurt, 1974).

2. See F. Kambartel, *Erfahrung und Struktur*; J. Mittelstrass, *Neuzeit und Aufklärung* (Berlin, 1970); Mittelstrass, *Das praktische Fundament der Wissenschaft und die Aufgabe der Philosophie* (Konstanz, 1972); K. Lorenz, *Elemente der Sprachkritik* (Frankfurt, 1970); C. Thiel, *Grundlagenkrise und Grundlagenstreit* (Meisenheim, 1972).

3. See P. Lorenzen, *Einführung in die operative Logik und Mathematik* (Berlin, 1955); *Formal Logic* (Dordrecht, 1965); *Metamathematik* (Mannheim, 1962).

4. P. Lorenzen, *Methodisches Denken* (Frankfurt, 1968), p. 28; cf. pp. 26, 43, and 58.

5. Kambartel, *Erfahrung*, p. 192; Mittelstrass, *Fundament*, p. 11.

6. See Lorenzen, *Methodisches Denken*, pp. 152–161; Kambartel, *Erfahrung*, pp. 251 ff.; Lorenz, "Die Ethik der Logik," in *Das Problem der Sprache*; Lorenz, *Elemente*, pp. 147 ff.; Kambartel, "Ethik und Mathematik," *Zum normativen Fundament der Wissenschaft*, ed. Kambartel and Mittelstrass (Frankfurt, 1973).

7. See Lorenz and Mittelstrass, "Die Hintergehbarkeit der Sprache," *Kant-Studien* 58 (1967): 187–208.

8. See L. E. J. Brouwer, *Collected Works* (Amsterdam, 1975), pp. 417–428, 151–222, and 246–267; A. Heyting, *Intuitionism* (Amsterdam, 1956); J. Klüver, *Operationalismus* (Stuttgart, 1971), pp. 83–113.

9. Dingler, cited in Klüver, *Operationalismus*, p. 176.

10. See H. Dingler, *Aufbau der exakten Fundamentalwissenschaft* (Munich, 1964).

11. See Lorenzen, *Methodisches Denken*, pp. 45 and 51.

12. See W. Kamlah and P. Lorenzen, *Logische Propädeutik oder Vorschule des vernünftigen Redens* (Mannheim, 1967).

13. Lorenz, *Elemente*, pp. 149 ff.

14. Ibid., p. 167.

15. J. Mittelstrass, *Die Möglichkeit von Wissenschaft* (Frankfurt, 1974), p. 201. "Formulated epistemologically, predication as an elementary action is that behind which we cannot go, an *a priori* of knowledge" (ibid., p. 74). Also see ibid., pp. 145 ff. and 158 ff.

16. See Kamlah and Lorenzen, *Logische Propädeutik*, pp. 70 ff.

17. This basic statement of the conception of a constructivist theory of science and of a dialogical-operative logic must be investigated more extensively in the framework of a systematic inquiry into the construction of a theory of communicative action.

18. For a quite accessible introduction see P. Janich, F. Kambartel, and J. Mittelstrass, *Wissenschaftstheorie als Wissenschaftskritik* (Frankfurt, 1974). For short summaries see Lorenzen, *Wissenschaftstheorie*, pp. 47–97; P. Lorenzen and O. Schwemmer, *Konstruktive Logik, Ethik und Wissenschaftstheorie* (Mannheim, 1973).

19. See Kambartel and Mittelstrass, *Fundament*; Mittelstrass, ed., *Methodologische Probleme einer normativ-kritischen Gesellschaftstheorie* (Frankfurt, 1975).

20. See Mittelstrass, *Möglichkeit*, p. 102.

21. Ibid., pp. 145 ff.

22. Kamlah and Lorenzen, *Logische Propädeutik*, p. 49.

23. Ibid., p. 169.

24. Ibid., p. 49.

25. It is clear from the text that *Logische Propädeutik* conducts an intensive debate implicitly and explicitly, with Heidegger; see for example pp. 12, 24, 96, 108, 128, 146, 148, 149, and 186 ff.

26. Kambartel interprets the *a priori* constitutive significance attributed to linguistic action insofar as in such action the rules of action as such are first posited, in analogy to Kant's schematism of the concepts of understanding and thus to Kant's conception of the understanding as a "faculty of rules" (*Critique of Pure Reason*, B 171), as a "faculty of the unity of appearances according to rules" (B 359). See Kambartel, *Erfahrung*, pp. 122 ff. Especially elucidating is the place of time and arithmetic, both of which play an important role in intuitionism. It is still doubtful that this exhausts the consequences of the temporality of the performance of operations. On this problem, from the perspective of Husserlian phenomenology, see T. Eley, *Metakritik der formal Logik* (The Hague, 1969).

27. With closer examination, it can be seen that these restrictive aspects are not connected to the nature of the approach itself.

Chapter 7

1. Apel, *Transformation* I, p. 21.

2. See Mittelstrass, *Möglichkeit*, p. 102.

3. See Lorenzen, *Konstruktive Wissenschaftstheorie*, pp. 11–21, 113–118.

4. See Apel, *Transformation* I, p. 43.

Chapter 9

1. On the following see Peukert, "Zur Einführung: Bemerkungen zum Verhaltnis von Sprachanalyse und Theologie," in D. High, *Sprachanalyse und religiöses Sprechen* (Dusseldorf, 1972); I. V. Dalerth, ed., *Sprachlogik des Glaubens* (Munich, 1974); P. T. Etges, *Kritik der analytischen Theologie* (Hamburg, 1973); J. A. Martin, *Philosophische Sprachprüfung der Theologie* (Munich, 1974).

2. See R. Carnap, "The Elimination of Metaphysics."

3. G. Pitcher, *The Philosophy of Wittgenstein* (Englewood Cliffs, 1964), p. 166.

4. See A. J. Ayer, *Language, Truth and Logic* (London, 1936).

5. See A. Flew, "Theology and Falsification," in *New Essays in Philosophical Theology*, ed. Flew and MacIntyre (London, 1955).

6. Ibid., p. 99.

7. Ibid., p. 97.

8. See A. M. Crombie, "The Possibility of Theological Statements," in *Faith and Logic*, ed. Mitchell (London, 1958).

9. See J. Hick, *Faith and Knowledge* (Ithaca, 1957); *The Existence of God* (New York, 1964); *God and the Universe of Faith* (London, 1973).

10. See W. F. Zuurdeeg, *An Analytical Philosophy of Religion* (London, 1959).

11. See Hare, "Theology and Falsification," in *New Essays*; R. Braithwaite, *An Empiricist's View of the Nature of Religious Belief* (Cambridge, 1965); R. W. Hepburn, "Poetry and Religious Belief," in *Metaphysical Beliefs*, ed. Toulmin, Hepburn, and MacIntyre (London, 1957). Van Buren takes over Hare's approach and his conception of "blik."

12. For a more precise discussion of this position see W.-D. Just, *Religiöse Sprache und analytische Philosophie* (Stuttgart, 1975).

13. M. Black, *Models and Metaphors* (Ithaca, 1962).

14. See F. Ferré, *Language, Logic and God* (London, 1962); "Mapping the Logic of Models in Science and Theology," in D. High, *New Essays on Religious Language*.

15. See the essays by Ian Ramsey in High, *New Essays*.

16. See W. Poteat, "God and the 'Private I,' " in High, *New Essays*.

17. On this lack of clarity, see Just, *Religiöse Sprache*, pp. 124–127. Grabner-Haider, in his attempt to construct a theory of the homily through I. T. Ramsey's conception of disclosure, overlooks precisely this difficulty; see A. Grabner-Haider, *Theorie der Theologie als Wissenschaft* (Munich, 1974).

18. See D. Evans, *The Logic of Self-Involvement* (London, 1963).

19. See also J. Ladriére, *Wissenschaft*, pp. 99 ff.

20. See L. Wittgenstein, *Lectures and Conversations*, ed. Barrett (Berkeley, 1955), pp. 53–72.

21. D. Z. Phillips, *The Concept of Prayer* (London, 1965); *Faith and Philosophical Inquiry* (London, 1970). On the ensuing debate see Dalferth, *Sprachlogik*, pp. 49–52.

22. This is precisely what Rhees accuses Phillips of; see Dalferth, *Sprachlogik*, p. 272.

23. See K. Nielsen, "Wittgensteinian Fideism," *Philosophy* 42 (1967): 191–209.

24. Perhaps more than anyone else, Apel has established the affinity of the later Wittgenstein and his followers to the questions of classical hermeneutics; see the pertinent essays in Apel, *Transformation* I, pp. 223–377.

25. The consequences of accepting these standards can be seen in the work of Grabner-Haider. He tries to escape the obvious contradictions that result from accepting these standards by

dividing theology into two realms, one that makes statements and another that does not. For the former, this sentence could be considered a basic metatheoretical axiom: "Everything that God has revealed and the Church teaches us to beleive is true." (*Theorie der Theologie*, p. 130) After the acceptance of this "basic dogma," the axiomatization of religious language is hardly problematic. But this ignores the entire hermeneutic discussion in which theology labors concerning this "everything that." If one attempts to determine the propositional part of theology in a theory of speech acts conceived independent of it, then there result both the problems of speech-act theory discussed above and the ultimate fixation of this false dichotomy in theology.

26. See Weizsäcker, *Einheit der Natur*.

27. Ibid., p. 288.

28. Ibid., p. 279.

29. Ibid., p. 16.

30. Ibid., p. 319.

31. The crystalizing point of a discussion of theology with Weizsäcker's thought would be the problem of time. See ibid., pp. 241 ff., 16.

32. N. Luhmann, "Religiöse Dogmatik und gesellschaftliche Evolution," *Religion—System und Sozialization*, ed. Dahm, Luhmann, and Stoodt (Neuwied, 1972), p. 21.

33. Ibid.

34. Luhmann, "Religiöse Dogmatik," p. 26.

35. Ibid., p. 22.

36. Ibid., p. 56.

37. Ibid., p. 91.

38. See N. Luhmann, "Die Weltgesellschaft," *Archiv für Rechts- und Sozialphilosophie* 57 (1971): 1–35.

39. "World . . . as a correlate of interaction—and therefore as a correlate of a system . . . is first constituted in interaction as the objectifiable horizon of experience which presents other possibilities, even if they are not exhausted or even explicitly negated." (Ibid., p. 31) Here are also hints of Luhmann's reinterpretation of Husserl in terms of interaction-systems theory.

40. Luhmann, "Dogmatik," p. 96.

41. Ibid., p. 92.

42. Ibid., pp. 96 ff.

43. N. Luhmann, "Die Organizierbarkeit von Religionen und Kirchen," in *Soziologische Beiträge zur Situation von Religion und Kirche in der gegenwärtigen Gesellschaft* (Stuttgart, 1972), p. 285.

44. Luhmann denies that the possibilities of variation in religion are unlimited, at least as far as the past is concerned. This can be seen in his remark that "they then did not have, for example, the possibility of trying 'money' should 'God' not exist any more." (Luhmann, "Dogmatik," p. 25)

45. W. Schulz, *Philosophie in der veränderten Welt*, p. 189.

46. Luhmann himself admits that he still has no adequate conception of the problems of modal logic. See Habermas and Luhmann, *Theorie der Gesellschaft*, p. 315.

47. R. Döbert, *Deutungssysteme*; see in particular p. 152.

48. See ibid., p. 140.

49. J. Habermas, *Legitimation Crisis* (Boston, 1973), pp. 11–12.

50. Habermas, *Profile*, p. 27.

51. Ibid., p. 28.

52. Ibid., p. 29.

53. Ibid., p. 28.

54. Habermas, *Legitimation Crisis*, p. 121.

Chapter 10

1. I. Kant, *Critique of Pure Reason*, B 25.

2. See W. Schulz's analysis of Fichte's *Vocation of Man* in *Philosophie*, pp. 326–334.

3. See the controversy between Gadamer and Habermas in Apel et al., *Hermeneutik und Ideologiekritik*, as well as Apel's view of the achievement and limits of hermeneutics in Heidegger and Gadamer, *Transformation* I, pp. 9–76.

4. The difficulties in reinterpreting traditional terminology only increase if the problem domain delimited here is called "transcendental dia-logic." See J. Heinrichs, "Transzendentales—dialogisches—politisches Denken. Thesen zu einer 'transzendentalen Dialogik," *Internationales Dialogisches Zeitschrift* 3 (1970): 375 ff.; "Sinn und Intersubjektivität. Zur Vermittlung von transzendental-philosophischen und dialogischen Denken in einer transzendentalen Dialogik," *Theologie und Philosophie* 95 (1970): 161–191.

5. This designation is derived from Max Weber. According to Weber, action is "human behavior when and to the extent that the agent or agents see it as subjectively meaningful." "By 'social' action is meant an action in which the meaning intended by the agent or agents involves a relation to another person's behavior and in which that relation determines the way in which the action proceeds." [Weber, *Economy and Society* (New York, 1968), p. 4] This conception of the concept of action has remained definitive to the present and was, for example, taken over by Parsons.

6. See G. E. M. Anscombe, *Intention* (London, 1957); S. Hampshire, *Thought and Action* (London, 1959); A. I. Melden, *Free Action* (London, 1961); A. Kenny, *Action, Emotion and Will* (London, 1963); S. Brown, *Action* (London, 1968); G. H. von Wright, *Explanation and Understanding* (Ithaca, 1971), pp. 34–82.

7. See von Wright, ibid., as well as the general discussion among Olafson, Dray, Toulmin, and Davidson. Von Wright perhaps best characterized the state of contemporary thinking in this area: "I would maintain that we cannot understand causation nor the distinction between

nomic connections and accidental uniformities of nature, without resorting to ideas about doing things and intentionally interfering with the course of nature." (pp. 65-66)

8. See J. Habermas, "Vorbereitende Bemerkungen zu einer Theorie der kommunikativen Kompetenz," in *Theorie der Gesellschaft*; "Stichworte zur Theorie der Sozialization," in *Kulture und Kritik*; "Notizen zum begriff der Rollenkompetenz," in *Kultur und Kritik*; "Können komplexe Gesellschaften eine vernünftige Identität ausbilden?" in *Zur Rekonstruktion des Historischen Materialismus* (Frankfurt, 1976).

9. See J. Piaget's *Psychology in Intelligence* and *Introdution a l'épistemologie génétique*.

10. See G. Nunner-Winkler and G. Rolff, "Theorie der Sozialisation," in *Erziehungswissenschaftliches Handbuch* III (Berlin, 1971).

11. R. Jakobson, *Child Language* (The Hague, 1968).

12. See A. Cicourel *Cognitive Sociology: Language and Meaning in Social Interaction* (Harmondsworth, 1973).

13. See N. Chomsky, "A Review of B. F. Skinner's *Verbal Behavior*"; R. Brown and U. Bellugi, "Three Processes in the Child's Acquisition of Syntax," *Harvard Educational Review* 34 (1964); R. Brown and C. Fraser, "The Acquisition of Syntax," in *Verbal Behavior and Learning*, ed. Cofer and Musgrave (New York, 1963); L. Bloom, *Language Development* (Cambridge, 1970); D. McNeill, "The Development of Language," in *Carmichael's Manual of Child Psychology* (New York, 1970); E. H. Lenneberg, *Biologische Grundlagen der Sprache* (Frankfurt, 1972); Lenneberg, *Neue Perspektiven in der Erforschung der Sprache* (Frankfurt, 1972).

14. See for example G. Bateson et al., "Toward a Theory of Schizophrenia," in *Steps to an Ecology of Mind* (San Francisco, 1972); M. Neumann-Schonwetter, *Psychosexuelle Entwicklung und Schizophrenie* (Frankfurt, 1973).

15. For example, in research into hospitals by Spitz, Bowlby, and others.

16. H. Garfinkel, *Studies in Ethnomethodology* (Englewood Cliffs, 1967).

17. See H.-G. Gadamer and P. Vogler, eds., *Neue Anthropologie* I and II (Stuttgart, 1972), especially the essays on the evolution of social and communications systems.

18. Mead himself deemphasized the biographical aspect of the formation of identity—an aspect only later incorporated by A. Strauss [*Mirrors and Masks* (Glencoe, 1959)]. This aspect seems to be neglected in American research. See W. I. Thomas, *Person und Sozialverhalten* (Berlin, 1965).

19. H. B. Grice, "Logic and Conversation," in P. Cole and J. L. Morgen, eds., *Syntax and Semantics*, vol. III: *Speech Acts* (New York, 1975). See also F. Schütze, *Sprache—Soziologisch gesehen* (Munich, 1976), especially pp. 568-595; D. Wunderlich, *Linguistik*, pp. 326-335. Wunderlich raises critical questions concerning Grice's concept of convention. Also see Wunderlich on the consequences of speech actions in *Sprachpragmatik und Philosophie*, ed. Apel (Frankfurt, 1976), pp. 441-462.

20. See Schütze, *Sprache*.

21. See L. Kohlberg, "From Is to Ought," in *Cognitive Development and Epistemology*, ed. Mischel (New York, 1971); Kohlberg, *Stages in the Development of Moral Thought and Action* (New York, 1969); E. Turiel, "Developmental Processes in the Child's Moral Thinking," in *New Directions in Developmental Psychology*, ed. Mussen, Langer, and Covington (New York, 1969).

22. The development of reciprocity—which naturally demands (since it is always socially mediated) an environment where full reciprocity, and thus the autonomy of the subject, is permitted and practiced, in order not to regress to a more "primitive stage"—follows its own logic of development. Kohlberg remarks: "Because such morality involves sacrifice, it has been consigned to the realm of the irrational by Nietzsche, Freud, Kierkegaard, and their followers. If, however, a mature belief in moral principles in itself engenders a sacrifice of the rational ego, apart from other personality and emotional considerations, we are faced with a conception of the rational and of cognitive structure which has no parallel in the realm of scientific and logical thought." ("From Is to Ought," p. 232)

23. In his communicative ethic Habermas postulates an additional stage of moral consciousness, and in it a sort of reciprocity in which the monological form of the judgment and determination of norms is taken into the communicative process. A new, additional evolutionary stage in the development of the individual and of society is thus outlined. See Habermas, "Rollen-kompetenz," pp. 213 ff.; Legitimation Crisis, p. 89.

24. Mead, Mind, p. 327. On the ideal of human society see p. 310.

25. See for example G. H. von Wright, An Essay in Deontic Logic and the General Theory of Action (Amsterdam, 1968); F. Von Kutschera, Einführung in der Logik der Normen (Freiburg, 1973). For an overview see W. Frankena, Ethics (Englewood Cliffs, 1963). Deontic logic is one of the most important fields of research in contemporary logic.

26. See H. Fahrenbach, "Ein programmatischer Aufriss der Problemlage und systematischen Ansatzmöglichkeiten praktischer Philosophie," in Rehabilitierung der praktischen Philosophie, ed. Riedel, vol. I (Freiburg, 1972).

27. Mead, Mind, p. 327.

28. See J. Habermas, "Kommunikative Kompetenz"; Legitimation Crisis; "What is Universal Pragmatics?" in Communication and the Evolution of Society (Boston, 1979).

29. See Habermas, "Kommunkative Kompetenz."

30. For this terminology see E. Goffman's use of the basic concept of "the presentation of self."

31. See Habermas, "Kommunikative Kompetenz," pp. 111 ff. Habermas's analyses are only here meant to serve as an example; similar or parallel distinctions can be found in Kamlah and Lorenzen, Propädeutik. On the state of the discussion in the Erlangen School see F. Kambartel, ed., Praktische Philosophie und konstruktive Wissenschaftstheorie (Frankfurt, 1974); see especially Kambartel's essay "Moralisches Argumentieren—Methodische Analyse zur Ethik." While Kambartel (in a letter to Lorenzen, ibid., p. 232) admits that Habermas has "unnecessarily narrowed his analyses to linguistic theses, Habermas's attempt is also misunderstood as the attempt to unite such analysis with anthropology and a critical theory of society.

32. In the Erlangen School the term is "Beratung" (consultation).

33. On the circular structure of this pointing back to other claims, see Habermas, "Kommunikative Kompetenz," pp. 123 ff.

34. For an important statement of this earlier debate, see K. Lorenz and J. Mittelstrass, "Hintergehbarkeit."

35. Habermas, "Kommunikative Kompetenz," p. 120.

36. Ibid.

37. Ibid., pp. 123 ff.

38. See D. Wunderlich, "Die Rolle der Pragmatik in der Linguistik," *Der Deutschunterricht* 4 (1970): 5-41. On the accusation of utopianism, also see Schulz, *Philosophie*, pp. 170 ff.

39. Habermas, *Legitimation Crisis*, p. 159.

40. Ibid. On the problems Habermas sees in incorporating the concept of the "transcendental," see "Universal Pragmatics," pp. 21 ff.

41. Habermas, *Legitimation Crisis*, p. 159.

42. Lorenzen, *Normative Logic*, p. 74.

43. Lorenzen, "Briefliche Diskussionsbemerkung," in *Praktische Philosophie*, p. 225.

44. Lorenzen, *Normative Logic*, p. 82.

45. Apel, *Transformation* II, p. 420; see also Habermas, *Legitimation Crisis*, p. 109.

46. F. Kambartel, "Wie ist praktische Philosophie konstruktiv möglich?" in *Praktische Philosophie*, p. 11.

47. See Kambartel, letter to Lorenzen, ibid., p. 232.

48. See Apel, *Transformation* II, p. 400.

49. Ibid., p. 419.

50. Ibid., p. 421.

51. See J. Habermas, *Theory and Practice* (Boston, 1971), p. 17; see also pp. 7 and 12.

52. See K. Raiser, *Identität und Socialität*, pp. 163-167.

53. Habermas, *Theory and Practice*, pp. 284-285.

54. Habermas, "Der Universalitätsanspruch der Hermeneutik," in *Hermeneutik und Ideologiekritik*, p. 154.

55. This seems to characterize the situation better than Habermas's formulation in "Kommunikative Kompetenz," pp. 140 ff.

56. See Apel, *Transformation* II, p. 225.

57. See Apel, *Transformation* II, pp. 157-178, 220-263, especially 223-225; Apel, *Charles S. Peirce: From Pragmatism to Pragmaticism* (Amherst, 1981), pp. 5-6.

58. See Mead, *Mind*, pp. 281-289, 327. Mead sees this idea as related to the basic assumptions of universal religions (pp. 271-272, 327).

59. See G. H. Mead, "The Philosophies of Royce, James and Dewey in their American Setting," in *Selected Writings*, pp. 371-391.

60. The foundational consequences of this approach must be discussed more precisely, as well as the problems resulting from turning it into a concrete program for empirical and nonetheless

normative-critical investigations. See the comprehensive studies in Schütze, *Sprache*. As an example of the empirical research of this sort, see R. Döbert and G. Nunner-Winkler, *Adoleszenzkrise und Identitätsbildung* (Frankfurt, 1975).

61. Habermas, "Kommunikative Kompetenz," p. 141.

62. See Apel, *Transformation* II, pp. 325, 429.

63. This foundation raises a number of questions already touched upon in our investigation of the basic problems of the philosophy of the social sciences. In this respect, the statements of a critical theory of society oriented toward communicative action must be compared to the Marxian approach on the dimensions of production, distribution, and consumption. (See Habermas, *Communication and Evolution of Society*.) The relevance of systems theory within a critical theory of society must also be tested, even if systems theory fails as the final metatheory of the social sciences. The place of individual empirical procedures and how they should be modified within the context already achieved by the theory of communicative action must also be investigated. A further desideratum of a foundational theory of the social sciences seems to be the development of rules for methodologically controlled hermeneutic understanding on the basis of the logic of interaction. See F. Schütze et al., "Grundlagentheoretische Voraussetzungen methodisch kontrollierten Fremdverstehens," in *Alltagswissen* II, pp. 433–495.

64. For a brief first orientation in this discussion see the introduction to G. Grewendorf and G. Meggle, eds., *Sprache und Ethik* (Frankfurt, 1974). See also B. Schuller, *Die Begründung sittlicher Urteile* (Düsseldorf, 1973).

65. Grewendorf and Meggle, *Sprache und Ethik*, p. 17.

66. See Hare, *Freedom and Reason* (Oxford, 1963).

67. Grewendorf and Meggle, *Sprache und Ethik*, p. 22. On the problem of universalization, see M. G. Singer, *Generalization in Ethics* (New York, 1961); Kurt Baier, *The Moral Point of View* (Ithaca, 1958); Habermas, *Legitimation Crisis*, pp. 86 ff. Also see the remarks above on the principle of "transsubjectivity" in the Erlangen School.

68. At this juncture it must be explained further what qualifies in this context as a need, as an interest, and as a subjective, objective, or transsubjective interest. This is not possible here. See Mittelstrass, *Gesellschaftstheorie*, especially the essays by Mittelstrass and Lorenzen. See also K. Lorenzen and O. Schwemmer, *Konstruktive Logik*, especially the terminology set forth in their "ortho-lexicon." The apparent unity of the Erlangen School should not lead one to overlook the enormous differences in the area of moral argumentation.

69. Compare the investigations in the logic of argumentation by Perelman, Bar-Hillel, Hare, and Toulmin. See Perelman, "Raisonnment Pratique," in *Contemporary Philosophy*, ed. Klibansky. Habermas bases his "Wahrheitstheorien" on Toulmin's *Uses of Argument*.

70. Habermas, "Wahrheitstheorien," p. 249.

71. Ibid., p. 250.

72. See Habermas, "Wahrheitstheorien," pp. 251 ff.; Lorenzen, "Scientismus versus Dialektik," in *Hermeneutik und Dialektik*; Mittelstrass, *Gesellschaftstheorie*; Apel, *Transformation* II, pp. 422 ff.

73. See Kambartel's and Lorenzen's statements in *Praktische Philosophie*, pp. 20 ff., 226 ff., 232 ff.

74. See Diederich, *Wissenschaftsgeschichte*.

75. See for example, R. Bubner, "Forschungslogik."

76. Diederich, "Einleitung," in *Wissenschaftsgeschichte*, pp. 39 ff. Compare G. Böhme, "Die Finalisierung der Wissenschaft," in ibid.

77. See Böhme, pp. 304 ff. The sentence "DDT has the effect of an insecticide" becomes untrue through its use, since it causes the selection of resistant species of insects.

78. See Peukert, "Systemstheorie."

79. See Peukert, "Theorie der Übersetzung," p. 309.

80. The decisive impetus for a reinterpertation of Freud has been developed by P. Ricoeur in *Freud* (New Haven, 1970). See the work of A. Lorenzer, such as *Kritik des psychoanalytischen Symbolbegriff* (Frankfurt, 1970) and *Sprachzerstörung und Rekonstruktion* (Frankfurt, 1970). Also see Habermas, "Universalitätsanspruch"; A. Mitscherlich, *Der Kampf um die Errinnerung* (Munich, 1975).

81. "Self-consciousness is *in* and *for itself*, when and by the fact that, it so exists for another. . . ." (*Phenomenology of Spirit*, p. 111) "The recognize themselves as mutually recognizing each other." (p. 112)

82. The classic text for this is still the "Master and Slave" chapter of *Phenomenology*.

83. "Each seeks the death of the other. . . ." (113)   See the Jena *Realphilosophie* II, p. 230: "And it is at the same time consciousness only in being recognized by another, and it is also consciousness as absolutely numerically one and must be recognized as such; that is, it must seek the death of the other and its own, and exists only in the reality of death."

84. "Universal self-consciousness is the affirmative knowledge of itself in an other self; each self as a free individuality has his own 'absolute' independence, yet is universal and objective in virtue of the negation of its immediacy or appetite without distinguishing itself from that other. Each has 'real' universality in the shape of reciprocity, so far as each knows itself recognized in the other freeman, and knows this insofar as it recognizes the other and knows him to be free." (*Encyclopedia*, paragraph 436)

85. *Phenomenology*, p. 114.

86. Ibid., p. 117.

87. Ibid., p. 119.

88. See A. Wellmer, *Critical Theory*, chapter 3; Habermas, "Arbeit und Interaktion" (in English in *Toward a Rational Society*).

89. This is not necessarily the path of a naive Enlightenment that unconsciously delivers itself over to the contradictions of history and does not reckon with the possibility that "after a period of advance, of the unfolding of human faculties, of the emancipation of the individual, after an enormous expansion of human power over nature . . . mankind finally falls back into new forms of barbarism." (M. Horkheimer, *Kritische Theorie* II, p. 169)   The insight of *The Dialectic of the Enlightenment* is then understood as a medium of this communicative process.

90. Metz, more than anyone else, has indicated the theological significance of Benjamin's work from his last decade of life; see Metz, *Faith in History and Society*.

91. Benjamin, letter to Gershom Scholem, April 4, 1937; Benjamin, *Briefe* II (Frankfurt, 1966), p. 729.

92. W. Benjamin, *Ausgewahlte Schriften* II (Frankfurt, 1955), p. 311.

93. M. Horkheimer, letter to Benjamin, March 16, 1937 (unpublished), quoted from R. Tiedemann, "Historischer Materialismus oder politischer Messianismus?" in *Materialen zu Benjamin*, ed. Bulthaup (Frankfurt, 1975), p. 87.

94. Horkheimer, *Kritische Theorie* I, p. 198 (1934).

95. Ibid., p. 372 (1936).

96. Benjamin, letter to Horkheimer, March 28, 1937, cited in Tiedemann, "Materialismus," p. 87.

97. This is Tiedemann's view (p. 88).

98. On the apocryphal character of this designation see Tiedemann, p. 115.

99. W. Benjamin, "Theses on the Philosophy of History," in *Illuminations* (New York, 1969), p. 260.

100. Ibid., p. 255.

101. Horkheimer, letter, March 16, 1937, cited in Tiedemann, "Materialismus," p. 87.

102. W. Benjamin, *Passagen*, cited in Tiedemann, p. 88. For this whole complex see R. Tiedemann, *Studien zur Philosophie Walter Benjamins* (Frankfurt, 1973), pp. 128 ff.

103. Benjamin, "Theses," p. 262.

104. Ibid., p. 256.

105. W. Benjamin, *The Origin of German Tragic Drama* (London, 1977), p. 166. [Steiner translates *Leidensgeschichte* as "Passion."]

106. W. Benjamin, "Zur Geschichtsphilosophie der Spätromantik und der historischen Schule (unpublished), cited in Tiedemann, *Studien*, pp. 144 ff.

107. See Christian Lenhardt, "Anamnestic Solidarity: The Proletariat and its *Manes*," *Telos* 25 (1975): 133–155. In this article Lenhardt attempts to demonstrate that "anamnestic solidarity" is the basic problem of many of the classics of the Frankfurt School, especially Benjamin, and relates it to religious phenomena (such as ancestor worship) and to the Marxian theory of labor value.

108. See Lenhardt, p. 137.

109. Horkheimer, *Kritische Theorie* I, p. 374.

110. Ibid., p. 372.

111. Horkheimer, letter to Benjamin, March 16, 1937, in Tiedemann, "Materialismus," p. 87. Adorno also expressed himself to Horkheimer concerning the latter's position in a letter of February 25, 1935 (cited in H. Gumnior and R. Ringguth, *Max Horkheimer in Selbstzeugnissen und Bilddokumenten* (Reinbek, 1973), pp. 84 ff.: "I find the essay on Bergson quite exceptional. Especially the passage on the historian as savior has affected me most. It is amazing how completely the consequences of your 'atheism,' in which I believe less the more completely it becomes explicit (since every explication increases its metaphysical power), are fully in agreement with those arising from my theological intentions, however discomforting they may be to you, but in any case their *consequences* cannot be distinguished from yours—I would have

to say that the motive of the rescue of the hopeless is the center of all my efforts, without there being something left over I still want to say. . . ." The basic problem remains how one is to think of this memory without then divinizing the one who is remembering—the historian.

Chapter 11

1. One could understand the entire investigation up to now as a systematic reconstruction of the questions Kant saw as unifying all the interests of reason: "1. What can I know? 2. What ought I do? 3. What may I hope?" (Critique of Pure Reason B 833) The question about possible knowing can only be answered today by way of a detour through the problems of the theory of science and in the return to the intersubjective basis of the search for truth. The question about what I ought to do must be answered in the return to the normative implications of communicative action and the possibility in this sphere of reaching consensus. It seems that any attempt to answer the third question (that even remotely has anything to do with the current state of theory of science and action) has not yet been undertaken. It must be reconstructed in the manner of and depending on the first two, on the basis of the theory of communicative action. It should no more be read "What may I hope—for myself?" but rather "What may I hope—for the other—in his death?"

2. Adorno, Negative Dialectics, p. 402.

3. Even for Habermas, it appears that here thought has in principle come to its limits: "Considering the risks to individual life that exist, a theory that could interpret away the facticities of loneliness and guilt, sickness and death is, to be sure, not even conceivable. Contingencies that are irremovably attached to the bodily and moral constitution of the individual can be raised to consciousness only as contingency. We must, in principle, live disconsolately with them." (Legitimation Crisis, p. 120) Certainly we are not concerned here with thinking that "interprets away" death, nor are we concerned with "the constitution of the individual," but rather with experiences that put in question communicative action as a whole and the identity of the individual achieved in it.

4. See M. Gatzemeier, Theologie als Wissenschaft? (Stuttgart, 1974). The question must be put to Gatzemeier whether his conception of action from the start excludes a normative concept of transsubjectivity, if the limit questions of action are not seen exclusively in terms of securing success of action and in this framework in securing the cooperation of others. The concept of action in Gatzemeier's work excludes a normative concept of the identity of subjects in communication. He cannot then shed any light on the experiences of the history of religion, or even on the Judeo-Christian tradition, and therefore he cannot reconstruct their rational core. This could be shown in a more extensive analysis.

5. See H. Kamp, Tense Logic and the Theory of Linear Order, dissertation, Los Angeles, 1968; N. Rescher and A. Urquhart, Temporal Logic (New York, 1971).

6. These are exactly the problems Mead wrestled with in the last years of his life; see Raiser, Identität, pp. 142 ff.

7. Kant serves as a model case for such critique. According to Kant, speculative reason misunderstands its own possibilities when it creates the ego or God and an absolute object. Critique must deconstruct such objectifying, objective constructions of pure theoretical reason and indicate the original possibilities of speech in this realm. God can only be spoken of in the context of the freedom of subjects, and thus in a context in which reason becomes practical.

8. If we have recourse here to the witnesses of the tradition and then explicate the structure of the intended fundamental theology, this naturally raises methodological difficulties. The

proposal for a fundamental theology must prove to be hermeneutically fruitful; that is, it must make possible the understanding of historical witnesses and experiences as well; on the other hand, it can only be developed on the basis of these experiences. The circle is inevitable. In order to protect the proposal of a conception of fundamental theology from hermeneutic naiveté, we have to attempt to develop it from the reconstruction of the discussion of both theology and the theory of science. Such a proposal must therefore be tested in many dimensions.

9. This is the way Buber translates Exod. 3:14. See also P. Weimar and E. Zenger, *Exodus* (Stuttgart, 1975).

10. Deut. 24:17 ff. Cf. Exod. 22:21–27; Deut. 10:17–19; 27:19; Isa. 1:16 ff.

11. See, for example, Hos. 6:6; Amos 4:4; 5:5.21 ff.; Isa. 1:10 ff. Mic. 6:6–8; Jer. 7:1 ff.

12. See W. Beyerlin, *Die Rettung der Bedrängten* (Göttingen, 1970).

13. See Neh. 9:26; O. H. Steck, *Israel und das gewältsame Geschick der Propheten* (Neukirchen, 1970), pp. 60 ff.

14. The title of a book by Klaus Koch still describes the state of research into this problem: *Ratlos vor dem Apokalyptik* [*Perplexed by the Apocalyptic Tradition*]. K. H. Müller speaks of a "macro-mutation of local hopes in the future toward apocalyptic eschatology," which he sees as the result of the dominance of Hellenism and the desire to relativize its claims to totality [Müller, "Ansätze zur Apokalyptik," in *Literatur und Religion des Frühjudentums*, ed. J. Maier and J. Schreiner (Würzburg, 1973)].

15. See Dan. 12:2; Isa. 25:8; 26:19; cf. 2 Mac. 7:9 ff.

16. See Mark 12:24–26 ff. and I Cor. 15:34 against those who deny the resurrection of the dead: "Certain people have no knowledge of God."

17. See the recent debates concerning the historical Jesus and the important thesis of E. Fuchs that "*Jesus'* action was itself the actual framework of his proclamation." [Fuchs, "Die Frage nach dem historischen Jesus," *Gesammelte Aufsätze* II (Tübingen, 1960), p. 155] See also Fuchs, *Jesus: Wort und Tat* (Tübingen, 1971).

18. See J. Maier and J. Schreiner, *Literatur*; W. Harnisch, *Verhängnis und Verheissung der Geschichte* (Göttingen, 1969).

19. Among such passages are Dan. 2:44; 7,13f; Ass. Mos. 10,1; OrSibIII, 767.

20. H. Schürmann, "Das Hauptproblem in der Verkündigung Jesu," in *Gott in Welt* I, ed. Metz and Kern (Freiburg, 1964), p. 579.

21. See Schürmann, pp. 579–607; A. Vögtle, " 'Theo-logie' und 'Eschato-logie,' " in *Neues Testament und Kirche*, ed. J. Gnilka (Freiburg, 1974); H. Flender, *Die Botschaft von der Herrschaft Gottes* (Munich, 1968); P. Hoffmann and V. Eid, *Jesus von Nazareth und eine christliche Moral* (Freiburg, 1975).

22. See J. Becker, *Johannes der Taufer und Jesus* (Neukirchen, 1972).

23. See Luke 11:20.

24. On the idea of the faith of Jesus, see Heb. 12:2; Thusing, essay in W. Thusing and K. Rahner, eds., *Christology*; Ebeling, "Jesus und Glaube," in *Wort und Glaube* I (Tübingen, 1967).

25. See E. Fuchs, "Alte und neue Hermeneutik," in *Gesammelte Aufsätze* III.

26. This is Fuchs's proposal. In the exegetical discussion of Jesus' own self-understanding, Bonhoeffer's formula in his *Ethics*—Jesus as "a man for others"—has played an important role. This formula was countered by one of Jesus as "a man for God." Neither formula brings to light the point of the matter in question. Jesus asserts God for others *in* his communicative action and bases his self-understanding on this event, in terms of others in this sense. Fuchs (ibid., p. 222) therefore asks: "Must we not then admit that this is a special case, so that we should not inquire so much into his self-understanding but into that of those who believed in him? Because it would be senseless to ask him about his 'extra nos,' when he himself is our 'extra nos,' that is to say, the one through whom we understand ourselves? But why could we not be precisely those through whom HE understood himself?" To this extent, what Fuchs (ibid., p. 203) asserts for faith in general would be even more radically true of Jesus: "In faith I understand myself from God's work in my neighbor." Attempts to formulate this context necessarily remain unsatisfactory. This is because the basic categories for the interpretation of such processes are inadequately developed. On the one hand, recourse to Biblical interpretations, such as titles attributed to Jesus, is scarcely helpful here. Their significance must also be culled from the basic event. A dilemma of classical christology consists in the fact that the actions of Jesus are secondarily added onto a statically conceived essence. A theological hermeneutics, or more precisely a foundation theory of theology, must determine the connection between communicative action and the reality of God.

The admittedly provocative use of the word "assertion" is an attempt to point out the following:

• This mode of discourse insists after tracing out the discussion in the theory of science that discourse in theology is not concerned with an illusory process of projection or an idealistic construction of meaning.

• This pointing toward a reality occurs not in purely verbal assertion but in the fact that a human being, in the temporally structured, mortal-finite performance of his existence, is directed to God as a reality for others and thus as a reality for himself, and in this way "asserts" God's reality. This excludes any reified understanding of the reality of God. The question of the "refutation" of God then arises in the annihilation of this form of existence.

• In this way, all theological discourse is connected to a specific communicative practice with a normative core that is discussable in the human sciences.

• The consequence of these reflections is to develop the basic conception of theology as a theory of action.

27. For the following remarks, the results of A. Jülicher, R. Bultmann, C. H. Dodd, J. Jeremias, E. Fuchs, E. Jüngel, E. Linnemann, G. Eichholz, D. O. Via, N. Perrin, E. Guttgemanns, P. Ricoeur, W. Harnisch, O. Bayer, and others must simply be presupposed.

28. See for example Luke 15:1 ff.

29. For a very different treatment of this disputed issue, see H. Schürmann, "Wie hat Jesus seinen Tod bestanden und verstanden?" in *Jesu ureigener Tod* (Freiburg, 1974). See also H. Kessler, *Die theologische Bedeutung des Todes Jesu* (Düsseldorf, 1970).

30. See O. H. Steck, *Das gewaltsame Geschick*.

31. See H. Gese, "Psalm 22 und das Neue Testament," *Zeitschrift für Theologie und Kirche* 65 (1968): 1–22; L. Ruppert, *Der leidende Gerechte* (Würzburg, 1972); Ruppert, *Jesus als der leidende Gerechte?* (Stuttgart, 1972).

32. See K. Lehmann, "Die Erscheinung des Herrn," in *Wort Gottes in der Zeit*, ed. Feld and Nolte (Düsseldorf, 1973).

33. See W. Kasper, *Jesus der Christus* (Mainz, 1974), pp. 162 ff.

34. One dilemma is that the categories previously used in systematic theology, as in the case of the idealistic conceptual frameworks of the analysis of "appearance," are developed more in terms of the dialectic of subject and object than in terms of the relation of human beings as they approach their death. This very same dilemma results from the use of the Hegelian analysis of death. For Hegel, the question is precisely whether the concept of death is really only a reflective one, since one's destruction [*Zugrundegehen*] is understood as coming to grounding [*Kommen zum Grund*] and thus to one's actual reality in the dialectical inversion of reflection. But then one has attained a reflexive concept of negativity, not a concept of death related to temporal, human existence. To this extent, a theory of intersubjectivity inclusive of the analysis of death and an analysis of the intersubjective experience of the death of the other remain fundamental requirements for a foundational theory of theology with a view to a theology of the resurrection and for a hermeneutics for the interpretation of the resurrection reports.

35. Metz, *Theology of the World*, p. 90.

36. The relation of a fundamental theology understood in this sense to classical fundamental theology must in any case be determined in such a way that the latter's ultimate task of giving an account of faith can be fulfilled only if it grounds itself as fundamental theology. Fundamental theology must thus be a theory of both methods and foundations. On the concept of fundamental theology see Rahner, *Investigations 1*, "Formale und fundamentale Theologie," pp. 205 ff. G. Söhngen has always understood fundamental theology as "the doctrine of theological principles," which as "the basic theological science" has to be done within "foundational research" in theology. ("Fundamentaltheologie," in *Lekikon von Theologie und Kirche*) Metz also understands fundamental theology in this sense as "formal dogmatics" and—since the subject matter of theology grounds the possibility of its discourse—of dogmatics as "material fundamental theology." (See Metz, *Faith in History and Society* and "Apologetik," in *Sacramentum Mundi*.) For a discussion of the concept of fundamental theology in Protestant theology see G. Ebeling, *Wort und Glaube* II (Tübingen, 1969), p. 104: "Under the problematic of fundamental theology, I understand the question of the grounding of the necessity of theology as such, accepting in an independent way a concept of fundamental theology that has up to now been used usually only in Catholic theology." See also W. Joest, *Fundamentaltheologie* (Stuttgart, 1975).

37. H. Krings, "Freiheit. Ein Versuch Gott zu denken," *Philosophisches Jahrbuch* 77(2), 1970; H. Krings and E. Simons, "Gott," in *Handbuch philosophischer Grundbegriffe*. Cf. J. B. Metz, "Freiheit," in ibid.; W. Pannenberg, *Gottesgedanken und menschliche Freiheit* (Gutersloh, 1972), especially pp. 23–41.

38. See W. Schulz, *Die Vollendung des deutschen Idealismus in der Spätphilosophie Schellings* (Stuttgart, 1955); W. Kaspar, *Das Absolute in der Geschichte* (Mainz, 1965); A. Portmann, *Das Bose—die Ohnmacht der Vernunft* (Meisenheim, 1966).

39. See O. Marquard, *Schwierigkeiten mit der Geschichtsphilosophie* (Frankfurt, 1973); H. Blumenberg, *The Legitimacy of the Modern Age* (Cambridge, Mass., 1983). Among the clearest and most insightful analyses of this situation are G. G. Grau's investigations on Nietzsche and Kierkegaard. Grau's basic thesis is that the Job situation of religious thought is not broken through in Christianity; rather, intellectually responsible speech demands a return to this situation; accordingly, the philosophy of religion after "the self-dissolution of Christian faith" must again begin with the experience of the persistence of suffering.

40. For empirical investigations on the danger of the loss of identity in the death of important interaction partners, see Spiegel, *Der Prozess des Trauerns* (Munich, 1981).

41. See the essays by E. von Weizsäcker in *Offene Systeme* I.

42. See, for example, R. Berlinger, *Das Werk der Freiheit* (Frankfurt, 1959); Berlinger, *Das Nichts und der Tod* (Frankfurt, 1961).

43. See appendix 1.

44. Heidegger, *Being and Time*, p. 307.

45. The critique of theology by the Erlangen School is directed against the fact that discourse on God cannot be transparently introduced; see F. Kambartel, "Theo-logisches," *Zeitschrift für Evangelische Ethik* 15 (1971): 309–311; Kamlah and Lorenzen, *Logische Propädeutik*, pp. 105 ff.; M. Gatzemeier, *Theologie* I, pp. 169–172. The elementary critique of Gatzemeier's attempt at reconstruction is that it does not at all consider the limit experiences we have analyzed as the paradox of anamnestic solidarity which are met in the action-theory approach. Despite the assertion of presupposing a concept of action directed toward transsubjectivity, Gatzemeier overlooks the temporality and the reciprocal reflectivity of action. Thus, he also cannot analyze the experience of death of the other (see p. 170), and he finally retreats to a monological and instrumental concept of action. It does not seem that this has to be the case in a constructivist theory of science. The structure of the reconstruction of the question of God proposed here can be clarified in contrasting with Kant. In the *Critique of Pure Reason*, Kant wanted to deconstruct an assertion of the reality of God derived from the principles of speculative reason, since it goes beyond the regulative function of the idea, as a transcendental illusion. In the *Critique of Practical Reason*, which proceeds from the assumption of the autonomy of the will and establishes the inherent tendency of reason to totality, the existence of God is postulated because it alone can guarantee that autonomous moral action will lead to the happiness of the acting subject. The alternatives considered by Kant are Stoicism and Epicureanism. In opposition to both positions, the "highest good" still consists for him in the unity of morality and happiness: the necessity in thought to postulate the existence of God results from the necessity of this unity. The cogency of this necessity proceeds from the concepts of the freedom and the autonomy of the subject. The postulate of the existence of God is established primarily on the basis of the subjectivity of the autonomous subject, not on the basis of the freedom of the other and the desire for his happiness. Another position could perhaps best be reached through Kant's *Foundations for a Metaphysics of Morals*, where, in the third formulation of the categorical imperative, Kant speaks of the generality or totality of the system of persons who are posited as ends in themselves. This offers possibilities to further interpret Kant's position. Redemption cannot be adequately conceived merely through the concept of pure subjectivity. Paul Ricoeur rightly points out in *Conflict of Interpretations* (Evanston, 1974) that, in light of the contemporary situation, the central themes in Kant must be taken up again through a kind of "post-Hegelian Kantianism." Adorno also returns to Kant at the end of *Negative Dialectics*: "That no inner-worldly improvement is sufficient to compensate the dead with justice; that none disturbs the injustice of death, motivates Kantian reason to hope against reason. The secret of Kant's philosophy is the inconceivability of despair."

46. See Metz, *Faith in History and Society*.

47. See the survey in Kasper, *Jesus*, 153–162. See also J. Moltmann, "Gott und Auferstehung," in *Perspektiven der Theologie* (Munich, 1968); E. Jüngel, "Thesen zur Grundlegund der Christologie," in *Unterwegs zur Sache* (Munich, 1972). Jüngel writes: "The responsibility of theology to Jesus Christ resurrected from the dead demands a hermeneutics of theological logic determining the discourse about the resurrection of Jesus Christ." (p. 285) It certainly remains unclear what sort of logic this is supposed to be. According to my presentation, it must be strictly determined through the dia-logic of an intersubjectivity to be understood as a temporal approaching unto death and the experience contained in it of the self-disclosing reality of God.

48. See U. Wilckens, *Auferstehung* (Stuttgart, 1957). See also the debate begun by R. Pesch [*Questiones Theologie* 153–154 (1973–74)].

49. K. Rahner, "Jesus Christ and Christology," in *A New Christology*, ed. K. Rahner and W. Thüsing (New York, 1980), pp. 10 ff.

50. Ibid., pp. 16–17. Also see W. Thüsing, ibid., pp. 49–51; K. Rahner, *Investigations* 6, pp. 247–248; K. Rahner, *Ich glaube an Jesus Christus* (Einsiedeln, 1968), especially pp. 15–53.

51. J. B. Metz, "Unsere Hoffnung," *Synode* 6 (1975): 25–41, I, 3 (in *Faith in History and Society*).

52. See Ladriére, *Rede der Wissenschaft*. Ladriére's analyses are among the most insightful and knowledgeable, but in the end they rest on a transcendental egology inspired by Husserl and suffer from all the aporias of such a view.

53. Ramsey's theory can never become the basis of a theory of proclamation, since it does not strictly determine the process of disclosure as a process within the horizon of intersubjective, anamnestic action unto death.

54. Rahner's theses "On the Unity of the Love of Neighbor and the Love of God" also point to a theory of communicative action as a foundational theory of theology. (*Investigations* 6, pp. 231–249). The transcending openness to the other is the openness to the absolute mystery of God, and conversely the opening to God as one self-communicating absolute mystery is possible only in the turning to others in love. For Rahner, "the readiness for death" is one of the "essential traits of *love* of another person." (6, p. 242) Rahner sees in communication in the face of death the point of departure for a contemporary conception of Christology in fundamental theology. (*Christology*, pp. 38–41).

55. *Summa Theologica*, Question I, 2a 3.

56. See Welte, *Der philosophische Glaube*, pp. 132 ff.

57. Rahner, *Investigations* 4, p. 54.

58. J. B. Metz, "Zukunft aus dem Gedächtnis des Leidens," *Concilium* 8 (1972): 399–407; see p. 406.

59. Ibid.

60. It should be clear that a theory of the narrative developed on the basis of such a fundamental theology (see Metz, *Faith in History and Society*) is clearly different from a structuralist theory of the narrative. The investigation of rigid forms, such as in the process of narration of sayings, fairy tales, and myths, was the impetus for the development of structural anthropology. It would then be a distortion of the possibility of "narrative theology" as the presentation of the breakthrough to the radically new to reduce it to typical forms of narrative research. A theological theory of narration can only be developed in the framework of a theory of innovative, situation-changing speech actions that transform one's understanding of both oneself and reality as a whole.

61. See Lorenzen and Schwemmer, *Konstruktive Logic*, p. 153.

62. A further analysis would be able to show that a theological theory of this sort can fulfill the requirements for a theory in the sense of the later Carnap. The basic theoretical concepts of theological theory could be connected through proper rules for the correlation of empirical statements of the concrete behavior of subjects engaged in communicative action. The character of this correlation must certainly be determined by the character of its realm of objects; that is, the rules of correlation must be of a hermeneutical sort, and so must be rules of interpretation. I have already indicated in principle the limits of this type of theory and the danger of objectivistic reduction. If one starts from the concept of theory developed in constructivist theories of science, then these requirements may be fulfilled in respect to the paradigmatic introduction of basic concepts and the systematic construction of vocabulary, insofar as the concept of action cannot finally be reduced to instrumental action.

63. Plato, *Parmenides*, 151e–157b.

64. See Heidegger, *Being and Time*, sections 62 and 76.

65. Benjamin, "Theses," p. 261.

66. Ibid., p. 256.

67. Ibid., p. 257.

68. Ibid., p. 255.

69. J. Habermas, "Consciousness Raising or Redemptive Criticism," *New German Critique* 17 (1979): 30–59; see p. 56. (Also in *Profiles*.)

70. See Peukert, "Theorie der Übersetzung."

Appendix 1

1. See G. Ebeling, "Hermeneutik," *Religion in Geschichte Gegenwart* (Tübingen, 1959); K. Lehmann, "Hermeneutik," in *Sacramentum Mundi* III (Montreal, 1969); N. Henrichs, *Bibliographie der Hermeneutik und ihrer Andwendungsbereiche seit Schleiermacher* (Düsseldorf, 1968).

2. *Ansatz* (here translated as conception) appears often in Peukert's vocabulary. It is most often here translated as "conception" or "approach," and more rarely as "view."—translator

3. See G. Hasenhüttel, *Der Glaubensvollzug* (Essen, 1963); M. Boutin, *Relationalität als Verstehensprinzip bei Rudolf Bultmann* (Munich, 1974).

4. Bultmann, *Kerygma und Mythos*, ed. Bartsch, III (Hamburg, 1948), p. 51. The Bultmann-Jaspers debate is translated under the title *Myth and Christianity* (New York, 1958).

5. On the relationship between Bultman and Heidegger see *Heidegger und die Theologie*, ed. Noller (Munich, 1967); J. Macquarrie, *An Existentialist Theology* (London, 1953); K. Lehmann, "Christliche Geschichtserfahrung und ontologische Frage beim jungen Heidegger," in *Heidegger*, ed. Pöggeler (Cologne and Berlin, 1969), especially pp. 146 ff.; Boutin, *Relationalität*. On the following see H. Peukert, "Bultmann and Heidegger," in *Rudolf Bultmann in Catholic Thought*, ed. O'Meara and Weiser (New York, 1968).

6. Throughout this chapter, there is a contrast between the two German words for "historical," *geschichtlich* and *historisch*. Although there is no clear way to make this distinction in English, it should be clear that *historisch* is limited to factual, chronological history, and that *geschichtlich* is broader and includes history as tradition.—translator

7. See R. Bultmann, *Das Verhältnis der urchristlichen Christusbotschaft zum historischen Jesus* (Heidelberg, 1960).

8. See R. Bultmann, *The History of the Synoptic Tradition* (New York, 1968), p. 348.

9. R. Bultmann, *Faith and Understanding* (New York, 1969), p. 40.

10. R. Bultmann, "Barths Römerbrief," *Christliche Welt* 36 (1922): 360.

11. Bultmann, *Faith and Understanding*, pp. 145–164.

12. On this development see O. Pöggeler, *Der Denkweg Martin Heideggers* (Pfullingen, 1963); K. Lehmann, "Christliche Geschichtserfahrung"; W. Schulz, *Philosophie in der veränderten Welt* (Pfullingen, 1972).

13. Pöggeler, *Denkweg*, p. 35. Pöggeler was the first to explicate this relationship. Also see Lehmann, "Christliche Geschichtserfahrung," p. 161, n. 4.

14. See Heidegger's own list of his lectures and seminars in W. Richardson, *Heidegger: From Phenomenology to Thought* (The Hague, 1963), pp. 663–671.

15. Pöggeler, *Denkweg*, p. 37.

16. Ibid., pp. 40, 43.

17. M. Heidegger, *Being and Time* (hereafter *BT*) (New York, 1962), p. 40.

18. *BT*, p. 41.

19. *BT*, p. 62.

20. See *BT*, section 40.

21. M. Heidegger, *Existence and Being* (Chicago, 1949), p. 369.

22. Ibid., p. 370.

23. *BT*, p. 67.

24. A precise investigation of these historical relationships is not yet possible, since Heidegger's works have been published very sporadically. See W. Schulz, "Über den philosophiegeschicht-lichen Ort Martin Heideggers," *Philosophische Rundschau* 1 (1953–54): 65–93, 211–232.

25. I. Kant, *Critique of Pure Reason*, B.384.

26. Ibid., B.391.

27. Ibid., p. 434.

28. Heidegger, *The Essence of Reasons* (Evanston, 1969), p. 41.

29. Ibid.

30. See E. Husserl, *Cartesian Meditations* (The Hague, 1964), pp. 7–25.

31. See Fink, "Die phänomenologische Philosophie E. Husserl in der gegenwärtigen Kritik," *Kantstudien* 38 (1938): 319–383; Diemer, *Husserl* (Meisenheim, 1956), pp. 33 ff.

32. See Husserl's remarks on *Being and Time*, cited in Diemer, p. 29, along with Husserl's objection to Heidegger's book on Kant that Heidegger belonged to "the anthropological tendency."

33. *Cartesian Meditations*, pp. 89–148.

34. See *BT*, sections 46–53. Heidegger declares in a footnote on p. 497 that the existential problematic remained foreign to Kierkegaard, but then he takes over Kierkegaard's essential distinctions without giving their source in Kierkegaard's 1845 "At the Side of a Grave" [*Thoughts*

on Crucial Situations in Human Life (Minneapolis, 1941)]: To imagine oneself dead is earnestness; to be witness to the death of another is a mood. (81); only in earnestness does death seem to be decisive (82), indeterminate (101), inexplicable (101). See Heidegger: "Death, as the end of Dasein, is Dasein's ownmost possibility—nonrelational, certain, and as such indefinite, not to be outstripped." (*BT*, p. 302)

35. *BT*, p. 374.

36. It is possible to see Heidegger's analysis of temporality as his own authentic discovery, even if it is inconceivable without its prehistory in Kant, Hegel, Schelling, Kierkegaard, and Husserl. However, its significance can best be seen through its relationship to Aristotle and Augustine. According to Aristotle, time is the "quantity of movement in terms of earlier and later." (*Phys.* 11, 219 b I) The question is, however, how earlier and later can be made into quantities. Would there be time at all without the soul? Numbers can only be counted by the soul, and in the soul only by *nous*. (233 a 25–26) Time can only be grasped in the positing of a now as an act of *nous*. "So it is impossible that time is, if the soul is not" (233a 26). To this extent, this now posited by the soul is the origin of time. (*An. Posit.* B 12 95b 18) The temporality and finitude of *nous* are unclarified by Aristotle. [See Jan van der Meulen, *Aristotles* (Meisenheim, 1951), section 22.]

Augustine is fundamental to any analysis of the problem of time, since it is Augustine who, in chapters 13–28 of book XI of the *Confessions*, saw, for the first time in the history of Western thought, the full scope of the dialectic of grasping time. (See Rudolf Berlinger, *Augustins dialogische Metaphysik* (Frankfurt, 1962).] Augustine asks: "What then is time? Who ever in his mind can grasp the subject well enough to be able to make a statement on it? Yet in our ordinary conversation we use the word 'time' more often and more familiarly than any other." (*Conf.* XI, 14) As one lives unreflectively within time, the past and the future seem self-evident. As soon as one inquires into its essence, it is evident that time cannot be determined like the essence of a table or a tree. The being of time becomes "the most complicated of enigmas" (*Conf.* XI, 22), threatening to dissolve into nonbeing. Since the past and the future are "non-esse," the present has "no duration or extension." (*Conf.* XI, 15) "Where therefore is time?" The self-awareness of the I, the self, proves to be time's point of origin. Past, future, and present are all given as "praesentia de praeteritis" in the "memoria," as "presentia de futuris" in "expectatio," as the "presentia de praesentibus" in "contuitus." Temporality manifests itself in the self-awareness of the I. The being of time and the being of this self are inextricably bound together. Inasmuch as man is the "punctum ipsum temporis," he remains exposed to the "angustiae temporis." (*Sermons* VI) For Heidegger, temporality remains in the difference of its finitude and does not dissolve in self-mediation; this can be shown in the formal-dialectical determination, marking the opposite pole to Hegel: Temporality is the original " 'Ausser sich' an und für sich selbst." *Sein und Zeit*, p. 329)

37. *BT*, p. 428.

38. *BT*, p. 437.

39. *BT*, p. 449.

40. *BT*, p. 450.

41. Before going into Bultmann's theology, I should at least point out the question whether Heidegger himself successfully attained the goal of his questioning. The explication of authentic temporality is supposed to develop the question of the sense of being. The third section of the first part of *Being and Time*, which was supposed to bear the title "Time and Being," was never published. The last sentences of *Being and Time* are: "How is this mode of the temporalizing of temporality to be interpreted? Is there a way which leads from primordial *time* to the meaning of *Being*? Does *time* manifest itself as the horizon of *Being*?" These questions remain unanswered. One must agree with Pöggeler when he says that "*Being and Time* remained a

fragment; the investigation was abandoned in the middle and never achieved its goal." (*Denkweg*, p. 64) Bultmann drew his hermeneutical reflections from these published parts of *Being and Time*; we must still ask what significance this has for his theology.

42. Bultmann in a letter of May 13, 1955, cited in Ittel, "Der Einfluss der Philosophie Martin Heideggers auf die Theologie Rudolf Bultmann," *Kerygma und Dogma* 2 (1956): 92. See Macquarrie's *Existential Theology* for particulars.

43. See Bultmann, *Essays* (London, 1955), pp. 234–261, 250 ff., and 252, n. 1.

44. See J. Maraldo, *Der hermeneutische Zirkel* (Freiburg, 1974); K. F. Gethmann, *Verstehen und Auslegung* (Bonn, 1974).

45. See *Essays*, p. 239.

46. *BT*, p. 195.

47. *BT*, p. 206.

48. *Glauben und Verstehen* III (Tübingen, 1960), p. 143.

49. *Essays*, p. 240.

50. *Myth and Christianity*, p. 67.

51. *Verstand* is here used to refer to the intellect, the merely cognitive —translator.

52. Bultmann, *Kerygma und Mythos*, II, p. 191.

53. *Faith and Understanding*, pp. 53–66.

54. See for example G. Hasenhüttel, *Der Glaubensvollzug* (Essen, 1963), p. 228. On the concept of the moment in Kierkegaard see K. Schäfer, *Hermeneutische Ontologie* (Munich, 1968), pp. 185 ff. In Heidegger see *BT*, pp. 385 ff. On the existential analysis of the moment see R. Berlinger, *Das Werk der Freiheit* (Frankfurt, 1959), pp. 24 ff.

55. Bultmann, *Kerygma und Mythos* I, p. 39.

56. Ibid., pp. 41 ff.

57. See Bultmann's exegesis of John 12: 27–32 in *The Gospel of John* (Philadelphia, 1971), pp. 427–433.

58. *BT*, p. 437.

59. *BT*, p. 438.

60. Bultmann, *Kerygma und Mythos* II, p. 197.

61. "To know Christ is to know his benefits."

62. R. Bultmann, *Theology of the New Testament* (New York, 1953), p. 250.

63. See the correspondence between Wolfhart Pannenberg and Gerhart Ebeling in *Zeitschrift für Theologie und Kirche* 70 (1873): 448–473, especially p. 473, concerning a new objectivism in theology.

64. Bultmann, *Kerygma und Mythos* II, p. 192.

65. Ibid., p. 194.

66. *BT*, p. 360.

67. *BT*, p. 434.

68. Ibid.

69. Bultmann, *Kerygma und Mythos* I, p. 37.

70. See Schulz, "Ort," p. 221; B. Welte, *Auf der Spur des Ewigen* (Freiburg, 1966), pp. 262–276; H. Danner, *Das Göttliche und der Gott bei Heidegger* (Meisenheim am Glan, 1971).

71. *BT*, p. 274.

72. *BT*, p. 308.

73. *BT*, p. 233.

74. M. Theunissen, *Der Anderer* (Berlin, 1965), pp. 176 ff.

75. Ibid., p. 181, n. 34.

76. Schulz, *Philosophie in der veränderten Welt*, p. 301.

77. Ibid., p. 300.

78. The question remains whether after the "turn" the conception of authentic intersubjectivity is fundamentally different; this still must be more precisely investigated. See K. O. Apel, *Transformation der Philosophie* I (Frankfurt, 1971), pp. 35 ff. [Selections in English: *Towards a Transformation of Philosophy* (London, 1981.)]

Appendix 2

1. *Investigations* 11, p. 71.

2. I do not hereby claim to outline "the extraordinary, immense and unprecedented nature of this theological work" (Metz, "Karl Rahner—ein theologisches Leben," *Stimme der Zeit* 99, p. 306). See H. Vorgrimler, *Karl Rahner* (Freiburg, 1963); K. Lehmann, "Karl Rahner," *Bilanz der Theologie im 20. Jahrhunderts* IV (Freiburg, 1970); K. Fischer, *Der Mensch als Geheimnis* (Freiburg, 1973); B. van der Heijden, *Karl Rahner* (Einsiedeln, 1973); P. Eicher, *Die anthropologische Wende* (Freiburg, 1970).

3. *Investigations* 11, p. 87.

4. Kant, *Critique of Pure Reason*, B 25.

5. See W. Schulz, *Der Gott der neuzeitlichen Metaphysik* (Pfullingen, 1957); C. Möller, "Antworten des neunzehnten Jahrhunderts," in *Wer ist das eigentlich—Gott?*, ed. Schulz (Munich, 1969).

6. J. Maréchal, *Le point de départ de la métaphysique* (Paris, 1922), especially volume 5, *Le thomisme devant la philosophie critique*. See also Eicher, *Wende*, pp. 22 ff.

7. See K. Rahner, *Spirit in the World* (New York, 1968). For the details of individual investigations and their historical genesis, see the presentations listed above.

8. *Vorgriff* (literally, pre-grasp) has also been translated as "pre-concept" in the English edition of Rahner's *Investigations*, and has the connotation of another of its German meanings, anticipation. Here it is rendered "anticipatory grasp."—translator

9. See *Hearers of the Word* (New York, 1969), p. 87 and chapters 7 and 8.

10. Rahner's analyses in *Hearers of the Word* seem to have a mostly ignored proximity to Kierkegaard's analyses of despair, anxiety, and the self in *Sickness unto Death*.

11. *Investigations* 4, 36–77.

12. See, for example, K. Rahner, "Observations on the Concept of Revelation," in *Revelation and Tradition*, ed. Rahner and Ratzinger (London, 1965), especially pp. 13, 22, and 26.

13. *Investigations* 11, p. 109.

14. See *Phenomenology of Spirit* (Oxford, 1977), p. 58.

15. See "On the Unity of the Love of Neighbor and the Love of God," *Investigations* 6, 231–249; "The 'Commandment' of Love in Relation to the Other Commandments," ibid. 5, 239–259; "One Mediator and Many Mediations," ibid. 9, 169–184; "The Church's Commission to Bring Salvation and the Humanization of the World," ibid. 14, 295–313, "Liebe," *Sacramentum Mundi* III, 234–251. This is not to say that for Rahner a theory of interaction is the only possible access to the reality intended in theology. It is nonetheless an access in terms of which the whole may be viewed and, if the problems of human interaction are followed to their radical conclusions, this reality necessarily comes into view. See the second formulation of "A Short Formula of Faith," *Investigations* 11, 240–241.

16. *Investigations* 6, p. 240.

17. Ibid., p. 241.

18. Ibid.

19. Ibid., p. 246.

20. Ibid.

21. Ibid., p. 245.

22. Ibid., p. 247.

23. The distinction between nature and grace can be explained in terms of this basic structure. It has its place in the framework of a theological theory of the communication of revelation. If one begins with a formal concept of the event of revelation in which God offers himself to be experienced, then this event can only be understood and thus communicated if the hearer takes part in this basic experience. "The act of hearing divine revelation as the word of God himself, as something more, therefore, than a word uttered about God and caused by God, presupposes, as the condition which makes it possible in the subject, that God himself through his own act of self-communication as an intrinsic principle cooperates in this act of hearing. And this is what we are accustomed to call the supernatural grace of faith." (*Investigations* 11, 91–92) If this communication is to be universal (that is, not arbitrarily limited), then this experience must be presupposed *a priori* with every possible communication partner.

24. See *Investigations* 13, 213–223.

25. Ibid.

26. See K. Rahner, "Der dreifältige Gott als transzendenter Urgrund der Heilsgeschichte," *Mysterium Salmundi.* II, 314–347; "Trinity," *Sacramentum Mundi* 6 (New York: 1970); "Theology of the Trinity," ibid., pp. 303–308; *Investigations* 11, 243 ff.

.

Index